# The
# HISTORY BUFF'S™ GUIDE
## to
# THE PRESIDENTS

*Also by Thomas R. Flagel*

THE HISTORY BUFF'S GUIDE TO THE CIVIL WAR

THE HISTORY BUFF'S GUIDE TO GETTYSBURG (with Ken Allers Jr.)

THE HISTORY BUFF'S GUIDE TO WORLD WAR II

· KEY PEOPLE, PLACES, AND EVENTS ·

*The*
# HISTORY BUFF'S™ GUIDE
*to*
# THE PRESIDENTS

## THOMAS R. FLAGEL

CUMBERLAND HOUSE
AN IMPRINT OF SOURCEBOOKS, INC.®

Published by Cumberland House Publishing Inc., an Imprint of Sourcebooks, Inc.®
P.O. Box 4410, Naperville, Illinois 60567-4410
(630) 961-3900
Fax: (630) 961-2168
www.sourcebooks.com

Cover design by Gore Studio Inc., Nashville, Tennessee

**Library of Congress Cataloging-in-Publication Data**

Flagel, Thomas R., 1966–
    The History buff's guide to the presidents / Thomas R. Flagel.
        p.   cm.
    Includes bibliographical references and index.
    1. Presidents—United States—History—Miscellanea. 2. Presidents—United States—Biography—Miscellanea. I. Title.
    E176.1.F58  2007
    973.09'9—dc22

                                                                    2007033003


Printed in the United States of America

VP  10  9  8  7  6  5

*For Riisy*

# Contents

## 5: THE INNER CIRCLE

# Prologue

IN THE LATE SPRING of 1787, fifty-five delegates gathered in Philadelphia to try and save the eleven-year-old nation from itself. Aimless and broke, nearly defenseless against enemies foreign and domestic, the country had ingested a lethal dose of diffusion, as each state was unwilling to compromise its own independence for the sake of the whole. A sign of the times, officials from Rhode Island refused to attend. The rest filed into the Pennsylvania State House—doctors, lawyers, planters, soldiers, artisans—with a single task before them. Repair the Articles of Confederation before the experiment dies.

Behind locked doors guarded by armed troops, with windows latched and curtains drawn, the delegation assessed the situation. Within days, the majority drifted toward a painful realization . . . the patient was terminal. Nothing could be done but to engineer an entirely new body politic, one that would bond the thirteen states and their myriad of militias, legal codes, postal systems, trade policies, revenues, and debts into a single entity. As the convention moved forward, an unsettling fact lingered—no one had given them the authority to do this. But they continued, secretly dismantling the old and weak Continental Congress. In its place they designed a federation to be led by something the country had gone without since 1776—a head of state.

At the end of four months, the delegates emerged and presented the Constitution to the states. When debating whether to ratify this unsolicited albeit bloodless coup, citizens were disturbed by several of its features. To begin with, the document was made by only fifty-five men out of a country of nearly four million, and yet it had the audacity to declare, "We the People . . ."

Far worse, the manuscript empowered an overriding legislature to collect taxes and form a standing army, the very offenses that sparked the Revolution in the first place. There was also no bill of rights. It all had a striking resemblance to a certain British Empire.

To many, the most unsettling part was the creation of a "President" who wielded the power of vetoes, federal appointments, and irreversible pardons. Plus he was to be commander of the armed forces. How could these delegates propose such an idea when thirty of them had personally signed the Declaration of Independence against a similar government such a short time ago? The whole affair smelled like a counterrevolution. Even some of the delegates themselves worried that the presidency could one day become "the fetus of a monarchy."

Today, we know the end result was a success. Ratification was achieved, the new federal system went into place without sectarian violence, and the president did not devolve into a king.

The fears of the eighteenth century appear naive to us in the twenty-first. We are the heirs of the system they denounced as too fragile. Their protests seem shortsighted, their skepticism misplaced against an office we have grown to respect, made by men whom we revere. We have a Washington State, several Adams counties, a Jefferson City. Our children might go to Monroe Elementary or Adams Junior High or Jackson Senior High or one of the other ten thousand schools named after a former leader. We travel to Mount Vernon and Mount Rushmore, go to college football games in Lincoln and Madison, and watch shuttles launch from the Kennedy Space Center. We buy history books and pay with cash and coins adorned with former chief executives.

When it comes to presidents, we are comfortable with the past . . . and yet uneasy with the present. Our recent executives look as if they are a completely different breed, far less noble than the ones who adorn our memory and monuments. We recall Vietnam and Watergate and claim a loss of innocence. We cite recent scandals, skyrocketing budgets, and the growth of big government to confirm that the executive branch has usurped an inordinate amount of power, far beyond what we think the Founding Fathers would have ever allowed. To us, the White House increasingly resembles a royal house (indeed, the executive branch has contained either a Bush or a Clinton since 1981). We have ungraciously named this era the *Imperial Presidency.*

Rest assured, we are looking at our living presidents in much the same way the first citizens of the Republic viewed theirs, with emotions ranging from adoration to loathing, and basing judgments mostly on which political faction the person belonged to. If this generation has lost anything when it comes to its relationship with the presidency, it is a sense of perspective, just like previous generations often lost theirs.

Thus is the beauty of studying history—it offers the chance to examine the phenomenon of change and to regain a sense of perspective. By no coincidence, some of the most effective chief executives diligently studied the past. Bookworm Harry Truman could hardly reflect on any current event without drawing comparisons to earlier times. Woodrow Wilson, PhD, taught history at Princeton, while Theodore Roosevelt published several works on military history (and his *Naval War of 1812* remains a standard on the subject). The Father of the Constitution, James Madison, brought crates of invaluable history books to the Philadelphia Convention, compliments of his friend Thomas Jefferson.

Has the presidency gained more power than could have ever been imagined? In short, yes. So have the Supreme Court, the Congress, and the general population. When it first began, the modest United States sat clutching the Atlantic coastline. It was less than a hundred miles deep, numbering a few million people, with only one in four white males empowered to vote. Today the Republic reaches five thousand miles across a continent and into the great Pacific, contains three hundred million inhabitants, and guarantees every law-abiding citizen the right to register and cast a ballot from anywhere in the world. It produces and consumes a quarter of the earth's resources, has bases and businesses across the planet, and endures as the lone superpower left after a century of global wars.

In tandem, the presidency and the country have transcended far beyond their original boundaries. To understand this monumental progression, one must closely examine the presidents themselves, which is why this volume was written.

The goal of *The History Buff's Guide* series is to make history comprehensive and comprehendible to the newcomer, while offering the wider-read enthusiast fodder for debate. The tool of choice is the succinct and enlightening top-ten list, which examines subjects in greater depth than a general overview, yet avoids the drowning minutiae of exhaustive works. The end result is a clear view of the big picture and a gateway to further study.

Every list overtures with background information and criteria for the respective topic. Some lists are chronological to illustrate progression. Others are quantitative or qualitative. Where appropriate, names and terms appear in SMALL CAPS to indicate a subject that appears in another list. All rankings are the result of thousands of hours of research, confirmations, consultations, and analysis.

THIS BOOK would not have been possible without the help and support of many outstanding individuals, and this historian would like to thank everyone involved, including his many colleagues at Kirkwood Community College, Michael Bryant of the U.S. Department of Education, and Bryon Andreasen and staff at the Abraham Lincoln Presidential Library and Museum. Thanks also to Charlie Becker and Dennis Bayne of Camp Courageous of Iowa, and their diligent crew, for their wonderful inspiration to this author and countless others. To the Prairie Writers of Iowa, for their direction and advice on content and writing, plus graduate student James Beins for content review on political philosophy. As always, many thanks to Ed Curtis, Ron Pitkin, and the rest of the patient and professional crew at Cumberland House Publishing, and to Barb Ross and John Wasson, the better angels of human nature.

# The HISTORY BUFF'S™ GUIDE to THE PRESIDENTS

# 1

# PRESIDENTIAL CHARACTER

## TOP TEN PREPRESIDENTIAL CAREERS

On average, presidents from the nineteenth century worked in seven or more occupations, whereas recent candidates rarely have experience in more than three different jobs. The same can be said of the general population. In 1800, a homestead often functioned as a schoolroom, seamstress shop, veterinary clinic, bakery, accounting office, and infirmary. In the year 2000, a home was more like a refuge from the workplace, which usually involved a single, specific career.

The transition occurred with the Industrial Revolution, where progressive technology created a fundamental shift from generalization to specialization. Blacksmiths were eventually replaced by sheet-metal workers, electroplating engineers, and electron-beam welders. Country doctors became diagnosticians, endocrinologists, or gastroenterologists. For better and worse, Americans have become less self-reliant and more interdependent.

Yet throughout this evolution, the electorate has preferred candidates from a rather narrow range of professions. In that long interview process known as the presidential campaign, a nominee's background often speaks volumes about the population that supports him or her, because it reflects what the masses value most in a potential leader. Listed below by volume are the job histories of those whom Americans deemed fit to hire.

## 1. MILITARY OFFICER (29)

WASHINGTON, JEFFERSON, MADISON, MONROE, JACKSON, W. H. HARRISON, TYLER,
POLK, TAYLOR, PIERCE, LINCOLN, A. JOHNSON, GRANT, HAYES, GARFIELD, ARTHUR, B.
HARRISON, McKINLEY, T. ROOSEVELT, TRUMAN, EISENHOWER, KENNEDY, L. JOHNSON,
NIXON, FORD, CARTER, REAGAN, G. H. W. BUSH, G. W. BUSH[1]

For generations, Americans assumed that a candidate with a military background, especially one with combat experience, was a natural political leader. Who better to take charge, so the logic went, than someone who was practiced in the art of command?

The tradition began with George Washington, who was admired more for his personal restraint and the discipline of his troops than for his moderate successes on the battlefield. Military hero worship truly took root with the seventh president, as supporters of Gen. Andrew Jackson recounted his teenage defiance of a saber-swinging redcoat during the Revolution and held a massive fund-raiser on the anniversary of his triumph against the British in the battle of New Orleans. Thereafter came Gen. William Henry Harrison in 1840, waltzing into the White House because of his "victory" against the pan-Indian settlement along Tippecanoe Creek in 1811. Apolitical Gen. Zachary Taylor was almost dragged into office because of his success in the Mexican War.

Two conflicts in particular produced a flood of candidates. Political novice Ulysses S. Grant was the first of six Union veterans to become president, five of whom were born in Ohio. The 23rd Ohio Infantry Regiment alone produced Maj. Gen. Rutherford B. Hayes and Maj. William

Then four-star Gen. Dwight Eisenhower grabs a quick lunch while commanding in Europe during World War II.

McKinley. Former Brig. Gen. Benjamin Harrison defeated Grover Cleveland in 1888 partly because the latter was chastised as "unversed in war."

Eight of the fifteen million men who served in the "Good War" of World War II ascended to the White House. First was five-star Gen. Dwight Eisenhower, followed immediately by a wave of naval officers: Lt. Jack Kennedy, Lt. Cmdr. Lyndon Johnson, Lt. Cmdr. Richard Nixon, Lt. Gerald Ford, and Annapolis graduate James Carter. Army Capt. Ronald Reagan shot training films in California, while decorated Navy pilot George H. W. Bush flew in the Pacific.[2]

Oddly, there have been eleven generals but not one admiral to reach the presidency. Nor has there ever been a representative from the marines, nor a veteran from Korea or Vietnam.

---

In 1976, to rank George Washington above all other U.S. officers, Congress gave him the posthumous promotion of "General of the Armies of the United States," a grade equivalent to a six-star general.

---

## 2.  LAWYER (26)

J. ADAMS, JEFFERSON, MADISON, MONROE, J. Q. ADAMS, JACKSON, VAN BUREN, TYLER, POLK, FILLMORE, PIERCE, BUCHANAN, LINCOLN, HAYES, GARFIELD, ARTHUR, CLEVELAND, HARRISON, McKINLEY, TAFT, WILSON, COOLIDGE, F. ROOSEVELT, NIXON, FORD, CLINTON

What is the federal government but a giant law office designed specifically to create, interpret, and enforce the country's legal code? The highest officer must take an oath to "preserve, protect and defend the Constitution of the United States," a sacred vow not to the nation but to its national law. Nearly every inaugural speech has paid homage to the rule of law—William Howard Taft's 1909 address was a virtual lecture on the subject, covering statutes on arbitration, child labor, commerce, tariffs, trust busting, and personal injury.

From the country's very beginning, legal eagles have been at the forefront of government. Approximately 50 percent of the signers of the Declaration and 60 percent of those who created the Constitution were trained in law. In any given Congress since then, about half the members have been attorneys or legal counsels.

Some of the more gifted in the profession included John Adams, who

Lincoln made his name and money through attorney services, occasionally working for major corporations like the Illinois Central Railroad.

successfully defended British troops who shot and killed five demonstrators at the March 5, 1770, Boston Massacre. William Taft was a far better lawyer than president, and in 1921 he attained his dream job of chief justice of the Supreme Court. A youthful Richard Nixon went from new hire to junior partner in a California firm in just two years. William Clinton achieved success as the attorney general of Arkansas, which he used as a springboard to the governorship.

Reflecting an increasingly litigious society, the West Wing is perpetually occupied by attorneys, but most of them are now staff members. Overall, lawyer-presidents are on the decline. In the 1800s, there were twenty presidents who had studied for the bar. In the 1900s, only seven had practiced professionally.[3]

---

In a law career that spanned a quarter century, Abraham Lincoln worked more than five thousand cases.

---

### 3.  STATE LEGISLATOR (21)

WASHINGTON, J. ADAMS, JEFFERSON, MADISON, MONROE, J. Q. ADAMS, VAN BUREN, W. H. HARRISON, TYLER, POLK, FILLMORE, PIERCE, BUCHANAN, LINCOLN, A. JOHNSON, GARFIELD, T. ROOSEVELT, HARDING, COOLIDGE, F. ROOSEVELT, CARTER

The axiom "All politics is local" certainly applied to the early Republic. Counting Washington and Adams, who served when their homes were still colonies, seventeen of the first twenty-one presidents worked as state legislators.

Prior to his service in the White House, James
Buchanan had been a lawyer, Pennsylvania legislator,
U.S. Representative, Andrew Jackson's minister to
Russia, U.S Senator, James K. Polk's secretary of state,
and Franklin Pierce's ambassador to London.

   Their power, relative to the federal government, was exceptional. For
more than seventy years, there was no such animal as the Internal Revenue Service; income taxes were paid to the state. No federal paper currency was then in use; everyday scrip bore the names of local banks, trusts,
and states. Taken together, state militias always outnumbered the regular
army, and there was no national draft. It was said that a person's exposure
to the federal government began and ended with the post office. Americans even acknowledged the relative power of states by referring to their
country in the grammatically correct fashion, "The United States are . . ."

   Ironically, that all ended with the "War for States' Rights." The sheer
magnitude of the conflict forced the federal government to exercise its
powers over the states like never before. The national budget exploded to
thirty times its yearly average, and the army grew sixty times its normal
size. Congress and the president imposed a national draft, a national railroad, federal income tax, the abolition of slavery, plus hundreds of other
laws and measures. Washington truly became the center of government.

   Consequently, candidates with ambition began to forgo grassroots
politics for higher offices. Only four men born since the Civil War have
risen from state houses to the White House. Calvin Coolidge was the last
state representative to do so, and James Carter was the last state senator.

In 1784, a signer of the Declaration of Independence lost a Virginia state
congressional race to a wealthy planter. Each had a son who also went on to
serve in state legislatures. Over time the two boys would run together for
the White House under the slogan "Tippecanoe and Tyler Too."

## 4.  GOVERNOR (20)

JEFFERSON, MONROE, JACKSON, VAN BUREN, W. H. HARRISON, TYLER, POLK, A. JOHNSON, HAYES, CLEVELAND, McKINLEY, T. ROOSEVELT, TAFT, WILSON, COOLIDGE, F. ROOSEVELT, CARTER, REAGAN, CLINTON, G. W. BUSH

Four distinct waves of governors have rolled into the White House, and all came in times of relative peace. From the end of "Mr. Madison's War" in 1815 to the start of "Mr. Polk's War" in 1846, six of the seven presidents had been state or territorial governors. After the Spanish-American conflict, it was four of four (counting Taft's civil governorship in the Philippines). Between the world wars, there was Lieutenant Governor Harding of Ohio, Governor Coolidge from Massachusetts, and New York's Franklin Roosevelt. After the fall of Saigon, four of the next five presidents had been heads of individual states.

Voters subconsciously prefer governors because they are effectively minipresidents. Governors are the head of a government, work with a legislature, manage a budget, act as commander in chief over militias or national guards (when they are not under direct federal authority), and nearly all have the power of vetoes and pardons. Before there was a federal executive, the young states of Delaware, Georgia, North Carolina, Pennsylvania, and South Carolina referred to their respective governors as "president."[4]

> One future president desperately wanted to be governor but never won. In 1962, Richard Nixon narrowly lost the California race to Democrat Pat Brown. The Republican subsequently announced his retirement from politics and told reporters, "You won't have Nixon to kick around anymore."

## 5.  U.S. REPRESENTATIVE (18)

MADISON, JACKSON, W. H. HARRISON, TYLER, POLK, FILLMORE, PIERCE, BUCHANAN, LINCOLN, A. JOHNSON, HAYES, GARFIELD, McKINLEY, KENNEDY, L. JOHNSON, NIXON, FORD, G. H. W. BUSH

Much like state legislators, U.S. representatives reached their apex of influence in the nineteenth century. More than half the presidents in the 1800s came from the lower house, compared to only five during the 1900s.

Nearly all of them had long stays on Capitol Hill. Lincoln became one of the few exceptions when he opposed the popular war with Mexico and was driven out. In contrast, James Madison served four terms as one of Virginia's first representatives. James Knox Polk worked for fourteen years and became the first (and to date only) Speaker of the House to become president. James Garfield served the Nineteenth District of Ohio from 1863 to 1880, until he became the GOP's pick for president.

The twentieth century witnessed a string of former representatives: Jack Kennedy, an aristocrat representing the working-class district of Boston; Lyndon Johnson, who placated his white constituents with several votes against civil rights; anticommunist Dick Nixon, who won many supporters through his hardhearted treatment of suspected spy Alger Hiss; and moderate George H. W. Bush, a supporter of the Vietnam War and tax incentives for independent oil companies.[5]

None were more respected than Michigan's Gerald Ford. He won twelve congressional terms, all by landslides. A fiscal conservative, he opposed minimum-wage increases, fought Medicare, and endorsed an all-or-none commitment to Vietnam. But he used logic over raw emotion, exuded honesty, and was genuinely considerate when discussing controversial issues, leading many to call him a "Congressman's Congressman."[6]

But no sitting member of the House has been elected to the White House in nearly 130 years. Today, the once prestigious chamber is commonly viewed as a mere apprenticeship for those seeking higher office.

---

In 1861, former U.S. Congressman John Tyler was elected by his fellow Virginians to the House of Representatives of the Confederate States of America. He died before he could take office.

---

James K. Polk is, to date, the only Speaker of the House to become president. In the nineteenth century, however, he was just one of thirteen veterans of the U.S. House of Representatives to reach the White House.

## 6. U.S. SENATOR (15)

MONROE, J. Q. ADAMS, JACKSON, VAN BUREN, W. H. HARRISON, TYLER, PIERCE, BUCHANAN, A. JOHNSON, B. HARRISON, HARDING, TRUMAN, KENNEDY, L. JOHNSON, NIXON

From its conception, the Senate possessed the air of lordship. Membership required U.S. residence of at least nine years (two more than the House), and senators were selected by state legislatures rather than by popular vote (a custom that lasted until 1913 with the Seventeenth Amendment). Inductees represented whole states rather than mere districts, and their terms were a courtly six years rather than a curtly two. There was also a greater presidential connection. Until 1886, the order of succession went from the president to the vice president to president pro tempore of the Senate. As Senator Lyndon Johnson said: "The difference between being a member of the Senate and a member of the House is the difference between chicken *salad* and chicken *sh*—."[7]

For a time, the chamber was known as the "Mother of presidents." From 1817 to 1849, all six executives had senatorial backgrounds. But since then, the upper house has seen a decline in the number of presidential victories. They are often well represented in elections but usually lose—and badly. On average, senators make up 35 percent of presidential candidates (more than any other group), and they win nomination 21 percent of the time. But up to 2008, no sitting senator has been elected since John F. Kennedy, often because their six-year terms and higher status give them the stigma of being "Washington insiders."[8]

Lyndon Johnson much preferred his former job of Senate majority leader over the banal position of vice president. Most deputy executives, with the possible exceptions of the grateful Chester A. Arthur and opportunist Dick Cheney, viewed the vice presidency as essentially a political demotion.

In 1957, Senator Jack Kennedy won the Pulitzer Prize for *Profiles in Courage*, a biographical sketch of eight U.S. senators, including John Quincy Adams, who refused to follow popular opinion on controversial issues.

## 7. VICE PRESIDENT (14)
J. ADAMS, JEFFERSON, VAN BUREN, TYLER, FILLMORE, A. JOHNSON, ARTHUR, T. ROOSEVELT, COOLIDGE, TRUMAN, L. JOHNSON, FORD, NIXON, G. H. W. BUSH

John Adams called it "the most insignificant office ever the invention of man contrived or his imagination conceived." Thomas Marshall, Woodrow Wilson's deputy, was partial to the joke about the woman who had two sons—one went to sea, the other became vice president, and neither was heard from again. "Not worth a pitcher of warm piss," said Franklin Roosevelt's first veep John Garner. When vice presidents died in office—which happened during the presidencies of Madison, Pierce, Grant, Cleveland, McKinley, and Taft—the government simply went without one.[9]

Yet in fourteen cases, deputy executives proved exceedingly important to their party and their countrymen. Eight provided invaluable continuity in the face of untimely deaths. Five were elected in their own right. One ably stepped up when his boss resigned.

The cold war elevated the vice presidency to an entirely new level. With the possibility of nuclear strikes, executives began to treat their second in command as potentially just that. Vice presidents became common fixtures in cabinet meetings and the NATIONAL SECURITY COUNCIL. In 1967, the Twenty-Fifth Amendment stipulated that all vacated vice presidencies had to be filled.

Recently, the office has gone through another transformation. Vice presidents were previously invaluable in "balancing the ticket" geographically. Up to the Civil War, nearly every pair of executives represented both the North and the South. From Reconstruction to World War II, a Northeasterner was almost always paired with a Midwesterner. Recently, however, the "balance" has been more political, joining moderates with slightly radical sidekicks, as exemplified by the Arkansas-Tennessee White House from 1993 to 2001 and the Texas-Texas pair from 2001 to 2009 (Dick Cheney lived in Dallas, but he claimed residency in his home state of Wyoming to be constitutionally eligible for election).

---

Franklin Roosevelt, undefeated in four presidential bids, failed in his only attempt to be vice president. Paired with Democratic nominee James Cox in 1920, they lost by a landslide to Warren Harding and Calvin Coolidge.

---

## 8. EDUCATOR (13)
J. ADAMS, JACKSON, FILLMORE, PIERCE, GARFIELD, ARTHUR, CLEVELAND, McKINLEY, WILSON, HARDING, EISENHOWER, L. JOHNSON, CLINTON

Until the late 1800s, the majority of teachers in the United States were male, and a few became president. John Adams, Millard Fillmore, Franklin Pierce, Chester A. Arthur, and Grover Cleveland taught to make ends meet while preparing for a career in law. Most viewed teaching as thankless grunt work, but most of them liked the kids, especially Adams. Fresh out of Harvard, he taught in a one-room schoolhouse in Worcester, where he believed: "In this state I can discover all the great geniuses."[10]

In the twentieth century, primary schools increasingly became a female domain, while males continued to dominate the world of collegiate academics. The only president with a PhD, Woodrow Wilson taught political science and history at Princeton, where he wrote *Constitutional Government in the United States*, a highly insightful volume on the hidden potential of the executive branch. After his service in World War II, Dwight Eisenhower became president of Columbia University. Bill Clinton enjoyed a brief professorship at the Arkansas University School of Law in the early 1970s.

Two future presidents planned on being teachers for life but were compelled to leave. James Garfield despised unruly kids, indifferent parents, and dilapidated schools, but he eventually became headmaster at a small academy in Ohio. He improved teacher quality, revolutionized the curriculum, and increased enrollment. The institute eventually became Hiram College. Lyndon Johnson became principal at a predominantly Hispanic elementary school in Texas, where he created academic competitions, speech tournaments, and a sports program, which he funded partly out of his own pocket. In addition to teaching, he also coached debate, softball, glee club, and volleyball. Disheartened by the lack of parental support, he left, coming to the same conclusion Garfield did a century before: "I want something that has the *thunder* in it more than this has."[11]

---

After retiring from the White House, Grover Cleveland went on to head the board of trustees at Princeton, where he often disagreed with radical changes proposed by the university's president, a professor named Woodrow Wilson.

---

## 9.  CABINET MEMBER (10)

JEFFERSON, MADISON, MONROE, J. Q. ADAMS, VAN BUREN, BUCHANAN, T. ROOSEVELT, TAFT, HOOVER, F. ROOSEVELT

Neither the word *cabinet* nor *secretary* appears in the Constitution. The document only mentions departments, which Congress is empowered to create. The president's relation with these units is defined in article 2, section 2, stating, "he may require the Opinion, in writing, of the principal Officer in each of the executive Departments, upon any subject relating to the Duties of their respective Offices."

In 1789 the Department of State was the first cabinet position constructed, followed by Treasury, War, and Justice with its attorney general. The prestige post was secretary of state, then commonly perceived as second in command of the government.

Before the age of specialization, many cabinet officials functioned interchangeably. While Lincoln's team is famed for being a well-managed hive of rivals, the same could be said for nearly every cabinet up to that time, including James Monroe's (himself the secretary of state under James Madison and, for a while, his secretary of war). Monroe's wise choices included John Quincy Adams, who as state secretary inspired the MONROE DOCTRINE and acquired Florida. Few despised Adams more than Monroe's secretary of war, John C. Calhoun, yet Adams and Calhoun became president and vice president in the election of 1824.

With the exception of State and Defense, secretarial status has waned in the public view. The only cabinet members from the twentieth century to eventually become president were the Roosevelts (both were former assistant secretaries of the navy), Taft (War), and Hoover (Commerce).[12]

---

In large official gatherings, such as the State of the Union Address, the Secret Service often removes and sequesters a representative, a senator, and cabinet member to be the "designated survivors." This ensures a presidential successor in case of a cataclysmic attack or disaster.

---

## 10. DIPLOMAT (8)
J. ADAMS, JEFFERSON, MONROE, J. Q. ADAMS, W. H. HARRISON, BUCHANAN, HOOVER, G. H. W. BUSH

Once upon a time, the foreign service was considered a presidential prerequisite. From the second through the sixth presidents, all but Madison had worked overseas, and all could speak French, the lingua franca of diplomacy.

It was a prestige assignment because the true powers resided across the Atlantic. Long before the United States could dictate its wishes upon other countries, its own national survival depended on the ambassadorial skills of a few good men stationed in Europe. During the Revolution, John Adams secured diplomatic recognition from Holland, along with several desperately needed loans. In 1782, Adams, Ben Franklin, and John Jay negotiated a peace treaty with Britain (much to the ennui of America's wartime ally France). James Monroe, Jefferson's envoy to Paris, played a critical role in closing the deal on the Louisiana Purchase. John Quincy Adams lived his entire adolescence in Europe, learning to speak several languages. In his adulthood he spent nearly two decades overseas, serving as the U.S. minister to Holland, Prussia, Russia, and Britain, negotiating trade agreements, fishing rights, neutrality on the high seas, and the peace treaty to the War of 1812.

In the twentieth century, only Herbert Hoover and George H. W. Bush served extensively in international affairs. Hoover and his wife worked as geological engineers across the globe before he entered politics (they both spoke German and Chinese fluently), and he headed relief programs in Europe after World War I. George H. W. Bush was Nixon's ambassador to the U.N. and Ford's envoy in China.

Oddly, as the United States has steadily climbed to the rank of global superpower, its leaders possess less and less international experience. As such, they are an accurate representation of their fellow countrymen. Fewer than one in four Americans own a passport.

---

While serving as the American emissary to the court of the Romanovs, John Quincy Adams witnessed Napoleon's invasion of Russia in 1814, and he was more than happy when it failed.

---

## TOP TEN PRESIDENTIAL PASTIMES

James Polk insisted, "No President who performs his duty faithfully and conscientiously can have any leisure." Three months after leaving office, an exhausted and emaciated Polk died of cholera at his Nashville home. He was fifty-three.

Though few were as driven as Polk, most chief executives of the age echoed his sentiments. Almost all described the job as a kind of altruistic suffering. With two years left in office, Thomas Jefferson lamented, "To myself, personally, it brings nothing but unceasing drudgery and daily loss of friends." Andrew Jackson equated being president with slavery. Benjamin Harrison once said of the White House, "There is my jail."

Twentieth-century executives painted a much different picture. "No other president ever enjoyed the presidency as I did," said Theodore Roosevelt, while his distant cousin Franklin later called it, "The grandest job in the world." Bill Clinton admitted, "I love this job. . . . Even in the worst of times—the whole impeachment thing—I just thank God every day I can go to work."[13]

So what happened from one century to the next? Part of it was cultural. Americans initially preferred altruistic leaders, borderline martyrs who showed no pleasure in power. Also, the work was arguably harder. Congress initially appropriated no money for staff, so executives had to schedule meetings, write speeches, answer mail, attend to office seekers, organize travel, and manage their residence largely on their own or with the help of relatives. Mostly, presidents changed their attitude because of something that emerged with the Industrial Revolution—the invention of leisure time.

Automation left an increasing amount of work to machines, and the masses were gradually introduced to such concepts as vacation, public parks, and spectator sports. The year 1895 alone saw the arrival of the motion-picture camera, the wireless radio, the founding of the American Bowling Congress, the first professional football game, and the first U.S. Open Golf Championship.

The pursuit of leisure, once the epitome of aristocracy, became the very essence of democracy. Not only had it become socially acceptable for presidents to seek the perks of prosperity, it had become downright patriotic. Consequently, voters gradually turned away from the "noble sufferers" and toward eager, aggressive leaders. Few embodied the image of the bon vivant president better than the Roosevelts, Jack Kennedy, and Ronald Reagan. In contrast, the likes of Herbert Hoover, Richard Nixon, and Jimmy Carter were ultimately seen as too prudent and grave to inspire confidence.

Following are the ten most common pastimes of the presidents while they were in office, listed in order of their overall popularity. As many illustrate, American culture was never accustomed to sitting still, and it continues to steadily accelerate.

## 1.  SMOKING AND DRINKING

This is a country virtually built on alcohol, tobacco, and firearms. In 1611, the settlement of Jamestown was on the fast track to failure just like every other English venture in North America—until John Rolfe discovered a way to cultivate a weed known for its slight hallucinogenic properties. The ensuing tobacco boom brought planters and fortunes to the Chesapeake (along with a demand for native lands and imported labor). Generations later, a tobacco planter inspired his soldiers to withstand the hardships of a revolution by giving them ample rations of rum.

Ever since, smoke and spirits have fueled many a president. Washington loved his rum, and he made sure to share a barrel at his 1789 inaugural. His vice president was fond of it as well, as was Thomas Jefferson. The man from Monticello was also a founding father of the American wine industry. Taken with the vineries of France and Italy, Jefferson encouraged growers to settle in the States, and he racked up a wine bill during his presidency that left him owing money to the government. Neither his pocketbook nor his palate could match John Quincy Adams, who could discern the region of nearly any bottle, a skill achieved through years of travel in Europe.

Vintage lost its vogue with the rise of Jacksonian Democracy, where hard cider and whiskey ruled. But most presidents of the middle 1800s tried to refrain, especially Pierce, Buchanan, and Grant. Grover Cleveland was not shy about consuming. The big man preferred beer, which he downed with piles of German food.

When a growing number of "dry" states ratified Prohibition in 1919, the presidents adjusted. Alcohol could not be bought or sold, but possession was not a crime, so Harding simply "acquired" cases of hard liquor and served it to his closest friends. Coolidge abstained, while Hoover discreetly visited various European embassies around town. The Belgians were most accommodating to his thirst for martinis. After repeal in 1933, the alcohol again flowed, as did millions of dollars in tax revenues.

Concerning tobacco, John Adams took up smoking by the age of ten. Andrew Jackson and later Gerald Ford were the only pipe aficionados, whereas Zachary Taylor was a chaw man. Through heavy advertising and copious free samples in World War II ration boxes, cigarettes reached their apex in the middle twentieth century. FDR, Eisenhower, and LBJ were all chain smokers, though the latter two quit for health reasons.

The most popular choice was cigars. U. S. Grant was famous for puffing down twenty or more a day. During the Civil War, admirers sent him thousands, which may have led to his eventual bout with terminal throat cancer. William McKinley almost never exercised, unless walking while smoking counts. Calvin Coolidge liked gargantuan Fonesca Coronas Fines de Luxe. Millionaire Herbert Hoover demanded large black Juan Alones Havanas, which he consumed at the rate of a hundred a week. Legendary is Kennedy's acquisition of more than a thousand Upmann Petit Coronas before he signed a total embargo against Cuba. Nixon, like Adams, smoked when he was nervous or celebrating. Bill Clinton's fondness for

JFK enjoys a cigar during the last summer of his life.

CECIL STOUGHTON, WHITE HOUSE

stogies became famous during the LEWINSKY AFFAIR, but he may not have lit up. Like most businesses and public buildings at the time, the Clintons followed the trend of an increasingly antitobacco nation and banned smoking throughout the White House.[14]

---

From the FDR administration through LBJ's, formal White House dinners often concluded with retirement into adjacent rooms, where the refreshments were coffee and cigarettes for women, brandy and cigars for men.

---

## 2.  READING

Before his eyesight failed him, George Washington liked to recite from newspapers to his wife before bedtime. But he made it a point never to read in the presence of company, as he thought it the pinnacle of rudeness.

John Adams read quickly, and in French, neither of which Washington could do. He was partial to science and mathematics, while Jefferson read almost everything he could find, though he found law to be uninspiring. James Madison enjoyed the purity of Greek and Latin rather than relying on English translations. All three amassed personal libraries numbering several thousand volumes, an expensive undertaking at the time. Jefferson's collection eventually became the core of the Library of Congress, while Madison donated the bulk of his collection to the University of Virginia.[15]

The White House would not have a library of its own until the 1850s, built by a couple who had met when she was a teacher and he was her student. Their lifelong pursuit of learning inspired Millard and Abigail Fillmore to ask Congress to fund a permanent executive library. Aided by a five-thousand-dollar grant, the Fillmores packed the second floor oval room with works on law, history, engineering, and the classics.[16]

Lincoln preferred Byron, Poe, and Shakespeare, especially *Macbeth*. Nothing enthralled him more than heavy satire, which often made him chuckle while reading. Not one to laugh alone, he would often recite long passages to anyone within earshot, which sometimes proved uncomfortable for those who were busy with more pressing matters. Certainly more refined than Lincoln, the well-read James Garfield enjoyed Jane Austen's subtle critiques of class-bound England. He also read ancient Greek and Latin.

For some, reading was a physical challenge. James Buchanan was far-sighted in one eye and nearsighted in the other, which made him unconsciously cock his head to the side. Theodore Roosevelt plowed through history, politics, biographies, Dickens, Poe, Shelly, and Tennyson. He read at night, the only time he was sitting still, but poor eyesight required him to read inches from the page. A boxing injury while president also damaged his left retina, which eventually rendered the eye blind. Cerebral Woodrow Wilson read nearly as much as TR, but far slower, because he struggled with dyslexia.[17]

Reflecting their culture, the later presidents either read quickly or not at all. Reagan and the Bushes rarely found time, whereas Truman and Nixon concentrated on biographies. Suitably, Nixon viewed tragic heroes as the most intriguing. For Kennedy it was newspapers, piles of them, and he could read fifteen hundred words a minute, nearly as fast as Jimmy Carter at two thousand words and more than 90 percent retention. One of Bill Clinton's favorite classics was Tolstoy's *War and Peace*, but he perused a wide variety of fiction and nonfiction, and he often had several books going at once.[18]

---

Lincoln once remarked, "My best friend is the man who'll git me a book I ain't read."

---

## 3. PETS

In the 1800s, most Americans had little spare time or extra food, so pets were relatively scarce. Chester Arthur and Millard Fillmore had none. Andrew Johnson fed house mice out of pity. Most of the first pets were

Of German descent himself, Herbert Hoover was partial to German Shepherds.

William Howard Taft's pet cow Pauline strikes a pose on the White House lawn. In the background stands the Old Executive Office Building.

working animals. Washington had his hunting hounds, including Sweet Lips, Drunkard, and Tipsy. Eccentric John Quincy Adams had silkworms. Confrontational Andrew Jackson raised fighting cocks. William Henry Harrison and William Howard Taft owned cows.

Horses, on the other hand, were the White House motorcade. John Tyler, U. S. Grant, and Abraham Lincoln were particularly kind to their steeds. Tragedy befell Lincoln's in 1862 when a fire broke out in their pens. Guards had to restrain him as he rushed to save the dying creatures. Among the fatally burned was a pony that had belonged to his late son William. Upon hearing of its fate, Lincoln wept.[19]

With the arrival of the internal combustion engine, a new breed took over. "If you want a friend in Washington," said Harry Truman, "get yourself a dog." Truman's friends were Feller the mutt and Mike the Irish setter. Ike liked Heidi the Weimaraner. Lyndon Johnson had his beagles. FDR and Hoover shared a love of canines, owning more than a dozen between them. Vice President Richard Nixon saved his career in 1952 with his sentimental Checkers speech on nationwide television. Dismissing accusations of financial impropriety, Nixon listed his assets, including a cocker spaniel recently given to the family. "I just want to say this right now," insisted the misty-eyed veep, "that regardless of what they say about it, we're gonna keep it." Dick wasn't clear if he meant the dog or his job.[20]

Then there are the virtual zoos. The Kennedys had a glut of animals great and small, from parakeets and hamsters to cats, rabbits, and a pack of dogs. The equestrian Jackie needed her prize mount Sardar. Caroline and John John owned ponies named Leprechaun, Macaroni, and Tex.

Before them was the strangely dynamic Coolidge family. Calvin preferred the company of animals, while his wife, Grace, simply enjoyed company, including a bobcat, a goose, an antelope, a stray cat, a donkey, and dogs aplenty. Among their favorite was Rebecca the Raccoon who liked to ride upon the shoulders of her masters while they strolled around the Executive Mansion.

No family accumulated more than the flying circus of the Theodore Roosevelts. Cats, rats, ponies, pigs, guinea pigs, a badger, a one-legged rooster, a slew of terriers and hounds, and a macaw. Avid travelers, the Roosevelts and their six kids seemingly adopted every animal that Teddy didn't shoot.

Situated within sight of the U.S. Naval Academy in Annapolis is the Presidential Pet Museum. Among the holdings is a cowbell once worn by *Pauline*, a bovine member of the Taft family who grazed upon the White House lawn.

## 4.  CARDS

Nearly every president in the nineteenth century played—except James Polk, whose wife, Sarah, forbade the pastime in the White House. The games were much like the general population of the Northeast, mostly of English origin and accompanied by French and German variations. The popular game early on was whist, a four-player contest involving tricks and trumps. After the Civil War, euchre became the national diversion and was a favorite of James Garfield, with pinochle and cribbage not far behind.

Saturday night was bridge night at the Eisenhower White House. As a soldier, Ike excelled at poker, but as president he chose less combative card games in order to keep the peace among friends.

EISENHOWER PRESIDENTIAL LIBRARY

Over time, whist evolved into the female-dominated bridge, while males turned toward competitive poker, an ancient game introduced into the United States sometime in the 1820s. Adept at reading people, Grover Cleveland thrived on it. FDR and Truman played for small pots. The most skilled players were Eisenhower and Nixon, who both made ample sums in their younger days but elected for friendlier games while in office.[21]

Warren Harding liked to play poker in the White House at least twice a week, though he wasn't particularly good at it. On one occasion he lost a set of china from the Benjamin Harrison administration. But he found the experience a wonderful diversion from the cares of office as well as a great way to stay connected with cabinet members and major campaign contributors. Frequent faces at the table included Treasury Secretary Andrew Mellon, Gen. John "Blackjack" Pershing, and William Wrigley Jr. Harding's commerce secretary, Herbert Hoover, sat in on a game once and was so offended by the seedy behavior of the president and his guests that he never came back.[22]

---

Along with playing cards, Martin Van Buren liked to place wagers. One of his favorite pursuits was to bet on the outcome of elections.

---

## 5. WALKING

When the country moved more slowly, so did their presidents. John Kennedy and Lyndon Johnson were the first executives born in the age of the automobile. Before them, most presidents grew up in rural areas or "walking towns," where hiking was the major mode of transportation.

Many developed a considerable amount of endurance. While in his sixties, John Adams could go five miles before tiring, insisting, "It sets my blood in motion much more than riding." His presidential son liked to start his day with a stroll to Capitol Hill and back. James Madison preferred setting out during midday, while night owl Chester Arthur preferred the quietness of Washington at 3:00 a.m. Calvin Coolidge enjoyed a brisk jaunt in the morning, followed by a slower stroll in the afternoon, where he would window shop to forget about his troubles.[23]

The fastest among them was Harry Truman, who moved abruptly for miles on end. After the attempt on his life in 1950, Truman had to tolerate a slower pace and a much higher degree of protection from the Secret

Service. Though he despised feeling insulated from the public and being forced to take shorter trips, he did enjoy conversing with "his boys" about almost everything except politics.

The last dedicated stroller was Jimmy Carter, who cemented his image as a frugal man by walking the last mile to his inauguration. He and Rosalynn also attempted to take leisurely saunters around Camp David, though the gaggle of Secret Service agents behind them invariably dampened the ambiance.

---

Most presidencies transpired before the automobile. Twenty-fifth president William McKinley was the first chief executive to ride in a car while in office.

---

## 6.  HUNTING AND FISHING

Washington hunted foxes, as did his look-alike, James Monroe. John Tyler was by many accounts an excellent shot. Grover Cleveland gunned for game with a rifle he named "Death and Destruction."

Making up for lost time as a sickly little boy, Theodore Roosevelt immersed himself in outdoor and combat sports—boxing, hiking, jujitsu, polo, rowing, wrestling. He also hunted extremely large game. Immediately after leaving office, TR and his son Kermit went on an extended African safari, where they proceeded to bag more than five hundred animals, including antelope, elephants, giraffes, hippos, hyenas, leopards, lions, rhinos, warthogs, waterbucks, wildebeests, and zebras. Conservationist Roosevelt made up for poor eyesight by shooting often. The legend

Winston Churchill observes while FDR fishes at Shangri-La, the presidential retreat that later was known as Camp David.

of the Teddy Bear is not entirely true. On a particularly unproductive hunting trip to Mississippi, President Roosevelt was presented with a small black bear that had been injured and restrained. Though he did refuse to shoot the exhausted animal, he had someone else kill it with a knife.[24]

Most other sportsmen chose the more placid pursuit of fishing. New Yorker Martin Van Buren was one of the first presidential fishermen. Franklin Pierce loved the recreation, and it was rarely far from his mind (he mentioned fishermen or fishing rights in all four of his State of the Union addresses). Chester A. Arthur preferred angling in Canada. Cleveland found the Adirondacks more to his liking, while Eisenhower was an avid fly fisherman. Unlike Ike, Herbert Hoover never took a sick day or a vacation during his entire presidency, opting instead to labor sixteen-hour days in an effort to fix the Great Depression. Only after defeat in the 1932 elections did he allow himself weekends in the Shenandoah, where he cast his line into the rushing streams.

---

Two presidents who thoroughly despised hunting were Lincoln and Grant. The former could not bring himself to kill, and the latter hated the sight of blood.

---

## 7. SWIMMING

Today commonly viewed as a sport of the upper classes, swimming was initially equated with poverty. Dipping in rivers and streams not only provided a simple form of entertainment for early Americans, it was often their primary means of bathing. Tubs and clean water were conveniences of the wealthier strata, and millions of citizens went without indoor plumbing until well into the twentieth century (the White House did not have indoor bathroom facilities until the Hayes administration in the late 1870s).[25]

The stigma of commonness did not bother John Quincy Adams, and he looked forward to swimming in the Potomac on a daily basis. In his fifties, President Adams could swim the river's breadth, so long as the weather and the water's pace were agreeable. Not until Theodore Roosevelt would the Potomac see another executive swimmer, and he liked it cold. In contrast, his polio-stricken cousin preferred the eighty-eight-degree waters of Warm Springs, Georgia, which he first visited three years after contracting polio in 1921. FDR also installed the first swim-

The media critiques Gerald Ford's form in the new White House pool. Portrayed as a clumsy man, Ford was actually one of the most athletic individuals ever to become president.

COURTESY GERALD R. FORD LIBRARY

ming pool in the White House, which he kept lukewarm. Not only were the balmy waters therapeutic for Roosevelt, he found them liberating, because they allowed him to do something that had been impossible since he was thirty-nine—stand under his own power.

Kennedy was a child of the sea, and he spent long hours sailing or swimming. The latter activity offered a cardiovascular workout without straining his ailing spine, and he too kept the pool at the Executive Mansion warm. LBJ also partook of the presidential waters, often conducting meetings with political figures while he waded. Never athletic as a child, Johnson was among the least-fit presidents, and swimming was essentially the only routine exercise he did while in office. Though the former naval officer was also a fine swimmer, Richard Nixon had the FDR pool covered over to make space for the West Wing pressroom. The Fords compensated by building an in-ground pool on the South lawn.

> John Quincy Adams and TR swam in the Potomac the same way JFK and LBJ swam in the White House pool—naked.

## 8. MUSIC

Oddly, very few presidents were blessed by the muse Euterpe. Thomas Jefferson practiced violin up to three hours a day and played duets with fellow Virginian Patrick Henry. He collected sheet music from across the East Coast and Europe, and as with food and wine, he preferred Italian and French but could play nearly anything. While a diplomat in Paris during the summer of 1785, he broke his wrist severely (possibly from a riding accident). He never played without pain again.

John Tyler was quite proficient at the violin and preferred American folk tunes. His favorite playing partner was his wife, Julia, who occasionally accompanied him on the guitar. Their White House was more musical than most, and she started the tradition of having the Marine Band play "Hail to the Chief" at official events.[26]

Nearly every president owned a personal piano, save for Gerald Ford and the Bushes, but few played. Undoubtedly the most proficient among them was the humble Harry Truman, who as a youth grumbled at being forced to rise at dawn to practice for hours and traveling up to twice a week into Kansas City for professional lessons. He was partial to Beethoven, Chopin, and Mozart, and he played often while in office. For a poor speaker and plain dresser, he was far more in tune with the fine arts that the regaled Kennedy or Reagan, neither of whom cared at all for haute couture in any form.[27]

Many presidents took pleasure in simply listening. McKinley was fond of the opera, Taft and Wilson liked musicals, and the swarthy Harding occasionally attended a Washington burlesque show. Perhaps the least musical of all was U. S. Grant. He claimed to only know two songs. "One was Yankee Doodle," said the general, "the other wasn't."[28]

---

Music may have saved the lives of John and Julia Tyler. Riding the gunship *Princeton* down the Potomac, the presidential couple went belowdecks to listen to celebratory songs, while guests above watched a large naval cannon shoot rounds. One of the firings burst the breech, killing eight onlookers, including Julia's father.

---

## 9.  GOLF

The pinnacle pastime of the business class, golf is centuries old, but it did not catch on in the United States until the late 1800s. The first chief executive to fully embrace the game was portly William Howard Taft. He was roundly criticized for spending time on the links, yet at the same time his high profile caused a surge in the game's popularity.

On doctor's orders, Wilson took up golf and had a hard time liking it. He described the game as "an ineffectual attempt to put an elusive ball into an obscure hole with implements ill-adapted to the purpose." Even on a good day, he was unable to crack a score of one hundred. His successor shot in the nineties, but Harding preferred to be a spectator.[29]

Golf and Eisenhower were almost synonymous in the 1950s, a fair assessment considering he played up to 150 rounds a year. He also installed a putting green near the Rose Garden and enjoyed hitting irons shots off the White House lawn. Some of his longer hits strayed outside of the grounds. On the links, he shot in the eighties consistently.[30]

Despite a bad back, Kennedy played better than Ike. A former member of the Harvard team, he was amazingly strong off the tee, and he occasionally shot in the high seventies. But he knew the public-relations risk of spending long hours on the links, having witnessed the public ire waged against Eisenhower, so Jack normally played in secret.[31]

Nixon golfed but was a better bowler, having a lane installed in the Executive Mansion, upon which he averaged a respectable 175. Often viewed as clumsy, Gerald Ford may have been the finest athlete ever to be president. A former football MVP at Michigan, he lifted weights in the presidential study, skied, loved water sports, played tennis, but he never quite mastered golf, playing with an eighteen handicap. A self-deprecating man, Ford was famous for saying, "I know I'm playing better golf because I'm hitting fewer spectators."[32]

---

Both of the Bushes were avid golfers, and they came from a long line of club men. George Herbert Walker, George H. W. Bush's grandfather, was president of the U.S. Golf Association.

---

William Howard Taft tees one up at Hot Springs, Virginia, during his first year as president.

## 10. TENNIS

In the spring of 1903, when her husband was away on a tour of the western states, Edith Roosevelt had a surprise waiting for Teddy on his return—the first tennis court at the White House. Originally it stood next to the West Wing. It was later moved to a more secluded spot just a few yards west of the grand fountain on the South lawn. Teddy found time to work and play by doing both simultaneously, and his cadre of players were sometimes called the "Tennis Cabinet."[33]

Wilson didn't care for the game, but his family did, a fate shared by Coolidge and Truman. All three men were rather pathetic at sports, but they married excellent athletes and enjoyed watching their family compete. Wilson's daughters played the occasional singles match, and Harding's wife, Florence, initiated an all-women's tournament at the executive complex. The Coolidge sons John and Cal Jr. were exceptionally active, partaking of the presidential court on numerous occasions. In the summer of 1924, they played each other on a particularly hot day, and sixteen-year-old Cal Jr. thought nothing of it when his foot blistered. A week later, the abrasion turned septic, and he died of blood poisoning. His father fell into a deep depression, often sleeping twelve hours a day.

The next active players were Carter and Ford, followed by tennis fanatic George H. W. Bush. To avoid public scrutiny, Bush would usually play at a private club in Washington, but he often invited professional players to hit a few on the White House court. Among Bush's oldest partners was his secretary of state, James Baker III—the two had met in 1959 when they were paired for a doubles match at the Houston Country Club. Bill

Edith's gift to Teddy was the first White House tennis court, which was right outside the original West Wing. Standing guard in the background is the Old Executive Office Building.

Clinton dabbled in the game. He also jogged and swam in an attempt to keep his weight down—to little avail.

> Calvin Coolidge's secretary of war was Dwight Davis. In his youth, Davis was a superb tennis player and a founder of the International Lawn Tennis Challenge. After his death in 1945, his tennis tournament was named in his honor—the Davis Cup.

## TOP TEN OVERTLY
## RELIGIOUS PRESIDENTS

Contrary to popular belief, the Founding Fathers as a whole were neither devoutly religious nor agnostic. The architects of the Republic were nearly as pluralistic as their four million constituents, from New England Puritans to Maryland Catholics, from rustic revivalists to urbane skeptics.

In 1776, only one out of six Americans belonged to a particular church, and many viewed providence with a sense of wonderment rather than doctrinal certainty. But when it came time to form a more prefect union, the Constitutional Convention in Philadelphia agreed that if they were to save both church and state, separation was absolutely mandatory. The United States, with its multitude of denominations, would never stay united under the guise of a national religion. In order to survive, the government had to rule through the consent of the people, not through the assumption of divine right.[34]

True to their word, the Founding Fathers protected faith as personal property. Nowhere in the Constitution was there an overt reference to God. Article 6 forbade any religious test for public office. In 1791, the very first sentence of the First Amendment read, "Congress shall make no law respecting an establishment of religion." Normally reserved in his language, President Washington was adamant when he told a citizen, "No one would be more zealous than myself to establish effectual barriers against the horrors of spiritual tyranny."[35]

So it was written for generations. U. S. Grant proclaimed, "Not one dollar . . . shall be appropriated to the support of any sectarian schools." His successor Rutherford Hayes considered proposing a constitutional amendment to that effect. Theodore Roosevelt thought it sacrilegious to have "In God We Trust" on coins, a phrase adopted during the turmoil of the Civil War, and he lobbied for its removal. His protégé William Taft refused to discuss religion at all in the 1908 election.[36]

Most presidents firmly believed in a supreme being, and many invoked the blessings of heaven in public. But there have been some who actively blurred the separation between God and government. Initially they were the exception. But a transformation occurred after World War II, when the country faced an archenemy in the officially atheistic Soviet Union. To demonize the opposition—a standard tactic in wartime—the White House began to resemble a house of faith, a bastion of believers against a godless foe. When the strategy proved popular among voters, faith-based government slowly became a possibility. The wrath of Vietnam and Watergate further enticed the electorate to seek candidates with religious conviction, and openly spiritual presidents have been in place ever since.

Below are the chief executives who were the most explicitly devout in their public service, based on the rhetoric of their speeches, actions in their daily lives, and the inclusion of religion in their policies. Not surprisingly, most of them are recent, and they have consciously challenged the moral boundaries established by the Founding Fathers.[37]

## 1.  DWIGHT D. EISENHOWER (PRESBYTERIAN)

He began his inaugural speech with "a little private prayer" and then proceeded into a sermon of rapture, fired by references of gods and wars, light and darkness, and warnings that "forces of good and evil are massed and armed and opposed." After swearing the oath on two Bibles, Eisenhower announced: "Science seems ready to confer upon us, as its final gift, the power to erase human life from this planet. At such a time in history, we who are free must proclaim anew our faith."

It was a bit dark for such an otherwise cheery fellow. The message was also atypical of him. Until he reached the White House, Eisenhower had not been particularly religious in his life. After election, he transformed into the valiant crusader, dedicated to stand firm against the specter of faithless communism.

During his childhood, Ike's mother was a member the Watchtower Society, later known as Jehovah's Witnesses. For nearly twenty years, the
Eisenhower home in Abilene, Kansas, served as a meetinghouse. Threaded
into many of the gatherings were portents of Armageddon, due sometime
around 1915. When the end of time came and went, all the Eisenhower
boys drifted away from their mother's sect, rarely to speak of it again.

However, by Inauguration Day 1953, the possibility of global annihi-
lation seemed all too real. The metaphorical darkness of communism had
spread across half of Europe and all of China. Southeast Asia seemed
poised to fall, and the Soviet Union possessed the bomb. Americans had
recently learned that their own scientists had engineered an entirely new
device: a "hydrogen bomb" hundreds of times more powerful than what
had leveled Hiroshima and Nagasaki.

In his war against "godless communism," Eisenhower opted for con-
tainment overseas but an offensive at home. Twelve days after his address on the apocalypse, he was baptized, confirmed, and made a
communicant in the Presbyterian Church. On Flag Day 1954, he signed
a bill adding "under God" to the Pledge of Allegiance. He consecrated
the moment with the statement, "We are reaffirming the transcendence
of religious faith in America's heritage and future; in this way we shall
constantly strengthen those spiritual weapons which forever will be our
country's most powerful resource in peace and war." In 1956 he helped
make "In God We Trust" the official motto of the United States, and in
1957, the phrase was added to federal paper currency. Support for his
actions were considerable, especially in the Deep South and the Northeast, where more than two-thirds of public schools engaged in daily
Bible readings.[38]

The man who considered himself "the most intensely religious man I
know" also set the precedent of starting cabinet meetings with a prayer,
and he created the interfaith White House prayer breakfast. Eisenhower
also started a tradition that ran through the administrations of Johnson,
Nixon, Reagan, and the Bushes, when he called on evangelist Billy Graham to be his unofficial spiritual advisor.[39]

---

In retirement, Dwight Eisenhower became a member of the Gettysburg
Presbyterian Church, the same church Abraham Lincoln visited after giving
a short address at a nearby cemetery on November 19, 1863.

---

## 2.   GEORGE W. BUSH (METHODIST)

 No doubt the question was meant to be a plumb-line measure of intellect. Most of the Republican candidates could hardly name one, let alone pretend to have a preference. But when debate moderator Tom Brokaw asked them in a 2000 Primary debate which political philosopher influenced them most, the oft-stumbling governor of Texas quickly offered an answer. It was a statement not of brains but of conviction, the one ingredient he held in abundance.

"Jesus Christ, because he changed my heart." Since age thirty-nine, Bush professed to be born again, and his advertised creed, viewed by the pundits as a quirk, gave him a decisive push from the religious Right that would carry him into the White House.

After winning the GOP nomination in August, his running mate was to be Pennsylvania Governor Tom Ridge. Bush dumped the pro-choice Catholic for pro-life Methodist Dick Cheney. On Election Day, he won 77 percent of the evangelical Protestant vote, nearly a fourth of the electorate. More than 85 percent of those who described themselves as religious conservatives chose him. When he became president, Bush was not exaggerating when he said, "I am here because of the power of prayer."[40]

David Frum, a Bush speechwriter, described the revived White House as a "culture of modern Evangelicalism." The chief executive led Bible studies. Every cabinet meeting began with a prayer. Several staff and cabinet members wore their faith on their sleeves, particularly Secretary of Education William Bennet and speechwriter Michael Gerson (who would later coin the phrase "axis of evil"). Nine days into his term, Bush established the White House Office of Faith-Based and Community Initiatives, offering grants to private organizations that provided social services.[41]

In hindsight, it can be said that the attacks of September 11, 2001, greatly intensified a preexisting condition, and Bush consecrated the new War on Terror with ecclesiastical language. Standing before a joint session of Congress on September 20, he stated, "Either you are with us, or you are with the terrorists. . . . One cannot serve two masters."

Throughout his administration he argued against abortion and gay marriage on moral grounds. His first veto was against the funding of stem cell research. As of 2007, funds from his faith-based program had only gone to Christian organizations. Continuing to wage war in the Middle East, he was often called into question for his heavily religious moralizing, yet Bush never hid his worldview from the American public. "My style, my focus, and many of the issues that I talk about," Bush firmly insisted, "are reinforced by my religion."[42]

---

Among George W. Bush's fellow Methodists are U. S. Grant, Rutherford Hayes, and first lady Hillary Rodham Clinton.

---

## 3.   JAMES EARL CARTER (BAPTIST)

The religious Right truly became a part of American politics with the emergence of a conservative, devout Democrat. In 1976 a Gallup poll calculated that nearly half of American Protestants considered themselves "born again." Included among them was soon-to-be-president Jimmy Carter.[43]

His brand of unconcealed faith struck a chord with the long-dormant and diffuse fundamentalist lobby. It also appealed to a large portion of the general electorate seeking a clean break from the demagoguery of LBJ and Tricky Dick. It was a Third Great Awakening of sorts, and religion stepped into the political waters with both feet. In his home church in Plains, Georgia, the candidate insisted, "We have a responsibility to shape government so it does exemplify the teachings of God." Said one individual at the Democratic Party Convention, "Surely the Lord sent Jimmy Carter." While President Gerald Ford later wrote, "Carter talked about his religious convictions in a way that I found discomfiting," many voters believed Carter when he said, "I'll be a better president because of my deep religious convictions."[44]

The *New York Times* dubbed Carter's inaugural address a "sermon," and he continued to teach Sunday school while president. Respectful of the Old Testament, he was hawkish in his support of Israel, a nation-state he considered to be "a fulfillment of Biblical prophecy." When discussing his pursuit of peace in the Middle East, Carter frequently used the phrase "sacred work."[45]

But as a moralist, Carter was largely unsuccessful. He brought the revival, and then he asked the congregation to think secularly on prayer in public schools, family planning, and abortion. His moral will appeared all the more suspect when tested against the "godless" Soviet Union in Afghanistan and the rise of Islamic fundamentalism in Iran.[46]

Yet his was largely a faith of introspection, a perpetual effort to cleanse the self rather than convert others. Emblematic was his thoroughly religious "Crisis of confidence" address of July 1979. He spoke of a citizenry that had lost its way, and he lamented that self-worth was "no longer defined by what one does, but by what one owns." His message was initially greeted with widespread approval, but in time the testament became known as the infamous "Malaise Speech," roundly rejected by a populace that felt they had suffered enough to consider themselves worthy of salvation. In 1980, many of them chose to look for a less complicated faith, one that provided an unequivocal feeling of righteousness.[47]

---

Secret Service code name for President Carter: "The Deacon"

---

## 4.  WILLIAM McKINLEY (METHODIST)

At a camp revival meeting in Poland, Ohio, a ten-year-old boy stood up among the congregation and declared his everlasting devotion to his God. By sixteen, he had attained the rank of communicant, much to the delight of his devout parents. In adulthood he became a Sunday-school director and president of a YMCA. He was so driven by his faith that he openly declared Christianity as "the mightiest factor in the world's civilization." A year later, he became the twenty-fifth president of the United States.[48]

Americans liked their candidates to be upstanding, but preachy types were still considered suspect in the late nineteenth century. One of the reasons McKinley won the election of 1896 was that he was the *lesser* of two evangelicals. Nebraska Democrat William Jennings Bryan (later Woodrow Wilson's secretary of state and the prosecuting attorney in the 1925 Scopes trial) was so forthright in his Presbyterianism that he effectively alienated the largest religious minority in the country—Roman Catholics.

The comparative moderate, McKinley was still the most openly religious president the country had yet elected. His inaugural address nearly sounded like an excerpt from the Old Testament. "Our faith teaches that there is no safer reliance than upon the God of our fathers," moralized McKinley, "who will not forsake us so long as we obey His commandments and walk humbly in His footsteps."

Yet he was sincerely penitent. Warmhearted, humble, tender, and faithful to his afflicted wife (Ida suffered from random crippling seizures), McKinley was the model believer. While in the White House, he attended Metropolitan Methodist Church, prayed daily, and often invited guests to sing hymns in the Blue Room.[49]

McKinley was no imperialist, but he did support the growing network of Christian missionaries across the globe. Attending an ecumenical missionary conference in Carnegie Hall, the president blessed their work with a convocation: "May this great meeting rekindle the spirit of missionary ardor and enthusiasm [for] the continuous proclamation of His gospel to the end of time."[50]

Much of that missionary zeal had spread to the Philippines, which the U.S. armed forces had recently pried from the clutches of Imperial Spain. Compelled to explain why he decided to conquer and occupy the country and promote Protestant missions therein, McKinley explained to a group of fellow Methodists, "I went down on my knees and prayed Almighty God for light and guidance." He then told his audience of the epiphany, "There was nothing left to do but to take them all, and to educate the Filipinos, and uplift and civilize and Christianize them, and by God's grace do the very best we can by them, as our fellowmen for whom Christ also died."[51]

McKinley's well-intended exploits received a great deal of criticism, especially from those who feared America was simply replacing Spain as the new ruler of the archipelago. Indeed, it would be another war and another forty-five years before the United States granted Filipinos their independence, but McKinley would not live to see it. His assassination in 1901 spared him of any further criticism for his reluctant crusade and made him a martyr to nationalists and missionaries alike.

Before he finally succumbed to his mortal wounding, William McKinley's last words were: "It's God's way. His will, not ours, be done. Nearer my God to Thee."

## 5.  RONALD REAGAN (PRESBYTERIAN)

 In 1980 Reagan became president by being the anti-Carter. Patriotism over penitence, the swift sword over the olive branch, the self-assured over the self-denied. Whereas the peanut farmer portrayed himself as unique, Reagan made himself out as the All-American, possessing something in common with all fellow members of "God's Country," and in no venue did he better achieve this than in the rough waters of religion.

Doctrine was not a major part of Ronald Reagan's early life, nor would it ever be. He often mentioned how his father was a Catholic and his mother a Protestant, but aside from a sense of tolerance for the God-fearing, they imbued in him no strict code or scriptural familiarity. He dabbled in the Disciples of Christ and Presbyterianism but preferred the ambiguity of revival transformation—to feel saved is to be saved. And in his mature years, he swaddled the cross in the flag, espousing a belief he called "faithful patriotism."[52]

Fundamentalists who had backed Carter four years earlier widely supported his questioning of evolution, his advocacy of school prayer, and his opposition to abortion. His staff and cabinet included hard-line evangelicals, such as special assistant Morton Blackwell and Education Secretary Robert Billings. Cold warriors cherished his zeal against the agnostic Soviet system, which Reagan described to an Orlando church group as "a sin and evil in the world, and we are enjoined by Scripture and the Lord Jesus to oppose it with all our might." In his annual addresses to Congress, Reagan broke with tradition and repeatedly used the word *God*. It was with sincerity that Jerry Falwell, president of Moral Majority Inc., considered Reagan's victory in 1980 "my finest hour."[53]

However stirring he may have been, Reagan often ran into trouble with clerics. Many groups, including the National Council of Churches, openly rejected his reduction of social services, his favoritism toward the wealthy, and his tendency to support right-wing dictatorships in third-world countries. In 1983 Reagan claimed the papacy supported his pro-Contra operations in Nicaragua. It did not, and the Vatican publicly corrected him.[54]

Nor were historians fond of his rewriting the spiritual past. He often depicted Puritans as champions of religious freedom, the same Puritans that openly persecuted Jews, Catholics, and Quakers. The president also painted Benjamin Franklin and Thomas Jefferson as devout believers, while they were actually the most skeptical of the Founding Fathers. In recounting the Philadelphia Convention of 1787, Reagan liked to state that the framers "opened all the constitutional meetings with prayer." In fact the framers almost unanimously rejected such a proposal.[55]

But the general public welcomed Reagan's message of American righteousness. In the 1984 elections, he won more than 65 percent of the Methodists, 66 percent of Lutherans, 68 percent of Presbyterians, and 81 percent of white evangelicals.[56]

---

Ronald Reagan was the first divorcee ever elected president.

---

## 6. WOODROW WILSON (PRESBYTERIAN)

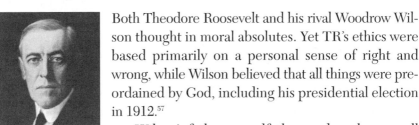

Both Theodore Roosevelt and his rival Woodrow Wilson thought in moral absolutes. Yet TR's ethics were based primarily on a personal sense of right and wrong, while Wilson believed that all things were preordained by God, including his presidential election in 1912.[57]

Wilson's father, grandfather, and uncle were all Presbyterian ministers. In his youth, Woodrow felt no great desire to follow in their footsteps until his college years. One night, the eighteen-year-old scribbled in his journal about a life he viewed as misspent. "I have increased very little in grace," wrote the troubled man, "and have done almost nothing for the Savior's Cause here below."[58]

Initially conservative, Wilson gradually adopted the sentiments of his predominantly progressive family, who viewed social reform rather than prayer as the clearest path to salvation. As an adult, Wilson summarized his new worldview in a speech before a YMCA assembly, insisting, "If you will think about what you ought to do for other people, your character will take care of itself. . . . And that is the lesson of Christianity."[59]

He never wavered in his rhetoric. To a White House visitor in 1915, he said, "My life would not be worth living if it were not for the driving power of religion, for faith, pure and simple." While president he served as an elder in Washington's Central Presbyterian Church, went to prayer meetings every Wednesday, and read the Bible nightly. To him, Christianity was "the most vitalizing thing in the world."[60]

Nowhere were his convictions more apparent and annoying to others than in his diplomatic mission to Versailles, where the savior-American proceeded to preach upon the warring Continentals. Taken aback by Wilson's hubris, French president Georges Clemenceau said, "He thinks he is another Jesus Christ come upon the earth to reform men." Equally surprised was British prime minister David Lloyd George, who thought Wilson was acting like "a missionary" who had come "to rescue the poor European heathen." Directing European relief programs at the time, philanthropist Herbert Hoover knew Wilson could not turn it off, calling the president "a born Crusader."[61]

Wilson's rigor at Versailles was heartfelt but ineffective. Europe pulled the teeth from his progressive Fourteen Points, and the U.S. Senate refused to ordain his League of Nations. But he did score a major victory in terms of his faith. He lent his support to Britain's Balfour Declaration, a secret policy statement backing the formation of a Jewish state in the old Ottoman Empire. Shortly before his death, he believed Israel was about to become a political reality, and he viewed its creation in purely religious terms. "To think that I, a son of the manse," he said in confidence to an associate, "should be able to help restore the Holy Land to its people."[62]

---

To demonstrate "due regard for the Divine Will," Woodrow Wilson ordered U.S. forces in the First World War to work and fight as little as possible on Sundays.

---

## 7.  BENJAMIN HARRISON (PRESBYTERIAN)

"He is a cold-blooded, narrow-minded, prejudiced, obstinate, timid old psalm-signing Indianapolis politician." Theodore Roosevelt may have been a tad callous in his assessment of Benjamin Harrison, but he was not alone in the sentiment. Harrison was hard to like, in part because he was such a contradiction. He could charm crowds with his brilliant oratory, but in person he was tactless and aloof. He would skip out of the White House to play with his grandchildren, yet squeeze twelve-hour workdays out of his staff. Apt to change his mind often, he chastised anyone who dared contradict him.[63]

Harrison was born in 1833 in the hinterlands of Ohio, a time and place deep in the evangelical throws of the Second Great Awakening. His parents were devout, as was his presidential grandfather. By age twenty-seven he was an elder in the church, a Sunday-school teacher, and a deacon. He intended on going into the ministry until he surmised that an eager Christian could do more in politics. As he once told his fellow students at Miami of Ohio, "Civil society is no less an institution of God than the Church."[64]

The chance to become the nation's premier civil servant came in the election of 1888. He won primarily due to the relentless efforts of a well-organized and well-funded Republican hierarchy. Harrison, however, chalked his win to something else. Hearing he had won, Harrison vigorously shook the hand of national Republican chairman Stan Quay and beamed, "Providence has given us victory." Angered by the candidate's lack of gratitude, Quay later said, "He ought to know that Providence hadn't a damn thing to do with it."[65]

In office he began every day with a short service, where his father-in-law, the Reverend John Scott, led the family in prayer. A self-described born-again, Harrison alienated prominent Republicans by selecting a rather anonymous and unaccomplished cabinet; vital to Harrison's criteria, nearly all of them were declared Presbyterians.[66]

Like his grandfather, he was a Sabbatarian, refusing to conduct any official business on Sundays. The national media couldn't help notice that while the moralizing Harrison cherished the day by not working, he would occasionally play pool or go on extended treks in the countryside.[67]

Ultimately, the popular Harrison lost favor. Certainly intelligent, industrious, and committed to conducting the basic necessities of his job, he failed to win the hearts and minds of his fellow Americans in part because his paradoxical behavior looked so much like hypocrisy.

---

Benjamin Harrison's promotional campaign biography was written by Lew Wallace, author of the religious epic *Ben Hur*.

---

## 8.   GEORGE H. W. BUSH (EPISCOPALIAN)

Tenacious is the legend that George Washington added the words "so help me God" when he first took the oath of office. Actually there is no firsthand evidence of an executive uttering the addition until Chester A. Arthur in 1881. Arthur's invocation, said at a time when only 20 percent of Americans regularly attended church services, did not become an inaugural tradition until the late 1930s, when 50 percent of Americans were routinely going to the pews.[68]

By 1989, the "oath after the oath" was customary, and George H. W. Bush took the piety one step further in his inaugural address. "And my first act as President," he announced to the world audience, "is a prayer. I ask you to bow your heads . . ."

Fundamentalists were initially cold to his puritanical Northeastern roots and his relative restraint compared with the prophesizing Reagan. Not surprisingly, Bush finished third in the Iowa caucuses behind Kansas senator Bob Dole and televangelist Pat Robertson. But as the campaign progressed, he pushed good-versus-evil rhetoric, championed prayer in public schools, and mentioned God in nearly every campaign speech. On November 8, 1988, the Episcopalian scored an astounding 88 percent of the evangelical vote.[69]

As president he continued to pray daily and attend services weekly, yet Bush viewed his faith much like he viewed his politics: "I'm a conservative, but I'm not a nut about it." His prayer-in-school statements never

Not until Chester A. Arthur was there a verified instance of a president concluding his oath of office with the phrase "so help me God."

manifested into action, nor did his attempt to order the Pledge of Allegiance in schools. To the Supreme Court he appointed David Souter and Clarence Thomas, both of whom were right of center but not to any extreme, and neither were adamantly opposed to the religious Right's nemesis, *Roe v. Wade*.

Only when it was time for reelection did Bush replay the God card, and the message had lost its edge. In the polls, nearly every denomination reduced its support. The largest hit came from evangelicals—nearly 40 percent eventually voted against him.[70]

---

George H. W. Bush and eight other presidents were Episcopalians. Eight more were Presbyterians. Together the two denominations represent more than 40 percent of the past chief executives but less than 5 percent of the American population.

---

## 9. RICHARD NIXON (QUAKER)

When Hubert Humphrey conceded the 1968 election, Nixon summoned a longtime spiritual confidant to his suite at the Waldorf Towers in Manhattan. When the guest of honor arrived, the president-elect, daughters Tricia and Julie, and wife Pat joined hands with Billy Graham, formed a circle, and praised "God's plan for the country."[71]

In his first weeks in office, Nixon started nondenominational services in the White House. According to Nixon, it was intended to keep his devotion private. His aide John Ehrlichman considered it a political display. The Sunday gathering in the East Room soon became a prestigious event, attended by the elites of religion and Washington alike, with church choirs, organists, and Billy Graham as common fixtures.[72]

Such was the enigmatic Nixon, private yet public in worship, straitlaced yet profane, utterly faithful to a wife he rarely acknowledged. Somewhat forgiving of his joining the navy in the Second World War, fellow Quakers heavily opposed his militarism in Indochina. At the same time, the chairman of the Joint Chiefs of Staff, Thomas Moorer, was somewhat beleaguered when Nixon insisted that no bombing raids on

Vietnam should occur on a Sunday, whether the Sabbath was hovering over East Asia or North America.[73]

Nixon was not an evangelist. A Quaker in name all his life, he sporadically praised many faiths, from the unassuming honesty of his mother's Society of Friends, to the grand ritual of Catholicism, to the political prestige of Presbyterians. During the darkest hours of Watergate, he sought a rabbi for spiritual guidance. Much like his relationship with the Constitution, he explored the depths of religion but was uncomfortable with its strict guidelines.[74]

Perhaps nothing summarized his religious convictions or his innate complexity more than a statement he made to his trusted chief of staff, Bob Haldeman. Sequestered at Camp David in the last days of his presidency, Nixon confessed: "You know, Bob, there is something I've never told anyone before, not even you. Every night since I've been president . . . I've knelt down on my knees beside my bed and prayed to God for guidance and help in this job. Last night before I went to bed I knelt down, and this time I prayed I wouldn't wake up in the morning."[75]

---

Thus far two Quakers have become president—Richard Nixon and Herbert Hoover, which is two more than Lutheranism, the largest mainline Protestant denomination in the United States.

---

## 10. JOHN QUINCY ADAMS (UNITARIAN)

Of the early presidents, John Quincy Adams was the most public in his expressions of faith, and he was also the most cerebral. It was therefore no accident that he wrestled with matters of theology, for he treated faith as a wondrous enigma to be openly discussed as with any mystery of the universe.

While president he scoured the Bible often, and on Sundays he attended services twice: Unitarian in the morning and Presbyterian later in the afternoon. Religion for him was investigation, and while Adams embraced the concept of a divine being, he questioned the probability of a divine human on earth or the possibility of a virgin birth. Miracles, parables, and practices were all intriguing avenues for contemplation. He felt welcome in almost any religious environ, though the long and quiet services of Quakers bored him immensely. Later in life, he found radical departures such as Ralph Waldo Emerson's Transcendentalism to be too ethereal, even for him.

Adams did not join a church until he was president. It was to be Unitarian Congregationalism, the church of his less pontificating father. The two men would come to share many traits in faith—admiration for a human Jesus, skepticism toward a Holy Trinity, and dismissal of predestination. Yet while the senior Adams was content to be a good person, his son possessed an innate restlessness, a desire to search eternally for an absolute truth, one that could only be achieved through resolute and open pontification.

> John Quincy Adams and his father are among the very few presidents who are buried in a religious setting. The Adamses and their brides are interred beneath the Congregational Church in Quincy, Massachusetts.

## TOP TEN
## MACHIAVELLIAN PRESIDENTS

If the institution has mutated from a subdued patronage into an imperial presidency, then it would stand to reason that the presidents have gone from being fatherly figures to resembling *The Prince*, Niccolo Machiavelli's archetype of the power-hungry politician. In actuality, there have been autocratic presidents from the Republic's beginning, and these Machiavellian types have been among the most revered.

While it is true that recent candidates have been far more aggressive than their forbearers in running for the office, they generally have not ruled with a firmer hand once they were in power. If anything, modern presidents have become hypersensitive to the wants and needs of the country as a whole. More than ever, their job security depends upon their ability to appeal to the masses. George Washington presided over a population of four million, but his electorate was 4 percent of that—a small portion of the white, male property owners in the country. Seventy percent of George W. Bush's America had the right to vote in 2004, including every race, ethnicity, religion, literacy level, and income bracket imaginable, male and female, age eighteen and above.[76]

When given the choice, Americans do not care for gentle souls atop the executive branch. Possibly the nicest presidents were Chester Arthur,

William Howard Taft, and Gerald Ford. Of these three, only Taft was elected in his own right, and none of them won a second term.

Consistently, the country has preferred "strong leaders," individuals who are much like the Prince. Although their personalities vary widely, the most authoritarian presidents shared a few basic traits. Nearly all possessed a temper and were acutely sensitive to criticism. Close friends were almost nonexistent. Oddly, nearly all of them were also bone fide mama's boys. And all but one were voted into office for a second term. They are ranked here by the intensity of their Machiavellian traits: sense of superiority, preference of force over mercy, level of secrecy, and fixation with their own legacy. They are paired with the act that best illustrates how far they were willing to go to retain power.

## 1.  FRANKLIN ROOSEVELT
### THE JAPANESE INTERNMENTS (1942–45)

He was neither introspective nor terribly sentimental, and he felt no desire or ability to pour his soul out to anyone. Even those who were near him on a daily basis were amazed by his ability to be simultaneously warm and detached. Roosevelt liked to call people by their first name, which put them at ease as well as in their place. He could also be devious. A favorite axiom of his was "Never let your left know what your right hand is doing."

Soon after Imperial Japan attacked Pearl Harbor (and Hong Kong, Malay, the Philippines, Wake Island, the coast of China, and Guam on the same day), Roosevelt's left hand of the U.S. Army was telling him to detain everyone of Japanese descent on the West Coast. His right hand of the cabinet, especially Attorney General Francis Biddle, strongly opposed this move, finding no viable threat of espionage or sabotage among the Japanese community, 64 percent of whom were American citizens. Initially the president agreed with Biddle as well as the first lady and J. Edgar Hoover. Regardless of the legal and moral implications, the idea was a logistical nightmare. The country could not spare the money and manpower required to gather, process, and incarcerate possibly two hundred thousand people.[77]

But growing pressure from the War Department, West Coast newspapers, and much of the white population in California began to weigh upon the pragmatic president. To win the war, he needed the political and industrial support of the West, and he was not about to let the Constitution

In 1942, Japanese and Japanese Americans await shipment of their belongings and transport for themselves to internment camps.

interfere with wartime needs. On February 19, 1942, Roosevelt signed Executive Order 9066, which empowered the War Department "to prescribe military areas . . . from which any and all persons may be excluded," namely ethnic Japanese. More than 111,000 would be detained, the majority of whom would remain in rudimentary camps for the duration of the war and lose most of their jobs, homes, and possessions in the process. Curiously, no such detentions were performed in the Hawaiian Islands, where nearly a third of the local population was of Japanese descent.[78]

Once the order was drawn, FDR did not pay much attention to the plight of the interned. The draconian act, after all, was intended to maintain the obedience of the majority *outside* the camp rather than the minority inside. Still, his overall detachment, bordering on indifference, seemed to prove the caustic remark that writer H. L. Mencken made of him years before: "If [FDR] becomes convinced tomorrow that coming out for cannibalism would get him the votes he so sorely needs, he would begin fattening a missionary in the White House backyard come Wednesday."[79]

> The Roosevelt administration briefly considered interning citizens of German descent, until they realized there were sixty million of them.

## 2.  ANDREW JACKSON
### THE NULLIFICATION CRISIS (1832)

While presiding over the Senate, Vice President Thomas Jefferson could not help but notice the agitated senator from Tennessee. The man was six feet tall and only 145 pounds, with the appearance and personality of a vengeful cadaver. Adding to the effect was his thatch of tombstone-gray hair and a pair of blue-flame eyes leering from their sockets. "His passions are terrible," Jefferson observed, "he could never speak on account of the rashness of his feelings. I have seen him attempt it repeatedly, and as often choke with rage." Jefferson might have been unnerved to learn that Andrew Jackson was at the height of his maturity.[80]

Tennessee's first congressman, the first president born west of the Appalachians, the first to use the pocket veto, and the first from the Democratic Party, Old Hickory viewed the world in black and white. To him, people were either dear friends (of which there were a handful) or scheming enemies. He was marvelously charismatic, incurably passionate, and blindly loyal to the lower classes. Women found him alluring.

Yet as president, he treated the nation as he did his many slaves, with paternal kindness, unless they disobeyed. Adversaries came to call him "King Andrew" for his despotic unwillingness to compromise. The trademark inflexibility sometimes backfired, as in the case of the PETTICOAT AFFAIR and in his many skirmishes with Congress. When the charter of the Bank of the United States came up for renewal, Jackson adamantly vetoed it, claiming the federal depository helped the rich become richer. It did. The private holding firm also stabilized currency and brought discipline to lending. When the charter died, so did the bank, and the ripple effect devastated the economy for years.

The greatest anger he reserved for the Nullification Crisis of 1832. In the face of exorbitant tariffs (more than 60 percent on some products), cash-poor South Carolina and its fiery native son—Vice President John C. Calhoun—declared the tariff law null and void. Jackson diplomatically dismissed the nullification, arguing that if such a power existed for the states to veto federal laws, no law would ever go into effect. In response, Calhoun resigned from the executive branch and joined the Senate, while his state threatened secession. Jackson volleyed back by promising to raise a massive army, up to two hundred thousand troops if need be, and arrest every leader involved for treason. If Calhoun were found guilty, Jackson vowed he would be hanged. In a letter to political cohort Martin Van Buren, the president admitted, "I expect soon to hear that a civil war has commenced."[81]

Such was the rage of Jackson. The president was within hours of ordering a nationwide call for volunteers when South Carolina capitulated. A compromise bill followed, and Speaker of the House James K. Polk announced a much-needed adjournment. While contemplating what might have been, Jackson was satisfied that the clouds had passed, but only temporarily. "The nullifiers in the south intend to blow up a storm . . . to destroy this union and form a southern confederacy bounded, north, by the Potomac river." He was right, of course, but fortunately for South Carolina, he would also be dead for fifteen years when it happened.[82]

---

As a dig against Jackson's ruthless stubbornness, political opponents nicknamed him "Andrew Jackass." The tag stuck, and over time, the image of the kicking donkey became the unofficial symbol of the Democratic Party.

---

### 3.   ABRAHAM LINCOLN
#### THE EMANCIPATION PROCLAMATION (1863)

The impression that Lincoln was caring and sensitive is plausible, because it is partially true. From an early age he displayed a gentleness blatantly out of place in the unforgiving wilderness of frontier Kentucky. Kind to animals, he viewed hunting as barbaric. He wrote poetry. Neighbors recalled that, as a young man, he would brood for hours, and he occasionally became preoccupied with thoughts of death.

Throughout the Civil War, which consumed all but the first five weeks of his presidency, he was no less repulsed by the misery around him. He became prone to nightmares and severe headaches. He lost weight. But during the entirety of the conflict, Lincoln displayed a behavior that can be classified as obsession. Nothing under his presidency, including constitutional law, the federal treasury, and the general welfare of millions, was deemed more important that the maintenance of an ethereal "union."

Within a week of South Carolina's firing upon Fort Sumter, Lincoln ordered the assembly and arming of seventy thousand troops, suspended the writ of habeas corpus in Maryland, and issued a naval blockade against the entire southern half of his own country. All of this was done without the consent of Congress, which he did not call into session until July 4, 1861, nearly three months after the shooting had started.

Today, his most acclaimed act is the Emancipation Proclamation. In

1862, it was widely unpopular, manipulative, and opportunistic, but it was a work of Machiavellian genius. In his famous public letter to abolitionist Horace Greeley in August 1862, Lincoln confessed his loathing for human slavery, yet he acknowledged it was only a chess piece in his quest for military victory: "If I could save the Union without freeing any slave I would do it; and if I could save it by freeing all the slaves I would do it; and if I could save it by freeing some and leaving others alone I would also do that. What I do about slavery, and the colored race, I do because I believe it helps save the Union."[83] He chose to free some—in the areas of rebellion. For others, he continued to suggest colonization elsewhere and contemplated promoting a bill that would free slaves in loyal states by the year 1900.[84]

The opportunity to unveil his executive decree came after the battle of Antietam on September 17, 1862, a marginal Federal victory. On September 22, Lincoln issued a public statement proclaiming that all slaves residing in areas that were still in rebellion as of the New Year "shall be then, thenceforward, and forever free." Though moral, it was not necessarily legal, even as a war powers act.

Yet as an effective weapon, it was unparalleled. With the power of the pen, Lincoln did not immediately free a single person. But he did strike fear and anguish in the South, allowed the federal government to eventually recruit nearly 180,000 free and slave African Americans into the Union armed forces, and eliminated any chance of seeing Britain or France enter the war on the side of the Confederacy. No battle, no general, no other act of government had cemented his power so far so fast.

---

In the preliminary Emancipation Proclamation, Lincoln gave each Confederate state the option of keeping slavery within its borders if it surrendered by January 1, 1863.

---

### 4. LYNDON JOHNSON
#### THE GULF OF TONKIN RESOLUTION (1964)

His constituents called it the "Johnson Treatment," also known as bullying. From hearty backslaps to little kicks to the shins, paternal advice, and constant invasions of personal space, LBJ knew how to maneuver people into a corner—his corner. Biographer and longtime confidant Doris Kearns Goodwin noted that conversations with him were like unending tests of submissiveness. Press secretary George Reedy said of him, "He may have been a son of a bitch but he was a colossal son of a bitch."[85]

In August 1964 he was a popular SOB, and he was ready to use his political capital on two targets. The first concern was the approaching November elections. The second was, in his words, "the woman I really loved," his Great Society, a social-assistance program that was to dwarf the New Deal. Not part of the relationship was Vietnam.[86]

Then on August 2, 1964, North Vietnamese gunboats fired on two U.S. destroyers in the Gulf of Tonkin. The *Maddox* took a single bullet to the topside. Days later, another alleged assault occurred (it was more like a panic attack). An event of no real consequence or relevance, it was still an opportunity for Johnson to make an audacious request to Congress: "to approve and support the determination of the President as Commander in Chief to take all the necessary measures to repel any armed attack against the forces of the United States to prevent further aggression. . . . The United States regards Vietnam as vital to its national interest and to world peace and security in Southeast Asia." Johnson was asking Congress to violate the Constitution and give him total authority on whether to enter into a war. The House voted unanimously in favor of Johnson. Only two senators voted against the measure, both of them Democrats.[87]

With blank check in hand, LBJ did something even more remarkable, something almost dictatorial in its absoluteness. He did nothing. Month after month, he rejected plans from the Department of Defense to carpet bomb North Vietnam. He also refused any substantial buildup beyond the seventeen thousand troops already present in South Vietnam. Not

A pensive Lyndon Johnson signs the Gulf of Tonkin resolution. For the next nine years, the executive branch assumed legislative authority over war making.

until his power was secured through his election in November, and his Great Society was set in motion, did he decide to address the seemingly minor issue of Southeast Asia. Fortunately for Johnson, his options were wide open, thanks to the infinite latitude he quickly and easily wrested from Congress in the Gulf of Tonkin Resolution.

A title befitting his character, LBJ's nickname in college was "Bull."

## 5.  WOODROW WILSON
### THE SEDITION ACT (1918)

On the surface, Wilson was an accomplished and revered academic, a rousing public speaker, and worldly. In private, he was a rather crass and lonely figure. He struggled with intimacy on all levels, he demanded absolute loyalty from an ever-shrinking circle of friends, and he found humor in mimicking other ethnicities.[88]

His speeches made him sound like an idealist, as demonstrated in his first inaugural address in 1913. "The feelings with which we face this new age of right and opportunity sweep across our heartstrings like some air out of God's own presence," he assured with his scholarly, melodic tone, "where justice and mercy are reconciled and the judge and the brother are one." Taken in context, he was no more optimistic than most well-educated progressives at the time, trained in the flowery language of the Gilded Age, and facing a new century of unparalleled promise.

But he could be medieval when it counted. His late and reluctant entry into the World War unearthed his basic instincts of survival, and while he planned to fight for democracy in Europe, he suspended it indefinitely at home. Under his heavy pressure and precise direction, Congress passed the Trading with the Enemy Act (still in effect today), the Espionage Act (ten-thousand-dollar fine and twenty years in jail for doing or saying anything against the military draft), and the Alien Act (immediate deportation of any suspected anarchist).

As wartime patriotism surged, Wilson forged ahead with the most virulent edict of his administration: the Sedition Act of 1918. The law made it illegal for anyone to "utter, print, or publish disloyal, profane, scurrilous, or abusive language about the form of government, the Constitution, soldiers and sailors, flag, or uniform of the armed forces." Several

Woodrow Wilson actively persecuted freedom of speech and press under the wartime Sedition Act.

citizens pointed out that the law itself was abusive toward the Constitution, and they were summarily arrested.[89]

Under the Sedition Act alone, more than fifteen hundred Americans were taken into custody under the guise of national security, and more than one hundred of them were convicted and imprisoned. One of the more ludicrous cases involved a member of the clergy from Vermont who suggested that Jesus of Nazareth was a pacifist. For spreading such a treasonous rumor, the pastor was sentenced to fifteen years behind bars.[90]

---

Woodrow Wilson's draconian laws during the Great War inspired the creation of the American Civil Liberties Union in 1920.

---

## 6.  RICHARD NIXON
### "THE PLUMBERS" (1971–73)

His first four years confirmed he would do whatever it took to reach desired ends: freeze government wages, desegregate schools, abandon the gold standard, bomb rice patties, visit Communist China. For his cold, calculating, slightly vengeful work, the nation rewarded the conservative and secretive leader with a four-year extension to his contract.

What the electorate did not know . . . yet . . . was that he was able to run a tight and efficient White House because he had hired his own palace guard. In the wake of the embarrassing PENTAGON PAPERS incident, Nixon instructed domestic policy advisor John Ehrlichman to form a "Special Investigations Unit." After some hunting, Ehrlichman created a group that would be known as "the Plumbers," so-called because their job was to stop all internal leaks. The central figures were David Young, a former assistant to Henry Kissinger, and Bud Krogh, a lawyer and close family friend of Ehrlichman. The team expanded to include former FBI agent G. Gordon Liddy and former CIA employee (and Bay of Pigs operative) E. Howard Hunt.[91]

Rather than prevent information from seeping out, the group began to bring large amounts of intelligence in. Colluding with others, including the dubious Committee to Re-elect the President (a.k.a., CREEP), the Plumbers engaged in wiretapping, examining tax returns of political opponents, pilfering CIA records, and scheming to illegally photograph classified information in the National Archives. The cell even created an enemies list to better target the suspected opposition, which included individuals in Congress as well as the private sector. Most of these activities were unknown to the president, yet he was generally aware that much of what they were doing was not legal.[92]

To what extent any of their covert activities helped Nixon remain in power is difficult to determine. Still popular among moderates and conservatives at the end of his first term, the incumbent Nixon probably would have won reelection by a wide margin regardless of the Plumbers. But their existence reflected the extent of hubris that had permeated the secretive Nixon White House, and their botched break-in of the Democratic national headquarters at the WATERGATE led to the destruction of the very institution they were breaking the law to protect.

---

Founder of the Plumbers John Ehrlichman and Nixon's chief of staff H. R. Haldeman were both Eagle Scouts.

---

## 7.  GEORGE W. BUSH
### THE WMD PRESENTATION TO THE U.N. SECURITY COUNCIL (2003)

Closer to his mother than his father, who was often away on business, George W. Bush assumed the role of family protector at an early age. In many respects, he acted like a morale officer rather than a leader, a persona he maintained throughout his life. At Phillips Academy and Yale, he enjoyed the social aspects of school, including cheerleading, but he developed a deep suspicion of intellectuals. Though inherently friendly and outgoing, he was not terribly open or conscientious. Like his father, he learned to fly fighter planes and entered the oil business. Unlike his father, he trusted his emotions more than his intellect.[93]

As an adult, G. W. Bush displayed a curious tendency to smile in awkward situations. The habit became most prominent during his presidency, especially when responding to questions about war, terrorism, or natural disasters. Largely involuntary, the trait is a defensive response to the stimulus of pain or discomfort. His father did not have this inclination, but Richard Nixon and Lyndon Johnson did, both of whom frequently smiled broadly after talking about emotionally difficult subjects. A wince more than a grin, it is a telltale sign that a person is not being straightforward.

Bush and his administration never actually tried to emphasize honesty as their overriding quality. Instead, the operative words were "leadership," "strength," and "commitment." Bush was also personally fond of the word *freedom*, using the word twenty-seven times in his second inaugural. It was under the premise of making the world "free from terror" that he initiated a preemptive strike on Iraq in 2003.

Evidence to justify such an operation was not available, so the Bush administration did the next best thing: they guessed. Vice President Richard Cheney and the assistant secretary of defense, Paul Wolfowitz, engineered a sales pitch based on allegations that Iraq was manufacturing weapons of mass destruction and was directly connected to terrorist organizations. To deliver this war message, they chose the most trusted member of the administration, Secretary of State Colin Powell. Hopefully the ensuing Second Gulf War would go as well as the First, and if it did, the ends would justify the means.

In hindsight, they were trying to pull an Adlai Stevenson. At the height of the Cuban Missile Crisis, Kennedy's U.N. ambassador presented photographic proof to the Security Council that the Soviet Union was assembling tactical and medium-range nuclear missiles in Cuba. The overwhelming evidence and clear images brought virtually all of South America and Western Europe on the side of the United States.

At the height of the War on Terror, on February 5, 2003, Bush's secretary of state entered the Security Council and provided "irrefutable and undeniable" evidence that Iraq was assembling weapons of mass destruction in secret locations. With surveillance technology forty years ahead of what Stevenson had, all that Powell showed were blurry images of "weapons factories" that looked more like shopping malls from ten thousand feet. The computer-generated drawings of the mobile "biologi-cal agent" trucks were even less impressive. Unconvinced, the nations that had sided with the Kennedy administration in 1962 were reluctant to believe George W. Bush in 2003. Undeterred by the cold reception, the Bush invasion proceeded as planned. Though unsuccessful in finding any WMDs or proof of terrorist connections, the war did install a pro-West president in Baghdad and allowed George W. Bush to retain his job for a second term.[94]

---

In a television interview in 2005, a retired Colin Powell described his erro-neous presentation at the U.N. Security Council as "painful."

---

## 8. GEORGE WASHINGTON
### REPRESSION OF THE WHISKEY REBELLION (1794)

The stalwart and physically imposing Virginian rarely spoke, stood rigidly upright, and moved with a regal stride, bringing some to the false conclu-sion that he was pompous. Among the least educated of the Founding Fa-thers, George Washington took a great deal of time to reach a conclusion, but once the decision was made, he moved with the steady force of a river current. Though utterly trustworthy, he had a difficult time trusting oth-ers, and he let very few get close to him. He did not take criticism well.

"I walk on untrodden ground," Washington acknowledged. "There is scarcely an action the motive of which may not be subjected to double in-terpretation." His service was an exercise in restraint, and when dealing with untested issues, he preferred to err on the side of caution. There was one facet of the new government that needled him: the provision in the 1791 Bill of Rights that guaranteed freedom of the press. Galled by the liberal wing of the media who openly suspected him of wanting to be-come king, Washington said in 1792: "In a word if the Government and the Officers of it are to be the constant theme for News-paper abuse, and this too without condescending to investigate the motives or the facts, it will be impossible, I conceive, for any man living to manage the helm, or to keep the machine together."[95]

Obliged by law to tolerate dissent in the form of print, Washington de-nounced any threat of violence against the government. A neutral in foreign wars, he did not hesitate to play commander in chief on his own people.

And when farmers and merchants began to gather arms against a law they thought immoral, the president amassed an army larger than anything he brought to bear against the British and sent it to crush the resistance.

The issue was a tax. Designed by Treasury Secretary Alexander Hamilton to increase federal revenues, the levy imposed a nine-cent charge on each gallon of distilled spirits. The burden fell hardest on the frontier poor who viewed hard alcohol as their currency, commodity, tea, and the best way to squeeze high profits out of cheap grain. Protests were at first modest and covert, mostly by way of smuggling. By the summer of 1794, citizens in western Pennsylvania were physically accosting tax collectors. The Whiskey Rebellion turned into a shooting war soon after. When federal marshals killed three protesters, a mob of thousands began to form near Pittsburgh to contemplate their next move (within a few miles of where a very young Lt. Col. George Washington unleashed the French and Indian War exactly forty years before).

The president immediately called out the militia from Pennsylvania and the surrounding states. On some stretches, he led the marching columns in person, a total force in excess of twelve thousand (in 1776, he attacked the Hessians at Trenton with less than two thousand). The rebellion melted before them, and only twenty arrests were made, leading some to conclude that their commander had fabricated the whole thing as a demonstration of his supreme authority. Why else, they reasoned, would a man who made his name by rebelling against a tyrannical government, suddenly refuse the same right to his own people? Washington was correct in his answer: the Americans of 1794 had something the previous generation did not—elected representation. The law could now be changed by peaceful means, and he as president expected his people to understand, respect, and exercise that great privilege.

> Repression of the Whiskey Rebellion marked the first and only time a sitting U.S. president personally led soldiers in the field against his own countrymen.

## 9. THEODORE ROOSEVELT
### THE COAL STRIKE OF 1902

When Republican officials named New York governor Theodore Roosevelt to be William McKinley's running mate in the 1900 elections,

McKinley's closest advisor, Mark Hanna, exclaimed, "Don't any of you realize that there's only one life between this madman and the Presidency?" The statement would be prophetic, not that TR was particularly insane, but that he would become chief executive by way of assassination.[96]

Compared to the sheepish McKinley, Teddy was an unassailable wildebeest. A man's man to the nth degree, he possessed a rigid sense of right and wrong, was cordial and enchanting toward women, and he loved to play with kids, especially his own. The first president to fly in an airplane, to own an automobile, and to dive in a submarine, Roosevelt had a joie de vivre that either consumed or overwhelmed everyone around him. "You don't smile with Mr. Roosevelt," said a reporter from the New York Times, "you shout with laughter with him." To fuel his bulldozer lifestyle, TR downed about a gallon of coffee per day.[97]

He did not speak softly, nor did he wield a big stick. Quite the opposite, TR opted for iron-fisted rhetoric and white-glove compromise. A bitter critic of big business, the "Trustbuster" was not against monopolies per se, just against corruption and price gouging (William Howard Taft would dismantle twice as many monopolies as Roosevelt). His sweeping conservationism was more to regulate the use of natural resources than to preserve virgin lands. To help both the white collars and the workers, he created the comprehensive Department of Commerce and Labor.

This department was the offspring of a national crisis, one that threatened to literally freeze the major cities of the Northeast. In the summer of 1902, exhausted and endangered coal miners in Pennsylvania began to strike. Working more than ten hours every day in conditions that were often lethal, the miners demanded a 20 percent increase in wages and a 20 percent decrease in work hours. With winter approaching and coal being the primary source of heat for most every home and building in the country's major cities, the mine owners cried blackmail and refused to negotiate.[98]

Roosevelt initially invited both sides to the White House to talk (the first time a U.S. president personally intervened in such a labor dispute). When the meetings failed, riots in the mining towns became increasingly violent, leading to several deaths. It was already October. Homes, schools, and hospitals were going without heat. Rumors of a nationwide strike were becoming more and more credible. If he sided with labor, Roosevelt would play into the hands of the growing socialist movement, numbering in the low millions already. Should he abide by the wealthy owners, he would lose the confidence of the working class. In the end, Roosevelt calmly chose neither, instructing his secretary of war to begin preparations for the invasion of Pennsylvania. Ten thousand troops were called at the ready. Roosevelt prepared to have federal soldiers take over operations of the anthracite coal mines. Labor and management would get nothing.[99]

Faced with the most aggressive presidential performance since the Civil War, both sides caved. In a masterful move to the center, Roosevelt successfully tamed a growing national division, brought a renewed prestige to his office, and taught the warring parties that it was possible for all sides to achieve victory. Renewed negotiations brought higher wages for the miners and, accordingly, higher prices for the owners. Shipments of heating coal resumed to the cities, and in 1904 Roosevelt became the first of five "accidental presidents" to be elected in his own right.

> TR was an exceedingly confident and persuasive individual. Not once in his long inaugural address in 1905 did he use the pronouns "I" or "me." Instead he preferred "we" and "us," which he said a total of seventy-one times.

## 10. JOHN ADAMS
### ALIEN AND SEDITION ACTS (1798)

Historian Alan Taylor observed, "The same qualities . . . that so offended colleagues have endeared Adams to scholars." Adams is definitely making a comeback, helped in part by David McCullough's bestselling (and exceedingly kind) biography of him in 2001. Not the most successful president, Adams still makes for good print, because he is such a fiery paradox.[100]

Prickly in public and charming in private, sickly in body and magnificent in intellect, the provocative Adams was never boring, but he was also excessively difficult, and he would rather be right than popular. One way for a president to always be right, and unpopular, is to make it illegal for people to criticize him, which is what Adams did in 1798, signing into law several bills that effectively negated the First Amendment.

The acts were born from the perennial Britain-France rivalry (a hatred that reached back to the Norman Conquest of 1066). In the tradition of the Washington presidency, Adams professed neutrality. In practice, his stance was blatantly pro-Brit. To crush growing dissent among some twenty-five thousand French émigrés, the legislature passed and Adams quickly signed the Alien Acts, one of which allowed the president to deport any foreigner he deemed a threat to national security during wartime (as of 2007, the Alien Enemies Act is still in effect). More extreme were the Sedition Acts, which made it a federal crime to write, print, or say anything that was "false, scandalous and malicious" against Congress or the president. Just what exactly constituted a false, scandalous, and malicious statement was never specified.[101]

The oppressive measures were written of, by, and for the Federalist Party, the ruling faction in the House, the Senate, the Supreme Court, and the presidency. Shackled by these laws (quite literally in some cases) were the Democratic Republicans, who openly wondered if the government was turning into a dictatorship or, at the very least, returning to the British Empire. Vice President Thomas Jefferson was so appalled by what was happening that he abruptly left Philadelphia and remained in seclusion at Monticello for nearly two months. Suspecting his mail was being searched, he used private messengers to communicate with his colleagues. Several states contemplated leaving the Union.[102]

Defenders of Adams, including biographer McCullough, argued that the president exercised considerable restraint when applying the laws. It is true that Adams never deported a foreigner under the Alien Acts, but hundreds and perhaps thousands feared for their lives and left on their own, especially at the height of the QUASI WAR with France. Only a few dozen people were ever arrested under the Sedition measures. But all of them were Republicans, more than twenty of them were newspaper editors, and one was a member of Congress.[103]

---

Under the Sedition Acts of 1798, it was not a crime to say or write "false, scandalous and malicious" things about the vice president—who just happened to be Democratic Republican Thomas Jefferson.

---

# 2

# ELECTIONS

## TOP TEN CLOSEST RACES

In the fight to gain a decisive edge, political parties invented an ever-widening array of tactics to put their candidate ahead. Massive parades and rallies emerged in the late 1820s. Promotional novelties appeared with frequency in the 1840s, maturing into a wholesale gadget, button, and banner industry by the end of the century.

One of the most striking innovations was to have candidates campaign for themselves. For generations, most Americans distrusted anyone who appeared hungry for power. Accordingly, presidential contenders were silent runners, cautious even when their name surfaced for nomination. A shift occurred in the 1880s, when personal "stumping" grew in earnest, mostly from a candidate's front porch. Wanting to see their man in person, thousands visited James Garfield at his Mentor, Ohio, home. Two races later, a total of two hundred thousand called on Benjamin Harrison in Indianapolis. Noting the power of personal contact, Nebraskan William Jennings Bryan conceived the mobile campaign in 1896, riding the railroads for an astounding eighteen thousand miles, the equivalent of crossing the continental United States six times.[1]

With bigger efforts came greater expenses. In the 1860s, major parties ran successful campaigns on one hundred thousand dollars or less. In 1896, William McKinley's war chest filled to an unprecedented three million dollars. Budgets exploded with the introduction of television in the 1960s and the expanding role of caucuses and primaries in the 1970s. Even with adjusted dollars, John Kerry spent more money in his losing

71

bid in 2004 than Grover Cleveland, Woodrow Wilson, FDR, and Harry Truman did in ten successful races combined.

In the 2008 race, for the first time, major contenders launched their campaigns from cyberspace. In their innovation, they were simply following an old pattern. From punch bowls and parades, to conventions and smoke-filled rooms, to yard-cards and airtime, the race has often gone to the most inventive.

Following are several examples of those who persevered by design. Ranked by percentage differences in electoral votes, these are the ten closest presidential contests in U.S. history.[2]

## 1.  1800

| | | | |
|---|---|---|---|
| THOMAS JEFFERSON (D-R) | 73 | AARON BURR (D-R) | 73 |
| JOHN ADAMS (F) | 65 | CHARLES C. PINCKNEY (F) | 64 |

To keep peace among the family of states, article 2, section 1 of the Constitution mandated that electors had to choose two persons "of whom one at least shall not be an Inhabitant of the same State with themselves." There was no stipulation on which vote would be for president or vice president; whoever finished second would be offered the deputy position. The framers did not foresee the rise of political parties and, with them, the invention of "running mates."

Germinating in the political pool were two embryonic, diametrically opposed factions. The Federalist cell endorsed the wealthy, a strong central government, and commercial ties with Britain. Their antibodies were the egalitarian Democratic-Republicans, who praised agrarianism, a subdued federal government, and the Revolutionary ally in France.

In the exceedingly malicious race of 1800 (see CONTROVERSIAL ELECTIONS), the Federalists ran President John Adams and Revolutionary War veteran Charles Cotesworth Pinckney against the Democratic-Republicans' Thomas Jefferson and New York state attorney Aaron Burr. In a process that lasted from summer into late autumn (Election Day was not established until 1845), the tide shifted back and forth, until South Carolina, the last state to submit its results, cast all eight electors for Jefferson and Burr.

As president of the Senate, Jefferson himself opened the electoral certificates in February 1801 to confirm what had been known for quite some time. Both he and Burr were tied at seventy-three votes, sending the decision into the House of Representatives, where partisans for the defeated Adams were waiting.

Each state in the House was to cast one vote. Whichever candidate received the majority would become president. It was common knowledge that Burr was the inferior candidate in rank, but anti-Jefferson camps saw an opportunity to embarrass the "Sage of Monticello." Six states went with Burr, eight with Jefferson, with Maryland and Vermont unable to decide.

And so it went, for seven days and thirty-five ballots, all with the same result. There appeared to be no end to the deadlock, and the Constitution did not permit a repeat election. Jeffersonians suspected the Federalists of scheming to keep Adams as president, and others wondered if Adams would proclaim himself president for life. The concern was credible enough to prompt two pro-Jefferson states to organize their militias.[3]

Sincerely fearing a civil war, and for the "political existence" of his small and defenseless state, Delaware's lone representative, James Bayard, switched his vote to Jefferson. Both sides criticized the long and arduous wait, but they accepted the final outcome, allowing the fourteen-year-old United States to survive yet another crisis in its troubled pubescence.[4]

---

The postelection fiasco of 1800 prompted the introduction of the Twelfth Amendment, mandating electors to specify their choice for chief executive and vice president. Several controversies surrounded the law's wording, and a final version was not ratified until 1804.

---

## 2.  1876

RUTHERFORD B. HAYES (R)        185
SAMUEL J. TILDEN (D)           184

More than eight million men voted, and it all came down to three states, two candidates, and one Supreme Court justice. At first, the election looked as if it belonged to Governor Samuel Tilden of New York. After eight years of the corrupt and ineffective Grant administration, the Democrats were one electoral ballot shy of victory with three states left.

An apprentice of Martin Van Buren, breaker of the Tweed Ring, and enemy of the spoils system, Tilden was praised by fellow Northerners for his antislavery past and favored by white Southerners for simply not being a Republican. Such popularity gave him nearly 4.3 million votes to his opponent's 4 million and a virtual lock on the Electoral College. Both he and his opponent went to bed on election night assuming Tilden had won.

Over the coming days, Republican nominee and Ohio Governor Rutherford B. Hayes took hope that the game was not yet lost. Election results had been called into question in Florida, Louisiana, and South Carolina. Republicans and Democrats both claimed victory in each state and sent conflicting electoral ballots to the Senate. At stake were nineteen electoral votes, and Hayes needed all of them to win. Though less famous and politically less influential than Tilden, Hayes possessed two critical advantages over his fellow northerner—he was a Union veteran, plus his party still controlled much of the occupied South through Reconstruction.

Thrown into a dangerous stalemate, for which the Constitution had no answer, the divided Congress fabricated a committee of fifteen delegates, including five members each from the House, Senate, and Supreme Court. Evenly divided between Democrats and Republicans, the committee voted precisely along party lines. The last and critical voice belonged to Justice Joseph Bradley, independent in name but vaguely Republican in practice.

After insinuating he would rule in favor of Tilden, Bradley awarded the three states and all nineteen of their electors to Hayes. Democrats could not help but notice that those three states were the only ones in the entire South that the Republicans managed to win. The backlash was so overwhelming that President Grant had Hayes secretly take the oath of office two days before Inauguration Day, for fear that a violent mob might prevent the official swearing-in from taking place.[5]

---

Never vindictive against the voters at large, Samuel Tilden willed much of his wealth and extensive book collection to the general public, an endowment that would become the New York Public Library.

---

### 3.  2000

| | |
|---|---|
| GEORGE W. BUSH (R) | 271 |
| AL GORE (D) | 266 |

The campaign of 2000 was a sleeping pill right up to the closing of the polls. Pundits called the election *Gush vs. Bore*, a flaccid bout between a president's son who had a friendly face and no gift for oratory and a sitting vice president who had all the charm of a mild headache. Dismal voter turnout—barely 50 percent—attested to their collective inability to inspire the masses. But then came Election Night.

In 2000, as in 1876, a Democrat outpolled a Republican by hundreds of thousands in the popular vote and led the Electoral College for weeks, standing just shy of the required majority. In both elections, Florida was in dispute, prompting review boards to conduct recounts, resulting in a microscopic lead for the Republican (45 votes in 1876, 537 in 2000). In both instances, the final word came from a solitary member of the Supreme Court who ruled in favor of the Republican. And after both decisions, the beneficiaries considered the outcome fair and just, the defeated party cried conspiracy, and the losing candidate asked for, and received, public calm.[6]

Minor parties again played the role of spoilers. As with the Pro-Greenbacks and Prohibitionists in Tilden's day, the environmental Green Party and the conservative Reform and Libertarian parties trimmed precious ballots from the two major contenders.[7]

---

In 2000, Al Gore lost his home state of Tennessee. Not since Woodrow Wilson in 1916 had a candidate been defeated in his native state and managed to win the presidency.

---

## 4.  1796

| | | | |
|---|---|---|---|
| JOHN ADAMS (F) | 71 | THOMAS JEFFERSON (D-R) | 68 |
| THOMAS PINCKNEY (F) | 59 | | |

In his Farewell Address (written with considerable input from Alexander Hamilton), the departing President Washington forewarned "the baneful effects of the spirit of party. . . . It agitates the Community with ill-founded jealousies and false alarms, kindles the animosity of one part against another, foments occasionally riot and insurrection."

Published during the country's first truly competitive election, the president's advice went unheeded. Congressman Fisher Ames noted that, instead of having a calming effect, Washington's address was "like dropping a hat, for the party racers to start."[8]

Though the newly forming Federalists and Democratic-Republicans were soon to grow into mortal enemies, their chosen candidates were less enthusiastic. In early December, as he awaited news of the outcome, Federalist favorite John Adams wrote to his son John Quincy, "I look upon the Event as the throw of a Die, a mere Chance, a miserable, meager Triumph to either Party." For the irritable Adams, the embarrassment of losing outweighed the desire to win, as he longed to close a lengthy and arduous career that kept him far from home. So, too, retired Secretary of State Thomas Jefferson hoped to finish second or lower, often insisting, "I cherish tranquility too much."[9]

In an age when electors used their own discretion and long distances meant piecemeal information, the final tally took months to calculate. Observing from nearby Montpelier, James Madison wrote his friend Jefferson that he believed South Carolina's soldier and diplomat Thomas Pinckney had won, with Adams finishing second. All would soon learn that a few key swing votes provided a completely different outcome. In heavily pro-Jefferson North Carolina, Pennsylvania, and Virginia, one rogue elector from each state voted for Adams. He needed sixty-nine electoral votes to win; he took seventy-one.[10]

Jefferson finished close behind with sixty-eight, and to the surprise of his devotees, the Republican decided to serve alongside the Federalist. In an attempt to reassure his political allies, Jefferson noted that subordination to Adams was neither dishonorable nor unfamiliar to him: "I am his junior in life, was his junior in Congress, his junior in the diplomatic line, his junior lately in our civil government."[11]

Adams would be the last president to serve in Philadelphia. Unbeknownst to him and his party, Adams would also be the only Federalist to ever be chief executive, and his long friendship with Jefferson was about to come to an unpleasant end.

---

The 1796 election marked the highest number of candidates ever to receive electoral votes—thirteen. Among them were George Washington, Samuel Adams, John Jay, Aaron Burr, and George Clinton.

---

## 5.   1916

WOODROW WILSON (D)        277
CHARLES EVANS HUGHES (R)   254

As he opened the Republican Convention in Chicago, Senator Warren Harding made a plea for party unity, reminding his colleagues that defeat in 1912 came largely from their internal feud over William Howard Taft and

Teddy Roosevelt. The assembly agreed and refused to nominate either one of their former presidents. The two men were not surprised. Contentedly teaching law at Yale, Taft knew his political career was "resting in a tomb." Suffering from recurring malaria, TR also realized his time had passed. "The People as a whole are tired of me and of my views," he observed.[12]

The GOP instead backed former New York governor and presiding justice of the Supreme Court Charles Evans Hughes. From the venerable bench, the moderate Hughes could offer no direct comment on his political outlook, and thus he could offend no one. Upon receiving the unsought nomination, Hughes accepted and immediately notified the president of his resignation from the High Court. Democrats backed the incumbent Woodrow Wilson.

At the time, differences between Democrats and Republicans were minimal. Both sides promoted stronger defense, women's suffrage, a ban on child labor, and closer ties with Latin America. The critical question involved warring Europe. Democrats backed their incumbent with the effective slogan, "He kept us out of war," which was high praise from a nation repulsed by the abattoirs of Verdun and the Somme, the "innovation" of poison gas, and a death toll growing by millions. Also committed to neutrality, the Republicans openly questioned if Wilson was doing enough to protect American interests. Demanding greater mobilization and accelerated arms production, Hughes and his constituents appealed to those impatient for resolution to the world war.

On election night, the GOP strategy appeared to have worked. Early returns indicated a near sweep of the Northeast for Hughes, while the Virginia-born and Georgia-raised Wilson took the less populous South. Hughes went to bed assuming he had won, and New York papers began printing headlines of his triumph.

As precincts farther west submitted their results, momentum shifted to the Democrats. Wilson scored crucial wins in Ohio and Texas, most of the Plains states, all of the Rockies, plus Washington and Oregon. Everything then hinged on California's thirteen electoral votes. By a scant thirty-eight thousand ballots, the Golden State went with Wilson. The president kept his job, but he would soon fail to keep his country out of war.

---

Charles Evans Hughes eventually reached the White House, serving as secretary of state to Warren Harding and Calvin Coolidge. Appointed chief justice of the Supreme Court by Herbert Hoover, Hughes went on to become the only person to administer the oath of office to the same president three times—Franklin Roosevelt in 1932, 1936, and 1940.

---

**6.  2004**

| | |
|---|---|
| GEORGE W. BUSH (R) | 286 |
| JOHN KERRY (D) | 251 |

The appearance of being "electable" has catapulted several back-markers to the front. In 1860, Republicans dropped Senator William H. Seward and former Ohio Governor Salmon P. Chase for being too outspoken against slavery, favoring instead a moderate one-term congressman from Illinois. In 1848, both the Democrats and the Whigs recruited Maj. Gen. Zachary Taylor, although he belonged to neither party. Preceding both the 1948 and 1952 elections, President Harry Truman privately asked Dwight David Eisenhower to run for president as a Democrat.[13]

Early in the 2004 campaign, the clear Democratic frontrunner had been Howard Dean. A Vermont governor who oversaw eleven balanced budgets and two reductions of state taxes, Dean stood well clear of nine other candidates, with Missouri Representative Dick Gephardt a distant second. As the caucuses and primaries neared, Dean's main rivals began to call him "unelectable," primarily because of his vocal opposition to the 2003 invasion of Iraq. In a matter of days, his massive lead dissolved into an embarrassing third-place finish in the Iowa Caucus, behind Senator John Kerry of Massachusetts and Senator John Edwards of North Carolina. Within a month, Dean was out, and Kerry and Edwards went on to represent the party.

As it turned out, Kerry wasn't quite electable either. When the senator criticized the war in Iraq, after voting to support the invasion, his critics labeled him a "flip-flopper." The Catholic Kerry also vacillated when speaking of his religious convictions (a tightrope John F. Kennedy knew well). By comparison, Bush's unwavering stance on his "global War on Terror" earned him points among those who favored decisiveness, while his patent evangelism brought him continued support from the religious Right.

On election night, Kerry initially did well, taking the entire Northeast, plus Illinois, Michigan, and Wisconsin. Then the South, Plains, and Rockies went to the incumbent. A late rally gave the Democrat the West Coast, and when reports came in that Ohio was experiencing widespread problems with voting machines, the contest looked like a replay of Florida in 2000. The day after the election, however, further scrutiny revealed that the margin in the Buckeye State was well over one hundred thousand votes in favor of Bush, enough to convince Kerry to abruptly concede the race.[14]

> George W. Bush won and lost almost the exact same states in 2004 as he had in 2000. The only differences in his reelection were first-time victories in Iowa and New Mexico and defeat in New Hampshire.

## 7.  1884

| GROVER CLEVELAND (D) | 219 |
|---|---|
| JAMES G. BLAINE (R) | 182 |

Not since James Buchanan in 1856 had the Democrats won a presidential election, but they believed they had a winner in the incorruptible Grover Cleveland. Physically imposing at a beefy 280 pounds, tough, and honest, Cleveland rocketed through the political ranks in Buffalo. From ward supervisor, to assistant DA, to sheriff, to mayor, Cleveland ran his posts with iron-fisted efficiency. He could work thirty-six hours straight without sleep, hated yes-men, and openly attacked the party bosses of Tammany Hall. By 1884 he had risen to governor, where he championed the cause of political reform.[15]

Running against him was GOP leader James Blaine of Maine. Even more vibrant and popular than Cleveland, he was known as the "Plumed

A Democratic poster in the 1884 election entitled "Saviours of Our Country" featured Washington, Lincoln, and Cleveland.

Knight" for his patriotic rants against former Confederates, many of whom were Democrats. Twice he had run for the Republican nomination, and twice he lost narrowly to dark horse veterans of the Civil War (Garfield and Hayes). In 1884 it was his turn to be president, and many assumed he would be, considering the Republican winning streak.[16]

News that Cleveland had a premarital affair seemed to herald a Republican landslide. Polls showed the governor trailing in his own state by as many as fifty thousand voters. But Blaine made mistakes of his own late in the campaign, alienating Catholics in the North and former Confederates in the South (see CONTROVERSIAL ELECTIONS).

The drastic shift in momentum cursed Blaine's third and final try for the presidency. Despite taking most of the Midwest and all of the Pacific Coast, he was defeated in several key Republican states in the Northeast, and none more critical than Cleveland's New York, which decided the election. In the Empire State, out of more than one million voters, Blaine lost to Cleveland by a miniscule 1,049 ballots.[17]

---

James Blaine is the only presidential candidate ever to win Illinois, Ohio, and Pennsylvania and still lose the election.

---

## 8. 1976

| | |
|---|---|
| JAMES CARTER (D) | 297 |
| GERALD FORD (R) | 240 |

Aside from the much-anticipated bicentennial Fourth of July at home and two successful *Viking* landings on Mars, the United States had little to celebrate in 1976. Lingering trauma from Vietnam and Watergate, 10 percent unemployment, 12 percent inflation, and the unnerving weight of the thirty-year cold war left the nation in a state of political fatigue. Consequently, Democrats and Republicans faced a mutual dilemma in the presidential campaign: how to motivate a highly disillusioned electorate.

The GOP had the advantage of incumbency, although the sitting president had not been elected. Representative Gerald Ford had fallen into the executive chair through Vice President Spiro Agnew's resignation on charges of tax evasion and Richard Nixon's painful abdication. After barely a month in office, Ford burned most of his political capital by granting Nixon a full and absolute pardon. Further eroding Ford's image, he barely survived a nomination battle against arch-conservative Ronald Reagan.[18]

The opposition appeared just as troubled. From a herd of fourteen unexceptional candidates, the best the Democrats could offer was a former Georgia governor who had been elected out after one term. Presenting himself as a Washington outsider and devoutly religious, Jimmy Carter appealed to those wracked with Beltway skepticism. But his evasive stance on issues straddled the line between avoiding controversy and appearing indecisive. Appropriately, he finished a distant second in the Iowa Caucus, trailing a solid block who voted "Undecided." At the party convention in New York, Carter won on the first ballot despite a strong "ABC" (Anyone But Carter) movement among his fellow Democrats.

In their first televised debate, both candidates verbally wandered, leaving many viewers disappointed and unsure. Subsequent debates allowed the struggling Ford, who had trailed by as much as 30 percentage points, to stage a last-minute comeback.

Election Day was far more exciting than the campaign. Carter took 40.8 million votes to Ford's 39.1 million. Eighteen states were decided by 2 percent or less. Fittingly, the race came down to the large pool of last-minute undecideds, 61 percent of whom eventually went with the peanut farmer–nuclear physicist. Reflecting the national malaise already in place, voter turnout was 54 percent, the lowest since the Korean War.[19]

---

President Ford's campaign manager was his chief of staff, future Vice President Dick Cheney.

---

## 9.  1848

| | |
|---|---|
| ZACHARY TAYLOR (W) | 163 |
| LEWIS CASS (D) | 127 |

Lewis Cass was a prolific writer from the prestigious Exeter Academy. Zachary Taylor had little formal education, rarely read, and had difficulty spelling. Cass had served as governor of the Michigan Territory, secretary of war, ambassador to France, and U.S. Senator. Taylor had never voted or held a political office in his life. The Democratic Cass wanted to be president. The independent Taylor insisted, "I am not at all anxious for the office under any circumstances."[20]

A phrenologist tries to determine the political disposition of the apolitical Zachary Taylor. Many guessed wrong about the slave-owning Southerner. As president, Taylor proved to be a diehard unionist who thoroughly distrusted the proslavery lobby, and he vowed to march on any state that threatened to secede.

The Whig Party didn't care. They needed Taylor badly. They had opposed going to war with Mexico in 1846, and when the invasion turned out to be relatively short, victorious, and profitable, the Whigs went looking to adopt a war hero. Brig. Gen. Zachary Taylor, conqueror of Antonio Lopez de Santa Anna at the battle of Buena Vista, would do nicely. He reluctantly accepted their nomination.

On the single-most contentious issue of the day—expansion of slavery into the new territories—Taylor remained silent, despite the fact he owned more than a hundred human beings. In contrast, the Northerner Cass openly defended the constitutionally protected institution and encouraged settlers of newly acquired New Mexico, Arizona, and California to determine for themselves whether to allow slavery within their borders.[21]

An 1848 Democratic broadside, "The One Qualification for a Whig Candidate," shows a general atop a mound of human skulls. While the Whigs indeed courted Mexican War heroes such as Winfield Scott and Zachary Taylor, it was the Democrats who pushed for the military invasion of Mexico in 1846.

Cass's diplomacy may have cost him victory. In response to his conciliatory tone, many antislavery Democrats ditched Cass and formed the
Free Soil Party, nominating the aging former president Martin Van Buren
as their candidate.

In the first presidential balloting to be conducted on a single day, the
Free Soilers siphoned more than 10 percent of the popular vote, most of
which came out of the Democratic pool. The largest, wealthiest, and oldest political party in the land, armed with the experienced Cass, lost to a
weakened faction who ran a total political novice. Of all the disappointed
Democrats, perhaps none was more so than the sitting president, James
Polk, who said of the totally inexperienced Taylor, "The country will be
the loser by his election."[22]

---

Each state of the Union has one prominent citizen represented in the National Statuary Hall in the U.S. Capitol Building. Michigan's selection is
Lewis Cass.

---

## 10. 1960

| | |
|---|---|
| JOHN F. KENNEDY (D) | 303 |
| RICHARD M. NIXON (R) | 219 |

In the race between an eight-year vice president and a fourteen-year congressman, one of them vigorously embraced the revolutionary medium of
television. That person, of course, was Richard Milhous Nixon.

A considerable amount of lore surrounds the first televised presidential debate in U.S. history. For starters, the live face-off between the
debonair Jack Kennedy and the dour Dick Nixon was the first such debate, period. Such tête-à-têtes were normally intraparty affairs conducted
during primaries and were not popular with the candidates. The next set
of presidential debates would not occur until 1976.

Certainly, the broadcast did signal a new age. When Nixon and
Kennedy began their Washington careers back in 1946, scarcely one hundred thousand televisions existed in the entire country. On September 26,
1960, more than seventy million viewers tuned in.

Legendary was Nixon's poor complexion—stemming from a recent
knee operation and subsequent loss of twenty pounds. His ashen appearance and five o'clock shadow contrasted sharply with the fit and rested

Kennedy. Yet polling indicated that the event was not decisive. In three televised debates that followed, the California Republican actually closed a considerable gap on his opponent.

As with any campaign, this one was contentious. Kennedy accused the Eisenhower administration of permitting "a missile gap" between the United States and Soviets. GOP ads claimed the Democrats had given up Eastern Europe, China, and atomic secrets to communists. Former president Harry Truman was especially harsh toward Nixon and predicted that Kennedy would "win overwhelmingly."[23]

It was possibly Nixon's most ethical campaign. In an age when anti-papal sentiments ran high, he refused to comment on Kennedy's Catholicism. Aware of his opponent's many ailments, including the potentially fatal Addison's disease, Nixon declined to make health an issue, although he was just four years older than Kennedy and physically far stronger. He fulfilled a campaign promise to visit all fifty states, flying to Alaska just two days before the election, and returning to the lower forty-eight in complete exhaustion. Some pundits hypothesized that his integrity may have won him Alaska but cost him several close races elsewhere.[24]

On Election Day, as Kennedy canvassed the friendly Northeast, Nixon purchased an unprecedented four hours of television time at an ABC affiliate in California, answering live calls and promoting the GOP platform. The director of the Roper Poll had Nixon leading by 2 percent, but he confessed, "I have never seen the lead change hands so many times." Gallop had Kennedy leading by 1 percent.[25]

As predicted, the result was close. Several days passed before the out-

At the famous first televised debate, Richard Nixon embraced the medium with greater zeal than his opponent.

NIXON LIBRARY

come was confirmed. California and Illinois were too close to call, and voter fraud was evidently rampant in the latter. The critical state proved to be Texas, which Kennedy narrowly secured through his selection of running mate Lyndon Johnson. Rather than ask for a recount, the fatigued and disheartened Nixon accepted the result and contemplated retirement.

---

Popularly perceived as the dawn of "Camelot," the 1960 election actually saw more women, college graduates, and independents vote for Nixon than Kennedy.

---

## TOP TEN LANDSLIDES

"Landslide" did not enter the American lexicon until the late 1800s, yet lopsided wins in the Electoral College were already commonplace. In the nineteenth century, most of the presidential races were not close, and in the twentieth century, eighteen out of twenty-five victors received twice as many electoral votes as their opponents.

Constitutional framers believed the opposite would occur, that few if any contests would produce a clear winner. The deduction appeared sound, considering their environment at the time. Only one in two hundred Americans subscribed to a newspaper. States were united only in theory, as interstate travel meant weeks of slow, back-road, back-breaking, horse-and-carriage drudgery. Once more, there were no political parties to speak of, and thus no machinery to produce consensus candidates.

Anticipating their diffuse communities would produce a flock of entrants, the framers invented a system in which the voting population would act like a large nominating committee. Either through male suffrage or legislatures, states would choose electors, who would then vote for president. To prevent a contest between favorite sons, each elector would get two votes, one of which had to go to a person outside the state. Assuming no one candidate would gain the necessary majority, the House of Representatives would then select a winner from the top five.

Unforeseen by the Constitutional Convention, emerging political parties quickly dominated the selection process. Steady growth in literacy, newspapers, and technology further transformed relatively obscure contestants into household names. Only twice in two centuries would the House choose a president. In all other cases, the public drifted toward two or three frontrunners. More often than not, one candidate would outdistance the rest by furlongs. Following, in terms of percentage of electoral votes, are the most conspicuous examples of landslides in over fifty presidential contests.

## 1. 1789

| | | |
|---|---|---|
| GEORGE WASHINGTON | 69 | (100% OF FIRST-CHOICE VOTES) |
| JOHN ADAMS | 34 | (49% OF SECOND-CHOICE VOTES) |

Thinking of a particular general from Virginia, Benjamin Franklin surmised: "The first man put at the helm will be a good one. Nobody knows what sort may come afterwards."[26]

Realistically, only two names were respected enough to be given the executive chair, and the good doctor from Philadelphia was one of them. Yet by 1789 he suffered from persistent kidney stones, memory loss, and the knowledge that his eighty-two-year-old body was far beyond its life expectancy. "I am grown so old and feeble in mind, as well as body," Franklin confessed to a friend, "that I cannot place any confidence in my own judgment."[27]

The alternative was thus a virtual automatic. At age fifty-six, George Washington was old enough to be venerable and young enough to survive at least one term. Better still, he hailed from the Old Dominion, the most populous state, resting comfortably between the commercial North and the agrarian South. Most important, he had been commander in chief during the Revolution and president of the Constitutional Convention

The man who did not want to be either king or president felt compelled to serve when he was elected to the office unanimously.

(both positions he attained by unanimous election). Undoubtedly the only true roadblock to Washington's appointment was the man himself.

Citing "growing infirmities of age," he wrote to fellow veteran Charles Pettit, "I have no wish, which aspires beyond the humble and happy lot of living and dying a private citizen on my own farm." To Benjamin Lincoln, his second-in-command at Yorktown and a leading supporter of his appointment, Washington pleaded, "I most heartily wish the choice to which you allude may not fall upon me."[28]

Some historians question whether he protested too much, feigning humility while assuming the prize was his. But he had good reason to believe his days were few. His father died at forty-nine, his paternal grandfather died at thirty-six. Of Washington's nine siblings, seven were deceased. Washington himself was nearly blind, growing deaf, with one solitary tooth left in his aching jaw. After the Revolution, the general informed his dear Marquis de Lafayette, that he "might soon expect to be entombed in the dreary mansions of my father's . . . but I will not repine—I have had my day." His day would be extended by a unanimous vote. With no primaries, conventions, or viable challengers, all sixty-nine electors voted for Washington.[29]

As stipulated by the selection process, the runner-up became vice president. Washington expected Massachusetts, birthplace and bank vault of the Revolution, to produce a favorite. One New Englander, whom he marginally knew, caught his attention as brash but particularly intelligent. "From different channels of information," Washington wrote from Mount Vernon, "Mr. John Adams would be chosen Vice President. He will doubtless make a very good one."[30]

---

Of the thirteen original states, only ten took part in the 1789 election. Rhode Island and North Carolina had not yet ratified the Constitution, and the New York house and senate disagreed on specific electors and cast no vote.

---

**2. 1792**

| | | |
|---|---|---|
| GEORGE WASHINGTON | 132 | (100% OF FIRST-CHOICE VOTES) |
| JOHN ADAMS | 77 | (58% OF SECOND-CHOICE VOTES) |

Before embarking on his first term, Washington said to Henry Knox, "My movements to the chair of Government will be accompanied by feelings not unlike those of a culprit who is going to the place of his execution."[31]

Life as president confirmed his trepidations. Though it began with fireworks and accolades, his administration soon fractured from infighting, particularly between his idealistic secretary of state, Thomas Jefferson, and his elitist treasury secretary, Alexander Hamilton. Unresolved problems with Britain, including redcoat garrisons on the frontier and the Royal Navy threatening American seafarers, left the lifespan of his country in doubt.

Washington also found himself the frequent target of a free press. Principle among his accusers were the *National Gazette*, a Republican-Democrat paper tangentially connected to Jefferson, and the *Philadelphia General Advertiser*, run by Benjamin Franklin's grandson. Reading accounts of his supposed desire for monarchy, misquotes and forgeries bearing his name, and column titles such as "The Funeral of George W—n," he openly feared a disintegration of public support, insisting: "These articles tend to produce a separation of the Union, the most dreadful of calamities."[32]

Adding to his pains were the reminders of his own mortality. For his innumerable ailments he took laudanum, a tincture of alcohol and opium. Early in his first term, a sizable tumor grew from his left thigh, requiring an invasive and painful operation. As old comrades died one by one, a bout of flu nearly killed him in the spring of 1790.[33]

In spite of his condition, and because of the failing health of his country, the man reluctantly accepted the possibility of what he dejectedly called "another tour of duty." Once again, Washington was every elector's first choice for president. He returned to the helm with the hope of retiring midterm. Within months of his second inauguration, he confided in a letter to James Madison his overwhelming desire to leave politics for Mount Vernon, "to spend the remainder of my days (which I can not expect will be many) in ease and tranquility."[34]

---

Despite refusing to run for a third term, George Washington still received two electoral votes in the election of 1796.

---

## 3.  1820

| | |
|---|---|
| JAMES MONROE (D-R) | 231 |
| JOHN QUINCY ADAMS (D-R) | 1 |

In April 1820, Maryland Representative Samuel Smith called his fellow Democratic-Republicans to gather in Congress for a presidential caucus.

Barely forty legislators bothered to attend, and they immediately disbanded for lack of quorum. By default, the sixty-year-old pragmatic President James Monroe was nominated for reelection.[35]

So went the dubiously titled "Era of Good Feelings," when one party thoroughly dominated affairs. Absent was any heir of the old guard Federalists. Monroe's congenial and diplomatic style did much to prevent the rise of a new opposition party or a new war with Britain. The Compromise of 1820 added Missouri and Maine to the Union, maintaining Senate parity between slave and free states. Only the Panic of 1819 remained unsolved, as bank failures sent the country into its first true economic depression. Yet the dispossessed—urban laborers and frontier farmers—remained outside the political sphere, and Monroe ran almost unopposed.

For years the legend persisted that a rogue ballot was cast to maintain George Washington's record as the only unanimously elected president. Yet electors submitted their choices at different locations and dates, and they were generally unaware of how others were voting. The lone ballot for John Quincy Adams, unsolicited at that, came from New Hampshire's William Plumer. It turned out that the elector wasn't concerned about Washington's legacy. Plumer sincerely disliked Monroe, whom he said had "not that weight of character which his office requires."[36]

Regardless, indifference beset the general public, prompting the *Ohio Monitor* to warn: "In most of the States the elections occur with great quietness, too great, perhaps, for the general safety of the Republic." Certainly anyone outside the privileged circles of the Old Dominion had cause for concern. Of the first ten executive terms in the nation's history, Monroe's reelection made it nine terms and counting for Virginia.

---

James Monroe could possibly have won by a larger electoral margin. Out of 235 electoral votes, only 232 were cast, because electors from Mississippi, Pennsylvania, and Tennessee died before they could submit their selection.

---

## 4.  1936

FRANKLIN D. ROOSEVELT (D)    523

ALFRED LANDON (R)                    8

Republican Governor Alfred Moosman Landon of Kansas embodied the median. Average in height and build, middle-aged, "Alf" was a moderate

In 1936, FDR was coolly confident that he could defeat Alf Landon in the November election. The result was more like a severe beating, a landslide greater than Roosevelt ever envisioned.

ROOSEVELT LIBRARY

in word and deed. He made his money in industry, oil in particular, mostly through the engagement of a solid work ethic. An uninspiring speaker with a modest intellect, Landon, however, held one unique characteristic—he was the only Republican governor to win reelection in 1932.

Essentially a sacrificial lamb, Landon faced the mammoth alliance of FDR and the New Deal. A tacit progressive, the Kansan personally supported the New Deal, yet he argued that the inherently inefficient colossus could be better managed at the state level. He also warned against the climbing national debt and the "extraordinary powers" exercised by the incumbent. Much to his demise, he openly criticized Social Security, FDR's most popular new program. In contrast, Roosevelt played Robin Hood, bashing big corporations, opulent securities, and major banks, consequently winning over the less privileged majority.[37]

By November, the Civilian Conservation Corps and the Emergency Relief Appropriations Act was employing millions. Joblessness went down, grain prices slowly went up, and the repeal of Prohibition allowed spirits to legally flow again. Roosevelt calculated he would get 360 electoral votes and Landon 171. The polls of Gallop and Roper predicted a wider sum, estimating the president would carry every state but three.[38]

Election night saw an astounding 83 percent voter turnout. Sequestered in his private study at Hyde Park, FDR listened to the early returns. Within an hour he emerged to celebrate with family and friends, his countenance beaming from the beating he was giving the GOP.

In the end FDR collected nearly 28 million votes to Landon's 16.7 million. The Democrats took 331 of 435 House seats and 76 of 96 chairs in the Senate. All forty-eight states, save Maine and Vermont, went to Roosevelt, giving him the widest margin of victory of his presidential career and the most lopsided electoral vote in the era of universal suffrage.[39]

---

Among those who endorsed Alf Landon in the 1936 campaign were media giant William Randolph Hearst and track star Jesse Owens.

---

**5. 1984**

| | |
|---|---|
| RONALD REAGAN (R) | 525 |
| WALTER MONDALE (D) | 13 |

On paper the former vice president had a chance. A 1983 Gallop Poll revealed that 44 percent of Americans considered themselves Democrats, and only 25 percent sided with the GOP. Reagan's soaring military expenditures and reduced taxes pushed yearly deficits to $200 billion, while social and educational programs were consistently reduced or eliminated. Divisions between moderate and conservative Republicans threatened to split the party, and Reagan continued a habit of embarrassing miscues. One such remark summoned international condemnation. During a radio sound check months before the election, the president jested, "I am pleased to tell you I just signed legislation which outlaws Russia forever. The bombing begins in five minutes."[40]

Diluting Reagan's minuses was an apparent recovery from a lengthy recession, one that had reached its depth during Mondale's vice-presidential years in the White House. Primed in part by renewed defense spending,

Even Ronald Reagan was surprised at the overwhelming support he received when he accepted the renomination of his party in 1984.

unemployment steadily declined, the Federal Reserve Board lowered prime lending rates below 10 percent, and the Gross National Product rose to an annual rate of an exceptional 7.6 percent.[41]

Yet statistics mattered little in a campaign based on sentiment. Both candidates inundated voters with primal themes of patriotism, family, and morality. In this contest, Reagan was clearly the superior. Naturally warm and optimistic, his indissoluble confidence bonded well with voters, whereas Mondale's serious countenance and stiff demeanor exhumed memories of Jimmy Carter's dark delivery style. Mondale's selection of a female running mate, a first for a major party, also failed to produce widespread support. New York's Geraldine Ferraro did invoke a reaction, however, especially among evangelicals and conservative Roman Catholics, who disdained her lenient stance on abortion.[42]

On November 6, all polls pointed to a Republican victory. Only the margin remained in doubt, and some observers openly wondered if Reagan would win all fifty states. Early returns were not close. The incumbent won states by 20 percent and more. By 8:00 p.m. eastern time, barely into the election night broadcast, CBS announced Reagan as the victor. Within thirty minutes, ABC and NBC followed suit, despite the fact that polls were still open in nearly half the states. Though abrupt, the predictions proved accurate. When all was counted, Mondale only managed to take his home base of Minnesota plus the District of Columbia.[43]

---

The Democrats were not breaking new ground in selecting Geraldine Ferraro in 1984. The first woman to run for an executive position was New York's Victoria Woodhull, who received the People's Party nomination for president in 1872. Twenty-six women in various small parties followed in her footsteps until Ferraro's more famous attempt.

---

## 6. 1972

| RICHARD M. NIXON (R) | 520 |
| GEORGE MCGOVERN (D) | 17 |

Robert Kennedy once referred to George McGovern as "the most decent man in the Senate." A decorated veteran of World War II, a history PhD, supportive of the impoverished and elderly, he was bitterly opposed to

Voters flocked to Nixon in 1972 because of his political strength and personal integrity. Within a year, public perceptions of the stoic Nixon changed considerably.

NIXON LIBRARY

the war in Vietnam and was running against a political machine that had recently conducted the WATERGATE break-in.[44]

Though overtly liberal, McGovern benefited from a radical shift in the Democratic nomination process, one he personally championed. Traditionally, party leaders dominated the selection of presidential candidates. By 1972, caucuses and primaries became the forums for nomination, largely turning national conventions into rubber stamps and morale boosters.

If the new method "democratized" nominations, it also alienated the party elite. Exemplifying McGovern's weakened position, he only managed to raise half as much money as Nixon (thirty million dollars to sixty million dollars), and he struggled to find a running mate.[45]

Rejection followed rejection, until Missouri Senator Robert Eagleton accepted the offer. Weeks later, information surfaced that Eagleton had suffered bouts of depression, was currently on medication, and had received two rounds of electroshock therapy in the 1960s. McGovern initially vowed to support him "1,000 percent," then dropped him from the ticket.[46]

The embarrassed candidate weathered yet another series of public failures to find a deputy, until Sargent Shriver of Maryland accepted. The energetic Shriver was a noble choice. Though best known as an in-law to the Kennedys, Shriver was a cofounder of the Peace Corps, Head Start, Job Corps, and the Special Olympics.

Regardless, McGovern's popularity dropped from the fortieth percentile to the twenties, while Nixon's climbed. Successfully distancing himself from the slow-moving Watergate investigation, bumped by publicity in the August Republican Convention, and aided by Henry Kissinger's late October statement that "peace is at hand" in Southeast Asia, Nixon went into November leading the polls by two-to-one margins.

In the final popular vote, Nixon took forty-seven million to McGovern's twenty-nine million. Not surprisingly, the incumbent won 94 percent of registered Republicans, yet he also garnered nearly 70 percent of moderates, 61 percent of blue-collar workers, and 42 percent of Democrats. McGovern even lost his home state of South Dakota, taking only Massachusetts and the District of Columbia.[47]

---

The 1972 election marked the initiation of the Twenty-sixth Amendment, which granted eighteen- to twenty-one-year-olds the right to vote in national elections. The majority of them declined the privilege.

---

**7.   1804**

| THOMAS JEFFERSON (D-R) | 162 |
| CHARLES C. PINCKNEY (F) | 14 |

Having narrowly won in 1800, through a contest marred by scathing antagonisms right and left, Thomas Jefferson attempted to calm the warring parties at the outset of his presidency. In his inaugural address, he reminded his countrymen, "Every difference of opinion is not a difference of principle. . . . We are all Republicans, we are all Federalists. If there be any among us who would wish to dissolve this Union or to change its republican form, let them stand undisturbed as monuments of the safety with which error of opinion may be tolerated."

Though tolerance remained elusive in a country still struggling with the right to dissent, prosperity all but assured reelection for Jefferson. His first term marked years of relative peace. The navy and army were reduced by more than half. The surprise Louisiana Purchase doubled the size of the nation. Taxes on whiskey were repealed.[48]

In opposition stood Charles Cotesworth Pinckney, a South Carolina–born and Oxford-educated lawyer, a planter, and a former aide to George Washington during the Revolution. Running with him was Rufus King, a Harvard-primed veteran of the Continental Congress and the

Constitutional Convention and a minister to Britain. Despite their credentials, their fellow Federalists neglected to explicitly endorse them.[49]

In contrast, Democratic-Republicans were far better organized, staging parades of local officials and militia, penning radiant articles in the *National Intelligencer* and other pro-Jefferson papers, and dumping the do-nothing Vice President Aaron Burr for the first governor of New York and a longtime Washington confidant, George Clinton.

Reflecting the democratization of the country, only six states chose electors through their legislatures, while eleven opted for general male suffrage. The result overpowered the exclusive Federalist clique, and Jefferson won all but Connecticut, Delaware, and Maryland. Afterward, Jefferson wrote to a friend in France, expressing hope that the decisive outcome signaled the end of political parties, observing that "the two parties which prevailed with so much violence . . . are almost wholly melted into one."[50]

---

Of all the states, New Jersey was most friendly to Jefferson, voting in favor of the president 13,039 to 19.

---

## 8.  1864

ABRAHAM LINCOLN (NU)        212
GEORGE B. MCCLELLAN (D)       21

"Seldom in history," wrote Ralph Waldo Emerson, "was so much seated on a popular vote." Barely four score and seven years old, the United States looked to be on its deathbed. A third of its states were in rebellion. Federal coffers were nearly empty. Suspension of the writ of habeas corpus cast a tyrannical hue upon the White House, while the total number of dead in the war was approaching a half million.[51]

Abraham Lincoln was somewhat surprised in June 1864 to learn that his Republican Party had endorsed him for reelection. His solace soon died with the chilling news from Virginia that U. S. Grant had launched a massive frontal assault upon heavy Confederate defenses at Cold Harbor and lost seven thousand men in twenty minutes. With no foreseeable end to the bloodletting, the president issued a sullen memorandum to his cabinet in August: "This morning, as for some days past, it seems exceedingly probable that this Administration will not be re-elected."[52]

Poised to replace him was the handsome, confidant, former commander of the Army of the Potomac, Maj. Gen. George B. McClellan. The Democratic Convention announced its selection of "Little Mac" from the echoing Wigwam in Chicago, the very hall in which Lincoln was nominated four years previous.

Scurrying to fashion wider support, Lincoln ran under the banner of the "National Union Party," a compendium of loyal Republicans and war Democrats. For vice president, party officials dumped Maine abolitionist Hannibal Hamlin for Tennessee's military governor, Democrat Andrew Johnson. The government also provided a service for the first time in American history—absentee voting for soldiers.

Fortunately for Lincoln, McClellan continued his old military habits and failed to act boldly. He allowed the Democrats to pair him with an antiwar plank and George H. Pendleton of Ohio, both of which endorsed a permanent division of the Union. Refusing to label the war a failure and thus disgrace the work of his former troops, McClellan consequently alienated his own party. Meanwhile, the Union army achieved a surprising run of successes. In September, Atlanta fell, as did coastal areas of Alabama and North Carolina. Days before the election, Philip H. Sheridan scored a dramatic victory in the Shenandoah, securing the whole of the valley for the North.[53]

Still, as Lincoln watched soldiers vote on the White House lawn, he was unsure. He was likely to lose the Border States. New York and Pennsylvania, which accounted for half the electoral votes needed for victory, were too close to call.

For the first time in U.S. history, soldiers in the field voted in a presidential election. Overwhelming troop support for Lincoln and the National Union coalition, especially among troops in the eastern theater, turned the 1864 election into a rout.

When all was done, the president did lose his birth state of Kentucky, plus Delaware and McClellan's New Jersey. The popular vote was close— a little over 2.2 million to 1.8 million. Lincoln narrowly won New York. Of nearly 750,000 votes cast, he edged Mac by 6,749. Yet a sweep of the Northeast and Midwest gave the incumbent a decisive count in the Electoral College, bolstered in part by massive support from the troops. Seventy-eight percent in blue went with their president. The decisive mandate devastated McClellan. "For my country's sake, "he wrote to a friend, "I deplore the result."[54]

---

Shortly after his stinging defeat in the 1864 election, George McClellan left the United States for Europe and stayed away for three years.

---

## 9. 1980

| | |
|---|---|
| RONALD REAGAN (R) | 489 |
| JAMES CARTER (D) | 49 |

Ten Republicans entered the starting gate, chomping at the bit to race against a hobbling administration. Among the candidates was Ronald Reagan, who many dismissed as too old at sixty-nine to be a genuine contender. Yet Reagan's acting background, the very butt of political jokes, became his most valuable asset in the audition for leading man.

"Dutch" knew how to draw sympathy, recounting his family's hardships in the Great Depression, his life as a soldier in World War II (albeit on sound stages in sunny California), and his conversion to the Republican Party (after voting for FDR four times and Truman once). Though Reagan was upstaged in the first act, losing the Iowa Caucus to Texan George H. W. Bush, he came back with vigor in the subsequent primaries. By convention time, the actor won the nomination on the first ballot.

Carter also won his party's nomination on the first count, yet he was still plagued by inflation above 12 percent, interest rates hitting 20 percent, stifling energy shortages, and a Soviet invasion of Afghanistan. Dwarfing them all was a lingering hostage crisis in Iran, destined to reach its first anniversary on Election Day 1980.

Ironically, the militant Islamic takeover of the U.S. Embassy in Teheran marked a highpoint in Carter's approval ratings, as the nation rallied around its leader in the early days of the standoff. But as weeks turned to months, and only a few of the sixty-nine American citizens and diplomats were released, Carter's numbers began to slip, from nearly 60 percent down to the low 30s. Polls indicated that participants were more likely to vote against Carter rather than for Reagan, whose popular messages of patriotism came with frequent miscues, such as insisting that trees caused pollution and labeling the Vietnam War as a "noble cause."[55]

Weeks before the November showdown, analysts predicted a close race. *Newsweek* had Carter edging the Californian. Yet when election night arrived, many former Carter supporters stayed home, while last-minute undecideds voted predominantly for the alternative.[56]

Carter took Georgia's twelve electoral votes, plus five smaller states. Many Democrats lamented the presence of third-party candidate John Anderson of Illinois, who collected 5.7 million votes, or 7 percent. Had all of Anderson's supporters turned to Carter (unlikely because Anderson was a former Republican), the president would have taken sixteen states, none of which rivaled the Reagan-Bush trophies of California, Ohio, Pennsylvania, and Texas.[57]

In a bittersweet moment for the incumbent, the American hostages in Iran were freed on the very day of Reagan's triumphant inauguration.

---

James Carter was the first incumbent Democrat to lose the White House since Grover Cleveland in 1888.

---

## 10. 1964

| | |
|---|---|
| LYNDON B. JOHNSON (D) | 486 |
| BARRY GOLDWATER (R) | 52 |

Riding a wave of sympathy from the assassination of John F. Kennedy in Dallas, Lyndon Johnson easily secured the official blessing of his party at the 1964 convention in New Jersey. Submitting his name for nomination was Texas governor John Connally, who was still recovering from the bullet that had first passed through Kennedy's neck. Amid the convention's tributes to the late president, LBJ stopped short of naming Robert Kennedy as his running mate. Later on, Johnson said that young Robert had "skipped the grades where you learn the rules of life." He instead chose the equally liberal Hubert Humphrey of Minnesota, assuring his base of support that Jack Kennedy's pledge of social reform would remain intact.[58]

Offering a countermeasure, Republicans nominated arch-conservative Barry Goldwater. Born in Arizona when it was still a territory, Goldwater was a living artifact of the Old West. Roughhewn in thought and appearance, he stressed rugged individualism as the cure to society's ills. Congressman William Miller of New York became his running mate, despite receiving zero delegate votes at the national convention in San Francisco.

Goldwater, a.k.a. "Mr. Conservative," condemned civil rights legislation as reverse discrimination. Also voting against the censure of Joseph McCarthy, Goldwater insisted that the senator's hunt for communists made the United States a "safer, freer, more vigilant nation." In accepting his party's nomination, he uttered the now famous "extremism in the defense of liberty is no vice," a mantra backed by offhand comments endorsing the use of thermonuclear weapons in Vietnam.[59]

In response, the Johnson campaign aired the controversial "Daisy Girl" commercial, showing a playful child's world erased by nuclear war. Such scare tactics were politically unnecessary. Johnson's approval ratings were holding steady at 70 percent, while unemployment, crime, and Vietnam still appeared to be manageable issues.[60]

The election was never in doubt. Most voters found Goldwater too radical to be plausible. Though he did attain support from conservatives like Ronald Reagan, the senator also received unwanted endorsement from extreme rightists such as the John Birch Society and the jingoist "Americans for America." Moderates, labor, and minorities voted overwhelmingly against him, and he barely won his home state. Looking back, one of Johnson's speechwriters called the landslide of 1964 "one of the silliest, most empty, and most boring campaigns in the nation's history."[61]

---

For vice president, Lyndon Johnson heavily considered naming Defense Secretary Robert McNamara.

---

## TOP TEN MOST CONTROVERSIAL ELECTIONS

It only takes a generation or two to turn a battle into nostalgia. Such is the case with presidential elections, when blood feuds are forgotten, and all that remains are faded cartoons, quirky slogans, and kitschy buttons. Enter the next campaign, and the mudslinging seems uniquely vulgar, as if politics had never been so rabid.

In reality, elections have never been so lawful and civilized as they are at present. Parties have learned the risks of wiretapping, slander, and slush funds. Journalists employ fact checkers and fear committing libel. Never has campaign financing been so tightly monitored.

This evolution took time. At first there was just the voice ballot, when citizens stated their choice in front of potentially hostile bystanders. Paper balloting was no better, as parties printed their own forms, often using symbols and colors similar to their opponents' in order to fool the illiterate. When polling did not go as they wished, district officials often "misplaced" whole boxes of returns. Much of this petulant behavior was exorcized by the secret ballot in the late 1800s. The first voting machines in 1892 marked a further decline in fraud.[62]

Voting itself is more democratic than ever. In the first elections, fewer than one-fourth of white males could participate. By 1860, every state except South Carolina essentially had universal white male suffrage. Women won the right to vote in national elections in 1920, as did Chinese Americans in 1943 and Japanese Americans in 1952. A century after emancipation, the 1965 Voting Rights Act guaranteed the opportunity to all African Americans. Since the Bill of Rights, there have been seventeen amendments to the U.S. Constitution—more than half of which involve the expansion of voting rights.

When all is said and done, however, elections are still fundamentally competitions, some of which have beaten the better angels of our nature. Listed below are the ten most divisive presidential races in the nation's history, based on the overall amount of civil unrest, voter fraud, vote tampering, media libel, and acts of public litigation that each generated. A testament to how far democracy has progressed, the majority occurred in the nineteenth century.

## 1.  "THE IRREPRESSIBLE CONFLICT"—1860

| | | | |
|---|---|---|---|
| ABRAHAM LINCOLN (R) | 180 | JOHN C. BRECKINRIDGE (SD) | 72 |
| JOHN BELL (U) | 39 | STEPHEN A. DOUGLAS (ND) | 12 |

The bloodiest war in American history did not start over the bombardment of a federal fort nor during a pitched battle along the banks of Bull Run. Disintegration began immediately after a presidential election.

The chance of disunion had been present since the nation's found-

An 1860 nonpartisan cartoon depicts the four presidential candidates tearing the country apart. For once, sensational journalism was correct.

ing. Southerners George Washington and Thomas Jefferson sincerely feared it. Northerners Benjamin Franklin and John Marshall expected it sooner rather than later. Yet the experiment survived several economic breakdowns, rebellions of citizens and slaves, the burning of its capital, and a dozen wars. Crises came and went, while an unanswerable question lingered.

North and South, the vast majority of Americans owned no slaves, but most tolerated the institution as a deeply rooted reality. The spread of slavery was an entirely different issue, of which there seemed no middle ground. In the 1860 election, Northern Democrat Stephen Douglas argued for new territories to decide for themselves, a policy already invalidated by sectarian violence in Kansas. Southern Democrat John Breckinridge, the nation's vice president, ran on a pro-slavery platform, while Unionist and former Secretary of War John Bell hoped that silence would win him the presidency. The Republican Lincoln flatly believed that all new states admitted into the Union should be free soil.

The four-horse race quickly devolved into a public stampede of slander, libel, and fraud. Month after month, parades, rallies, and the media played on base fears. Rumors spread that Lincoln was part black. Texas newspapers fabricated stories of slave uprisings to scare people into voting for Breckinridge. The pro-Bell *Richmond Whig* warned that a Breckinridge victory would bring "all the horrors of civil, social, and servile war," and a Kentucky paper reported, quite falsely, that there was no use voting for him because he had a terminal illness. The *St. Louis News* printed fake poll numbers showing Bell winning the state by a mile, while in fact Douglas was far ahead in the polls. In New York City, thousands of Douglas supporters marched with signs denouncing the Republican Party, including one banner that read "free love and free n[—]s will certainly elect Old Abe."[63]

The country fractured soon after Election Day, because the Republican won without receiving a single vote in ten states—all in the South. He even finished dead last in his birth state of Kentucky.[64]

An outraged South Carolina was first to revolt against the government, mere weeks after the election. The official article of secession proclaimed: "A geographical line has been drawn . . . and all the States north of that line have united in the election of a man to the high office of President of the United States, whose opinions and purposes are hostile to slavery."[65]

Mississippi, Florida, Alabama, Georgia, Louisiana, and Texas soon followed, declaring a betrayal of democracy. Seizing federal arsenals, foundries, and forts, forming their own constitution, electing their own president, the Confederate States of America determined to have their new nation up and running before the "Black Republican" took the oath of office. As one Georgia newspaper affirmed: "Let the consequences be what they may—whether the Potomac is crimsoned in human gore, and Pennsylvania Avenue is paved ten fathoms deep in mangled bodies . . . the South will never submit to such humiliation and degradation as the inauguration of Abraham Lincoln."[66]

---

Of the defeated candidates in 1860: Douglas died the following year from typhoid; Breckinridge fought in the Confederate army; Bell eventually supported secession, while his running mate, Edward Everett, was the keynote speaker at the dedication of the Soldiers Cemetery at Gettysburg just prior to Lincoln's delivery of the Gettysburg Address.

---

## 2. "THE MONSTER FRAUD OF THE CENTURY"—1876

| | |
|---|---|
| RUTHERFORD B. HAYES (R) | 185 |
| SAMUEL J. TILDEN (D) | 184 |

"Reconstruction" was a misnomer. A decade after the largest war ever waged in the Western Hemisphere, Americans were still trapped in the wreckage. Soldiers continued to occupy much of the Deep South, recession and corruption flourished, racial tensions prevailed, and shaky relations between Republicans and Democrats turned absolutely virile.

To maintain their hold on the presidency, many Republicans resorted to "waving the bloody shirt," reminding voters that the late Confederacy was largely of Democratic construct. They also attacked Democratic nominee Samuel Tilden (a highly ethical individual) of racketeering, tax evasion, and anti-Unionism.

In turn, Democrats spread rather interesting rumors about the Republican candidate. Reportedly, Rutherford B. Hayes had pocketed the pay of deceased soldiers under his command during the Civil War, embezzled millions as Ohio's governor, and killed his mom. The accusations were partially true. Hayes had been an officer in the Union army, served as governor of Ohio, and had a mother.[67]

Conditions were far worse in the South. Democratic "rifle clubs" began to harass Republicans, white and black. Vicksburg witnessed a bloodbath right before a local election in 1874—thirty-five blacks and two whites were killed in the wake of a political riot. In 1875, neighboring states began to adopt the "Mississippi Plan," a combination of blacklisting and physical harassment against "carpetbagger" Northerners and African Americans. In South Carolina, on the hundredth anniversary of the Fourth of July, a confrontation between white gentry and black militia led to the "Hamburg Massacre." Five of the militia were captured and summarily shot "while trying to escape."[68]

Predictably, the election of 1876 became a spectacle of voter intimidation and falsified counts, to the point where another civil war seemed inevitable. Neither candidate won a majority of the Electoral College (see

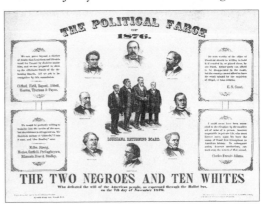

Sour grapes for the Democrats in 1876 were directed against the bipartisan committee that gave the White House to Republican Rutherford B. Hayes.

CLOSEST ELECTIONS), because Florida, Louisiana, and South Carolina submitted multiple, contradicting results. In a show of force, President Grant sent thousands of additional troops to the South. Questionable re-counts produced swings of ten thousand votes and more. Squads of fac-tional "Minute-Men" began to arm themselves. Democrats demonstrated across the country shouting "Tilden or Blood," while their representatives on Capitol Hill presented a resolution naming Tilden as president.[69]

One day before the end of Grant's term, a bipartisan committee placed the Republican Hayes in the White House. Miraculously, war was averted. Though the Democrats lost the presidency, they retained control of the House and subsequently cut off all funding for Reconstruction. Fac-ing a divided Congress and a divided country, Hayes opted to postpone civil rights in return for Southern cooperation, and he ended the military occupation of the former Confederacy.[70]

> Refusing to accept Hayes as their president, militant Democrats displayed flags at half-staff and referred to the chief executive as "His Fraudulency" and "Rutherfraud B. Hayes" throughout his four-year term.

## 3. REVENGE FOR "THE CORRUPT BARGAIN"—1828

| | |
|---|---|
| ANDREW JACKSON (D) | 178 |
| JOHN QUINCY ADAMS (NR) | 83 |

The election of 1824 was civil enough. Finishing last was House Speaker Henry Clay, with Treasury Secretary William Crawford third and Secre-tary of State John Quincy Adams second. Reflecting the country's physical and political drift westward, Senator Andrew Jackson of Tennessee won a plurality of the popular vote, but his 99 electors were well short of the 131 required for a majority.

Mandated by law, the decision went to the House of Representatives. Under Clay's watch, they chose the experienced Adams. At first, Jackson expressed surprise but not suspicion, until Adams gave Clay the presti-gious post of secretary of state. Already prone to a volcanic temper, Jack-son raged against the "corrupt bargain," and his fellow westerners began scheming to oust Adams in 1828.

They had an easy target. John Quincy was much like his father, only more haughty, cerebral, and distant. He spoke in ideals, of building a na-

The revered Henry Clay of Kentucky was in the middle of the fiery election of 1824. Initially Andrew Jackson had no reason to suspect House Speaker Clay of any wrongdoing when the House made John Quincy Adams president in 1825. That all changed, however, when Adams named Clay to be his secretary of state.

tional university and an astronomical observatory, items of marginal appeal to the 90 percent of Americans who lived in the rural world. Pouncing on the pompous intellectual, Jackson partisans spread rumors that "King John II" was turning the Executive Mansion into a palace of intrigue, filling it with "gambling equipment" (in truth, a billiard table). They also alleged that he secretly despised anyone who was not of English blood. Stories surfaced that while Adams was ambassador to St. Petersburg, he coerced a young woman into an affair with Czar Alexander I, a lie that mutated into accounts of Adams "the pimp" gathering prostitutes and virgins for the entire royal court.[71]

Revolted by this new political party of frontier mudslingers who took the name "Democrats," Adams's National Republicans responded in kind. They derided Jackson as a cruel slave master, uneducated, partial to cockfights, and a murderer (he executed two British captives during the War of 1812). They also attacked his wife. An ailing woman of sixty-one, Rachel Donelson Robards Jackson had once been married to an abusive husband. He eventually left her, though he neglected to finalize their divorce. Assuming otherwise, Rachel married Jackson, who adored her. In 1828, when an unfriendly press caught wind of the ancient (and long rectified) problem, they incessantly accused her of adultery.

The attacks failed to shake Jackson's appeal to the masses, and he won in a landslide, but he would lose his wife. Two weeks after the election, the emotionally shattered and publicly defiled Rachel suffered a severe heart attack. Doctors bled her, and she recovered slightly, only to succumb to a cardiac arrest. Under orders from her husband, doctors bled her again, this time from the temple. Rachel had been dead for hours before her husband stopped checking for her pulse.[72]

Weeks later, Jackson left for Washington. As he entered the city where his rivals were still in office, Jackson declared, "May God Almighty forgive her murderers as I know she forgave them. I never can." Perhaps wisely, both Clay and Adams did not attend the inauguration.[73]

---

On Christmas Eve, 1828, Rachel Jackson was laid to rest wearing the dress she had bought for her husband's inauguration day.

---

## 4.  "MURDER, ROBBERY, RAPE, ADULTERY, AND INCEST"—1800

| | |
|---|---|
| THOMAS JEFFERSON (D-R) | 73 |
| JOHN ADAMS (F) | 65 |

The two had once been dear friends, having met at the Second Continental Congress. John Adams marveled at the spindly Virginian's literary brilliance. Soft-spoken Thomas Jefferson was quickly impressed by the forceful and confident little stove from New England, seven years his elder. Their bond lasted twenty years, until they were president and vice president. Belonging to rival factions, the two abruptly drifted apart and rarely spoke to each other during the whole of their administration.

The bitter election of 1800 only widened the fissure. Awaiting the outcome back home in Massachusetts, Adams confided, "I am determined to be a Silent Spectator of the Silly and Wicked game." Jefferson busied himself with endless modifications to Monticello. The factions fought anyway.[74]

The pivotal question involved which superpower to embrace: Britain or its mortal enemy France. The Federalist Adams favored the former, and his enemies consequently branded him a royalist. James Madison cursed the Federalists as "the British Party," while others claimed that a reelected Adams would rejoin the monarchy and make himself royal governor of North America.[75]

Jefferson won several enemies for his well-known favoritism of France, a place that had turned to mob rule in the 1790s. As Europe sank once again into fratricide, Jefferson's enemies recounted a statement he had made years before: "I like a little rebellion now and then."[76]

Then there was the question of Jefferson's own faith, summarized in his famous statement, "for my neighbor to say that there are twenty gods, or no god. . . . It neither picks my pocket nor breaks my leg." His foes construed this as a profession of atheism, and Alexander Hamilton branded him "an Atheist in Religion and a Fanatic in politics." Another Federalist proclaimed that a Jefferson victory would mean "religion will be destroyed and immorality will flourish," while the *Connecticut Courant* declared: "Murder, robbery, rape, adultery, and incest will be openly taught and practiced."[77]

Fears only worsened when Jefferson and his running mate, Aaron Burr, tied in the electoral vote, and the Federalist-controlled Congress refused to name either one as president (see CLOSEST ELECTIONS). Citizens openly wondered if the Federalists were planning a coup. Rumors spread in January 1801 that a civil war was imminent after a mysterious fire broke out in the Treasury Department. Jefferson himself warned Adams that there would be "resistance by force, and incalculable consequences" if Congress did not choose a successor—and soon.[78]

At the last possible moment, the system worked, and an eleventh-hour vote lofted Jefferson into the presidency. Departing First Lady Abigail Adams rejoiced that the crisis had finally subsided, but she agonized that it was all too temporary: "I fear America will never go through another Election without Blood Shed. We have had a paper War for six weeks past, and if the Candidates had not themselves been entirely passive, Rage and Violence would have thrown the whole Country into a Flame."[79]

Thomas Jefferson received his swearing in at Congress Hall in Philadelphia, only a few hundred meters from the Pennsylvania State House, where

A Federalist cartoon depicts Satan and a drunk Thomas Jefferson trying to pull down the federal government during the contentious campaign of 1800.

twenty-four years previous, Adams and Jefferson worked together on producing the Declaration of Independence.

---

## 5.  THE DARK HORSE AND XENOPHOBIA—1844

| | |
|---|---|
| JAMES K. POLK (D) | 170 |
| HENRY CLAY (W) | 105 |

With President John Tyler unwilling to follow party directions, the Whigs dropped him for congressional icon Henry Clay of Kentucky, the swaggering, persuasive master of negotiation. The race was to be Clay's third try for the prize. Democrats struggled to choose between former president Martin Van Buren and states' rightist John C. Calhoun. After forty-nine exasperating ballots, the anonymous James K. Polk became their compromise choice.

The campaign quickly settled into a battle of libel and slander. Democrats accused Clay of breaking "every one of the Ten Commandments." Whigs painted Polk as a warmonger who was willing to fight Britain and Mexico to get Oregon and Texas. They also condemned Polk for being a slave owner (though Clay was one too). For much of the population, the issue of the day was neither slavery nor expansion. It was immigration.[80]

In 1820 there were only about sixty thousand immigrants out of some ten million Americans. By 1830 the number of foreign-born had doubled. The following decade the total quadrupled, consisting mostly of impoverished European Catholics.

THE HUNTER OF KENTUCKY.

Henry Clay and Theodore Frelinghuysen hunt Democrats in this 1844 image. Frelinghuysen holds John C. Calhoun and Thomas Hart Benton, while Clay beheads Van Buren, Polk, plus the sitting president, former Whig John Tyler.

The influx prompted a rise of ultranationalism, mostly among evangelical Protestants, who blamed rising crime and falling wages on the "Papists" pouring in from the Old World. In the late spring of 1844, a small altercation between Americans and Irish in Philadelphia set off a week of brawls, shootings, and arson. When it was over, scores of shops and homes were destroyed, two Catholic churches lay in ashes, and seven people were dead. The violence spread to other cities, including Charlestown, Massachusetts, where arson leveled a Catholic convent. To assure "law and order" in the upcoming election, Nativists in several states tried to restrict voting to U.S.-born citizens.[81]

Always the compromiser, Clay tried to play the middle ground. In turn, he was attacked from both sides. Protestants chastised him for courting Rome and immigration, whereas Catholics feared his running mate, Theodore Frelinghuysen, who advocated Protestant Bibles in public schools.[82]

Polk avoided the issue of ethnicity altogether, concentrating instead on promoting an aggressive foreign policy. The Democratic dark horse handily won the election. Yet it is possible that Polk achieved victory because of immigration rather than in spite of it. In the critical state of New York, which Polk barely won, corrupt Tammany Hall had naturalized thousands of Europeans almost as fast as they were leaving the boats. Encouraged to vote for Polk early and often, they did. In New York City alone, voter turnout was a curious 115 percent, vastly in favor of the Democrat.[83]

---

In a failed effort to gain Irish votes among the heavily immigrant population, New York Whigs hinted that their candidate's real name was "Patrick O'Clay."

---

## 6.  "GESTAPO TACTICS"—1968

| RICHARD M. NIXON (R) | 301 | HUBERT H. HUMPHREY (D) | 191 |
| GEORGE C. WALLACE (I) | 46 | | |

For once, Nixon was not the center of a controversy. In the space of eight months, the Democratic Party went from dominating national politics to losing control of its own convention hall, and it all began in Saigon.

Vietnam looked winnable until January 30, 1968, when North Vietnamese forces launched the Tet Offensive. The following day, bloodied

U.S. soldiers and marines were fighting hand-to-hand to retake their own embassy in the South Vietnamese capital.

Two months later, mentally and physically consumed by the war, Lyndon Johnson astonished the nation on live television with a sudden notice: "I shall not seek, nor will I accept, the nomination of my party for another term as your president." Four weeks later, Martin Luther King Jr. was murdered outside a hotel in Memphis, and race riots broke out in Detroit and Washington, D.C. Months after that, leading antiwar candidate Robert Kennedy was gunned down immediately after he had won the California Democratic Primary.

Had the presidential election occurred a year before, Richard Nixon would not have won his own party's nomination, let alone the presidency. But his promise to restore law and order in his country and make peace in Vietnam struck a chord with millions of Americans ready for a change. Democrats struggled to find a challenger, and at their national convention in Chicago, they quickly broke into two factions—those who supported the war and those looking for immediate withdrawal. Outside, thousands of antiwar protesters gathered, ranging from pacifists to radical leftists. To contain the crowds, Democratic Mayor Richard Daley mobilized the whole of the city's police force and put the Illinois National Guard on high alert.[84]

The tipping point came when prowar candidate Hubert Humphrey won the nomination on the first ballot, and crowds outside cried out in protest. In Grant Park, thousands of demonstrators and law officers started to turn on each other, and the violence immediately spread to nearby Lincoln Park. Rocks and tear gas incited panic on both sides. Bystanders were drawn into the ensuing chaos as police charged into the mobs, and rioting spread into the streets. Inside the convention hall, delegates watched in stunned silence as the riots were broadcast on live television. Horrified by what he was seeing, Senator Abe Ribicoff accused Richard Daley of "Gestapo tactics." There were calls to dissolve the assembly. It would take Daley and his security forces more than twenty-four hours to restore order in the city.[85]

The Democratic implosion in Chicago marked a national shift to the right. Though Humphrey rallied to make the election close—31.3 million votes to Nixon's 31.8 million—his defeat signaled the end of an era. Before 1968, Democrats won seven out of ten presidential elections. Starting with Nixon, it has been seven out of ten for the GOP.[86]

---

Reflecting the deep racial tensions in the 1968 elections, independent candidate George Wallace ran on a platform of segregation. He subsequently won forty-six electors and nearly ten million popular votes.

---

## 7. "BETWEEN LUST AND LAW"—1884

GROVER CLEVELAND (D)          219
JAMES G. BLAINE (R)           182

Mixing pulpit and politics, a reverend from Buffalo told his congregation that the upcoming election was a simple choice "between the brothel and the family, between decency and indecency, between lust and law."[87]

It is an incontrovertible truth that, from time to time, some Americans partake in premarital sex. Beer-drinking, cigar-smoking, card-playing bachelor Grover Cleveland certainly did. While he was practicing law in Buffalo in 1873, he was practicing other skills with a widow, Maria Halpin. In 1874, she bore a son. Whether Cleveland was the actual father was a tertiary point for Cleveland, and he provided for the child through the ensuing years.

Running for president in 1884, Cleveland received the endorsement of the *New York World* on the basis of four qualities: "He is an honest man. He is an honest man. He is an honest man. He is an honest man." But when a Buffalo newspaper leaked the story of Cleveland's love child, the accusations flew. Papers called him a "moral leper," "wretch," and "libertine." Cartoons showed a screaming baby with the title "Another Voice for Cleveland." Apocryphal stories surfaced of attempted kidnappings to silence mother and child. Others morphed into eyewitness accounts of "Grover the Good" engaging in physical relations with harems of women.[88]

Cleveland and his staff lessened the blow by readily admitting to the brief affair with Halpin and that he was providing financial assistance for the boy's care. As bad as it was for Cleveland, Blaine had it worse, as stories surfaced that he had engaged in shady business deals with railroad corporations. The former secretary of state, House Speaker, and senator weathered months of deflowering editorials and mounting evidence. At one point, a rally of forty thousand gathered in New York City and shouted, "Blaine, Blaine, James G. Blaine, the Monumental Liar from the State of Maine!" Other chants were less tasteful.[89]

Back and forth the sneers flew. When Nativists accused Blaine of being soft on Catholic immigration, a Protestant minister came to his defense, proclaiming the Republican stood firmly against "rum, Romanism, and rebellion." The xenophobic endorsement cost Blaine dearly, especially among Catholics and Southerners. In response, Republicans spread fake reports that Cleveland was about to die from palsy or kidney failure. One rumor professed that he recently contracted contagious leprosy.[90]

Rising out of the mud, Cleveland narrowly won (see CLOSEST ELECTIONS). He would run twice more, losing the White House in 1888 and regaining it in 1892. In each campaign he faced a new set of false accusations, among them were stories that he was an alcoholic and that he beat his wife.[91]

---

Among the many "Mugwumps" in 1884—Republicans who voted for the Democrat Grover Cleveland—were Gettysburg veteran Carl Schurz, abolitionist Henry Ward Beecher, and author Mark Twain.

---

## 8.   CORRUPTION AND DEATH—1872

| ULYSSES S. GRANT (R) | 286 |
| HORACE GREELEY (LR) | VOTES WITHDRAWN |

Georgia's former Confederate vice president, Alexander H. Stephens, viewed the candidates as a choice between "hemlock and strychnine." Running for reelection was U. S. Grant, personally above reproach, but head of an administration that fostered the BLACK FRIDAY and WHISKEY RING scandals.[92]

The field of Democrats was so weak that they turned to a Liberal Republican, *New York Tribune* editor Horace Greeley. Later generations would know him for the quote "Go west, young man." His contemporaries knew him to be intelligent but unwise, passionate to the point of irrational, and a veritable geyser of baseless accusations. During the Civil War, his *Tribune* equated Democrats with traitors, blamed unsuccessful Union generals for secretly backing slavery, and frequently accused Lincoln of cowardice. His words alone provided ample fuel for critics. His balding crown, rosy cheeks, frail glasses, and untamed neck beard made him a favorite of cartoonists. To his detractors, he had the look and sound of a panicky elf.

The David figure of newspaper editor Horace Greeley attempts to slay the warrior Ulysses S. Grant and his militarist backers. Goliath would win this battle by a landslide, and David would be the one to die.

Yet the campaign was anything but comical, a sordid season the *New York Sun* called a "shower of mud." Hard-right Republicans, claiming a monopoly on patriotism, depicted Greeley as soft on the South, while Grant was the triumphant warrior. Campaign photos invariably showed a much younger Grant in uniform.[93]

Most cynical was the work of *Harper's Weekly* illustrator Thomas Nast (inventor of the plump Santa, the Democratic donkey, and the Republican elephant). Nast and his fellow journalists portrayed Greeley as a servant of Jefferson Davis, based on the Confederate president's early release from prison in 1867, which Greeley helped facilitate. They also accused the editor of being friendly to the Ku Klux Klan, a most puerile falsehood. The longtime abolitionist had adopted a forgiving tone toward the defeated Confederacy, yet he remained as repulsed as any by the prolific incidents of arson, intimidation, and murder infecting the South since the Klan's birth in 1866.[94]

On Election Day, voter fraud was prevalent, especially in the South. Results from Arkansas and Louisiana were thrown out altogether. In the Northeast, hundreds of women suffragists tried to vote and were arrested, including Susan B. Anthony. At day's end, Grant's war record and Greeley's eccentricities made the result a foregone conclusion. The general won a second term with 286 electors out of a possible 352.

Greeley was to say, "I was the worst beaten man who ever ran for high office." His exaggeration would soon become fact. In the span of a month, Greeley lost his wife of thirty years, the election, then his job at the *Tribune*, after which he checked into a mental hospital and abruptly died.

Consequently, his votes were transferred to lesser candidates, making Greeley's total count in the Electoral College officially zero.[95]

---

Though many accused Grant of drinking again, the only confirmed alco-holic in the race was Greeley's running mate, B. Gratz Brown, a.k.a. "Boozy." After several rumored incidents, Brown became severely inebri-ated at a campaign banquet at Yale, where he proceeded to deliver a slurred, rambling tirade against Ivy League intellectuals.

---

### 9.  A WAR FOR THE LAWYERS—2000

| | |
|---|---|
| GEORGE W. BUSH (R) | 271 |
| AL GORE (D) | 266 |

Al Gore telephoned his adversary a few hours after midnight, believing George W. Bush had won the critical state of Florida. When an automatic recount showed a gap of a few hundred votes, the Tennessean retracted his earlier offer. The first of the attorney exchanges began the next day, when Gore's operatives requested a hand recount in key Florida districts. Two days later, Bush's legal advisors solicited a stoppage of the review. Thus began a rich circus of baneful rants, public cries of institutional racism, and a president's ransom in legal fees.

Starting things off, Florida Secretary of State Katherine Harris refused to extend a November 14 deadline for vote submissions. Though she later extended the cutoff by a day, she roused the ire of Gore people because she happened to be the cochair of Bush's Florida campaign staff.[96]

Next were the "Butterfly Ballots" of Palm Beach County, double-columned sheets with center-punch holes. When the election results came into question, county residents filed a protest in Florida's supreme court, deriding the ballots' design. Other counties experienced problems with their punch cards, many of which had incomplete perforations, adding the noun *chad* to the American vocabulary. While deriding the ballots as archaic, many pundits failed to mention that more than a third of the voting machines in the country were punch-type.[97]

Meanwhile, legal teams continued to file suits and appeals with reck-less abandon, and judgeships responded in kind—from a federal judge in Miami, to the Leon County Circuit Court in Tallahassee, to the Eleventh District Court of Appeals in Atlanta. The Florida Supreme Court alone rendered verdicts in seven different cases. Finally, the U.S. Supreme Court stopped the recounts, leaving Bush ahead in Florida by just over five hundred votes.

Both political parties acted less than democratically. Bush never trailed, yet his attorneys worked diligently to hinder recounts. Gore's advisors also moved to dismiss votes, specifically absentee ballots from the counties of Martin and Seminole. But the election itself was commendable for a number of reasons.

Differences were voiced through free speech, press, and assembly. Citizens petitioned their state and local governments, and though the country was divided in mind, the body politic peaceably abided by the rule of law. Partisan violence was virtually nonexistent. If any party was guilty of an offense, it was the one hundred million voters who declined to cast a ballot.[98]

---

The infamous butterfly ballot of Palm Beach County was designed by a Democrat, approved by both major parties, and published in local newspapers before the election.

---

## 10. WILLIE HORTON AND THE PLEDGE OF ALLEGIANCE—1988

| | |
|---|---|
| GEORGE H. W. BUSH (R) | 426 |
| MICHAEL DUKAKIS (D) | 111 |

Until the late twentieth century, candidates rarely dirtied themselves on the schoolyard of personal attacks, leaving that work to news media, party bosses, and the general public. Much of that changed with the invention of presidential debates, and the nominees took on the role of party chieftain. Witness the race between Vice President George H. W. Bush and Massachusetts Governor Michael Dukakis, a contest that began with Bush promising "a kinder, gentler nation."

It started blandly, with both sides selecting weak running mates. The Dukakis camp went with Texas Senator Lloyd Bentsen, an aging and distinguished congressman, but exceedingly reserved and plain. Bush followed with a choice that utterly confused his constituents—James Danforth Quayle, a meek, unaccomplished senator from Indiana.

During the campaign, the nominees drifted away from major issues, opting instead for platitudes on flags, country, a strong defense, and the death penalty, enunciated with toxic strikes against their opposition. Bush emphasized the Pledge of Allegiance, a thinly veiled attack against Dukakis's veto of a state law making the pledge mandatory in Massachusetts schools. But then came the story of Willie Horton, a convicted murderer who brutally raped a woman while he was on furlough from a Massachusetts prison. The Republicans saw their opening.

Bush's campaign manager, Lee Atwater, vowed to "strip the bark off that little bastard [Dukakis]" and "make Willie Horton his running mate." Ads featuring the Horton incident ran nonstop, along with other "evidence" that Dukakis was soft on crime. A GOP party chairman in Maryland, where the rape occurred, also distributed campaign literature featuring separate images of Dukakis and Horton with the caption: "Is This Your Pro-Family Team for 1988?"[99]

The Democrats were slow to point out that Dukakis's predecessor, a Republican, started the furlough system, and that forty-two states had similar policies. California's dated back to the governorship of Ronald Reagan, when two separate incidents of temporary release resulted in murder. Yet rather than exercise restraint, Democrats shot back with negative ads of their own, including the report of a halfway house program in Bush's Texas, where a resident had molested and murdered a minister's wife.[100]

For much of the disgusted population, neither candidate was worth a vote. Turnout hit a fifty-year low, as half the electorate stayed home. The other half leaned toward staying the course, and the vice president moved into the White House with 426 electoral votes to his opponent's 111.

---

At the 1988 Democratic National Convention, Texas Governor Ann Richards won thunderous applause when she said George Bush "was born with a silver foot in his mouth." Richards would later lose her governorship to another Bush, in part because she debated poorly against him.

---

# THE DOMESTIC SPHERE

## TOP TEN DEBT PRESIDENCIES

In 1800 the federal government was spending ten million dollars per year. In 1900 the rate was ten million dollars every two days. In 2000 it was ten million dollars every three minutes. Even with adjusted dollars, Washington at present consumes money forty thousand times faster than when it first began. With such an open purse, it is not surprising that the country has seen periods of cost overrun.

The tradition is for one party to blame the other for the growing debt. In reality, the reasons are manifold, but there are two chief causes. One involves a rapidly growing population that demands a more perfect union, with established justice, ensured domestic tranquility, unrivaled defense, and copious amounts of general welfare. Through revenues, bureaucracy, technology, and a great deal of borrowing, political leaders have largely delivered on these demands and have been eager to do so. The word *help* never appeared in the first seventy annual messages from the presidents. In the last fifty years, the term has utterly littered the State of the Union.[1]

By a large margin, the primary cause of debt has been warfare. Not "defense" per se, but major armed conflicts have swallowed public funds and resources faster than they could ever be replaced. As the following audit demonstrates, war has proven to be the ultimate nonprofit venture.

Listed below are the administrations that have overseen the greatest percentage increases in national debt. Notably, they are a relatively even mix of Democrats and Republicans, and they are joined by two Founding Fathers.[2]

## 1.  ABRAHAM LINCOLN (4,208%)
### NATIONAL DEBT IN 1861: $65 MILLION
### NATIONAL DEBT IN 1865: $2.8 BILLION

When he was a congressman, Abraham Lincoln fundamentally believed in pay-as-you-go government, covering expenses with increased tariffs, duties, and sales of public lands. He acknowledged, however, that deficits were "reasonably to be expected in time of war." Farsighted as he was, Lincoln did not foresee that the federal debt would grow forty-three times larger during the course of his presidency.[3]

When the Civil War began, the federal budget was a modest seventy million dollars. Over the next four years, the Union navy alone would eventually consume over four times that, building an armada of more than one hundred steamships and ironclads. An army of fewer than seventeen thousand in 1860 grew to more than one million. There were more Union generals in 1865 than there were government employees in 1800.

Both the presidency and the Republican Congress attempted to control the cost of the conflict by enacting the first-ever federal income tax in 1861—3 percent on all yearly income above eight hundred dollars (well above the average earnings of most farmers and laborers). Spiraling expenses forced Washington to impose a greater burden in 1862—surcharges on cigarettes, liquor, stamps, inheritances, plus income taxes on anyone making more than six hundred dollars a year.[4]

Before the money came in, it was already spent, prompting Treasury Secretary Salmon P. Chase to demand the issue of a first-ever federal paper currency. Backed by neither gold nor silver, printed money would at least allow the broke government to keep operating. Congress agreed, and the Legal Tender Act of 1862 dumped $150 million in "greenback" notes into the economy. Nearly $300 million more would soon follow. When tax and paper failed to cover the margins, the government sold billions of dollars' worth of bonds, selling them through brokers who gladly pocketed millions in commissions.[5]

By 1865 the Union military machine was fully operational, arming, feeding, clothing, and paying the largest army on the planet to essentially

During the Civil War, the federal and state governments had to train, feed, and equip two million Union soldiers. A private's rifle cost sixteen dollars, his shoes were twenty dollars, his monthly pay was thirteen dollars, and the cost to bury him was two dollars.

destroy its own southern infrastructure. Fearing the war would continue for another year, Lincoln contemplated offering Southerners $400 million to cover Confederate debt, damages to public property, and the emancipation of all slaves in exchange for surrender. His cabinet rejected the idea in total.[6]

By war's end, the price tag to the Union side alone was roughly $3.2 billion, most of it borrowed. After decades of Reconstruction, rebuilding, and veterans' pensions, the cost tripled.[7]

---

The national debt was higher at the time of Abraham Lincoln's assassination in 1865 than it was at the time of William McKinley's assassination in 1901.

---

## 2. WOODROW WILSON (2,500%)
NATIONAL DEBT IN 1913: $1 BILLION
NATIONAL DEBT IN 1921: $26 BILLION

Wilson had cause to avoid the Great War, aside from its horrific effusion of blood. As the Balkan crisis escalated into a Continental Armageddon, the empires were not only losing millions of able-bodied young men, they were also bleeding cash.

Along with "perfecting" new weapons such as combat aircraft, tanks, and poison gas, industrialization produced the tools of war in phenomenal bulk. In 1914, Britain made three hundred machine guns. Three years later the Brits were manufacturing nearly eighty thousand annually. Artillery output went from ninety-one field pieces in 1914 to more than five thousand in 1917. Countries were spending 50 percent of their GDP and more on their military machines.[8]

Initially the United States benefited from the melee, providing loans and foodstuffs to the capital-hungry conflict. But when Imperial Germany initiated unrestricted submarine warfare on an already fragile Atlantic trade network, Wilson called for a declaration of war against the Central Powers. The decision spawned the creation of a four-million-man armed force and a flurry of federal spending never before seen in U.S. history.

To pay for it, the government reintroduced federal income taxes. The added revenues only covered 40 percent of costs. The rest had to be borrowed. Much of it came through "Liberty Loan" drives, offering bonds at around 4 percent interest.

The relatively successful bond drives fueled an industrial boom. Between 1914 and 1918, the nation's steel production went up 235 percent, and shipbuilding increased over 1,000 percent. But the relative cost of fighting had also exploded. In the rifle-dominated Civil War, it took about one hundred pounds of spent ordnance to produce one battlefield fatality. In World War I, where heavy artillery ruled, it took four tons per KIA. The Allied Powers were killing by the millions, and each killed enemy cost an average of $36,485.[9]

Nine months after the war ended, the U.S. national debt peaked at an astounding $26,594,267,878.45. The government was hoping to recoup some of this by selling surplus grain and pork to the starving nations of Europe. Federal Food Administrator Herbert Hoover dismissed the idea,

NATIONAL ARCHIVES

The Wilson administration tried to keep the Allies afloat through massive bond drives.

arguing it was unethical and impractical to let food rot on the docks while waiting for countries to give money they did not have.[10]

In addition to its own deficits, the United States had loaned billions of dollars to more than twenty different countries, many of which were unable or unwilling to pay. After many years of negotiating, the largest debtors agreed to yearly payments lasting several decades. Greece was set to payoff its loan by 1948; Germany by 1981; Finland, France, Estonia, and Great Britain by 1984; and Austria by 1990.

For one American economist, this was ideal. Predicting the Roaring Twenties would go on for some time, he argued "the United States will retire all its debt by about 1950 . . . receipts from foreign debtors will run on to 1985 or to 1990. Therefore for a period of 35 to 40 years the future generations will enjoy a subsidy." Indeed, those generations would live to see a great many subsidies, most through money borrowed rather than money lent.[11]

---

In the last four years of the Wilson presidency, the federal government spent more money than it had in the previous 128 years combined.

---

## 3.   FRANKLIN DELANO ROOSEVELT (1,326%)
NATIONAL DEBT IN 1933: $19 BILLION
NATIONAL DEBT IN 1946: $271 BILLION

FDR may have spent a bundle on the New Deal, but the price tag for World War II made the cost of his social programs look like chump change.

Oddly enough, Roosevelt ran as a fiscal conservative in the 1932 elections. "I accuse the present administration," the Democrat said of Herbert Hoover, "of being the greatest spending administration in peacetime in all our history. It is an administration that has piled bureau on bureau, commission on commission." Achieving a landslide victory, Roosevelt initially planned to reduce spending. He hired Congressman Lewis Douglas, a diehard financial tightwad, as his first budget director. For his treasury secretary, he chose Republican businessman William H. Woodin, followed soon after by the equally conservative diplomat Henry Morgenthau.[12]

As his administration began to experiment with employment and pension programs, his New Deal began to run in the red. Roosevelt

FDR signs the congressional declaration of war against Japan and consequently turns the federal debt into a mammoth and permanent fixture.

accepted the deficits, but many of his contemporaries did not, including Douglas. By 1934 Douglas was out. In came more relief programs.

The plan was to recharge the economy rather than create a culture of dependency. Young men who worked in the Civilian Conservation Corps, preserving and reclaiming usable land, were required to send twenty-five dollars of their thirty-dollar weekly checks back to their families. Social Security was to be paid primarily by employers and their employees. Internal improvement programs like the Tennessee Valley Authority were meant to turn underdeveloped rural areas into revenue-producing towns and cities. During the 1936 presidential campaign, Roosevelt acknowledged the national debt had more than doubled, but he insisted, "There is much to show for it." Gross domestic production had returned to pre-Crash levels, and joblessness had been reduced by nearly 30 percent.[13]

The opportunity to tame the debt, for Roosevelt or for any president to follow, effectively vanished with the outbreak of the costliest and deadliest war in world history. Hoping to stay neutral, then to simply supply friendly nations through LEND-LEASE, the administration succumbed to full involvement in 1941, after the Japanese navy inflicted billions of dollars' worth of damage upon bases in Oahu, the Philippines, Guam, and Wake Island. Federal spending went from 40 percent of GDP to a rapacious 120 percent, the highest rate ever in the nation's existence. Citizens accustomed to paying 7 percent tax were soon paying 28 percent, and it was nowhere near enough to cover the cost. For the first time in its history, the government began deducting money directly from its citizens' paychecks.[14]

By 1942, 73.2 percent of the federal budget was going to the war, and the country was pumping out more industrial goods than all of the Axis nations combined. In 1944, 86.6 percent of all government expenditures went into military operations, as the nation trained and outfitted fifteen million troops. Shipyards eventually produced ten major battleships, twenty-seven aircraft carriers, over one hundred escort carriers, more than four hundred cruisers and destroyers, and over sixty-six thousand smaller craft. Factories rolled out more than thirty thousand heavy bombers, over sixty thousand tanks, land mines and small arms by the millions, and bullets by the billions. In 1945 half of all industrial goods in the world were made in the United States, and most of it was military hardware. But to fuel the industrial giant, the country increased its debt 500 percent in four years. Technically, a large part of the existing debt in 2008 still consists of money and interest owed since 1945.[15]

> Lend-Lease, established in 1941, provided food, fuel, and munitions to forty Allied countries. By itself, the program eventually cost in excess of fifty billion dollars, a total 20 percent greater than the entire federal debt amassed by the United States in its first 150 years of existence. There was no repayment plan.

## 4.   RONALD REAGAN (188.4%)
NATIONAL DEBT IN 1981: $994.8 BILLION
NATIONAL DEBT IN 1989: $2.87 TRILLION

Upon taking office, Ronald Reagan removed the portraits of Thomas Jefferson and Harry Truman from the White House cabinet room. In their stead he placed an image of Dwight Eisenhower "because I beat him for $10 the first time we played golf," Reagan said, and a painting of Calvin Coolidge, because he reduced the debt.[16]

But Silent Cal did not have to contend with Social Security, Medicare, Medicaid, or many other social programs, which constituted nearly half the federal budget in 1981. Nor did Coolidge have much of a military to support, while Reagan inherited the largest military budget in the world at $192 billion.

Reagan still chose to fight the debt with a Coolidge strategy, which actually belonged to Cal's treasury secretary, Andrew Mellon (who also served under Harding and Hoover). Mellon firmly believed in driving taxation down to stimulate private investment. Reagan emulated the idea with a series of breaks across the board, mostly to large corporations. While the government acquired approximately 45 percent of its revenue from individual income taxes (a level consistent since the Eisenhower administration), the Gipper reduced the burden on big business down to 8 percent and less (compared to 25 percent under Eisenhower and others). In turn, the president demanded Congress make cuts to entitlements (that is, commit political suicide) while he beefed up the cold war military.[17]

Falling revenues and increased expenditures worried a great many people, including budget director David Stockman, who noted that Reagan's military buildup was more expensive in adjusted dollars than Lyndon Johnson's tab for Vietnam. He also noted that his boss had chastised Jimmy Carter for running an eighty-billion-dollar deficit yet proceeded to double that amount in short order. When discussing these matters with his chief executive, Stockman noticed Reagan "ignored all palpable, relevant facts and wandered in circles."[18]

In effect, Reagan could afford to do so. After the recession of 1982–83, the economy began to benefit from the huge influx of federal dollars. Corporate profits were on the rise, unemployment was falling, and the welfare state remained relatively intact. In 1984 Reagan won reelection by a landslide, despite nearly two-thirds of Americans claiming to disapprove of his deficit spending.[19]

Regarding the growing debt, Reagan blamed Congress. Under Democratic control for his entire eight years and the Senate for his final two, the legislature made modest cuts to education, veterans affairs, health, wel-

Reagan's budget director, David Stockman (left), and the Gipper hashed out ways to rob Peter to pay Paul during regular Oval Office meetings.

fare, and the environment. At the same time they offered minimal opposition to increased defense spending and tax cuts. While both the White
House and Capitol Hill exchanged bitter rhetoric over expenditures, neither risked losing votes to address the issue. Their eight years of hesitance
nearly tripled the yearly cost of interest on the debt, but their inaction
also greatly benefited themselves and the voting public—at least for the
short term.[20]

---

In just his second year in office, Reagan's deficit was higher than the entire
federal budget in 1970.

---

## 5.   RICHARD NIXON–GERALD FORD (100.1%)
NATIONAL DEBT IN 1969: $ 353.0 BILLION
NATIONAL DEBT IN 1977: $ 706.4 BILLION

The obvious missing link in the debt chain is Lyndon Johnson with his
double-headed beast of "the Great Society" and the Vietnam War. Yet
LBJ was able to curb federal borrowing by increasing its income. In 1968
the president asked for and received a taxation surcharge to help pay for
the conflict in Southeast Asia, and he scaled back aspiration for his war on
poverty. Fiscal 1969 actually produced a budget surplus of nearly $3 bil-
lion. In his five-plus years as president, Johnson saw the debt rise, but
only from $317 billion to $353 billion, a total of 11.4 percent. In contrast,
the Nixon and Ford years experienced an increase of 100 percent, with
the last four years being the worst.[21]

Part of the problem was Nixon's war expenditures. On top of the
yearly defense bill, Nixon spent an additional fifty-nine billion dollars on
Vietnam, more than LBJ, Kennedy, Eisenhower, and Truman combined.
Postwar unemployment also rose. LBJ's jobless rate averaged less than 4
percent. Nixon managed to keep his at 5 percent. Ford suffered 7 percent
and up, and payouts to the unemployed more than doubled over the
course of his short stay.[22]

The breadth and depth of public entitlements were also growing. In
just eight years, the cost of funding Medicare went up 78 percent and Social Security increased 82 percent. Gerald Ford also had the misery of
dealing with the aftershocks of Watergate, Nixon's abandonment of the
gold standard, a six-month OPEC oil embargo, a doubling of inflation, the

fall of Saigon, two assassination attempts, and a yearly fee of $100 billion that went purely to service the interest on the federal debt.

> Gerald Ford wanted Congress to continue funding the South Vietnamese government, and he blamed the legislature for Saigon's collapse in 1975. At the time, Saigon was home to the fourth largest air force in the world and the fifth largest navy, thanks largely to money and equipment provided by the United States.

## 6. GEORGE WASHINGTON (~100%)
### NATIONAL DEBT IN 1789: UNKNOWN
### NATIONAL DEBT IN 1797: $83.7 MILLION

The first administration did not create a huge debt as much as adopt it. George Washington and his secretary of state, Thomas Jefferson, were uncomfortably familiar with personal debt. Land and slave rich but cash poor, both men were in constant arrears with lenders. Washington had to borrow money to travel to his first inauguration. As such, they viewed a national debt as the sum of all fears, something to be avoided if not dismissed.

Treasury Secretary Alexander Hamilton thought the opposite. Years before, when the feeble Continental Congress wallowed in financial straights, Hamilton contended: "A national debt, if it is not excessive, will be to us a national blessing." A crusader for strong central government, Hamilton viewed good credit as the one and only means for national survival. And credit could only be established by paying back every penny the United States owed its people and bankers abroad—some fifty million dollars. In addition, Hamilton insisted the government also assume the balances of every state, a total of twenty-five million dollars more.[23]

Jefferson vehemently opposed the plan. So did the legislatures of Virginia and Pennsylvania, states that had already repaid much of their wartime liabilities. But Washington and others slowly warmed to the logic of establishing a firm financial base for the otherwise unbalanced economy. Pennsylvania became less hostile when Hamilton brokered a deal to have the national capital moved from New York to Philadelphia, where it would stay for a decade. Tensions with Virginia eased when plans were made to create a permanent "Federal City" along its northeast border.[24]

---

Alexander Hamilton was a founder of the Bank of New York, which is still in operation.

---

## 7. GEORGE W. BUSH (96.6%)
NATIONAL DEBT IN 2001: $5.8 TRILLION
NATIONAL DEBT IN 2009: $11.4 TRILLION

For the first time in nearly fifty years the Republican Party held the Executive Mansion and both houses of Congress. Looking forward to a respite from opposition politics and a continuation of economic prosperity, the Congressional Budget Office predicted a federal revenue surplus of $5.6 trillion for the following decade. The White House concurred and set about contemplating how to best use the inevitable windfall.

Rather than address the debt, George W. Bush opted to fulfill a campaign promise to cut income and estate taxes. The only question was by how much. Democrats demurred against any reduction but offered no more than $900 billion over ten years. Bush wanted twice as much, but he settled on $1.35 trillion. It was the largest tax reduction in U.S. history.

Months later, the terror attacks of September 11, 2001, prompted the United States to invade Afghanistan and oust the Taliban government. With the war still underway, Bush worked to make his initial tax cuts permanent.[25]

Warhawks in the Bush administration also lobbied to launch a preemptive strike with a much larger force into Iraq, which they initiated with overwhelming public support in March 2003. Bush still pressed for more substantial tax cuts. Congress approved a $350 billion reduction, an amount Bush called "little bitty."[26]

Teensy weensy was the initial White House cost estimate for the removal of Iraqi dictator Saddam Hussein and the democratization of Iraq—$74.7 billion. Hussein was eventually captured, tried, and hanged, and elections were held in the new Republic of Iraq. Yet U.S. military operations did not progress as well as first hoped. Later official projections for securing and stabilizing Iraq exceeded $200 billion. Economists and budget experts calculated the end total would be well above $1 trillion (with adjusted dollars, about three times the military and financial support the United States provided Great Britain in World War II).[27]

---

George W. Bush's deputy defense secretary, Paul Wolfowitz, initially believed the reconstruction of Iraq would cost the United States nothing, as the liberated republic would ideally fund its own recovery through oil revenues.

---

## 8.  JAMES MADISON (94.3%)
NATIONAL DEBT IN 1809: $53 MILLION
NATIONAL DEBT IN 1817: $103 MILLION

In 1812, the United States was emotionally ready to declare war for the first time in its young life. Financially, it did not have the capital. Britannia ruled the waves, and its failure to respect American naval neutrality during the Napoleonic Wars had robbed the U.S. Treasury of its life blood—tariffs and duties on imported goods. Constricted in its budget, the U.S. Navy owned but six frigates, each with forty-four guns, mere sea bass to the sharks of the British "ships of the line" with seventy-four-plus cannons each. The army consisted of barely twelve thousand men, poorly paid. The only chance was to seize Canada fast and win on the cheap.

When the invasion failed miserably, losing not only the initiative but also Detroit, James Madison scrambled to find the resources for a protracted war. He asked for twenty thousand more troops. Congress belatedly agreed. But many observed that all the patriotism in the world would not coerce recruits to fight. Money, on the other hand, might help. Said one lawmaker, "Nothing short of a little fortune will induce our Farmers or their sons to enter on a life which they cordially despise: that of a common soldier." To fill the ranks, the government offered hefty cash bounties and 160 acres for each volunteer.[28]

Going bankrupt fast, Madison then turned to Treasury Secretary Albert Gallatin, the financial wizard who had helped Jefferson finance the Louisiana Purchase. The war could be executed, Gallatin told him, for a price. "This can be best done," he insisted, "by a well digested system of internal revenue." Fearing the voter backlash of such an unpopular measure, legislators began calling Gallatin "the Rat in the Treasury." But the taxes went into effect on salt, sugar, land sales, and paper, eerily similar to the fees Imperial Britain once imposed on the colonies. Angered by the abuse he was receiving from Congress and citizens alike, Gallatin requested a leave of absence and never returned.[29]

When redcoats invaded the Chesapeake Bay area and burned Washington, the federal government understandably became more desperate, borrowing millions through high-interest loans and offering bonds to any takers. They slapped taxes on liquor, paid privateers to raid British merchant ships, and desperately hoped that pro-British Massachusetts would not leave the Union.[30]

By 1814, the parties were fought out. The United States was near bankruptcy. Britain had been battling in Europe for more than a decade. War had lost its luster. The ensuing peace treaty resolved almost none of the original disputes, but a cessation of hostilities allowed both sides to declare victory and begin the long road to recovery.[31]

---

The final tally for the War of 1812 came to $68,783,122, more than the United States would spend on a war with Mexico a generation later.

---

## 9.  GEORGE H. W. BUSH (51.5%)
NATIONAL DEBT IN 1989: $2.87 TRILLION
NATIONAL DEBT IN 1993: $4.35 TRILLION

The federal debt, which had tripled in the previous eight years, required $200 billion in interest payments alone. An unprecedented peacetime buildup of the armed forces raised the Department of Defense's take from the treasury to nearly three hundred billion dollars a year.[32]

George H. W. Bush had the ironic misfortune of belonging to the very administration that saddled his presidency with enormous bills. Consequently his opportunity to shift blame to its source was effectively nonexistent. Nor did he have the political capital or the personal willingness of his former superior to continue pouring money into the national economy. In the course of his four-year term, he successfully captured and convicted the military president of Panama on a number of charges, oversaw the fall of the Soviet Union, forged a coalition of thirty countries to win a decisive seven-month war against Iraq, and saw approval ratings above 80 percent. Yet he would not win reelection.

For all the positives of his foreign policy, Bush could not effectively combat an economic recession at home. Unemployment neared 7 percent.

Annual deficits initially went down, only to grow and surpass the Reagan era. The Gipper's worst deficit was $221 billion in 1986. By 1990 Bush was doing just as badly, and the ensuing years were destined to be worse.[33]

Initially he hoped to reduce the losses by cutting into the solidly entrenched entitlements to the American public. But a Democratic Congress resisted, opting instead for a raise in revenues. To keep the government in operation, Bush agreed to raise taxes—in violation of his 1988 vow never to do so. The strategy worked, partially. For the first time ever, the U.S. Treasury received more than one trillion dollars in receipts in 1990. But expenditures also reached a record high, surpassing $1.25 trillion for the year.

---

When Medicare was established in 1965 to offer health coverage for the elderly, its projected cost was supposed to be less than $10 billion by 1990. The price tag for the Bush administration in 1990 ended up being more than $100 billion.

---

## 10. JIMMY CARTER (41%)

NATIONAL DEBT IN 1977: $706.4 BILLION
NATIONAL DEBT IN 1981: $994.8 BILLION

When Jimmy Carter was born in 1924, the federal debt was in its fifth straight year of decline. When he became president in 1977, the debt had risen seven years in a row, a trend he would fail to break.[34]

The economy continued to grow under President Carter, slowly, between 1 and 2 percent a year. Federal proceeds meanwhile expanded, quickly, from $355 billion in 1977 to nearly $600 billion by 1981. But the costs of operation were simply outpacing the economy, a condition made worse by foreign affairs.

By the late 1970s the epicenter of the cold war moved from Southeast Asia to the Middle East, where much of the planet's oil reserves lay in wait. For the first time, the United States was importing as much oil as it produced. Prompted by worldwide demand, the growing exporters were raising prices, from six dollars to fifteen dollars a barrel. Worsening the situation, the 1979 Iranian Revolution not only caused a hostage crisis for the Carter administration, it also created an energy crisis for the entire United States.

During the Carter years, a sluggish economy—made worse by escalating oil prices—bridled federal revenues.

Iran by itself was a relatively small oil producer. Though rich in reserves, the country produced less than 5 percent of the world's oil. But perception often outweighs fact, and the ensuing fears of a global oil shortage drove crude prices above thirty dollars a barrel. For the United States, the result was crippling "stagflation"—reduced productivity and climbing inflation. While the GDP grew by inches, inflation grew by miles, hitting double digits and forcing the costs of governmental programs upward. In an effort to monitor the situation, Carter requested the creation of the Department of Energy. He also promoted the idea of creating synthetic fuels, a politically popular concept, but a process many times more expensive than simply buying foreign crude. Ultimately he endorsed a nationwide conservation movement, which further lowered public confidence in the economy.

By 1980, the newly completed Alaskan pipeline was in full operation, providing the contiguous Unites States a quarter of its oil needs. But by then, the ineffective Carter had lost the chance to keep his job.[35]

During the Carter administration, the amount of money spent on interest toward the national debt was more than the cost of education, Medicare, unemployment payments, and the Veterans Administration combined.

## TOP TEN VETO PRESIDENTS

Woodrow Wilson called it a president's "most formidable prerogative." The less eloquent Harry Truman considered it, in relation to Congress, "one of the greatest strengths that the president has . . . if he doesn't like something that *they're* cooking up." Latin for "I forbid," the word *veto* does not appear in the Constitution, yet it exists as one of the most recognizable expressions of executive authority.[36]

When the 1787 Philadelphia Convention schemed to form a more perfect Union, delegates quickly endorsed the concept of a "qualified negative." New York's Alexander Hamilton and Pennsylvania's James Wilson favored an absolute veto. In opposition were Virginia's George Mason and Pennsylvania's Benjamin Franklin, the latter insisting that if one person could completely override a legislature, "the Executive will always be increasing here, till it ends in a monarchy."[37]

James Madison argued convincingly for a middle ground. Congress should have the option of overriding, he said, but a veto was essential to prevent some "popular or factious injustice." His plan carried the day, with a subtle wrinkle—the pocket veto. If Congress adjourned within ten working days of submitting a bill, a president could simply not sign it, in essence making his rejection absolute.[38]

To avoid appearing despotic, early presidents rarely employed it. Washington denied only two bills, both on grounds of their constitutionality. John Adams and Thomas Jefferson didn't block any. Those who tried were often rebuffed. In 1834 the Senate censured Andrew Jackson for his virulent refusal to recharter the Bank of the United States. For his ten vetoes, John Tyler was nearly impeached by the Twenty-Seventh Congress, which accused him of "withholding his assent to laws indispensable to the just operations of the government." Franklin Pierce and Andrew Johnson saw the majority of their vetoes overridden (five of nine and fifteen of twenty-nine respectively).[39]

Gradually, executives asserted themselves against Congress, and overrides became rare. A few presidents went undefeated (none better than William McKinley at 42–0), and most enjoyed a 95 percent success rate. Of more than twenty-four hundred vetoes, slightly over one hundred have failed to carry through.

Below are the ten most prolific presidents in the use of the qualified negative, ranked by the total number of their official rejections. Reflecting the growing power of the executive branch, eight of these ten administrations are from the twentieth century.[40]

## 1.   FRANKLIN D. ROOSEVELT (635)

REGULAR VETO:              372
POCKET VETO:               263
OVERRIDDEN:                  9

For some, the veto is a paring knife to shave away excess pork fat. For others, it is an axe to smash whole programs. For Franklin Delano Roosevelt, it was the dress sword, a symbol of authority over Capitol Hill.

In twelve years, Roosevelt never faced a house in opposition, yet he managed to make vetoes a weekly event. This occurred, in part, because the Democratic Congresses did not mind. Many legislators obliged the president's famous request, "Send me a bill I can veto," understanding that each rejection could cast the party in a positive light. Legislature or president, the noble defender was always a Democrat. It was masterful stagecraft.[41]

The partisan high tide came with the Seventy-Fifth Congress (1937–38), in which Senate Democrats outnumbered Republicans 75 to 17. In the House, the ratio was an astounding 333 to 89. And still Roosevelt's vetoes came, reminding both Capitol Hill and the nation just who was in charge. As was his style, he worded most vetoes in grand moral themes. A perfect example involved the Senate's simple request to rename the Chemical Warfare Service to the "Chemical Corps." Rather than just say no, FDR publicly declared, "I do not want the Government of the United States to do anything to aggrandize or make permanent any special bureau of the Army or the Navy engaged in these studies. I hope the time will come when the Chemical Warfare Service can be entirely abolished."[42]

In his final years, as FDR's health deteriorated, so did his hold on Congress. A showdown emerged over the Revenue Act of 1943, a hopelessly convoluted measure that favored the wealthy. Roosevelt angrily vetoed it, saying, "It is squarely the fault of Congress of the United States in using language in drafting the law which not even a dictionary or thesaurus can make clear." He added, "These taxpayers, now engaged in an effort to win the greatest war this Nation has ever faced, are not in the mood to study higher mathematics."[43]

Deeply offended by FDR's scolding, Senate majority leader Alben Barkley immediately resigned from his post. In response, his associates

No one dismantled the authority of Congress more than FDR, and the veto was among his favorite cutting tools.

unanimously reappointed him, and both houses overruled the president's veto within forty-eight hours.[44]

---

In 1943, FDR vetoed a joint resolution to designate December 7 as "Armed Services Honor Day." He called the measure "singularly inappropriate," as he believed the anniversary should be remembered as "one of infamy" rather than a national holiday.

---

## 2.  GROVER CLEVELAND (584)

| | |
|---|---|
| REGULAR VETO: | 346 |
| POCKET VETO: | 238 |
| OVERRIDDEN: | 7 |

In Buffalo, they called him "Veto Mayor." In Albany, it was "Veto Governor." Elected to the White House in 1884, partly for his reputation of stemming frivolous legislation, he became "Old Veto." Whereas FDR later killed one out of every twelve bills, stubborn Grover Cleveland stopped one out of every six. In his first term alone, the New York Nix rejected 414 legislative acts, twice as many as all preceding presidents combined.[45]

More than 80 percent of his targets involved personal disability pensions, mostly from Union veterans of the Civil War. While the Pension Bureau handled over half a million of these submissions, many of the rejected cases found new life as private bills in Congress, submitted by legislators looking to gain favor back home.[46]

Most pensions were modest and justified. Enlisted men who lost both feet were eligible for a pension of twenty dollars a month. Loss of both hands or both eyes meant five dollars more. Yet several requests were extremely dubious, pricey, and piling up. On a single day in mid-1886, Cleveland received no fewer than 240 pension bills, many of which belonged to, in Cleveland's words, "bums" and "blood-suckers."[47]

Among these was "an act granting a pension to John Hunter." The subject claimed permanent disability from "May, 1864, [when] he received a gunshot wound in the right leg while in a skirmish." Cleveland found no army record of the injury, but the man had indeed hurt his leg—fifteen years after the war—while picking dandelions. In another case, Senate Bill 363 was to reward Edward Ayers, who claimed his hip had been permanently damaged from shellfire in the battle of Days Gap, Alabama. The president passed on the idea, considering that Ayers had deserted his unit shortly after the battle.

Not surprisingly, veterans took offense at Cleveland's zealous scrutiny. In the 1888 elections, critics also noted that he had hired a substitute in the Civil War, whereas his opponent, Republican Benjamin Harrison, reached the rank of general in the Union army. Harrison won the old soldier vote and the election.[48]

Harrison, in deference to his support base, signed the Dependent Pension Act of 1890 (which Cleveland had vetoed in 1887), granting monthly stipends to all honorably discharged Union veterans, their widows, and their children. Soon after, the U.S. Treasury went from a one-hundred-million-dollar surplus to a huge deficit. Shocked pundits

To prevent a few thousand goldbricking Union veterans from sapping the national treasury, Grover Cleveland conspicuously vetoed hundreds of dubious pension applications. His diligence offended thousands of old Union soldiers, who subsequently voted en masse against him in the 1888 elections.

calculated that the new pension program would eventually cost far more than the Civil War itself.

To stop the bleeding, the nation returned Cleveland to the White House in 1892. For his comeback inaugural address, "Old Veto" was gracious but direct. The country was in trouble, he said, because it was guilty of "wild and reckless pension expenditure, which overleaps the bounds of grateful recognition . . . and prostitutes to vicious uses the people's prompt and generous impulse." His second term brought forth a scything of 170 more bills.[49]

---

Average number of vetoes per president before Cleveland: 9.6

Average number of vetoes per president after Cleveland: 90.1

---

### 3. HARRY S TRUMAN (250)

| | |
|---|---|
| REGULAR VETO: | 180 |
| POCKET VETO: | 70 |
| OVERRIDDEN: | 12 |

Republican Arthur Vandenberg described Friday the Thirteenth as his lucky day. A fellow senator had just become president. "Truman came back to the Senate this noon to have lunch with a few of us. . . . It means that the days of executive contempt are ended; that we are returning to a government in which Congress will take its rightful place."[50]

The following Monday, Truman gave his first address to a joint session of Congress. Millions listened via live radio, as Vandenberg and company interrupted Harry with seventeen rounds of thunderous applause. Across the nation, Truman's approval ratings topped 80 percent. Three weeks later, the Third Reich collapsed. Later that summer, the Japanese Empire surrendered, two years sooner than expected.[51]

But after the burst of celebration came the recoil. The country was up to its flagpoles in debt. The job market became flooded with returning soldiers. Military factories closed. Employment spawned ugly labor strikes. In the 1946 midterms, Vandenberg and the Republicans turned on their old colleague and won majorities in both Houses. A war of vetoes ensued.

Congress churned out a string of tax cuts favoring the upper class. Truman accused them of pandering to the rich and vetoed them all. Capitol Hill answered with a series of overrides. In 1947, Congress passed the

Taft-Hartley Act, virtually neutering organized labor. Truman vetoed that as well. They overrode him again, leading Truman to call the Eightieth Congress "good for nothing" and the "worst ever."[52]

Though he often lost, Harry started to look like the underdog, an image that paid huge dividends in the 1948 presidential race. Not only did he score a miracle win over dashing Thomas Dewey, his party also regained the House and Senate.

His joy was short lived, though. The following year, the United States lost its nuclear monopoly to the Soviets. Then came the "loss" of China, sparking a nationwide Red Scare and a fight over the definition of liberty itself. First came the Internal Security Act, requiring communists and their "sympathizers" to register with the Justice Department. It also empowered the government to forcibly detain anyone suspected of being a subversive. The bill was, in Truman's eyes, "even more un-American than communism." He refused to sign it. Congress answered with a crushing override.[53]

War in Korea only deepened the crisis, leading to a resurgence of the witch-hunting Committee on Un-American Activities in the House and the rise of Joe McCarthy in the Senate. Pandering to the fearmongers, Congress passed the Immigration and Nationality Act, denying all former communists entry into the country, including those who had fought against the Third Reich. For Truman, fighting reds in Asia was one thing, but turning on old allies was inexcusable. He vetoed the act in no uncertain terms. Congress rejected him yet again, and the measure became law.[54]

---

Though federal courts eventually struck down much of the 1952 Immigration and Nationality Act as unconstitutional, portions involving detainment or deportation of people based on their political views were reinstated through the Patriot Act of 2001.

---

## 4.  DWIGHT D. EISENHOWER (181)

| | |
|---|---|
| REGULAR VETO: | 73 |
| POCKET VETO: | 108 |
| OVERRIDDEN: | 2 |

In the rich lexicon of American slogans, "I like Ike" may be the most deceptively insightful, because Dwight Eisenhower rarely inspired primal emotion. The very reason for his meteoric rise in the blood sports of war and politics was his freakish ability to suppress passion—his and everyone else's.

So went his vetoes. Most were private relief initiatives, quietly pocketed or returned to the appropriate house with a sensible note. A handful involved the minting of commemorative coins—fifty-cent pieces for the tricentennial of Northampton, Massachusetts, for example. In 1958 he politely denied the Coast Guard sixty million dollars for the development of a nuclear-powered icebreaker.

He was only overturned twice, and they both came late in his second term. The first rebuff involved the Tennessee Valley Authority, the flagship of the New Deal. Ike wanted to privatize it; Congress wanted to keep it afloat on government money. Then came the last regular veto of Eisenhower's presidency, a pay hike to federal employees. He thought it was inflationary, and legislators thought it was overdue.

---

Vetoing S1901(1959), a bill that heavily subsidized the tobacco industry, might have brought mixed feelings for Eisenhower. Ten years previous, Ike had to give up smoking cold turkey, because his physician expressed concern over his four-pack-a-day habit.

---

## 5.  ULYSSES S. GRANT (93)

| | |
|---|---|
| REGULAR VETO: | 45 |
| POCKET VETO: | 48 |
| OVERRIDDEN: | 4 |

Within the first minute of his first inaugural address, U. S. Grant made his intentions abundantly clear: "On all leading questions agitating the public mind I will always express my views . . . and when I think it advisable will exercise the constitutional privilege of interposing a veto to defeat measures which I oppose." Grant kept his word, rebuffing more bills than the previous seventeen presidents put together. He was also the first to rely heavily on the pocket veto, again producing more than anyone before.

Most vetoes involved private relief funds, including compensations for property destroyed during the Civil War. Congress allotted twenty-five thousand dollars, for example, to one Paducah, Kentucky, homestead torn

Relatively weak when it came to protecting the civil
rights of blacks and Native Americans, Grant took a hard
line against soft money and heavy federal spending,
using his veto power early and often against a
spendthrift Congress.

down in battle (at a time when large farmhouses cost six thousand dollars). Another involved awarding East Tennessee University several thousand dollars in war-related damages to its campus. In vetoing its claims, Grant expressed sympathy, but he said loss was part of war, and if he signed the bills, "the ends of the demands upon the public Treasury cannot be forecast."[55]

Grant's most famous veto involved money. When the Panic of 1873 triggered a global depression, bankrupt businessmen and indebted farmers called for an increase in the public supply of greenbacks. Congress agreed. The resulting "Inflation Bill" of 1874 ordered a release of one hundred million dollars into the economy to boost the money supply by roughly 25 percent. Grant initially supported the idea, then he changed his mind.

The president, who had been flat broke many times in his own life, argued that the only way to regain financial stability was to return to the gold standard, however painful the journey might be. The impoverished public lashed out against him, but major investors applauded his "hard money" courage. Conservative media went so far as to call him a hero, and the *London Post* equated Grant's veto of the Inflation Bill with his triumph at Vicksburg. True to his prediction, the depression ended, but like the Civil War, it took four long years to happen.[56]

---

U. S. Grant was the first of a dozen presidents to officially request a line-item veto. Only William Jefferson Clinton would get the privilege, striking eighty-two items from eleven bills before the Supreme Court declared the practice unconstitutional.

---

## 6.  TEDDY ROOSEVELT (82)
REGULAR VETO:              42
POCKET VETO:               40
OVERRIDDEN:                 1

Like his cousin to follow, this Roosevelt never saw an opposition legislature, and he reveled in being the president. As many noted, the insatiable TR aimed to be "the bride at every wedding and the corpse at every funeral."

But "government by veto" repulsed him. "I have a right to veto every bill," he told a senator in 1905. But he added: "If we do not manage to work together on these matters it will be a bad thing for the country. . . . This system is postulated on self-restraint."[57]

True to form, Roosevelt was careful on what he vetoed. Most, like Grant's and Cleveland's, involved private pensions. Others blocked favorable treatment of large corporations. Some bills he may have rejected for being utterly mundane, such as *To refund certain tonnage taxes and light duties levied on the steamship Montara without register*; or the infamous *Granting to the city of Durango, in the State of Colorado, certain lands therein described for water reservoirs*; or the strangely appropriate, *To amend an act for the prevention of smoke in the District of Columbia.*

His only defeat came in May 1908, when he refused a deadline extension for construction of a dam along the Minnesota-Canada border. The fiscally conservative Roosevelt argued that the American public should not have to pay more simply because the Rainy River Construction Company could not get a job done on time. The House sympathized with the company, which had struggled during a recent recession. The extension passed with a 240–5 vote in the House and a unanimous 49–0 in the Senate.[58]

---

While he was a New York assemblyman, Theodore Roosevelt helped craft a Tenure of Office bill. It was vetoed in earnest. "Of all the defective and shabby legislation which has been presented to me this is the worst," wrote Governor Grover Cleveland.

---

## 7.  RONALD REAGAN (78)

| | |
|---|---|
| REGULAR VETO: | 39 |
| POCKET VETO: | 39 |
| OVERRIDDEN: | 9 |

Presenting himself as a conservative crusader against a spendthrift Congress, the fortieth president actually demonstrated considerable restraint. Ronald Reagan could talk a good game, but he personally hated confrontation, and he chose few battles. Rather than rule by veto, he preferred to sway Capitol Hill through less belligerent tactics, such as budget proposals and public appeals.

Congress consented to his demands for an expanded military. In turn, he shelved plans to eliminate the Small Business Administration, permitted over six hundred million dollars per annum for the Job Corps, and backed away from his campaign promise to eliminate the cabinet post of Secretary of Education.[59]

Few of his vetoes went unchallenged, and when Reagan tried to reject bills for health and human rights, he usually lost. He denied two extensions of the Clean Water Act, research funding for the National Institute of Health, and extensions to several civil rights laws. Congress passed each one anyway. On foreign aid, Reagan rejected a bill that mandated protection of human rights in a military aid package for El Salvador (the veto was later reversed by the U.S. Circuit Court of Appeals). The following session, he vehemently opposed sanctions against the apartheid government of South Africa, arguing for a less belligerent approach. Congress overruled him.[60]

In one of his more controversial moves, Reagan lobbied to sell one hundred antiship missiles, hundreds of small antiaircraft weapons, and more than one thousand Sidewinder missiles to the kingdom of Saudi Arabia. Congress volleyed back with a joint resolution to stop the sale, which Reagan vetoed. Noting Saudi Arabia's tacit connections with Syria and the Palestinian Liberation Organization, the Senate once again moved to override Reagan's negative. This time the Gipper won—by a single vote.[61]

---

Among the politicians who publicly supported Ronald Reagan's sale of arms to Saudi Arabia was former president Jimmy Carter.

---

## 8.  GERALD FORD (66)

| | |
|---|---|
| REGULAR VETO: | 48 |
| POCKET VETO: | 18 |
| OVERRIDDEN: | 12 |

Gerald Ford contended, "The veto's not a negative thing. . . . And a president ought to use it more freely if he doesn't like what Congress is doing. . . . The only way you're going to get the budget under control is for a president to establish whatever priorities he believes in, fight for them, and veto, veto, veto."[62]

Several of Ford's deputies were less comfortable with his confrontational approach against a Democratic Capitol Hill. As one aide saw it: "No president can afford to veto twenty-five bills a year. . . . It's too damn much, and Congress won't stand for it." Congress, in fact, did not stand for it. Legislators officially challenged more than half his regular vetoes and successfully reversed twelve of them. In the history of the presidency, only Andrew Johnson and Harry Truman experienced an equal or greater number of overrides.[63]

Several vetoes appeared rather callous on the surface, yet the fine print often revealed a compassionate rationale. Ford refused additional funding for the Rehabilitation Act, which provided vocational training to the handicapped, because it added 250 bureaucratic positions to the Department of Health, Education, and Welfare yet reduced services to its clientele. He tried to stop a new G.I. Bill from giving Vietnam veterans more money for schooling, because the allotment was disproportionately

Gerald R. Ford established a reputation of blocking Congress at every turn, despite the fact that he had served in the House for nearly a quarter century.

higher than what Korean War and World War II veterans received. Ford also rejected a National School Lunch Act, as it subsidized families who were above the poverty level and cost billions more than a program he introduced months earlier.[64]

One veto in particular proved costly. In accepting the presidency, Ford vowed "openness and candor" with the American public, and two months later he blocked an enhancement of the Freedom of Information Act. He rejected it on the advice of staffers Donald Rumsfeld and Dick Cheney, who believed the bill posed a national security risk. Ford agreed, though he knew there was bound to be resistance. True to his prediction, citizens grilled him in editorials, Democrats on the Hill rebuked the "undue secrecy in government," and Congress negated his veto by a landslide.[65]

> Though Ford was aggressive with Congress, he never lost his sense of modesty. Among his pocket vetoes, Ford refused a bill that would have renamed a government building in Grand Rapids, Michigan, the Gerald R. Ford Federal Office Building.

## 9. CALVIN COOLIDGE (50)

| | |
|---|---|
| REGULAR VETO: | 20 |
| POCKET VETO: | 30 |
| OVERRIDDEN: | 4 |

Legend contends that a woman attending a White House dinner said to Calvin Coolidge, "I made a bet today that I could get more than two words out of you." The president replied, "You lose." So goes the image of the thirtieth president.

In reality, "Silent Cal" was far more complex. He despised small talk, but his 1925 inaugural speech is the fifth longest on record, and he held more press conferences than any chief executive before him. Far from laissez faire, he often resisted Congress, though his party was in the majority for the whole of his administration.

In some cases, denials were effortless. One bill offered pensions to war widows and their dependents who lost loved ones in the War of 1812, a conflict that had ended 110 years prior to this legislation. Other vetoes came with risk and trepidation. Twice he alienated struggling farmers by refusing to have the government buy their surplus grain.[66]

His most fateful veto came against the 1924 Bonus Bill, which provided monetary compensation for those who served in the Great War while their countrymen found lucrative jobs in their absence. Coolidge endorsed a similar law while governor of Massachusetts, but he thought it would only create ill will on a national scale. He was overturned, and as he feared, the law caused problems. In 1932, destitute veterans marched as a Bonus Army upon the national capital and demanded immediate payment from Coolidge's successor, Herbert Hoover. As thousands of men and their families began to build shantytowns throughout Washington, asking for money the government did not have, Hoover felt compelled to drive them out by bayonet, a miserable task executed by officers such as Maj. Gen. Douglas MacArthur and Majs. George S. Patton and Dwight D. Eisenhower.

---

During Coolidge's five-plus years in office, Congress overrode four of his vetoes all on the same day.

---

## 10. GEORGE H. W. BUSH (44)

| | |
|---|---|
| REGULAR VETO: | 29 |
| POCKET VETO: | 15 |
| OVERRIDDEN: | 1 |

In rhetoric, George H. W. Bush was less belligerent toward Congress than his old boss. In practice, he was more aggressive, particularly with his use of vetoes. He also enjoyed a higher success rate. Except for a few budget proposals, Bush was officially challenged on every one of his regular vetoes, and he won every time, with the exception of a minor bill involving cable television providers.

Yet his victories damaged him politically. Bush vetoed the Family and Medical Leave Act, though nearly 70 percent of the American public supported the bill. He offended the working poor by blocking a measure to raise the minimum wage. He gave the impression of being antidemocratic when he blocked a voter-registration initiative, and he looked worse when he vetoed sanctions against China after the Tiananmen Square Massacre. Though highly successful in a war against Iraq, Bush was less appealing in domestic affairs, and his "rule by veto" left voters wanting someone more progressive in the presidential election of 1992.[67]

Though George H. W. Bush engaged the veto often, his president son did not follow in his footsteps. George W. Bush served his first four years without rejecting a single bill, the first chief executive to go an entire term "sans veto" since John Quincy Adams.

## TOP TEN CONFLICTS WITH
## THE SUPREME COURT

The Supreme Court began as an afterthought, formed during a marginal amount of discussion in the Philadelphia convention, and explained in a handful of paragraphs in the Constitution. When Washington, D.C., was built, the third branch of the government wasn't even given a building of its own. The high court initially resided in various rooms beneath the House and Senate, relocating no fewer than six times. Justices had no bench per se, nor private chambers. Not until 1935 would they receive their present stately abode, 146 years after the Court was born.[68]

For a body so clearly marginalized in the early going, it has demanded and received a remarkable level of respect. Presidents often disagree with its decisions but will rarely risk direct confrontation. As demonstrated by the following cases, when the two entities have gone head to head, the Court usually wins. With a comparatively tiny budget and no military force, justices can still bring presidents to heel, in part because the two parties empower each other.

Presidents nominate justices to lifetime positions. In turn, justices often refrain from negating executive actions, especially ones supported by the public. For example, Jefferson's Louisiana Purchase, Lincoln's Emancipation Proclamation, and Lyndon Johnson's Gulf of Tonkin Resolution were all unconstitutional. But the courts chose to exercise prudence for the sake of practicality.

Yet there have been clashes in the past, where checks and balances devolved into turf wars. Nearly all of them involved presidents with backgrounds in law, many of whom felt qualified to question the will of the justices. Following in chronological order are ten landmark battles that have strained, as well as defined, the relationship between the White House and the Black Robes.

## 1.   MARSHALL CLAIMS THE CONSTITUTION
*MARBURY v. MADISON* (1803)

President Thomas Jefferson and Chief Justice John Marshall honestly loathed each other. In private, Jefferson once called the authoritarian Marshall a man of "profound hypocrisy" and a member of "the Alexandrian party and the bigots and passive obedience men." The Federalist in turn considered the disheveled Republican "unfit" to be president. Their disagreements were frequent and deep, and one established a legal precedent of monumental consequence.[69]

Before John Adams departed the presidency, he made several late judicial appointments, all of them Federalists. A like-minded Senate approved them before retiring. The final step required the secretary of state to deliver the appointments, a task only partially completed in the forty-eight hours left in the Adams administration. When faced with the unsent appointees, newly sworn President Thomas Jefferson chose not to send them. Instead he cut several of the posts out of the judiciary altogether, believing that a smaller government was a better one.[70]

Several of the eliminated appointees complained bitterly, including William Marbury, who was looking forward to being Justice of the Peace for Washington, D.C. Marbury sued to have the new state secretary, James Madison, deliver his employment papers, but neither Madison nor Jefferson were eager to obey his demands.

When the case reached the Supreme Court, Chief Justice Marshall knew he had no legal authority to force the executive branch, and his nemesis Jefferson, to give Marbury a job. But he also did not want to

Jefferson despised Supreme Court Chief Justice John Marshall with all his being, but as president he could never bring himself to stand up against the dominant jurist

hand Jefferson a victory and rule in his favor. Instead, Marshall took the opportunity to define the separation of powers and stake a major claim for the judicial branch.

In a majority decision, he ruled that the Court did not have jurisdiction over the duties of the executive. But Marshall proclaimed that the executive and legislative branches could not interfere with the one great responsibility inherent in the courts—the right of "judicial review." From that point onward, the judiciary alone had final say as to what was constitutional and unconstitutional. "It is emphatically the province and duty of the judicial department to say what the law is," wrote Marshall, and neither Capitol Hill nor the White House could ever deny that authority so long as the United States existed.

---

John Marshall established the tradition of having Supreme Court justices wear black robes. John Jay, the first chief justice, preferred red.

---

## 2.   THE BURR CONSPIRACY AND EXECUTIVE PRIVILEGE
### UNITED STATES v. BURR (1807)

As a rule, the government does not care much for treason, and when former vice president Aaron Burr became a suspect in an alleged conspiracy to create a rogue country west of the Appalachians, Jefferson and others called for his head, or at least his body in court, and a conviction looked probable.

By 1807, Burr had almost no credibility. In the ELECTION OF 1800 he declined to step aside and let his running mate claim the presidency. In 1804, the sitting vice president killed rival Alexander Hamilton in the country's most infamous duel. By 1806 he was said to be orchestrating an invasion of Mexico, with plans of creating a vast empire astride the Mississippi. The evidence, though sparse, was enough to have Jefferson stand before Congress and conclude that Burr's guilt was "beyond question."[71]

Two of Burr's supposed accomplices were reviewed before the Supreme Court. Chief Justice John Marshall, refusing to bend to the will of sensationalist newspapers, found insufficient proof to accuse them of treason; he let them go. Marshall then rode to the circuit court in Virginia to try Aaron Burr in person. A furious Jefferson determined that if Marshall set Burr free, then the chief justice would have to be impeached.[72]

All but demanding a conviction, the president suddenly turned somber when his own name was subpoenaed. Twice Marshall demanded he testify, and twice Jefferson refused, claiming he could not possibly attend a trial, lest "such calls would leave the nation without an executive branch." Claiming executive privilege, Jefferson also refused to relinquish records in his possession that were pertinent to the case. "Some of these proceedings," the president said of the documents, "should remain known to their executive functionary only."[73]

In the end, Jefferson angrily relented and sent the requested material. None of the papers, no witnesses, nothing convinced Marshall that the government had a valid argument against the defendant. Burr walked. Jefferson half expected the decision. Yet the disappointment of one more Marshall victory led the president to lament what he called "the original error of having a judiciary independent of the nation."[74]

> In 1836, Aaron Burr was somewhat amused to hear that a band of Americans had started a war with Mexico to form an independent country. He found it ironic that Jim Bowie, Davy Crockett, and Sam Houston were declared heroes, while he was tried for treason for allegedly trying to do the same thing.

## 3.  JACKSON IGNORES THE COURT
### WORCESTER v. GEORGIA (1832)

By the early 1800s, the white population in the United States was doubling every twenty years. Most Native Americans were less than enthused about the trend. Their misery worsened when Andrew Jackson signed the Indian Removal Act of 1830, requiring "voluntary" relocation to unsettled lands west of the Mississippi. But the Cherokee of Georgia had reason to believe they had won a stay of extradition.

In 1832 the state of Georgia arrested several white missionaries living with the Cherokee. Two of them, Samuel Worcester and Elizur Butler, sued the state for violating the sovereignty of their hosts. Surprisingly, the Supreme Court sided with the Native Americans and their guests, ruling that only the federal government, not the states, had authority over Indian affairs. In the majority opinion, an ailing John Marshall labeled Georgia's

Andrew Jackson felt no need to assist the Supreme
Court in forcing the state of Georgia to observe its
rulings—especially when it came to Indian affairs.

actions against the Cherokee "repugnant to the Constitution, laws and
treaties of the United States."[75]

Tribal members reportedly danced after hearing the decision. One
member proclaimed the verdict proved "for ever as to who is right and
who is wrong." In contrast, Governor Wilson Lumpkin swore to his legislature that he would defy the ruling "with the spirit of determined resistance."[76]

Legend has it that President Jackson, the famed Indian fighter, responded by saying, "John Marshall has made his decision. Now let him
enforce it." In reality, Jackson chose to ignore the ruling, and he hinted
that the state of Georgia should do the same. "It [the Supreme Court]
cannot coerce Georgia to yield to its mandate," said Jackson. "It is better
for them [the Cherokees] to treat and move."[77]

Governor Lumpkin did ignore the ruling, and the Cherokee were
soon forced from their land. John Marshall saw the defeat as the death
knell of the Court's credibility and possibly the end of the government
upon which it rested. Lamenting the seemingly limitless power of the
Jackson administration, the chief justice bemoaned, "I yield slowly and reluctantly to the conviction that our Constitution cannot last."[78]

---

In 1838, the U.S. government began to forcibly relocate more then seventeen thousand Cherokee from their homes in Georgia and Alabama to the
Oklahoma Territory. Approximately four thousand died on the ensuing Trail
of Tears.

---

## 4.  LINCOLN, TANEY, AND HABEAS CORPUS
*EX PARTE MERRYMAN* (1861)

Eleven states seceded. By all accounts, Maryland looked to be next. Ninety-seven percent of the Old Line State had voted against Lincoln in 1860. When Fort Sumter fell, residents lofted Rebel flags in celebration. Days later, citizens of Baltimore attacked the Sixth Massachusetts Regiment as it entered the city, resulting in the deaths of four soldiers and twelve civilians.[79]

In desperation, Lincoln ordered Winfield Scott, commanding general of the army: "If at any point . . . you find resistance which renders it necessary to suspend the writ of Habeas Corpus for the public safety, you, personally or through the officer in command . . . are authorized to suspend that writ." Neither Lincoln nor Scott had such authority. Only Congress could grant a suspension, and the legislators were not in session.[80]

The right of citizens to petition against imprisonment has been a mainstay of free societies. Without it, governments can arrest without warrant, hold without charge, and imprison without trial. Certainly Lincoln was uneasy about his decision, but he rationalized his action. "I felt that measures, otherwise unconstitutional, might become lawful, by becoming indispensable to the preservation of the constitution," an act he equated to removing an arm to save a body.[81]

The arrests proceeded. In Baltimore alone, the Union army jailed news editors, a court judge, and the chief of police. Members of Maryland's legislature were taken prisoner, along with several private citizens.[82]

One of the first to protest was John Merryman, a Baltimore resident suspected of being an officer of Rebel militia. Taken from his home at 2:00 a.m. on May 25, 1861, he was thrown into Fort McHenry and held without charge. Appealing to a local circuit court, he filed for a writ of habeas corpus and won. The presiding judge happened to be eighty-four-year-old Roger B. Taney, slave owner, Marylander, and chief justice of the Supreme Court.[83]

In his verdict, Taney tersely stated, "The President has exercised a power which he does not possess under the Constitution." He sent his ruling to the commander of Fort McHenry and to Lincoln himself. Both men ignored it.[84]

Many Unionists fully supported the administration. "Of all the tyrannies that afflict mankind," claimed the *New York Tribune*, "that of the judiciary is the most insidious, the most intolerable, the most dangerous." The *New York Times* wrote that Justice Taney "uses the powers of his office to serve the cause of traitors." Attorney General Edward Bates worried that the Supreme Court would challenge every arrest and "do more to paralyze the executive . . . than the worst defeat our armies have yet sustained." Taney began to fear he would soon be arrested, and in fact Lincoln considered doing so.[85]

Nearly two years passed before Congress granted Lincoln the power to suspend the writ. The right was deemed retroactive to the beginning of the rebellion and permitted to remain until the end of hostilities, whenever that would be. Yet Taney's decision would ultimately prevail. In the related case of *Ex parte Milligan*, the Supreme Court ruled unanimously that neither Congress nor Lincoln had the right to suspend the writ of habeas corpus in Maryland, because it was not a state in rebellion. But the verdict came in 1866, when the war was over and both Lincoln and Taney were dead.

> Five of the justices in the 1866 case of *Ex parte Milligan* were Lincoln appointees, including the former secretary of the treasury, Chief Justice Salmon P. Chase.

## 5. COURT-PACKING FDR (1937)

Twelve times the heavily Republican Supreme Court ruled his New Deal initiatives unconstitutional, including his debt relief to farmers and the creation of a minimum wage. In response, Franklin Roosevelt accused the Court of denying the needs of the country. The justices answered by refusing to attend FDR's 1937 State of the Union Address.[86]

The president had seen enough. Weeks later, in a nationwide radio broadcast, FDR called the Court a "super-legislature . . . reading into the Constitution words and implications which are not there." He mentioned that forty-five of the forty-eight states had term limits for judges, and perhaps it was time to do likewise with the High Court.[87]

Roosevelt offered something akin to forced retirement. "What is my proposal? It is simply this: whenever a judge or justice of any federal court has reached the age of seventy and does not avail himself of the opportunity to retire on a pension, a new member shall be appointed by the president then in office." He also wanted the maximum number of justices to be increased to fifteen.[88]

The shock announcement offended even his most devout supporters. Hatton Sumners (D-TX), chairman of the House Judiciary Committee, called the plan "infamous." The Senate refused to vote on it, while Vice President John Garner opposed it outright. The Bar Association condemned the idea, and former president Herbert Hoover considered it "subordination of the court to the personal power of the Executive." In examining the overwhelming opposition, Interior Secretary Harold Ickes figured that FDR either had to win the court-packing fight or resign.[89]

One senator remained relatively neutral. "I knew from my study of history that there was nothing sacrosanct about the number nine, that the memberships of the Supreme Court had fluctuated from five to ten. President Lincoln wanted to enlarge the Supreme Court to eleven," observed Harry Truman.[90]

Ultimately, time rescued Roosevelt. In June 1937, conservative justice Willis Van Devanter announced his retirement. The following year, Harding appointee George Sutherland left, followed by the death of Hoover-appointed Benjamin Cardozo. FDR would eventually place eight new justices on the Supreme Court. Only George Washington appointed more, with ten. Had he only waited, Roosevelt could have prevented one of the worst public relations mistakes of his long legacy.

---

FDR's biggest ally on the court-packing bill was Senate Majority Leader Joseph "Arkansas Joe" Robinson, whom FDR promised to appoint to the

Faced with a gaggle of Republican appointees in the Court, FDR schemed to fill the bench to the left. He should have waited for Father Time to do it for him.

ROOSEVELT LIBRARY

bench if the measure passed. Neither the bill nor the senator lived to see the day. Robinson succumbed to a massive heart attack on July 14, 1937, right before the measure died in committee.

## 6. TRUMAN SEIZES THE STEEL MILLS
### *YOUNGSTOWN SHEET AND TUBE CO. v. SAWYER* (1952)

At 10:30 a.m. Washington time, on Tuesday, April 8, 1952, Harry Truman addressed the nation on radio and television. In the interest of national security, for the safety of NATO allies and nearly four hundred thousand U.S. troops fighting in Korea, the president announced that the government was going to seize the nation's steel mills in ninety minutes.

The shocking announcement was in reaction to an imminent nation-wide strike of steelworkers. Truman blamed the owners, who had not granted their laborers a single pay raise since 1950. Though he abhorred the idea of taking control of their factories, he could not allow their stubbornness to jeopardize the safety of his troops.

It so happened that the general population, including the Supreme Court, would not allow Truman to have sole discretion on what constituted a "national emergency." Public backlash was nothing short of lurid. Truman was called a usurper, a bully, a dictator. Some compared him to Hitler. Newspapers openly attacked his extremely broad definition of commander in chief. Thoroughly tired of the war in Korea, Americans everywhere were in no mood to make further concessions. Impeachment became the watchword on Capitol Hill.[91]

The steel corporations immediately sued. Within weeks, *Youngstown Sheet and Tube Co. v. Sawyer* reached the Supreme Court. There was some possibility Truman would win. All nine justices were Roosevelt and Truman appointees, including Truman's old friend and former treasury secretary Fred Vinson, the chief justice.[92]

In an abrupt six-to-three vote, the Court decided that the president had in fact violated the Constitution. Such a confiscation of private property, ruled the majority, could only be done if the country was in a state of emergency and if Congress mandated it, neither of which applied. The defeat simply accelerated Truman's decline and confirmed the impossibility of his running for reelection.[93]

To a certain extent, Truman was correct in his predictions about a shutdown of the steel industry. The strike eventually lasted seven weeks and temporarily put more than one million people out of work.

## 7.   FREEDOM OF SPEECH AND THE PENTAGON PAPERS
### *NEW YORK TIMES CO. v. UNITED STATES* (1971)

No president has come close to Nixon's terrible record with the judicial branch. Most executives had but one or two High Court rulings go against their administration. Lincoln lost five, FDR twelve. Nixon lost no fewer than twenty-five.[94]

One such case involved an attempt to block the *New York Times* from publishing excerpts from the so-called Pentagon Papers, a top-secret Defense Department report detailing American involvement in Indochina from 1945 to 1968. Written during the Johnson administration, the report reached the *Times* in the summer of 1971 by way of Daniel Ellsberg, a former defense analyst for the State Department. Ellsberg helped craft the Pentagon Papers, but the war's continuation, and a climbing death toll of forty thousand U.S. servicemen, motivated him to leak several key passages.

The first segments appeared in the Sunday edition of June 13, sparking an immediate reaction. Nixon called it "the most massive leak of classified documents in American history." The *Times* countered that it was morally obligated to publish the excerpts. The Justice Department, then under John Mitchell, filed a restraining order against the *Times*, claiming "the nation's security will suffer immediate and irreparable harm" should any more segments be made public.[95]

A more immediate threat was to the government's credibility. The report recounted how policy makers repeatedly ignored the intelligence community, exaggerated threat levels, and conducted acts of terror and sabotage in North Vietnam as early as 1954.

While a temporary order restrained the *Times*, Ellsberg went to the *Washington Post*, which began to run its own summaries of the Pentagon Papers on June 18. The government acquired a restraining order on that publication the following day. By June 26, all parties were in the Supreme Court, arguing their case.

The press won in a six-to-three decision. Outraged, Nixon blamed Ellsberg, the media, and the Court's "undue haste" for sabotaging the war effort. "Our military policy was working on the battlefield," he believed, but "the Pentagon Papers were published, and on June 22 the Senate voted its first resolution establishing a pull-out timetable for Vietnam. Before long, the North Vietnamese would slam the door on our new [peace] proposal and begin building up for a new military offense."[96]

> In an attempt to discredit Daniel Ellsberg, White House operatives G. Gordon Liddy and E. Howard Hunt broke into the Los Angeles office of Ellsberg's psychotherapist. Much to their disappointment, they found nothing incriminating.

## 8.   THE WHITE HOUSE TAPES
### *UNITED STATES v. NIXON* (1974)

Every president since Franklin Roosevelt used recording equipment to keep track of official business. Kennedy was the first to install a system in the Oval Office. Johnson became so accustomed to taping his phone conversations that he often forgot the machines were on. Not unfamiliar with the art of bugging, Nixon had listening devices placed in several locales, including the cabinet room, Camp David, and the Oval Office. Each president viewed such recordings as a convenient means of dictation, but the tapes were never meant for public consumption.[97]

Consequently, neither the American people nor the Supreme Court knew about the practice. That is, until July 16, 1973, when Nixon's deputy assistant Alexander Butterfield happened to mention it to a Senate committee investigating WATERGATE. Stunned and more than a bit curious, the Senate demanded Nixon's Oval Office tapes—all of them. Nixon refused. Thus began a yearlong fight over the critical evidence.

Nixon's counsel argued executive privilege, national security, and right to privacy. None of it swayed the Court, including the four Nixon appointees. One of them, Chief Justice Warren Burger, wrote the majority opinion that the president did have the right to keep certain conversations private, but not when it interfered with the duties of the judicial branch in a criminal hearing.

The verdict came on July 24, 1974. Much to the surprise of his harshest critics, who expected him to either resist the decision or destroy the evidence, the president obeyed and handed over the tapes. Less than three weeks later, with evidence mounting against him, and with Congress proceeding toward impeachment, Richard M. Nixon became the first-ever chief executive to resign from the presidency.

> The Supreme Court decision against Nixon was unanimous, with one abstention. Justice William Rehnquist withdrew himself from voting because he had previously worked as the defendant's assistant attorney general.

## 9.  REAGAN AND CIVIL RELIGION

On the bicentennial of the Constitution's founding, President Ronald Reagan came to Independence Hall to commemorate the event, which he proceeded to do with all the fervor of a preacher before a congregation. He regaled the Constitution as "a covenant with the Supreme Being to whom our Founding Fathers did constantly appeal for assistance." In his eyes, the document was nothing short of a "miracle" and "the triumph of human freedom under God."[98]

Reagan possessed a great many attributes, but constitutional law and American history were beyond him. Nonetheless, he had a deep sense of what he felt was right, and this included bringing church and state together.

On several issues, the Court generally leaned Reagan's way, particularly regarding the increase of states' rights and reduction of affirmative action. Yet on the "moral scorecard" the justices repeatedly went against him. In *Wallace v. Jaffrey* (1985), the Court struck down an Alabama law for prayer in public schools. *Grand Rapids v. Ball* (1985) and *Aguilar v. Felton* (1985) forbade public teachers from also teaching in parochial schools.

Irritated but undaunted, the president used his 1986 State of the Union speech to make a direct appeal to the Supreme Court to ban abortion. "America will never be whole," argued Reagan, "as long as the right to life granted by our Creator is denied to the unborn." The bully pulpit had no effect. Later that year, the Court ruled in *Thornburg v. American College of Obstetricians* that states could not "intimidate women into continuing pregnancies."[99]

Reagan countered by appointing prolife, far-right justices. After the moderate Sandra Day O'Connor came conservative Catholic Antonin Scalia and the promotion of archconservative William Rehnquist to chief justice. Reagan added Anthony Kennedy, another conservative Republican Catholic, in 1988.[100]

---

Chief Justice William Rehnquist and Associate Justice Sandra Day O'Connor were classmates at Stanford Law School.

---

## 10. PREMATURE ADJUDICATION
### CLINTON v. JONES (1997)

In yet another case involving the definition of executive privilege, the president's legal counsel maintained that the unique position of chief executive precluded said person from participating in a civil hearing. The argument didn't work for Thomas Jefferson in *United States v. Burr*, and it wasn't going to work for Bill Clinton in *Clinton v. Jones*.

In an attempt to placate the Court and to reduce exposure to an already embarrassing story, the defense team requested a delay in Paula Jones's sexual harassment suit until the accused was no longer in office. The case involved an alleged solicitation of sex in 1981 from then Arkansas Governor Clinton upon state employee Jones inside the Excelsior Hotel in Little Rock. The plaintiff did not file until three years later. In the interim, the marginally successful governor had become president of the United States.

A series of blocks and appeals elevated the case up the judicial chain, until Clinton's motion for a delay reached the Supreme Court in January 1997, a week before the incumbent was about to take his second oath of office. The Court took four months to reach a decision, but it would be unanimous. The president's counterclaim was invalid, and the case became a landmark in U.S. law. The ruling on *Clinton v. Jones* determined that no person stood above the law, regardless of rank in the government.[101]

---

*Clinton v. Jones* did not go well for either party. Clinton paid a settlement of nearly one million dollars, had his law license suspended, and was impeached for statements made during deposition. Jones underwent a divorce, posed nude in *Penthouse*, and took part in a celebrity boxing match to pay for legal expenses.

## TOP TEN NOTABLE
## PARDONS AND COMMUTATIONS

Two little boys were playing with a toy soldier when they decided it would be fitting and proper to execute him, because he had been sleeping on guard duty. While they began to dig his final resting place in the lawn, the family gardener commented that perhaps forgiveness was in order. Not long after, a note arrived from the boys' father: "The doll Jack is pardoned. By order of the President. A. Lincoln."[102]

Article 2, section 2 of the U.S. Constitution gives each chief executive "Power to grant Reprieves and Pardons for Offences against the United States, except in Cases of Impeachment." To date, more than ten thousand people—plus the aforementioned Jack—have received presidential pardons. Thousands more have attained commutation of sentences, remissions of fines, and general amnesties. Their crimes, alleged and proven, have covered the spectrum, from tax evasion and gaming violations, to perjury, drug trafficking, murder, military desertion, espionage, and treason.

Among the few powers explicitly granted to the executive, clemency is the only one that is irreversible, and yet it is the least analyzed. Even the Philadelphia Convention barely expressed concern when giving presidents the ability to place almost anyone above the law. Their rationale stemmed from tradition, as several governors already had the authority (a holdover from the English monarchy). They also viewed clemency as a tool of prudent peacekeeping rather than a weapon of tyranny.

Over the years, the Founding Framers have been correct, generally. Most clemencies transpire quietly, often at Christmastime, with minimal notice or opposition from the public at large. But there have been moments of great controversy, where presidents seemed to conspire against due process. In hindsight, a few were wise decisions, resulting in the calming of troubled waters. Others incited entirely new hurricanes, and one led to the downfall of an administration. Following are the landmark cases, listed in chronological order, that rank as the most contentious acts of clemency ever offered from the inkwells of the chief magistrates.

### 1. PARTICIPANTS IN THE WHISKEY REBELLION (TREASON)
PRESIDENT: GEORGE WASHINGTON
CLEMENCY: FULL PARDON, JULY 10, 1795

In spite of his vengeful nature, Alexander Hamilton was the most ardent supporter of empowering presidents with the right of clemency. Through his famous defense of the Constitution in the Federalist Papers, Hamilton suggested, "In seasons of insurrection or rebellion, there are often critical moments, when a well-timed offer of pardon to the insurgents or rebels may restore the tranquility of the commonwealth."[103]

To his surprise, Hamilton found himself fighting against an insurrection not seven years later, leading thousands of federalized troops against the WHISKEY REBELLION in western Pennsylvania. Commanding in the field as President Washington monitored events from Philadelphia, Hamilton and his columns marched into the dissentious woodlands in the late autumn of 1794. They encountered almost no resistance, save for the ghostly liberty poles standing anonymously along their route, each crowned with blood-red caps, a symbol of revolution.

Impatient to get their work done before winter, officers and scouts began pulling suspects from their homes in the dark of night, detaining them in barns and cellars. Some 150 civilians were questioned at gunpoint. Two were mortally wounded by accident, while others went days without food. Hamilton interrogated several captives personally, and he soon discovered that the ringleaders had long disappeared into the frontier. With no one of consequence in their possession, the army nonetheless attempted to save face by marching scores of "prisoners" eastward to Philadelphia. The journey began in November and lasted five weeks. Several of the detainees were barefoot. One man died of exposure.[104]

On Christmas Day, the victorious army paraded their exhausted captives through the City of Brotherly Love. They were met with cheering crowds, ringing church bells, twirling flags, and the president, fully pleased that the rebellion had been tamed.

The ensuing trials dragged on, with no plausible evidence emerging, leaving many of the accused to rot in squalid jails for months. In the end, nearly all were acquitted except for John Mitchell, a small-time farmer, and Philip Wigle, a pauper, both of whom were described as "simple" and were perhaps mentally slow.[105]

Mitchell and Wigle were convicted of treason and sentenced to hang, but Washington realized their deaths would only turn harmless men into martyrs for another rebellion. Nine months after their capture, the incarcerated and the rest of their supposed accomplices received "a full, free, and entire pardon" from their president, though none were ever compensated for their suffering.[106]

---

One of the commanding officers in the surge against the Whiskey Rebellion was Gen. Henry "Light Horse Harry" Lee, future father of Robert E. Lee.

---

## 2.  MEMBERS OF THE CONFEDERACY (TREASON)
PRESIDENT: ANDREW JOHNSON
CLEMENCY: FULL PARDON AND AMNESTY (DECEMBER 25, 1868)

To balance their Union Party ticket for the 1864 presidential elections, Republican officials chose Andrew Johnson of Tennessee over Vice President Hannibal Hamlin of Maine. Along with being pro-Union, Johnson was a southerner and a Democrat, and party leaders figured that the broad appeal of both Lincoln and Johnson all but assured an election victory in November.

The following April, Lincoln was dead, murdered by a Southern Democrat no less. In an attempt to hold on to the presidency, Republicans immediately realized they had made a serious miscalculation in 1864 and would have to wait until 1868 to rectify it.

Andrew Johnson was a steadfast Unionist, but of the old order, insisting on the supremacy of whites in the political arena and supporting states' rights in local affairs. While Radical Republicans in Congress, such as James Garfield of Ohio, pressed for harsh retributions against the former Confederacy, Johnson supported a more conciliatory approach. In short, he sought to win back the white South by rejecting major changes on race relations.

The president vetoed the extension of the Freedman's Bureau and a bill on civil rights. He also lobbied against the Fourteenth Amend-

Despite decades of political experience, Andrew
Johnson was unable to build common ground
between the victorious North and the defeated South.

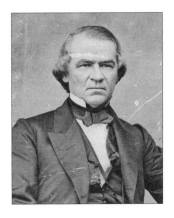

ment that provided full citizenship to African Americans. His dismissal
of Lincoln's secretary of war Edwin Stanton in 1868 only finalized a
steadily growing movement to impeach him, a crisis he famously survived by a single senatorial vote. Johnson's personal train wreck finally
ended when his own party refused to nominate him for the 1868 elections.[107]

In a last-ditch effort to heal North-South division, he instead sliced
them back open. On Christmas Day 1868, he granted "unconditionally,
and without reservation, to all and to every person who directly or indi-
rectly participated in the late resurrection or rebellion, a pardon and
amnesty for the offence of treason against the United States." Only the
highest-ranking officials and military officers were excluded. To Johnson,
he saw the sweeping gesture as the best way "to secure permanent peace,
order, and prosperity throughout the land, and to renew and fully restore
confidence and fraternal feeling among the whole people." The effect was
far different than he had hoped. Republicans became convinced that
their president was soft on treason, while former leaders of the Confederacy continued to introduce "black codes" that curtailed the newly won
civil freedoms of the former slave population.[108]

Along with the sweeping amnesty Andrew Johnson gave on Christmas Day
in 1868, he also issued 654 individual pardons during his term, more than
any other president before him. His successor, U. S. Grant, easily broke that
record by allotting 1,332 pardons, mostly to former Confederates.

### 3. EUGENE DEBS (SEDITION)

PRESIDENT: WARREN G. HARDING
CLEMENCY: COMMUTATION, DECEMBER 25, 1921

The wiry and righteous Woodrow Wilson took offense of anyone who dared oppose him, while the easygoing Warren G. Harding did not have a rancorous bone in his pudgy middle-aged body. Their differences reached all the way to the First Amendment, a law Wilson blatantly disregarded after U.S. entry into the Great War, when he imposed a slew of congressional acts designed to crush all public opposition to military involvement.

It was under Wilson's Espionage Act that labor activist Eugene Debs had been arrested. In a public speech in Ohio, Debs had criticized military conscription as undemocratic. He had mentioned the war only once, but it was enough to have him jailed and sentenced to ten years behind bars and his citizenship revoked for the rest of his life. Even after the war ended, Wilson adamantly refused to show mercy for the sixty-three year-old Debs, whose health was failing inside a federal prison in Atlanta. For as long as he was in office, Wilson promised never to let the man go free, in part because Debs had run against him in 1912 as the candidate of the Socialist Party and slammed the well-to-do Wilson as a tool of big business.

When Harding won the White House in 1920, he saw no reason to continue the incarceration. The accused was a reformer, not a radical, and Debs had already served more than two years. Several labor and religious leaders were petitioning for Debs's early release, and the president agreed.

Harding initially wanted to issue a pardon on July 4, until the Ameri-

Aging labor leader Eugene V. Debs walks out of the White House shortly after Warren Harding grants him clemency.

can Legion and other patriotic leagues found out. To them, Debs was still a traitor, undeserving of any compassion. Never one for confrontation, Harding waited until Christmas Day. He invited the federal prisoner to meet him at the White House, unguarded and in private, for an official termination of the "traitor's" sentence. The pardon was unpopular, especially with the American Legion, the Veterans of Foreign War, and the nationalistic Mrs. Harding. But the president believed the act was a necessary gesture of goodwill toward the working class and a symbolic end to the suppression of free speech in a democratic society.[109]

> Five times Eugene Debs ran as the Socialist Party presidential candidate. His highest vote tally was more than 910,000, which he attained in 1920 while in prison.

## 4.  JIMMY HOFFA (JURY TAMPERING, FRAUD, CONSPIRACY)
PRESIDENT: RICHARD M. NIXON
CLEMENCY: COMMUTATION, DECEMBER 23, 1971

Since 1957, when he was the chief counsel for the Senate Permanent Subcommittee on Investigations, Robert Kennedy had been gunning for James Riddle "Jimmy" Hoffa. The head of the Teamsters had long been known as a corrupt and belligerent individual. He was also tangentially connected to the mafia, but Kennedy could never get a conviction.

As both men began to rise to prominence, they developed a passionate and sincere loathing for each other. The hatred only intensified when Kennedy became attorney general in 1961 and made the Teamsters Union one of his primary targets of inquiry. In 1964, while investigating Hoffa for embezzlement of union funds, Bobby secured a conviction on jury tampering, resulting in an eight-year sentence. Additional convictions of fraud and conspiracy lengthened the punishment to thirteen years.

Long before he stepped into the Lewisburg Federal Prison in Pennsylvania, Hoffa had been a supporter of Richard Nixon, who shared Hoffa's animosity toward the Kennedys. After four years of incarceration, the godfather of truckers received a commutation of his sentence from first-term President Nixon, who released him right before Christmas in 1971.

In his memoirs, Nixon never once mentioned Hoffa. But he did highlight with great pride an event that occurred not long after Hoffa's release.

During the 1972 presidential campaign, the board of the International Brotherhood of Teamsters voted overwhelmingly to endorse the Republican for reelection—the only major labor organization to do so. Thrilled by winning over the traditionally Democratic union, Nixon invited the whole board to his home in San Clemente, a meeting he later called "one of the most important watershed meetings in American politics in this century."[110]

---

Richard Nixon and Jimmy Hoffa started their careers the same way—working as stock boys in a grocery store.

---

## 5.  RICHARD M. NIXON (OBSTRUCTION OF JUSTICE)
PRESIDENT: GERALD FORD
CLEMENCY: FULL PARDON, SEPTEMBER 8, 1974

"We are not a vengeful people," said Gerald Ford. He was correct for the most part. Not long after the Second World War, many Americans were driving German automobiles and purchasing Japanese electronics. Nixon's visit to China tamed fears of the communist dragon almost overnight. But Ford forgot the fundamental ingredient required for any change of heart—timing is everything.[111]

"I wasn't prepared for the allegations that the Nixon pardon prompted," admitted the unelected president, but he might have known it was too soon. Only a month had passed since Nixon's resignation. No charges had been filed against him. There was no pending court date. Furthermore, Ford decided to give his old boss total absolution for the entirety of Nixon's tenure in the White House, "for all offenses against the United States which he, Richard Nixon, has committed or may have committed or taken part in during the period from January 20, 1969, through August 9, 1974." In announcing the pardon, Ford paraphrased Harry Truman, Abraham Lincoln, and the book of James, but none of it rang true.[112]

Immediately Ford's approval rating took a twenty-two-point dive. His own press secretary, Jerald TerHorst, resigned in protest. The Senate quickly passed a resolution to stop any further pardons concerning Watergate. "You're crazy," said Speaker of the House Tip O'Neill to an apologetic Ford. "I'm telling you right now this will cost you the election. I hope it's not part of any deal."[113]

There was no deal. The former House minority leader simply be-

President Ford tries to explain to the House Judiciary Subcommittee exactly why he chose to give former president Nixon a full and absolute pardon. The subcommittee, and much of the nation, viewed the pardon as an act of favoritism rather than forgiveness.

lieved that clemency would spare a depressed Nixon from further anguish and allow the country to move forward. Right away it was clear that he had guessed wrong. What may have hurt him most was Nixon's unwillingness to admit some amount of wrongdoing. Even Ford was offended by the lack of remorse. "I was taking one hell of a risk," Ford said, "and he didn't seem responsive at all."[114]

Ford's fellow Republicans were most distressed, wondering why he could not save this little time bomb for sometime after the midterm elections, a mere eight weeks away. It was all for naught for the GOP. They lost four seats in the Senate and took a forty-eight-seat beating in the House. Two years later, Ford was elected out of office as well.[115]

> After Ford's pardon of Nixon, several legislators backed a proposed amendment that would mandate congressional approval for all future pardons. The author of the amendment was U.S. Senator and future vice president Walter Mondale.

## 6. VIETNAM DRAFT RESISTERS (VIOLATION OF THE SELECTIVE SERVICE ACT)
PRESIDENT: JAMES CARTER
CLEMENCY: CONDITIONAL PARDON, JANUARY 21, 1977

In their first presidential debate, incumbent Gerald Ford and Democratic hopeful Jimmy Carter were asked how they would handle more than one hundred thousand draft resisters of the Vietnam conflict, many of whom had fled the country. "I think we gave them a good opportunity," said the defensive president. "I don't think we should go any further."[116]

Ford already had a resolution in place, whereby clemency would be given to anyone who would turn himself in, work two years of community service, and sign a loyalty oath to the United States. About one in six resisters took the offer, leaving more than ninety thousand in limbo.[117]

Carter responded that he endorsed an immediate pardon for all violators, adding that the poor were disproportionately punished in the United States, while "the big shots who are rich, who are influential very seldom go to jail," a thinly veiled reference to the Nixon pardon. In reality, most who had fled conscription were white and middle class, many of whom had voting parents who were eager to see their sons return with a clean record.[118]

Upon winning the presidency, Carter honored his promise of a pardon. In his first executive order, he granted full clemency to anyone who had violated the Selective Service Act between August 4, 1964, and March 28, 1973, provided they had not committed a violent crime in the process. Conspicuously absent from the pardon were those already in the military who had deserted or gone temporarily AWOL during the course of the war, a group that consisted of some five hundred thousand individuals. His administration reviewed those dissenters on a case-by-case basis and rejected the majority of applicants.[119]

> During his four years in office, President Carter was relatively prolific in granting clemency. Among those who received executive commutations were Watergate burglar G. Gordon Liddy, bank robber Patti Hearst, and Harry Truman's would-be assassin Oscar Collazo.

## 7.    W. MARK FELT (ILLEGAL SEARCH AND SEIZURE)
PRESIDENT: RONALD REAGAN
CLEMENCY: FULL PARDON, MARCH 26, 1981

It rarely troubled Ronald Reagan to know only the basics. Briefs were to be no more than a page and a half, doubled spaced. Details were left to his inner circle, whom he trusted implicitly. Consequently he had no real reason to doubt his key advisors, particularly White House Counsel Ed Meese, when they recommended a full and absolute pardon for former associate FBI director and convicted federal criminal W. Mark Felt. After gathering some cursory information, Reagan determined that Felt deserved clemency and was in fact a hero.

The president's praise was based on the information that Felt, along with fellow FBI agent Edward S. Miller, had authorized illegal break-ins and wiretaps of suspected Vietnam protesters and their families in the early 1970s. Under the Carter administration, the two men had been charged and fined for violating the Fourth Amendment (unwarranted search and seizure) along with several other privacy laws. In his pardon statement, Reagan noted, "thousands of draft evaders and others who violated the Selective Service laws were unconditionally pardoned by my predecessor. America was generous to those who refused to serve their country in the Vietnam War. We can be no less generous to two men who acted on high principle to bring an end to the terrorism that was threatening our nation."[120]

Regardless that their "high principle" went against the U.S. Constitution, and their domestic espionage unearthed absolutely nothing, Felt and Miller were nonetheless exonerated. Richard Nixon, who was in office when Felt committed the crime, sent him a congratulatory bottle of champagne with a note that read, "Justice ultimately prevails." Those more familiar with the specifics of the trial roundly criticized Reagan for his abrupt clemency and high praise.[121]

Unbeknownst to all of them, Felt was "Deep Throat," the legendary informant who had leaked details of the Watergate cover-up to journalist Bob Woodward. Not until 2005 did Felt reveal his role in bringing down an entire administration. By that time Nixon and Reagan had both passed away and would never learn how the fully pardoned Felt had indeed become somewhat of an American hero, albeit to many Democrats.

> One of W. Mark Felt's character witnesses in his 1980 trial, and a contributor to his defense fund, was Richard Nixon.

## 8.  CASPAR WEINBERGER (PERJURY, FRAUD, CONSPIRACY)
PRESIDENT: GEORGE H. W. BUSH
CLEMENCY: FULL PARDON, DECEMBER 24, 1992

George H. W. Bush was not prone to exaggeration, which made the language of his pardon of Caspar Weinberger appear all the more unusual in its embellishments. According to Bush, Reagan's former secretary of defense was "a true American Patriot," a hero of the Second World War, a flawless family man who engineered the dismantling of the Berlin Wall and caused the collapse of the Soviet Union. Also according to the pardon, Weinberger's buildup of nuclear warhead stockpiles and the failed Star Wars program had given the United States "a new birth of freedom." In addition, Weinberger was a victim, "tormented" by what Bush incorrectly called "the most thoroughly investigated matter of its kind in our history."[122]

Contrary to Bush's assertion, IRAN-CONTRA had not been fully investigated. Weinberger had been convicted because he did not disclose to congressional investigators that he had kept notes during several key meetings involving the arms-for-hostages deal. At the time of the pardon, the former secretary had also been charged with lying to independent counsel about Iran-Contra.[123]

Almost in passing, Bush's pardon also included five other individuals who were heavily involved in transferring weapons to Iran and money to the Contra insurgents in Nicaragua, including former NATIONAL SECURITY ADVISOR Robert "Bud" McFarlane. The president commended them all for their participation, stating, "The common denominator of their motivation—whether their actions were right or wrong—was patriotism." Most Americans did not believe him. A Gallup Poll indicated that only 27 percent of the public approved of the pardons.[124]

---

Caspar Weinberger has something in common with Mother Teresa, Helen Keller, and Rosa Parks—they are all recipients of the Presidential Medal of Freedom.

---

## 9.  MARK RICH (TAX EVASION, ILLEGAL ARMS TRADING)
PRESIDENT: WILLIAM CLINTON
CLEMENCY: FULL PARDON, JANUARY 20, 2001

He issued no pardons or commutations in his first two years. Had he not been reelected, Bill Clinton would have had only 56 acts of clemency to his name, well below average among his contemporaries. Into his final year, his total rested at 178, miniscule compared to Reagan's 393, Carter's 534, and Eisenhower's 1,110.

Claiming the dearth was due to backlog, Clinton accelerated the review process in his last months, often bypassing the pardon attorney's office in examining cases. Showing questionable tact in his last day as president, the departing Clinton signed 140 separate pardons plus 36 commuted sentences. Many of his fortunate beneficiaries were accused of rather mundane offenses—odometer rollbacks, false tax returns, mail fraud. Several had already served their time, including his half-brother ROGER CLINTON for drug possession.

And then there was seedy billionaire Mark Rich. A fugitive living in Switzerland since 1983, his alleged crime was tax evasion—forty-three million dollars' worth. He also acquired oil from Iran during the Teheran hostage crisis, which he sold at greatly inflated prices illegally to the United States during an oil embargo. Exactly why Clinton felt compelled to grant a full reprieve to a fugitive Jewish émigré from Belgium was not immediately apparent. It was later revealed that the Israeli government insisted that Clinton show leniency toward Rich, because the oil trader had donated large amounts of money to Jewish causes. Rich's former wife was also found to be a major contributor to the Democratic Party.

"Pardongate" would haunt Clinton as yet one more stain on his tumultuous last term. In contrast, Rich was still rich, living in opulence among the elite circles of Europe, and free from any further prosecution for his indiscretions in oil and money.

Charges against Mark Rich were first issued in 1983 by U.S. Attorney Rudi Giuliani. Rich's counsel in the pardon application process was attorney Lewis "Scooter" Libby.

## 10. LEWIS "SCOOTER" LIBBY (OBSTRUCTION OF JUSTICE, PERJURY)
PRESIDENT: GEORGE W. BUSH
CLEMENCY: COMMUTATION, JULY 2, 2007

George H. W. Bush and his eldest son were markedly different presidents: the diplomat and the crusader, the conservative and the spendthrift, the reticent and the recalcitrant. But in one aspect they were in lockstep. Both were absolute misers when it came to forgiving crime, unless it involved someone from within their White House.

In the War on Terror, the George W. Bush administration was adamant about connecting the Saddam Hussein regime with weapons of mass destruction. When evidence did not support their view, they generally ignored or dismissed it, including a report from diplomat Joseph Wilson that refuted a rumor that Iraq had purchased yellowcake uranium from Niger. Either through miscommunication or by design, Bush nonetheless claimed in his 2003 State of the Union address that Iraq had indeed acquired the prenuclear material.[125]

Wilson publicly criticized Bush's miscue (and the administration later admitted it was mistaken). But at least one Bush official, possibly in retaliation against Wilson, leaked the fact that the diplomat's wife, Valerie Plame, was an undercover CIA operative. Whether or not the disclosure was malevolent, it was nonetheless seen as a major breach of security.

An ensuing investigation indicated that Dick Cheney's chief of staff, Lewis "Scooter" Libby, was one of the possible sources and that Libby had been told of Plame's covert status by the vice president. During questioning, Libby claimed that he learned of Plame's role in the CIA through the media and only after the leak had been committed. Both statements were false. For these and other infractions, prosecutors convicted him of perjury and obstruction of justice. Ordered to spend thirty months in prison, he was about to begin serving his time when the president commuted the sentence.[126]

Controversial leaks have been part of the executive world since New York was the national capital, and Bush was certainly not the first to grant clemency for a prominent member of the government. But Libby's case was unique in that he was one of the highest-ranking White House officials ever tried, convicted, and sentenced for a federal crime.[127]

---

When George W. Bush was governor of Texas, he granted the fewest acts of clemency of any governor in that state since the 1940s.

---

## TOP TEN ASSASSINATIONS AND ATTEMPTS

James Garfield once said, "Assassination can no more be guarded against than death by lightning." He knew from experience how quickly lightning could strike, having lost so many comrades and his president during the Civil War. In the fifteen years after Abraham Lincoln's death, assassins killed twenty public officials in the United States and seven foreign heads of state. In 1881, Garfield would be next.[128]

The Constitution includes no assurances of, or funding for, executive safety. For the first twenty-five presidents, a paltry security detail varied from year to year. For James Monroe, protection consisted of a few civilian guards and a doorkeeper. Congress permitted the often-threatened John Tyler to have four police officers (called "doormen") at the White House. Franklin Pierce was the first to hire a full-time bodyguard.

Not until 1894 did the Secret Service enter the picture, in extralegal fashion. A division of the Treasury Department, the Secret Service initially investigated counterfeiting, fraud, bootlegging, and other revenue issues. Looking into threats from Colorado gamblers against Grover Cleveland, a few operatives began to watch over the president and his family, extending their assignment at the insistence of the first lady. One war, another assassination, and a score of rejected congressional bills later, the Sundry of Civil Expenses Act of 1906 authorized a portion of the Secret Service to guard "the person of the President" thereafter.[129]

Access to the "First Citizen" has lessened ever since, but the assaults have continued. In 1974, unemployed and distraught Samuel Byck tried to hijack a commercial airliner with the intent of crashing it into the White House to kill President Nixon. He instead shot and killed an airport guard, a pilot, and himself. George H. W. Bush's term witnessed sixteen separate cases of perpetrators jumping the White House fence. During Bill Clinton's tenure, the Executive Mansion experienced a suicide plane crash on the South Lawn, incoming shots from a 9mm handgun, and a barrage of automatic rifle fire that struck the building's north facade.

No executive has served without incident. A fourth of them have been personally assaulted, and four have been murdered. Without question, it is a dangerous job. But as the following cases illustrate, the country can be a dangerous place. Following in chronological order are the ten cases that can be classified as direct attacks upon the First Citizen of the country.[130]

## 1.   ANDREW JACKSON (JANUARY 30, 1835)

"I try to live my life as if death might come at any moment," claimed Andrew Jackson, neglecting to add that death came frequently in his life, only to other people. As an adult, Jackson amassed slaves and was quick to the lash. During his military service, he butchered Creeks, Seminoles,

Mentally unwell Richard Lawrence attempted to kill Andrew Jackson at the Capitol. Onlookers, including Davy Crockett, rushed to subdue the president's assailant.

and British soldiers with impunity. In cases of personal disputes, he readily dueled, killing a man on one occasion, but not before his opponent lodged a bullet within an inoperable inch of his vengeful heart.[131]

As chief executive, he could be just as authoritarian, threatening to attack South Carolina over a tariff issue, banishing the Cherokee to the Trail of Tears, and bullying congressmen into submission. Not surprisingly, he had received more than five hundred death threats by the middle of his second term. An attack finally came while Jackson was attending memorial services on Capitol Hill for a recently deceased legislator. The president, looking far older than his sixty-seven years, filed out of the Rotunda with the rest of the congregation, when a bearded thirty-year-old male approached him, raised a pistol, and fired.[132]

The percussion cap detonated with a staccato clap, but the gun did not go off. Stepping still closer, the assailant fired another pistol, and again the weapon failed. True to his militant nature, Jackson charged the man, ready to strike. Onlookers, including Tennessee Congressman Davy Crockett, violently piled on the would-be assassin.

The shooter turned out to be an English émigré named Richard Lawrence, an unemployed house painter. When questioned, Lawrence insisted that Jackson had killed his father three years before, when in fact his father died in England twelve years previous. Suspicions of his mental health were confirmed when Lawrence also claimed to be the rightful heir to the throne of England.[133]

Conspiracy theories germinated quickly. Jackson accused militant southerner John C. Calhoun, his former vice president. Calhoun denied the accusation and called Jackson a dictator. Others wondered if the entire assassination attempt had been staged to boost the president's status. Regardless, the death threats continued unabated. Six months after the attempted shooting, an unknown individual, who signed his name "Junius Brutus Booth," assured the president, "I will cut your throat whilst you are sleeping."[134]

> Richard Lawrence was found not guilty by reason of insanity. He was eventually committed to an asylum in Washington. The building was later named St. Elizabeth's Hospital and housed another would-be assassin, John Hinckley Jr.

## 2. ABRAHAM LINCOLN (APRIL 14, 1865)

Mary Todd Lincoln had reason to believe she and her husband were surrounded by enemies. They were. During the course of a four-year war, Washington had swelled from forty thousand people to one hundred thousand, nearly a third of whom were refugees from the battered South. But the danger seemed to have passed with the surrender of the Confederacy's largest army at Appomattox Court House. Later that week, on Good Friday, Mary and her husband attended their favorite playhouse, an establishment they had frequented many times before. In light of the warm occasion, invitations were personally extended to Lt. Gen. U. S. and Julia Grant, to chief of the War Department telegraph office Thomas Eckert, to House Speaker Schuyler Colfax—all of whom declined. Mary

The Presidential Box at Ford's Theatre was photographed shortly after the shooting of Lincoln. Note that the bunting to the right hangs lower, where assassin John Wilkes Booth caught his spur during his leap to the stage and ensuing escape.

then asked Clara Harris, the daughter of a New York senator. She accepted and brought along her fiancée, Maj. Henry Rathbone.[135]

Midway through the play, a dark plot would come to fruition. For months a cadre of Confederate sympathizers had planned to kill the Union heads of state, and the ringleader took it upon himself to remove the chief executive. Slipping into the balcony box, with its four silhouetted occupants, the perpetrator leveled a single-shot derringer at the president's occipital lobe and sent a .44-caliber ball into his brain. Startled by the noise, Mary Lincoln turned to see her husband's head droop forward. A waif of gunpowder entered her nostrils as a knife-wielding man bullied his way between her and her husband. Rathbone attempted to stop the assailant, only to have his arm slashed wide open. The man leaped to the stage and escaped through a backstage door as confusion, then mass terror, swept through the crowded theater.

Taken to a boardinghouse adjacent to the theater, the president died in nine hours. Though Lincoln would never gaze upon another face, he had seen his killer on stage before, in an 1863 production called *The Marble Heart*.

Sadly, the tragedy was not yet done. Rathbone survived his wound and eventually married Clara Harris, only to stab her to death years later. He was committed to an insane asylum, where he died. Mary would enter an asylum as well, soon after the death of her eighteen-year-old son Tad in 1871. Mentally shattered, she was sentenced in large part because of the testimony of her only surviving child, Robert, who stated under oath, "I have no doubt my mother is insane."[136]

---

Robert Todd Lincoln would go on to serve as James Garfield's secretary of war and be present at his shooting in 1881. In 1901, Robert was on his way to see President William McKinley when that president was gunned down. In 1928, his remains were laid to rest in Arlington Cemetery, near the future burial plot of John F. Kennedy.

---

### 3. JAMES A. GARFIELD (JULY 2, 1881)

By the audacity of the act, anyone who tries to murder a president is often assumed to be insane. More than likely, the assumption was correct with thirty-nine-year-old Charles Guiteau. He was of unstable lineage. At least

James Garfield is shot twice from behind by the delusional Charles Guiteau. The president initially believed he would die within minutes. Instead, he lingered for eighty days before succumbing to massive infection.

two cousins and an uncle perished in mental asylums. His abusive father claimed to be immortal. Himself a hyperactive but cerebrally slow child, Guiteau attained four things in adulthood: a dubious law degree, religious fanaticism, an incurable case of syphilis, and the belief that he would one day be president.[137]

His lofty aspirations seemed tangible after the elections of 1880. Guiteau had written a flavorless, wandering speech endorsing Republican candidate James Garfield. He mailed it to the nominee, passed out copies to strangers, and may have once or twice delivered the drowsy lecture to small audiences. When Garfield won, Guiteau believed his little writing caused the outcome, and he expected to be compensated.[138]

Throughout the spring of 1881, he wrote letters, grilled party officials, and pestered White House staff. No one would listen to him. Convinced that Garfield would know who he was, he lined up with other office seekers, met the president in person, and demanded an ambassadorship. When Garfield abruptly rejected him, Guiteau left and bought a .44 snub-nosed revolver. For weeks he stalked Garfield around Washington, waiting for the right moment, reassuring himself that Garfield would be "happier in Paradise."[139]

On July 1, at the Baltimore and Potomac Rail Station, just as the president, his family, and staff prepared to depart the capital for a summer respite, Guiteau approached the entourage from behind and fired. He stepped closer and fired again, just as nearby police and officials subdued him.

Hit in the arm and lower back, Garfield started to vomit profusely.

Between gasps for air, the president calmly surmised the situation—"I am a dead man."[140]

Garfield would never walk again. For eighty days he withered in his White House bed, rallying on occasion and quietly enduring ordered isolation. Though medical schools were beginning to grasp the concept of germ theory, a myriad of doctors repeatedly probed for the bullet using gloveless fingers and unwashed instruments, sometimes reaching a depth of twelve inches with their repetitious, forceful jabs.[141]

After a transfer to New Jersey, where Garfield sought the calming effects of the coastline, infections accelerated. He succumbed two weeks later, in severe pain, at the age of forty-nine. Weeks later, Guiteau was convicted of murder and sentenced to hang. He would be executed almost a year to the day, and quite near the location, of his crime.

---

Charles Guiteau purchased an expensive, ornate revolver for the shooting, assuming that it would be prominently displayed in a museum one day. The weapon has since been lost.

---

### 4.  WILLIAM McKINLEY (SEPTEMBER 6, 1901)

The "progress" of the Industrial Revolution brought newfound miseries for the working poor—tepid slums, morbid factories, child labor, and eighty-hour workweeks. Beneath the new shadows of high-rises coagulated a bog of abject poverty. This growing divide between rich and poor spawned a widespread anarchist movement enunciated by eloquent ide-

President McKinley takes a bullet in the stomach from point-blank range. Ever tender-hearted, the severely wounded McKinley first thought of his ailing wife. He then ordered his guards not to hurt the man who had just shot him.

alists and punctuated by the destitute. The goal was a world without politicians. The means was assassination.

In 1894, an anarchist fatally stabbed the president of France. In 1897, another anarchist shot and killed Spain's premier from point-blank range. In Geneva a jobless man, so poor that he could not afford to buy a knife, fashioned a homemade dagger and drove it into the heart of the empress of Austria. Two years later, an assassin gunned down King Humbert of Italy.[142]

News of King Humbert's murder aroused the imagination of Polish-American Leon Czolgosz, a twenty-eight-year-old unemployed factory worker who had recently experienced a caustic, mood-altering illness. Deeply troubled by American military involvement in the Philippines and the continuous specter of strikes, evictions, and poverty in his adopted country, the young man resolved to kill whom he later called "the enemy of the good working people."[143]

In early September 1901, Czolgosz traveled to the Pan American Exhibition in Buffalo, New York, to confront William McKinley. The president's security detail at the conference included three Secret Service operatives, four Buffalo municipal detectives, eleven members of the U.S. military, and eighteen policemen.

On the afternoon of September 6, after addressing a crowd of thousands on the benefits of international cooperation, McKinley received the general public as people filed through the exhibition's Temple of Music. Standing in line was Czolgosz, his right hand heavily wrapped in a white handkerchief concealing a revolver. As McKinley extended his arm to greet him, Czolgosz blasted two shots into the president's midsection. Assuming he had been fatally wounded, McKinley pleaded to his aides: "My wife. Be careful how you tell her."[144]

Hours later an operation failed to find the bullet, yet the patient emerged relatively free from pain. Days of steady improvement offered hope, until Friday, September 13, when a high fever and acute weakness signaled the onset of gangrene. Early the next morning, McKinley quietly passed away. Six weeks later, having admitted guilt at an abrupt trial, Czolgosz died in the electric chair at New York's Auburn Prison.

Newly promoted Theodore Roosevelt, in his first presidential message to Congress, demanded a halt to all immigrants who were extremely poor and/or illiterate. For the country to survive the wave of terror that claimed McKinley's life, Roosevelt argued, it had to "decrease the sum of ignorance . . . out of which anarchistic sentiment inevitably springs."[145]

To prevent admiring anarchists from stealing the assassin's body, prison officials filled Leon Czolgosz's coffin with quicklime and sulfuric acid.

### 5.   FRANKLIN DELANO ROOSEVELT (FEBRUARY 15, 1933)

President-elect Franklin Roosevelt came to Miami with a landslide victory behind him and troubles innumerable ahead. The already catastrophic Depression appeared to be worsening. Bank failures and property foreclosures continued unabated. World grain production, the foundation of nearly every national economy, had declined by a fourth. Joblessness neared 25 percent in the United States, Japan, and Britain, more than 30 percent in France, and almost 50 percent in Eastern Europe. Representative governments were falling everywhere. Two weeks before Roosevelt traveled to Florida, a xenophobic militarist declared himself dictator in Germany.[146]

Arriving in Miami after a long fishing trip on the Astor family yacht, FDR offered a few words of encouragement to a host of twenty thousand citizens gathered at Bay Front Park. In attendance was Chicago Mayor Anton Cermak, looking to secure the good graces of his party's ascending chief. After FDR spoke from atop the backseat of a stretch convertible, Cermak approached to shake his hand. As the two men spoke, rapid gun-

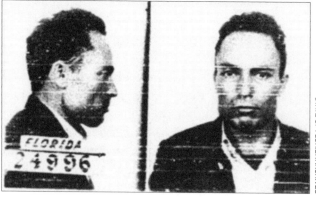

Giuseppe Zangara, an unemployed Italian immigrant, allegedly had a newspaper clipping of the McKinley assassination in his pocket when he attempted to murder Franklin Roosevelt.

STATE OF FLORIDA ARCHIVES

fire rang about them, emanating from the store-bought pistol of Giuseppe Zangara, standing just ten yards away.

Zangara hit five people with five shots, none of whom were Roosevelt. Clearly the most seriously injured was Cermak, and before the convertible could speed away to safety, Roosevelt demanded the mayor be placed in the car and driven to the nearest hospital.

When hearing the assailant was an unemployed bricklayer from Italy, FDR hypothesized that the attack was a mafia hit on Cermak. No such mob connection materialized. Yet Zangara officially became a murderer when the Chicago mayor died from his wounds three weeks later, just two days after FDR's inaugural promise of "the only thing we have to fear is fear itself—nameless, unreasoning, unjustified terror."[147]

By the end of the month, Zangara was dead as well, electrocuted by the state of Florida. He proclaimed to the end, in broken English, to hate the wealthy, the elite, and all presidents.

Though outwardly optimistic about the nation as a whole, FDR viewed his own chances of survival with pragmatic fatalism. He refused any additional security after the shooting, and no one recollected his ever mentioning the incident in Miami ever again.[148]

---

One of the first officials to question Giuseppe Zangara was Roosevelt advisor Raymond Foley, who as a child in 1901, stood very close to William McKinley at the time of the fatal shooting.

---

## 6.  HARRY S TRUMAN (NOVEMBER 1, 1950)

The end of the Second World War unleashed a wave of independence movements as former colonies and protectorates labored to rid themselves of deteriorating bonds. Among them was Puerto Rico, seeking liberation from its meek status as a U.S. territory.

On July 4, 1950, Harry Truman offered a compromise. He signed Public Law 600, which granted the island the rank of commonwealth. Residents could elect their own governor, engage in free trade with the United States, and have a nonvoting representative in Congress. For an ultrapatriotic minority of Puerto Ricans, this was not enough. Only full autonomy would suffice.[149]

Meanwhile, the Trumans sought independence of a different sort. Past

The Blair House housed the Truman family during the White House renovation. To the right stands the guard booth where Leslie Coffelt was mortally wounded during the attempt on Truman's life.

TRUMAN LIBRARY

its 150th birthday, the White House was falling apart, literally. While the building underwent extensive renovations, Harry and his family relocated to the Blair House across Pennsylvania Avenue. Accommodations were pleasant, but security was a concern. All that stood between the president and the public was a latched screen door and a few armed guards.[150]

For Truman, personal security was an afterthought. His base concerns were global in nature—tensions between East and West in Europe, possible entry of Communist China into the Korean conflict, a growing Red Scare at home, and a recent and bloody nationalist uprising in Puerto Rico.

On an unseasonably warm November afternoon, as Truman prepared for a memorial service at Arlington, two well-dressed men approached the Blair House. They were Oscar Collazo and Griselio Torresola, members of the Puerto Rico Independence Movement, who had decided to murder Truman. In their way were three guards posted outside the residence: policemen Donald Birdzell and Joseph Downs and Pvt. Leslie Coffelt.

The two assailants brandished semiautomatic pistols and began firing. First to fall was Coffelt, taking several shots to the chest and abdomen. Birdzell took a bullet to the leg and another to the upper body. Three slugs slammed into Downs, who was guarding the main door. Truman rushed to his second-story window in time to see his men disable Collazo with a shot to the chest, while Coffelt, though mortally wounded, killed Torresola with a shot to the head.[151]

It was over in seconds. Unfazed, Truman commented, "A president has to expect those things." He kept his appointment at Arlington and seemed indifferent to the shootings, until he heard that Coffelt had died, leaving behind a wife and stepdaughter. The president ordered that a plaque be placed on the Blair House to commemorate Coffelt's sacrifice. Days later, speaking to a crowd in his hometown of Independence, a visibly emotional Truman confided, "You can't understand just how a man feels when somebody else dies for him."[152]

The struggle for Europe and Korea continued, as well as for the troubled Caribbean island. Four years after the Blair House incident, four gunmen forced their way into the U.S. House of Representatives, shouting "Long live free Puerto Rico!" and opened fire, wounding five Congressmen.

---

Oscar Collazo was scheduled to be executed in July 1952, but with a week to spare, Truman commuted his sentence to life. Twenty-seven years later, Collazo walked out of prison, pardoned by President James Carter and later decorated by Cuban president Fidel Castro.

---

### 7.  JOHN F. KENNEDY (NOVEMBER 22, 1963)

First lady of Texas Nellie Connally turned to the backseat of the blue 1961 Lincoln Continental and assured her guest, "Mr. Kennedy, you can't say that Dallas doesn't love you." Less than twenty seconds later, Nellie was desperately pulling her severely wounded husband toward her, when she looked up and saw brain tissue splatter the interior of the vehicle.[153]

What followed in Dealey Plaza was utter chaos. Racing engines, screaming sirens, stunned witnesses, crying, shouting, running. Sensing the confusion as he read the incoming bulletins of the unfolding tragedy, an editor at the *New York Times* predicted, "The year 2000 will see men still arguing and writing about the President's death."[154]

Was it a conspiracy? Most certainly not, but the myriad of theories do contain a grain of truth. JFK had enemies, and not just jealous husbands.

The pro-Castro element, including Fidel himself, was less than pleased by the CIA-sponsored Bay of Pigs episode, the removal of Soviet missiles, and multiple CIA attempts to kill *el Presidente*. Conversely, anti-Castro factions had reason to be angry over Kennedy's last-minute stoppage of U.S. air support for the Bay of Pigs invasion, leaving more than a thousand expatriates to be killed or captured on the shores of their lost homeland.

Angry too were organized labor, organized crime, and the mafia, all targets of a painfully diligent U.S. Attorney General's office, led by Bobby Kennedy. The FBI and its bombastic director, J. Edgar Hoover, also loathed the intrusive and controlling Kennedy brothers. Plus, the CIA, military contractors, the Pentagon, and the Saigon government were growing impatient with Kennedy's slow approach to Vietnam. Add the vice president, a heartbeat away from his dream. Also among the accused are the Soviet Union, the Ku Klux Klan, the homosexual and bisexual communities, plus thirty alleged "second gunmen."

But motive does not equal murder. If it did, Kennedy's limousine would have had more holes in it than the conspiracy theories that claim Lee Harvey Oswald wasn't a lone assassin. Sadly, the maladjusted, disturbed former marine, who had failed in everything else he tried in life, happened to be a competent sharpshooter.

Armed with a functioning Mannlicher-Carcano rifle and nested on the sixth floor of the Texas School Book Depository, Oswald landed two of his three steadied shots, and they were not difficult. Elm Street slanted down and away from the building, making the target appear almost motionless from his angle. On the fatal hit, his four-powered scope made his victim look as if he were only twenty-five yards away. And at 12:30 p.m., Oswald found his mark.[155]

If viewed dispassionately, the evidence is overwhelming. A full-scale, bipartisan investigation lasted nearly a year. It questioned more than five hundred witnesses, gathered more than two dozen volumes of evidence and testimony, heard from specialists who performed the autopsy, rela-

Within moments of this photograph, John F. Kennedy was shot in the neck and parietal lobe. Texas Governor John Connally, seated to the front and slightly to the left of Kennedy, was also seriously wounded. Blood and brain tissue splattered mostly forward, indicating the shots came from above and behind the victims.

tives and friends of the chief suspect, ballistics experts, and eyewitnesses who saw the rifle barrel protrude from the sixth-floor window. The gun matched the bullets. The suspect owned the gun. Traces of the suspect and the gun itself were at the crime scene, from which the suspect escaped and killed a police officer. Rarely is a murder investigation ever so irrefutable.

Most damning are the exit wounds of the victims, indicating that the shots came from above and behind. Had the assassin been standing behind the fence on the grassy knoll, in full daylight, near hundreds of witnesses and two dozen cameras, and managed to hit a moving target shielded by street signs and several bystanders, the splatter would not have caked the windshield in front of Nellie Connally, it would have drenched the first lady's face.

It is no crime for the conspiracy theorists to pursue the case further. The hundreds of investigations, books, articles, and documentaries speak volumes about the noble human desire to find absolute truth. But there are times when it is not possible to find logic and reason in a senseless act.[156]

---

Until recently, the Conspiracy Museum operated a block away from Dealey Plaza, adjacent to the Kennedy Memorial. It folded in late 2006, and a sign on the window suggested the museum's closure was part of a conspiracy.

---

## 8.   GERALD R. FORD (SEPTEMBER 5, 1975)

Public acts of terror are recurrent in human history, but they spiked considerably in the late 1960s and early 1970s, spurred in part by the novelty of worldwide television and the global exposure it provided minor players. Eighty-two hijackings occurred globally in 1969, more than all previous years combined. In 1970, attempts were made on the lives of five international leaders. The following year, Palestinian militants murdered the prime minister of Jordan, Bengali rebels sparked a war between India and Pakistan, and separatist violence escalated in Northern Ireland and the Basque region of Spain.

In 1972, shocked by the massacre of eleven Israeli athletes at the Munich Olympiad, President Richard Nixon established the Cabinet Committee to Combat Terrorism, amassing the heads of ten federal

Moments after Lynette "Squeaky" Fromme pointed a gun at President Ford, he was rushed into the California capitol building, where he had just given a speech on social violence and gun control.

departments, including the FBI, Defense Department, and CIA. By 1975, Robert Fearey, the U.S. national coordinator for combating terrorism, surmised that conditions were steadily worsening, noting, "There's even concern that, at some point, terrorists might try using weapons of mass destruction."[157]

The same month of Fearey's dark predictions, President Gerald Ford traveled to Sacramento, California, to give an address in the state capitol on the dangers of rising crime and waning gun control. Waiting for his arrival, with a Colt .45 automatic pistol, was twenty-six-year-old, bright-eyed, auburn-haired Lynette "Squeaky" Fromme, an early and devout follower of cult leader and convicted mass murderer Charles Manson.

As Ford moved through a crowd of well-wishers, Fromme pushed her way toward the president, her disheveled crimson bathrobe and red floral dress almost as conspicuous as her aggressive behavior. Not two feet away from her goal, she raised her pistol and was immediately wrestled down by a Secret Service agent. Operatives rushed Ford into the capitol building and took Fromme into custody, where they discovered her gun was loaded but the chamber was empty.

Whether she truly wished to shoot Ford was never firmly established. Fromme did admit the act was an attempt to help the man she called "our Christ." Through her court trial, Fromme planned to name Charles Manson as a character witness, hoping it would allow him to deliver, via television, his cryptic messages of justice through violence. Her request was rejected, and she was sentenced to life in prison.[158]

Before becoming president, Gerald Ford was a member of the Warren
Commission that investigated the John F. Kennedy murder.

## 9.   GERALD R. FORD (SEPTEMBER 22, 1975)

Once again it would be a woman, and again in California, but this time
the gun would go off. Despite his brush with the Manson family not three
weeks previous, Ford refused to alter his hectic travel schedule, which
had taken him to thirty-nine states in his first thirteen months in office. "I
have no intention to allow the Government of the people to be held
hostage at the point of a gun," said Ford, although he started wearing a
cumbersome bulletproof vest on public outings and allowed a larger contingent of personal bodyguards. Subconsciously, he began to look at
hands before shaking them.[159]

Of all the types Ford might have suspected, the likes of Sara Jane
Moore was probably not among them. Forty-five years old, mother of
four, trained in nursing and accounting, her hobbies included reading,
needlework, and going to the opera. With a submissive countenance and
dozy brunette waves, Moore had the look of a careworn housewife. Her
past, however, was anything but docile.[160]

Estranged from an authoritarian father, she married and divorced five
men, abandoned three of her four children, bounced from job to job, and
became enamored by the radical fringe within San Francisco. Finding

Seventeen days after the first
attempt on his life, a second
would-be assassin stalked Ford.
The photographer caught the
president reacting to the sound
of the gunshot emanating from
the .38 Smith and Wesson of Sara
Jane Moore.

GERALD R. FORD LIBRARY

acceptance within several militant organizations, Moore gained enough access to merit the attention of the FBI.

In 1974, the FBI convinced her to become an informant. Flattered and willing, she accepted. But in her services, Moore began to fear the clandestine government rather than the younger, idealistic people she was encountering. She admitted to a friend her involvement with the FBI and was immediately ostracized by the counterculture community. Hoping to regain their trust, she contemplated shooting Ford, against whom she had no particular animosity. Not a natural-born killer, Moore actually phoned local police, admitting she was thinking of harming the president. Officers interviewed her, confiscated a .44-caliber pistol, and informed the Secret Service of her identity and Bay Area address. In light of her complicity, officials did not consider Moore a threat.[161]

Ford came to San Francisco soon after. One stop included a press conference at the St. Francis Hotel. Standing patiently in a crowd outside was Moore, with a new .38-caliber Smith and Wesson revolver tucked in her purse. Moore later claimed she debated whether to wait for her target or to pick up her son from school. The answer came when Ford walked out of the hotel. Moore brandished her weapon and pulled the hammer back. A bystander knocked her arm astray just as she squeezed off a single round.

Once again, Ford remained relatively unfazed. Interviewed afterward, he pledged to remain accessible to the people, insisting, "If we can't have that opportunity of talking with one another, seeing one another, shaking hands with one another, something has gone wrong with our society."[162]

In rebuttal, the disillusioned Moore offered her own commentary: "There comes a point when the only way you can make a statement is to pick up a gun."[163]

---

Both Lynette Fromme and Sara Jane Moore were sentenced to the federal prison at Alderson, West Virginia, from which both briefly escaped (Moore in 1979 and Fromme in 1987).

---

### 10. RONALD REAGAN (MARCH 30, 1981)

A bulletproof car nearly cost him his life. As Ronald Reagan stepped out of the Washington Hilton Hotel and greeted the small crowd outside, his ten-week stint as chief executive almost came to an abrupt end. In the

Reagan waves to the crowd seconds before John Hinckley Jr. sprays the area with bullets. A ricochet struck Reagan in the chest. Press Secretary James Brady, to the left and behind the president, was hit in the brain and mistakenly reported as dead after the shooting. Brady actually survived but never walked again under his own power.

RONALD REAGAN PRESIDENTIAL LIBRARY

span of two seconds, a sometimes psychiatric patient, John Hinckley Jr., littered the cool gray afternoon with a spray of six bullets. Every shot missed the intended victim—until one struck the right rear panel of the armored limousine, flattened to the size of a dime, ricocheted at a sharp angle, and spun straight into the president's chest.

Rushing to evacuate Reagan from the area, Secret Service agent Jerry Parr shoved him into the waiting car, driving his chest into the transmission hump with such force that Reagan was said to have yelled, "You sonofabitch, you broke my ribs."[164]

Reagan started to cough up a bloody froth, suggesting that a cracked bone had indeed pierced a lung. Quickly examining his charge, Parr noticed a small slit in the president's chest near the left arm and ordered the driver to nearby George Washington Hospital at maximum speed.

Back at the crime scene, officials had thrown down and rapidly disarmed the shooter, while others treated the injured. Agent Tim McCarthy and police officer Thomas Delehanty were seriously wounded. Press Secretary James Brady lay immobile. He had taken a bullet to the brain. National media would soon report that Brady had died.

Blocks away, Reagan walked into the hospital and then collapsed, unable to breathe. He had lost nearly half his blood. The jagged, spent round had lodged within an inch of his seventy-year-old heart.[165]

Remarkably, every one of Hinckley's victims survived. Reagan was in and out of surgery in less than an hour. Brady, however, sustained severe cerebral damage, leaving him confined to a wheelchair for the remainder of his life.

Stories of Reagan's calm demeanor and bright banter while going into surgery (along with less-publicized moments of genuine fear) endeared him to the American public. A rapid recovery also dispelled trepidations of his advanced age, and he experienced a surge of popularity.

Amid all of this was a strange underlying thread of pop culture. Hinckley later confessed he had shot the president, a former actor, in order to impress an actress he had seen in *Taxi Driver*, a film about a misguided would-be assassin.

In spite of his brush with death, Reagan continued to support the sale and ownership of personal firearms, whereas his severely disabled press secretary successfully lobbied for greater gun control, later earning him the Presidential Medal of Freedom from William Clinton.

Seven months after the attempt on Reagan's life, Egyptian president Anwar Sadat was gunned down in Cairo. For security reasons, Reagan refused to have himself or Vice President George Bush attend the funeral. He instead sent former presidents Richard Nixon, James Carter, and Gerald Ford.

# FOREIGN AFFAIRS

## TOP TEN DOCTRINES

Harry Truman was once asked how foreign policy was formed in the federal government. He answered with his typically abrupt candor, "I make foreign policy." Contrary to Truman's assertion, the variables involved in shaping international relations are infinite and ever changing. It is for that very reason presidents create, and their publics prefer, statements clarifying their position. Such pronouncements establish the impression of leadership, a character trait considered vital for presidential and national success. By the twentieth century, these mission statements became known as "doctrines."[1]

Latin for "belief code," a doctrine is usually traced to a particular presidential speech or resolution. Often presented as a sweeping plan for the future, it is always a response to a recent event and aimed squarely at a particular country or ideology. Almost every doctrine has been totally baseless in international law, claiming jurisdiction far beyond the boundaries of the United States.

The fact that most have come from recent administrations is a testament to the growing American presence in every corner of the world—politically, commercially, militarily. And rather than being buried in some secret document or clandestine backroom deal, they acquired their authority through congressional acts and popular appeal. With very few exceptions, the following declarations enjoyed a solid base of support when they were unveiled.

Listed here in chronological order are the most prominent doctrines of administrations past. They reveal a country eager from its infancy to police large portions of the globe. They also attest that presidents have been stalwart in their resolutions but extremely selective in their actions.

## 1.  MONROE DOCTRINE (1823)

James Monroe's seventh annual message to Congress was a rather dreary report, save for a pair of deafening thunderclaps. In a doctrine likely authored by Secretary of State John Quincy Adams, the president issued two clear warnings. First, Europe was not allowed to colonize any part of the Western Hemisphere ever again. Second, any attempt to do so would be considered a direct threat to the security of the United States.

Monroe's audacity came from two principle events—revolution in the Americas and counterrevolution in Europe. By 1822, nearly all of Central and South America had won independence from Spain and Portugal. Meanwhile, the old monarchies had successfully crushed Napoleon Bonaparte and were looking to expand imperial footholds overseas. Britain already held Canada and much of the Caribbean, Russia laid claim to Alaska and much of the Pacific Northwest, France had its French Guyana, and Spain (the biggest loser in the revolutions) wanted to revitalize its fading imperial greatness.

At the time, Monroe had almost no ability to enforce his word. No multinational treaty, summit, or agreement gave him the authority to proclaim hegemony in the region. Militarily, Europe collectively had more than forty times the army and navy he did. Besides, the only immediate threats to U.S. security in the region were buccaneers (in Monroe's tenure alone, American merchant vessels suffered more than two thousand pirate attacks in the Caribbean). But the proclamation contained a democratic air to it, while simultaneously demonstrating American bravado. It made for good print. For later generations, it also made for aggressive policy, as presidents adopted the "Monroe Doctrine" as if it were irrefutable international law. And therein lies its impact, as the primary justification for a litany of questionable endeavors.[2]

James Polk's administration used it to swallow Texas, supposedly to block Britain from taking the territory for itself. Rutherford B. Hayes invoked it in opposition to France's attempt to build a canal across

James Monroe, aided by Secretary of State John Quincy Adams, engineered a doctrine that Americans used for generations to come.

Panama. The doctrine was a cornerstone to William McKinley's declaration of war against Spain in 1898. Woodrow Wilson referred to it when he sent occupation forces into Cuba, the Dominican Republic, Haiti, Mexico, and Panama. Not surprisingly, on the doctrine's one-hundredth birthday in 1923, the American public marked the anniversary as a national holiday.[3]

> Since the establishment of the Monroe Doctrine, the United States has engaged in more than seventy military engagements in Central and South America, ranging from small expeditions to all-out wars. Nicaragua and Panama have seen the most interventions (twenty-two) followed by Mexico (eleven) and Cuba (nine).

## 2. MANIFEST DESTINY (1845)

Some view Manifest Destiny as a glorious demonstration of the pioneer spirit. Others see the process as an act of genocide against millions of Native Americans. Oddly, both extremes commonly fail to recognize that it was, in its base nature, a foreign policy.

Journalist John O'Sullivan coined the phrase in 1845, and the Democratic Party of James Polk took it as its mantra. The sentiment had been in place long before. Several of the original thirteen colonies had no western border, on the assumption their jurisdiction stretched to the end of the continent, wherever that was. After the victorious Revolution, Thomas Jefferson viewed the Republic as "the nest from which all America, North

& South is to be peopled." Providence itself appeared to have ordained the new nation to succeed, to expand as far as geography would allow, from pole to pole eventually. In 1845 it seemed destined. In less than a lifetime, the country had grown 100 percent in land area, 400 percent in population, and 700 percent in economic production. No other nation in the world, including Britain, could match such numbers.

Yet territorial expansion was not a major policy goal among presidents, until James K. Polk made it so in his 1845 inauguration. Standing in a pouring March rain, as thousands listened to his address from the Capitol's East Portico, Polk assured the nation and its neighbors: "Our Union is a confederation of independent States, whose policy is peace with each other and all the world." And then he added his doctrine: "To enlarge its limits is to extend the dominions of peace over additional territories and increasing millions." Ten times he mentioned the annexation of the Republic of Texas, which he misleadingly called a "reunion." Concerning land to the northwest, jointly controlled by the United States and Britain: "Our title to the country of the Oregon is 'clear and unquestionable,' and already are our people preparing to perfect that title by occupying it with their wives and children."

He told his audience that the safety of the United States was in peril, and the only way to ensure national security was to acquire Texas and Oregon—by force, if needed. Like a true expansionist, he argued that Manifest Destiny had now become the responsibility of his earthly government. "It is confidently believed," he shouted, "that our system may be safely extended to the utmost bounds of our territorial limits, and that as it shall be extended the bonds of our Union, so far from being weakened, will become stronger."

> The territory acquired during the four years of the Polk administration was approximately 1.19 million square miles, or greater than the land area of Belgium, Denmark, France, Germany, Great Britain, Holland, Ireland, Italy, Luxembourg, Poland, and Portugal combined.

## 3. THE ROOSEVELT COROLLARY (1904)

In 1901, Theodore Roosevelt wrote to the German ambassador, "If any South American state misbehaves toward any European country let the

European country spank it." He changed his mind two years later, when German gunboats sailed to Venezuela to collect a debt owed by dictator Cipriano Castro, involving a sum of seventy million marks—plus interest. Very publicly, a snide Castro refused to pay. Berlin eventually settled for arbitration, but the potential for more European armadas coming to the New World was too great for Roosevelt to accept.[4]

In December 1904, Roosevelt added a "corollary" to the Monroe Doctrine. He told Congress that if any Central or South American country defaulted on loans in the future, it would "force the United States, however reluctantly, in flagrant cases of such wrong-doing or impotence, to the exercise of an international police power."[5]

As much as Monroe distrusted Europe, TR despised Latin America more. To him, Western Europe was "civilized," while his neighbors to the south were more like spoiled children. The heads of Colombia were the "bandits of Bogota" and "homicidal corruptionists," while in the Dominican Republic, "the successful graspers for governmental power were always pawning ports and custom-houses."[6]

To ensure domestic tranquility, Roosevelt sent an expeditionary force to Santo Domingo in 1905, a nation more than thirty million dollars in debt to European creditors. By 1906 he was sending troops to Cuba in an attempt to stabilize the country (where they would remain for three years). In 1907, the U.S. Navy was heading to Honduras as the country descended into a border war with Nicaragua.

For his "Big Stick" diplomacy, Roosevelt was often accused of wanting to acquire an empire, which he repeatedly denied. When a rumor

As assistant secretary of the navy, Theodore Roosevelt labored intensely to modernize the fleet. As president, he was able to enjoy the fruits of his labor and enforce his policy of aggressive U.S. involvement in Latin America without fear of European interference.

surfaced that the Dominican Republic was his for the taking, TR insisted, "I have about the same desire to annex it as a gored boa constrictor might have to swallow a porcupine wrong-end-to." He also refused to take Cuba, stating, "Emphatically we do not want it," but he added privately that he was "so angry with that infernal little Cuban republic that I would like to wipe its people off the face of the earth."[7]

> In the fight between Theodore Roosevelt and Latin America, the latter may have gotten the last word. During a postpresidential expedition to the Amazon, Roosevelt contracted malaria, from which he never fully recovered.

## 4. TRUMAN DOCTRINE (1947)

Throughout the cold war, much of the American rhetoric in foreign affairs involved the dangers of "losing" countries to communism. The concept originated in the myth that a frail and exhausted Franklin Roosevelt willingly gave up Eastern Europe to Stalin at Yalta. Few bothered to acknowledge that the region was not Roosevelt's to lose; the Red Army had taken it meter by meter from the Third Reich at a cost of twenty-seven million dead.

But historical memory is selective. Rather than a brutal consequence of the Second World War, the Soviet occupation came to be seen as a gradual, subversive, and calculated attempt to take over the world one country at a time (a.k.a "Domino Theory"). Harry Truman established the doctrine that no further "losses" would occur on his watch, and he began

Like much of the photography at the time, Truman saw the world in black and white. In that world, communism was the manifestation of ultimate darkness.

by defending two unstable countries where communist parties were a major part of the political landscape—Greece and Turkey.

In March 1947, Truman requested four hundred million dollars in weapons and financial aid to bolster anticommunist forces in the two nations, but a Republican Congress and a savvy State Department were highly skeptical. The venerable Senator Robert Taft, son of the twenty-seventh president, protested that Truman was aiming to start a war with the Soviet Union. Russian expert and diplomat George Kennan, who initially believed the Soviets to be expansionists, began to view the situation in Europe as more stable than first thought. To win over his opponents, Truman overemphasized the danger, depicting the fall of both countries as imminent and disastrous if American assistance was not forthcoming.[8]

The strategy worked—with consequences. Greece and Turkey received military and economic assistance, but the shock and awe of "us versus them" sermons began to have a profound effect on the U.S. population. While the Soviet hierarchy gave little attention to Truman's dire statements, the American public started to accept the hypothesis as fact. The hyperbole soon grew into obligations on a global scale. After getting involved in the Balkans, the United States established a permanent naval presence in the Mediterranean. Then came the multibillion-dollar Marshall Plan for the rest of Europe. Intervention in Korea followed soon after. Truman also began sending advisors, weapons, and supplies to the French in Indochina. At home, fear of communism also had the unfortunate consequence of making Sen. Joseph McCarthy's accusations of communist infiltration of the U.S. government sound entirely plausible.

> One of the more popular items provided to Greece through the Truman Doctrine was twenty thousand strong and healthy Missouri mules. The United States initially intended them for use as pack animals in mountain warfare. The Greeks preferred to use them to plow their fields.

## 5.  EISENHOWER DOCTRINE (1957)

Ike promised money, men, and materiel for anyone willing to fight communism. "We face a hostile ideology," Eisenhower warned, "global in scope, atheistic in character, ruthless in purpose, and insidious in method. Unhappily the danger it poses promises to be of indefinite duration." By the 1950s, both the GOP and Democrats were beginning to believe that communism was aiming to take over the world. The only question was which political party was going to be more aggressive in fighting it.[9]

Far from the amiable golf addict he was often depicted to be, Eisenhower was a proactive campaigner against any traces of leftist thought. In 1954, he allowed the CIA to stage a coup in Guatemala, ousting progressive Jacobo Arbenz on the grounds that the land reformer was a communist (Arbenz was not a communist, and only four of the fifty-one members of his coalition government were). In 1955, the United States endorsed Ngo Dinh Diem to be the first president of South Vietnam. Diem was autocratic, repressive, and Catholic in a predominantly Buddhist country, but he won American support because he was a fervent anticommunist.

Back in the United States, Ike perpetually spoke of reducing the deficit and directing more money to civilian rather than military projects, but in 1956 nearly 60 percent of the federal budget was going to defense (compared with 45 percent during the Vietnam War and less than 25 percent during the Reagan administration).[10]

By 1957 Eisenhower widened his sights to the Middle East, where he requested two hundred million dollars from Congress to be spent as he saw fit to bolster anticommunist governments. He also insisted on immediate approval of any future deployment of troops to the region. Congress said yes to the money but no to what Senator Hubert Humphrey called "a predated declaration of war."[11]

The U.S. Sixth Fleet eventually did go to the Gulf region, landing fifteen thousand soldiers and marines to establish order in Lebanon. Ike also sent money and arms to Iraq, Israel, Jordan, Libya, and Saudi Arabia in an effort to isolate Egyptian president Gamal Abdel Nassar, whom Eisenhower considered to be a communist. Unfortunately, Eisenhower did not count on internal rivalries destroying what little unity he was able to provide temporarily in the region. By 1959, his doctrine was largely abandoned, but it did establish a strong precedent for U.S. military involvement in the Middle East.

---

In July 1958, the ruling monarchy of Iraq was overthrown by the Iraqi army. Eisenhower believed the coup was directed by Gamal Nassar and carried out by communists, despite the fact U.S. intelligence could find no proof that it was.

## 6.  KENNEDY DOCTRINE (1961)

"Let every nation know, whether it wishes us well or ill, that we shall pay any price, bear any burden, meet any hardship, support any friend, oppose any foe, in order to assure the survival and the success of liberty." No doctrine had ever been so ambitious. In his inaugural address, John F. Kennedy used the words *globe* and *world* no fewer than twelve times. Paradoxically, Soviet premier Nikita Khrushchev delivered an exceptionally similar speech that very same month, promising support for any nation seeking independence.

Kennedy's violent death three years later forever changed the course of American history. It also blurred American memory. He had been elected in 1960 in part because he had presented the Eisenhower administration, and its vice president, as being soft on communism. Often viewed as a compassionate idealist, Kennedy was a hawk of the highest order, a case he made patently obvious at his inauguration, and he maintained a federal budget where 50 percent went straight to the Pentagon. When the Democratic Party honored their fallen leader at the 1964 National Convention, their platform publicly declared some of the great achievements that JFK had made possible over the preceding three years, including a 44 percent increase in tactical fighter squadrons, 45 percent increase in combat-ready army divisions, 150 percent increase in thermonuclear warheads and 200 percent increase in overall megatonnage, and an 800 percent increase in special forces.[12]

Kennedy's dual doctrine of massive nuclear deterrence and multiple ground operations was a natural outgrowth of the preceding administrations,

He ran for office as an ardent anticommunist, and his inaugural address affirmed his oath to fight Marxism anytime, anywhere. After the fiasco of the Bay of Pigs however, Kennedy learned to temper his aggression, relying instead on modest troop buildups and huge nuclear stockpiles to demonstrate American might.

only stated in a brazen display of one-upmanship. His focus on Cuba, resting only ninety miles from the Florida coast, had a historic and geographic legitimacy by way of the Monroe Doctrine. Less defensible was Kennedy's steady escalation in Southeast Asia. The country of most concern was, of course, Laos.

Before Dwight Eisenhower left office, he was entertaining the possibility of invading Laos and reinstating a right-wing government. The nation, according to Ike, could "develop into another Korea," and the surrounding area would then succumb to the domino theory. Notably, in Ike's security briefing to the young president-elect in January 1961, South Vietnam never entered the conversation.[13]

But after the failed Bay of Pigs, Kennedy began to look toward Saigon, and its aggressively anticommunist government, as the best possible opportunity to score a low-cost victory against Moscow and erase the embarrassment of Cuba. A show of force was needed somewhere to prove he had the military chutzpa to back up his doctrine, a pledge he made on his first day on the job.

> Proof that Americans are unpredictable when it comes to foreign policy, Jack Kennedy's public approval rating hit a peak of 83 percent immediately after the failed Bay of Pigs invasion.

## 7. NIXON DOCTRINE (1969)

Richard Nixon campaigned in 1968 on the premise he could bring "peace with honor" to the Vietnam conflict. He failed to do either. But he did implement a new method of battling communism that would become the U.S. modus operandi for the remainder of the cold war.

July 25, 1969—Nixon was in Guam after meeting the returning crew of *Apollo XI*. In a small press conference, he mentioned a change in the way the United States would help friendly nations face external threats. Instead of sending troops, the United States would just send money, ordnance, and equipment. It was up to the nations themselves, he said, to supply the manpower. The idea was not unlike FDR's LEND-LEASE program at the start of the Second World War. "I made only one exception," Nixon stated in his memoirs, "in case a major nuclear power engaged in aggression against one of our allies or friends, I said that we would respond with nuclear weapons."[14]

Many citizens, including Senate majority leader Mike Mansfield, interpreted this to be the Vietnam exit strategy promised by the president. Nixon abruptly corrected them. The doctrine "was not a formula for getting America *out* of Asia," Nixon later wrote, "but one that provided the only sound basis for America's staying *in* and continuing to play a responsible role." He emphasized that point in a nationwide televised address on November 3, 1969, in what became known as his "Great silent majority" speech. The public reaction was overwhelming. Never before had the White House mailroom received so many letters and telegrams—eighty thousand in the course of a few days. Nearly all supported Nixon in full. An ensuing Gallop Poll registered a 77 percent approval rating for the president.[15]

Another four years would pass before troops were withdrawn from Southeast Asia. In the interim, the United States funneled an increasing amount of money and materiel into Saigon. By 1973, most of the weapons, aircraft, and ships in the South Vietnam armed forces were American-made. But all that firepower could not save a government that was, at best, dysfunctional.

Sound policy or not, Nixon applied his doctrine in other areas of the world, especially the Middle East. After the departure of British troops from the region in 1971, the State and Defense departments provided funds and weapons to the kingdom of Saudi Arabia. Also receiving assistance was Mohammed Pahlavi, the shah of Iran, a man whom Nixon had known since 1953. Though possessing a questionable human-rights record, the shah was viewed as a stabilizing force in the region, and he was allowed to purchase the most sophisticated conventional weapons available in the American arsenal.

It was through the Nixon Doctrine that Israel became a close ally to the United States, starting with the 1973 Yom Kippur War. Committing no troops, Nixon instead lobbied Congress to resupply Israel with billions of dollars' worth of tanks, artillery, combat aircraft, and ammunition. Capitol Hill acquiesced, and Israel won the war, turning a relatively distant relationship between Washington and Jerusalem into one of the most diehard alliances on the planet.[16]

---

At one point during the mid-1970s, half of all U.S. arms sales were to the shah of Iran. By the late 1970s, Israel received the majority of exported American arms.

---

## 8.   CARTER DOCTRINE (1980)

In 1903, Lord Lansdowne declared to Parliament, "We should regard the establishment of a naval base or a fortified port in the Persian Gulf by any other Power as a very grave menace to British interests, and we should certainly resist it by all the means at our disposal." In 1980, Jimmy Carter announced in his State of the Union address, "An attempt by any outside force to gain control of the Persian Gulf region will be regarded as an assault on the vital interests of the United States of America, and such an assault will be repelled by any means necessary, including military force."

History does not repeat itself, but human behavior does. President Carter echoed Lord Lansdowne because the United States and the Soviet Union were beginning to assume the role long held by Great Britain and France in the Middle East. For more than a century, the rival Western European superpowers hovered over the precious linchpin to their Asian colonies. For the Eagle and the Bear, the goal was the Middle East itself and its vast reserves of oil.[17]

Only nine months before his forceful doctrine statement (crafted in part by hawkish National Security Advisor Zbigniew Brzezinski), Jimmy Carter had played the peacemaker in the CAMP DAVID ACCORDS. His aggressive change of mind came by way of several unsettling events. In late 1979, Islamic fundamentalists staged terrorist attacks in Saudi Arabia, Ethiopia and Somalia fought a border war, and radical students captured the U.S. Embassy in Teheran. Soon thereafter, the Soviet Union invaded Afghanistan, an act that Carter embellished as "the most serious strategic challenge since the Cold War began."[18]

Strangely, the United States and the USSR failed where Britain and France at least endured. Indicative of the poor logic of the Carter Doctrine, the president found himself struggling against Muslim extremists in Iran and supporting them in the Afghan War, achieving little progress in either pursuit. The Soviets fared worse, losing fifteen thousand soldiers in ten years of miserable occupation of Afghanistan, unable to adapt to the harsh terrain and guerrilla warfare.

---

In protest of the Soviet Union's invasion of Afghanistan, Jimmy Carter mandated that the United States boycott the 1980 Summer Olympics in Moscow, and sixty-four other nations joined the protest. Eighty-one nations still participated, including Afghanistan.

---

### 9.  REAGAN DOCTRINE (1985)

The aged Republican closely mimicked the policy of a youthful Democrat. Though less eloquent, Ronald Reagan's anticommunism was just as intense as Jack Kennedy's. Both claimed, incorrectly, that the Soviet Union held a superior edge in nuclear weapons technology. Both increased defense spending by large margins (11 percent for Jack and 44 percent for Ron in his first three years). They even had their own famous Berlin sound bite—"Ich bin ein Berliner" (1963) and "Mr. Gorbachev, tear down this wall" (1987).

Not well versed in German, Kennedy basically said he was a jellyroll. Rather dim on history, Reagan was unaware that the Berlin Wall was conceived and constructed by the German Democratic Republic, not the Soviet Union.

What they lacked in accuracy, they made up in conviction, and both men were committed to roll back the "red tide" rather than simply contain it. To accomplish this, both looked to weapons of mass destruction to secure the territorial United States, and both relied on small conventional actions to win the fight in the developing world.[19]

The main difference between the two was how they viewed the Central Intelligence Agency. Kennedy lost faith after the CIA's poor performance in the 1961 Bay of Pigs operation. Reagan, in contrast, believed the CIA to be the very best tool to combat communism on the ground, and he ushered in what is known as the "golden age" of covert operations. In June 1980, he indicated—if elected—exactly where he would fight the cold war. In very simple terms, he explained the cause of instability in the world, especially in Central America and Africa. Ignoring the roles of poverty, disease, dictatorships, corruption, and ethnic hatred in the regions, Reagan declared, "Let's not delude ourselves; the Soviet Union underlies all the unrest that is going on." In his 1985 State of the Union address, he emphasized how he would fight: "We must not break faith with those who are risking their lives on every continent from Afghanistan to Nicaragua to defy Soviet-supported aggression and secure rights which have been ours from birth. . . . Support for freedom fighters is self-defense."[20]

To accomplish this, he gave the CIA exceptional latitude in determining who the freedom fighters were and in what ways they could be best assisted. By Reagan's second term, the CIA was involved in granting a combination of funds, weapons, communications equipment, military training, and intelligence to a number of "anticommunist" groups and regimes. Public pressure and the Iran-Contra scandal forced him to reduce activity in Nicaragua, but clandestine activities continued in Afghanistan, Angola, Cambodia, Chad, Ethiopia, Iran, Liberia, Nicaragua, Pakistan, and the Sudan.[21]

---

In 1986, the Reagan administration gave the Islamic Mujahideen of Afghanistan more than five hundred million dollars in weapons and supplies to fight the Soviet invasion. In 1951, the Truman government gave the same amount to rebuild Germany under the Marshall Plan.

---

## 10. BUSH DOCTRINE (2001)

"Allow the President to invade a neighboring nation, whenever he shall deem it necessary to repel an invasion," wrote a beleaguered congressman to a hawkish friend, "and you allow him to make war at pleasure." Representative Abraham Lincoln had no luck in dissuading his associate from backing a preemptive assault on Mexico in 1846. A minority of legislators were just as unsuccessful in trying to stop the invasion of Iraq in 2003.[22]

George W. Bush first justified his doctrine of "first strike" a week after the terror attacks of September 11, 2001. In the Authorization for Use of Military Force, the congressionally approved measure empowered the president to launch offensive operations to "deter and prevent any future acts of terrorism or aggression against the United States." The statute did not define terrorism. Nor did it require anyone but the president to determine what group or country constituted a threat. Public support for the bill was overwhelming, and Bush's approval rating reached 90 percent.[23]

In hindsight, the bill was not intended for use against Afghanistan, the suspected base of operations of the al Qaeda cell that orchestrated the 9/11 suicide missions. That attack had already taken place. In addition, international law already permitted the use of defensive force, so long as an unprovoked assault could be proven as imminent.[24]

In 2002, a year almost to the day, Bush augmented the doctrine with the Authorization for Use of Military Force Against Iraq. Containing false assumptions that Iraq was in possession of weapons of mass destruction and was harboring active terrorists, the joint resolution passed the House of Representatives by a comfortable 296–133 and the Senate by 77–23.

Bush would later add that the main aims of the ensuing offensives in Afghanistan and Iraq were to spread and defend democracy in the Middle East. In this endeavor, Bush was following a long tradition in American foreign policy. McKinley stated a similar goal in Cuba, as did Wilson with Imperial Germany, Truman in Turkey, Kennedy and Johnson in Vietnam, Ford in Angola, Carter in Iran, and Reagan in Nicaragua and Afghanistan. One consistency among all of these operations: they were ultimately unsuccessful.

---

The last time the United States officially declared war on any nation was June 5, 1942 (against Third Reich allies Bulgaria, Hungary, and Romania).

---

## TOP TEN ACHIEVEMENTS IN DIPLOMACY

As head of state, the president is the first citizen, the country's lead representative within the global community. While everyone from congressmen to town councils can claim jurisdiction in domestic affairs, there is the general consensus that it is the president who takes the lead in all things external, and several leaders have made their reputation almost exclusively on what they achieved beyond the borders of the United States.

Remarkably, the Constitution provides few duties and little latitude in international affairs, and any politician who claims to favor a strict interpretation of the document is either bending the truth or has never read article 2: "He shall have Power, by and with the Advice and Consent of the Senate, to make Treaties, provided two thirds of the Senators present concur; and he shall nominate, and by and with the Advice and Consent of the Senate, shall appoint Ambassadors, other public Ministers and

Consuls." Nothing more is said of executive authority in foreign relations, aside from war powers.

Naturally, the vital art of diplomacy demands far more than just creating treaties and making appointments, and through the years the second branch of government has employed a workshop of methods to mend fences and make deals. The most notable of these have gone far beyond the strict limits of article 2, and several have directly infringed upon the Constitution.

The best have brought prosperity when catastrophe seemed inevitable. Collected here in chronological order are the finest achievements in international diplomacy in which presidents were directly involved. They stand as monuments to skillful negotiation, where human reason engineered stability out of turmoil. Poetically, many were initially viewed as minor acts, and a few were dismissed as outright failures.

## 1.   GEORGE WASHINGTON'S ATLANTIC WALL
### PROCLAMATION OF NEUTRALITY (APRIL 22, 1793)

Washington was preparing to begin his second term when he received word that democratic radicals had guillotined the monarch of France. Weeks later, ships from Europe were bringing news of French revolutionaries marching against the royal houses of Austria, Britain, Holland, Prussia, and Spain. In response, Washington ordered an emergency cabinet meeting in Philadelphia. The crisis was clear. Britain was the nation's primary trading partner, but the United States was legally bound to fight alongside France, having signed a treaty of "perpetual friendship and alliance" with them during the American Revolution.[25]

Washington's cabinet and his country were passionately divided. Treasury Secretary Alexander Hamilton and his followers were fond of stable Britain, while Secretary of State Thomas Jefferson and like-minded Republicans backed France. Adding to the crisis, Washington had no Senate to consult. Congress would not be in session for another eight months. As the fighting escalated in Europe and began to lurk westward across the high seas, the president put forth a radical idea of his own: absolute neutrality—no aid to France, no arming of merchant ships, no trade in weapons, not even a foreign legion for either side. His cabinet unanimously agreed.[26]

On April 22, 1793, Washington issued a brief declaration, aimed mostly at his own countrymen, forbidding them from actively taking sides in any way. For this strict and unilateral decision, he was instantly attacked . . . by his own people. Pro-London merchants demanded a crushing blow against the Jacobin uprising. Francophiles accused Washington of abandoning a republic and a loyal ally. Both sides contended he had no constitutional authority to declare neutrality, just as he had no right to declare war.[27]

Deeply hurt by his assailants, the aging and exhausted Washington began to vent his anger through spontaneous rages. Secretary of War Henry Knox started to worry for the man's health. "He had rather be on his farm than be emperor of the world," said Knox, "and yet they were charging him with wanting to be a king." Thomas Jefferson was less sympathetic, suggesting the soon-to-retire president was "fortunate to get off just as the bubble is bursting, leaving others to hold the bag."[28]

But in establishing the precedent of neutrality, the reluctant warrior gave his infantile nation precious time to mature, to build its tiny army, to allow its commerce to take root, and to keep redcoats and radicals from once again battling on his continent. Though widely hated, the plan worked. Not until 1812 would the United States openly enter into a war. By then, its fledgling navy was strong enough to fight on its own. But as Washington predicted, the consequences of fighting Europe again were brutal.

---

Due to the unpopularity of the Neutrality Proclamation, Vice President John Adams requested weapons from the War Department to protect his own house.

---

## 2. THOMAS JEFFERSON'S "EMPIRE FOR LIBERTY"
LOUISIANA PURCHASE (OCTOBER 20, 1803)

It was the very definition of diplomatic success—going from the brink of war with Napoleon Bonaparte to peacefully doubling the size of one's own country for a measly three cents an acre. To be sure, Thomas Jefferson benefited immensely from extenuating circumstances. But he knew when to suspend his ideals in the face of a great opportunity, one so massive that even his great mind could barely imagine its consequences.

The heart of the matter was New Orleans. Without it, the Mississippi River was simply the West Coast of the United States from which no vessel

Cost of the Louisiana Purchase: three cents an acre.
Budget for the Lewis and Clark expedition into the territory: $2,500.
Avoiding war with Napoleonic France: Très bien.

could sail. Jefferson was entering his first term as president when he learned that the delta, previously owned by a rather agreeable Spain, had been secretly ceded to France and its thirty-two-year-old dictator, Napoleon Bonaparte.

On the verge of panic, Jefferson and Secretary of State James Madison contemplated an alliance with Britain and a declaration of war against France. A quick strike might take New Orleans before the French generalissimo could establish a foothold.[29]

Unbeknownst to the president and his secretary, Napoleon had already rethought his plans for the Americas. In 1801, he had sent a seemingly insurmountable twenty-thousand-man army to destroy an uprising in Saint Domingue (Santo Domingo), his one major staging area in the Caribbean. Within a year, his grand army was down to four thousand survivors, the rest having died from rebel attacks and yellow fever.

In contrast, the war option was still open for Jefferson when he instructed his emissary in France, Robert Livingston, to offer a buyout of the mouth of the Mississippi, plus any land on the Gulf Coast that France might be willing to sell for two million dollars. When negotiations stalled, Jefferson sent his close friend James Monroe to Paris on orders to threaten the French with an Anglo-American alliance if they did not cooperate. Surprising them all, the beleaguered Napoleon offered all of the Louisiana Territory, a massive and largely unknown expanse more than three times the size of France itself, for fifteen million dollars.[30]

Quite suddenly, Jefferson had inherited a wonderful problem. He had always been the champion of small government, the elimination of the national debt, and a strict interpretation of the Constitution. But to accept the offer would nearly double the federal debt, and he had no executive authority whatsoever to acquire territories. Yet to reject the offer would mean letting go of the greatest land deal in history. Fortunately for Jefferson, his emissaries had already agreed to the proposal, leaving to their president the awkward task of explaining the greatness of the deal to the American public and begging Congress for the phenomenal sum to cover the balance.[31]

Opposition was strong, but in the minority. Critics openly questioned the expense and the presidential right to make such a decision. Jefferson himself never stopped wondering if what he had done was legal. But the end result turned the United States from a coastal plot to a continental presence. Ever the democratic philosopher, Jefferson eventually rationalized the purchase on the grounds that it would serve as a great leap forward for representative government, step one in what he hoped would become an "empire for liberty."[32]

---

The treaty that secured the Louisiana Purchase did not specify the exact land area involved. Jefferson and Madison assumed that the deal also included the territory of Florida, until the ruling government of Spain eventually informed them otherwise.

---

## 3.  THEODORE ROOSEVELT'S CONTINENTAL DIVIDE
### PANAMA CANAL (1903–14)

"By far the most important action I took in foreign affairs during the time I was President," figured Theodore Roosevelt, "related to the Panama Canal. Here again there was much accusation about my having acted in an unconstitutional manner, a position which can be upheld only if Jefferson's action in acquiring Louisiana can also be treated as unconstitutional." Roosevelt's defensive tone stemmed from accusations that he had violated Colombia's sovereignty and abused his authority as commander in chief. But as far as Roosevelt was concerned, it was a crime against humanity to stand in the way of progress.[33]

Since the 1500s, European powers had dreamed of slicing the narrow isthmus connecting North and South America. A canal would cut voyages by as much as eight thousand miles and spare sailors the treacherous journey around "the Horn," where the incompatible Atlantic and Pacific churned against Argentina's Antarctic tail.

The two possible canal routes were across the wider but flatter Nicaragua or up and over the narrower but higher ridge of Panama. In the late 1800s, a French company tried slicing through Nicaragua, only to make minimal progress at the cost of more than twenty thousand dead employees, mostly from yellow fever and malaria.

The Colombian province of Panama was the only viable option in Roosevelt's view, and the United States was the only country capable of accomplishing the task. Seeking total control of the project, he offered Bogotá millions of dollars for a right-of-way through their northern region. Though wracked by corruption, poverty, and civil wars, the Colombian government refused to cooperate with Roosevelt. Well known for his contempt for Latin America as a whole, he denounced the Colombians as "impotent" and a "lot of jackrabbits." He contemplated invading the country and taking the isthmus by force.[34]

On November 3, 1903, the people of Panama did the work for him, staging an independence movement against a government they had long seen as repressive. Roosevelt wasted no time in giving them assistance, ordering the gunboat USS *Nashville* to the eastern coast of Panama to protect "American interests" in the area. Other vessels from the U.S. fleet were soon on their way. The Panamanians achieved victory in two days, and within hours, the White House was calling for de facto recognition of the new nation. Days later, the Republican-led Senate granted full diplomatic recognition.

An ensuing treaty gave the United States authority over a "Canal Zone" ten miles wide through the heart of the small country, for which Panama was to receive $10 million in gold plus $250,000 yearly rent. The French company that owned building rights in the region collected a cool $40 million. The Bogotá government received nothing, a point that satisfied Roosevelt immensely.

Predictably, Colombia was infuriated, but many Americans were equally appalled. The *New York Evening Post* called the acquisition of the Canal Zone "a vulgar and mercenary venture." Others feared the creation of an American empire, recalling the very recent and violent subjugations of Hawaii and the Philippines. Congress, including Republicans sympathetic to Roosevelt, believed he had grossly overstepped his authority, and many suspected he had secretly staged the Panamanian revolt. Democrats vowed to block the canal treaty with Panama, but to no avail.[35]

In the end, Congress capitulated because the public widely favored an American-built, American-controlled corridor through the continents. For the public and their president, the incalculable benefits to trade and naval power easily outweighed concerns over Colombian dignity and constitutional particulars. On February 23, 1904, the Senate ratified the agreement between Washington and Panama City, and the digging began.

---

In 1906, Theodore Roosevelt became the first sitting president to visit a foreign country when he traveled to Panama. While inspecting the canal dig in person, he decided to help the laborers by operating one of the steam shovels for a while.

---

### 4.  FRANKLIN ROOSEVELT'S ARSENAL OF DEMOCRACY
LEND-LEASE (MARCH 11, 1941)

By Christmas 1940, only Britain remained standing. The rest of Europe was either neutral or under the double yoke of Nazi Germany and the Soviet Union. Poland and France had fallen in six weeks, Norway in a month, Holland and the Baltic States in a week, Denmark in a day. Meanwhile, the empire of Japan had already gored Manchuria and was winding its way down the China coast.

Contrary to popular belief, Franklin Roosevelt was not eager to throw his country into the conflagration, especially on behalf of a China run by

The genius of Lend-Lease was that badly needed supplies—not American lives—were risked to aid the British and Russians in the war against Germany. This M4 Sherman tank was one of thousands that British tankers used to protect Middle East oil fields.

warlords and a Britain concerned with saving its own empire. The president well remembered the consequences of serving an ungrateful Europe in the First World War and losing 110,000 Americans and billions of dollars in defaulted loans in the process. But by 1940 the price of neutrality was overbearing. Trade partners and friendly nations were collapsing one by one, prolonging the interminable Great Depression. The question arose, how to save the world without sacrificing the country.

While Congress was in Christmas recess, Roosevelt used his last "fireside chat" of the year to offer a solution. He proposed to provide Britain and others with the weapons and materiel required to fight—guns, warships, transports, tanks. When the war was over, repayment would be made in kind. The nation was to become "the great arsenal of democracy," the economy would prosper, and the world could dutifully defend itself.

The response was overwhelming. Cables, calls, and letters poured into the White House, more than Roosevelt had ever received in his career. Nearly every correspondence expressed total approval and support. When an isolationist Congress reconvened, Roosevelt presented them with the Lend-Lease program, technically in violation of U.S. neutrality laws, but already too popular to stop.[36]

During the course of the war, United States provided over $50 billion in goods and services to forty countries (equivalent to $850 billion in 2008 dollars), most of it in the way of food and fuel. Britain received nearly half. The Soviet Union, joining the Allies later in 1941, received a quarter, amounting to about 7 percent of what the Soviets produced on their own. Third and fourth in line were Free France and Nationalist China.

The greatest beneficiary was the United States, which injected its economy with much needed funding, collected concessions from its partners, ramped its industry toward a war footing, and kept the country out of the conflict for a year. Lend-Lease also established a sense of cooperation among the Allies, replacing the bitter cycle of suspicion that prevailed during the Great War. Roosevelt would rightly look back at the program as one of the finest accomplishments of his presidency, and he ranked his "Arsenal for Democracy" address among the best speeches he ever made.[37]

---

At the end of the war, the Soviet Union disputed how much it owed the United States for Lend-Lease and did not agree to a payment settlement until 1990.

---

## 5.  HARRY TRUMAN'S WESTERN WALL
### NORTH ATLANTIC TREATY ORGANIZATION (APRIL 4, 1949)

Ideally, the Soviet Union and the United States would have withdrawn completely from Europe after World War II. But there is something about global war that tends to dent people's faith in one another. In hindsight, the best solution was a long waiting period, where neither side had to give up a meter of ground. The entity that made it possible was referred to as the Iron Curtain, and contrary to popular perception, its first solid manifestation was American-made.

Created six years before the Warsaw Pact and twelve years before the Berlin Wall, the North Atlantic Treaty Organization was born out of fear. But it had the unforeseen benefit of allowing Western Europe and the United States to move forward, away from the question of how to make peace with either Germany or Josef Stalin, and toward a military, political, and economic partnership that has lasted to this day.

Selling this idea to the American public was not an easy task for Harry Truman. Despite a record debt, he had already requested four hundred million dollars for the defense of Greece and Turkey under his TRUMAN DOCTRINE and billions more for the controversial Marshall Plan. Now he was asking the United States to enter into its first military alliance in 150 years, an agreement that effectively obligated the country to help Western Europe if and when it was attacked again. Once more, such an alliance challenged the authority of Congress to declare war.

Truman, who was not above stretching the Constitution "when emergencies or opportunities demand that it be stretched," assured Capitol Hill that the treaty allowed the legislature to maintain its authority, as the alliance asked for each country to come to one another's defense "as it deems necessary." He added that the only way to prevent another European war and to revitalize the American economy was through the close cooperation of its strongest allies.[38]

Fortunately for Harry, the Soviet Union obliged in playing the role of the imminent threat. Relenting on their promise to permit free elections in Poland in 1947, supporting a communist takeover in Czechoslovakia in 1948, and blockading Berlin later that year, the "Red Menace" gradually assumed the specter of an expansionist system, one that Truman painted as more dangerous than the recently deceased Third Reich.

Truman and his first NATO commander, Dwight David Eisenhower, confer over the particulars of the largest military alliance since World War II. By the time Truman left office, NATO consisted of fourteen member states. President Eisenhower would add a fifteenth in 1955—a sovereign and rearmed West Germany.

EISENHOWER LIBRARY

In 1949, Congress relented, and the United States formally joined Belgium, Britain, Canada, Denmark, France, Holland, Iceland, Italy, Luxembourg, Norway, and Portugal in a union of mutual security. In 1952, traditional rivals Greece and Turkey signed on as well. In 1955, West Germany formally joined, allowing the strongest economic force to bolster an already formidable conglomeration.

Over time, NATO proved to be a balancing force in a most uneasy era. In forty-five years, Europe was the only cold war theater where peace prevailed. Wars of ideology exploded in Africa, Asia, and South America, some of which devoured millions of lives. But the continent that had been the birthplace of the two deadliest wars in human history remained stable throughout. In celebrating the treaty's fortieth anniversary, President George H. W. Bush would rightfully proclaim the alliance to be the "second Renaissance of Europe."[39]

---

Established in 1949, NATO did not participate in a hostile engagement until 1994, when it fought against Serbian forces in the Bosnian War.

---

### 6. JOHN F. KENNEDY POSTPONES ARMAGEDDON
CUBAN MISSILE CRISIS (OCTOBER 14–28, 1962)

In the radioactive game of brinkmanship, Kennedy had the upper hand. Stationed in the NATO-member states of Italy and Turkey were a total of forty-five Jupiters, American intermediate-range missiles aimed directly at the Soviet Union. By March 1962, they were operational. Atop each was a nuclear warhead one hundred times more powerful that the uranium device detonated over Hiroshima.[40]

These missiles were hardly a mystery to Soviet intelligence. The dilemma for Moscow was having no viable equivalent. For all intents and purposes, the United States was out of range, and the only possible launch pad was the pro-Soviet island of Cuba. Accordingly, and without much foresight, Moscow shipped sixteen SS-4 medium-range nuclear missiles to Cuba in the summer of 1962. Twenty more were on the way, each capable of hitting Dallas or Washington, D.C. Also en route were sixteen SS-5 intermediates, all of which could strike any of the contiguous forty-eight states.[41]

On October 14, a U.S. spy plane photographed suspicious construction and equipment in the jungles of Cuba. Two days later, the Kennedy administration viewed the confirmed images of SS-4 missiles under assembly. If allowed to become operational, the rockets could hit the very city in which they were standing. The options were to bomb the sites, invade, or do nothing. The Joint Chiefs advised invasion. The president chose a fourth option, endorsed by Defense Secretary Robert McNamara and Attorney General Robert Kennedy. The U.S. Navy would stage a "quarantine" of incoming ships to Cuba (to call it a "blockade" was technically an act of war).

From that point onward, any number of events could have resulted in a rapid, catastrophic escalation. Communications were slow, sometimes taking hours for messages to be sent and received through antiquated means. Most ships respected the quarantine, but not all. A

To support U.S. claims, Ambassador Adlai E. Stevenson presented photographic evidence of ballistic missile installations in Cuba to the UN Security Council.

Soviet attack sub was discovered a few miles from the Florida coast. At least sixteen SS-4s went on line. Ten days into the standoff, a U-2 plane was shot down. Kennedy himself began to see invasion as his only option but allowed secret negotiations more time. Along with the missiles, the Soviets were also sending cruisers, destroyers, tanks, infantry regiments, artillery brigades, MIG fighters, nuclear bombers, and nuclear submarines. McNamara personally wondered if he would be alive the following week.[42]

To their credit, both Kennedy and Khrushchev eventually realized that the situation was largely a crisis of their own making, and on October 28, they readily accepted the first opportunity to resolve the situation. In exchange of U.S. pledges to end the quarantine, remove its fifteen missiles in Turkey, and never invade Cuba, the Soviets would remove all missiles and personnel from the island. Perhaps greater than the solution itself was the immediacy with which it was announced, virtually eliminating the risk of accident or rogue aggression from either side.

As with most diplomatic solutions, this deescalation had its critics. Even after the worst had passed, there were military figures in Cuba, the Soviet Union, and the United States calling for offensive operations. The withdrawal was a key reason for Khrushchev's downfall two years later, and Kennedy's pledge on Cuba made him look "soft on communism." But in their careful resistance to armed aggression, both Kennedy and Khrushchev spared at least several thousand lives, and at best prevented a possible war of global proportions.[43]

---

During the Cuban Missile Crisis, the U.S. Armed Forces went on DEFCON 2, the second highest level of Defense Readiness Condition, for the first and only time during the cold war. DEFCON 1 authorizes the use of nuclear weapons.

---

## 7.  RICHARD NIXON'S "JOURNEY FOR PEACE"
### COMMUNIST CHINA (FEBRUARY 21–28, 1972)

Nixon equated domestic programs with "building outhouses in Peoria," but he loved the intrigue of global affairs. Chairman of the Joint Chiefs, Adm. Thomas Moorer observed, "Once the president was very involved with Watergate, he would sit at the NSC meetings apparently in heavy

President and Mrs. Nixon mug for the cameras on the Ba Da Ling section of the Great Wall. While public events included several banquets, cultural exhibitions, and a tour of the Forbidden City, secret meetings covered hypersensitive subjects such as Taiwan and Vietnam.

thought until someone mentioned foreign policy, and it was just like giving him a needle; he would spark right up."[44]

His biggest hit came when he bridged the chasm between the United States and the most populous nation on earth, two countries that had been thoroughly estranged from one another for more than twenty years. To Americans, China was the great "lost" world, the stalwart ally against Japan in World War II, stolen away by communists in 1949. Mao Zedong's brutal Cultural Revolution of the late 1960s only cemented the specter of a ruthless system. To the Chinese, the United States was the worst of all enemies, an imperial power perched and ready to strike the People's Republic from bases in Okinawa, Japan, South Korea, and Taiwan. The United States was already bombing the living daylights out of Cambodia, Laos, and Vietnam.[45]

But China and America had a common foe in the Soviet Union, whom they both suspected of wanting to take over the world. For more than two years Nixon quietly investigated whether Red China might be open to a bilateral meeting. In secret negotiations conducted through Pakistan and Romania, the desired answer finally arrived in early 1971—Nixon was welcome to visit Peking (Beijing).[46]

News of his impending trip stunned the American public. No sitting president had ever visited China. But many quickly reasoned that only an anticommunist could politically make such a move, and most were supportive of the trip. Like their president, the public was curious but cautious. Plans were finalized for February 1972, and upon his departure, Nixon said he hoped the trip would become a "journey for peace."[47]

The weeklong agenda was feverishly eager—lavish dinners, theater productions, a tour of the Great Wall, and most significantly, several high-level meetings. Nixon met with the aging and sickly Mao Zedong shortly after he arrived. It was to be their only encounter during the trip. They spoke for about an hour, spending most of the time complimenting each other and belittling themselves.

The pivotal discussions were with Premier Zhou Enlai. Topics ranged from Sino-Indian relations to the status of Korean War POWs. Both sides were thoroughly grateful for the experience, but they were unwilling and unable to make any major commitments. On Vietnam, Zhou hinted China would never militarily intervene, but he refused to mediate a peace between North and South. Concerning Taiwan, Nixon expressed a belief that there should be "one China," but he was vague on whether it should be nationalist or communist. They mentioned the possibility of normalized relations, but full diplomatic recognition would not come for several years.[48]

The journey was a triumph nonetheless. The United States began to allow open travel to mainland China, and rudimentary trade agreements followed. The Soviet Union, fearing a Sino-American alliance, warmed to the idea of détente and invited Nixon to Moscow. By 1979, Beijing and Washington were exchanging ambassadors.

> Nixon's China trip led to the creation of a U.S. Liaison Office in Beijing. In 1973 David Bruce became the first American emissary to the People's Republic. He was succeeded the following year by George H. W. Bush.

## 8.  JIMMY CARTER TAMES A BLOODFEUD
### CAMP DAVID ACCORDS (SEPTEMBER 5–17, 1978)

The Arab-Israeli War of 1948, the Suez Crisis in1956, the Six-Day War of 1967, the War of Attrition from 1967 to 1970, the Yom Kippur War in 1973—those who claimed Israel was a stabilizing element in the Middle East were not checking the scoreboard. Many American presidents tried to establish some semblance of lasting peace between any Arab state and the Jewish homeland. None succeeded until Jimmy Carter all but forced it upon Egypt and Israel in the autumn of 1978.

Carter's initial plan was to invite Egyptian president Anwar Sadat and Israeli prime minister Menachem Begin to Camp David for calm discussions on Palestine, mutual diplomatic recognition, and a possible peace treaty. The optimistic Democrat was working on a number of false assumptions, primarily that such painful and divisive topics could ever be calmly discussed between Israel and its most powerful enemy. He also believed his close friendship with Sadat would encourage Begin to be more cooperative. Plus, the placid woodland setting was supposed to put both parties at ease.[49]

As the three first sat down, it was immediately clear that Carter had guessed wrong on everything. Sadat and Begin despised each other on a personal level. The Egyptian leader worsened the situation by demanding that Israel surrender all occupied lands in Gaza and the West Bank, pay reparations for past wars, and compensate refugees for their lost homes. Begin calmly informed both gentlemen that he had no desire to agree to anything, and he abruptly retired to his cabin.[50]

After two days and no progress, Carter started meeting with each side separately and invited Secretary of State Cyrus Vance to try his hand with other officials in attendance. A week passed, and Sadat eased his stance on Palestine, asking instead for Israeli withdrawal from the Sinai Peninsula. Nothing was achieved, and the camp's total isolation began to wear on the visitors. Sadat and his staff were packing their bags, threatening to leave, when Carter finally lost his temper.

The former naval officer warned his friend that leaving would do more than end their friendship, it would mean the end of U.S.–Egyptian relations. Carter then proceeded to threaten Begin. If the prime minister did not agree to some meaningful breakthrough, Carter would tell the

Carter threatened his old friend Anwar Sadat to either cooperate with Israel or lose all American support for the foreseeable future.

world media how Israel sabotaged the entire summit by refusing to negotiate. The tantrum worked.[51]

In return for U.S. assistance in building new airfields, Israel agreed to withdraw from the Sinai, and the adversaries pledged to sign a peace treaty with each other. The following year, they fulfilled that promise.

Though both Sadat and Begin were roundly criticized by their own people for capitulating too much to a longtime enemy, their relations with the United States stabilized thereafter, and the two nations have not directly fought each other ever since.[52]

---

In spite of their obstinate behavior at Camp David, both Anwar Sadat and Menachem Begin were awarded the Nobel Peace Prize in 1978.

---

## 9.   RONALD REAGAN'S BEST FAILURE
### REYKJAVÍK SUMMIT (OCTOBER 11–12, 1986)

Contrary to conservative belief, Ronald Reagan did not defeat the Soviet Union. As his former Secretary of State Alexander Haig noted, "For us to consider that standing tall in Granada, or building Star Wars, brought the Russians to their knees is a distortion of historic reality." Credit instead goes to resistance movements in Eastern Europe, the dual tragedies of the Afghan War and Chernobyl, and what Haig called "the internal contradictions of Marxism."[53]

What Reagan achieved instead, with the help of Soviet general secretary Mikhail Gorbachev, was a monumental reversal in the nuclear

Tense body language between Soviet premier Mikhail Gorbachev and President Reagan at Reykjavik reflected their nervousness as they changed history

arms race. It started at a meeting that was not supposed to take place, through an agreement that was initially perceived as a great failure by both sides.

Reagan and Gorbachev held their first summit in Geneva in 1985. To the surprise of their advisors, the two cold warriors got along relatively well. The Gipper liked this new type of Soviet leader, more open to dialogue than the traditional Politburo cronies. The Soviet leader was initially taken aback by Reagan's old-fashioned patriotism, but he quickly appreciated the president's sincere nature. A Soviet official observed, "Gorbachev respected Reagan, although he had some misgivings about Reagan's intellectual capacities."[54]

Based on their amicable encounter, another summit was scheduled for Washington. In light of what was destined to be a more substantive exchange, Gorbachev suggested a preparatory meeting to set the agenda. Reagan agreed. In October 1986, the leaders met in Reykjavik, Iceland. Reagan pushed for discussions on a wide range of topics. The Russian wanted to focus purely on arms control, as both nations were spending inordinate billions on nuclear weapons. Gorbachev was also concerned about Reagan's proposed Strategic Defense Initiative, a spaced-based missile-killing system dubbed "Star Wars," which threatened to create an arms race on earth and in space.

The two bickered back and forth, and it looked as if the Washington summit was never going to happen. In a moment of exasperation, Gorbachev offered to do away with all ballistic missiles. To the Russian's amazement, Reagan readily agreed. The only roadblock was SDI. Reagan refused to surrender what he believed was the ultimate missile shield. Gorbachev viewed the system as a surefire way for one country to win a nuclear war. Regrettably, both sides were unaware that the program was financially infeasible and technologically impossible. The two left Iceland despondent, lamenting to their constituents "what might have been" had the other side relinquished.[55]

They did not yet realize the monumental turning point they had reached. Previous arms-control agreements only slowed the progression of nuclear arsenals. This impromptu meeting revealed that both sides had lost their faith in the security of weapons of mass destruction. Reykjavik led directly to the Intermediate-Range Nuclear Forces Treaty in 1987, the first agreement of its kind, eliminating an entire class of weapons. The treaty also allowed each side to monitor the destruction of existing missiles on site, a major concession unthinkable in earlier years.

Numerically, the INF Treaty itself involved less than 5 percent of total stockpiles, but it did herald a string of unilateral reductions and program cancellations from then on. Looking back, State Department veteran Rozanne Ridgeway acknowledged what had been attained in a small and initially disappointing encounter: "Reykjavik, in nuclear history, must be seen as the two days in which the world stopped building up nuclear weapons . . . that was the mountain we were climbing. At Reykjavik, we got to the top and started down. To this day, that is not well appreciated."[56]

---

At their peak during the 1980s, the Unites States and the Soviet Union owned approximately eighty thousand nuclear weapons altogether, ranging from artillery shells to missile warheads. In 2008 the combined total is closer to twenty-five thousand.

---

## 10. GEORGE H. W. BUSH ENDS THE COLD WAR
### THE FOUR-POWER TREATY ON GERMANY (SEPTEMBER 12, 1990)

The Soviet Union was on the verge of collapse, and a divided Germany openly professed a desire for reunification. For older generations, a resurgent Fatherland did not exactly invoke the warmest memories. Several prominent leaders—including Soviet general secretary Mikhail Gorbachev, British prime minister Margaret Thatcher, and French president François Mitterrand—were hesitant to help Berlin regain its prominence. More important, countless Russians, Poles, Ukrainians, and not a small number of Jews were adamantly opposed to a reunified Germany, a nation that had cost them millions of lives barely a lifetime ago. But the chance of anything happening soon was remote. The Soviet Union still possessed twelve thousand nuclear warheads and posted nearly four hundred thousand troops in East Germany, and the Berlin Wall still stood firmly in place.[57]

During a European tour in 1989 commemorating the fortieth anniversary of NATO, George H. W. Bush departed from his normally cautious way of doing business and announced to Europe that it was time to grow up. Before a large crowd in Mainz, West Germany, the hometown of Chancellor Helmut Kohl, the president told his audience and the world:

"The Cold War began with the division of Europe. It can only end when Europe is whole." The United States was going to spearhead an immediate reunification, not only of Germany, but of the entire continent. To the worried populations east and west, Bush simply concluded, "The world has waited long enough."[58]

Under the advice of his brilliant secretary of state, James Baker III, Bush proposed "Two Plus Four" negotiations, bringing together East and West Germany plus Britain, France, the Soviet Union, and the United States to determine how to finally bury the fears of the past. Under the forceful direction of the U.S. State Department, and Bush's demand for measurable progress, age-old rivals soon established a common understanding.

The parties agreed that if a unified Germany were to exist, it must vow to never expand beyond its existing borders, its armed forces were to be downsized, and the country was to never possess weapons of mass destruction. In turn, Britain, France, and the United States were to reduce their troops in the country by no less than 20 percent, and the Soviet Union was to remove all of its occupational army by 1994.

On September 12, 1990, barely sixteen months after Bush initiated the idea, foreign ministers from each of the six countries signed the Treaty on the Final Settlement with Respect to Germany, effectively ending both World War II and the cold war. As Helmut Kohl celebrated the reunification of a sovereign and peaceful Germany and the first steps toward true reconciliation among the major powers, he showered praise foremost upon the United States "and above all President Bush."[59]

---

Upon George H. W. Bush's insistence, the former East Germany was removed from the Warsaw Pact and incorporated into NATO. Four months later, Czechoslovakia, Hungary, and Poland announced they were leaving the pact as well, and the once-feared communist alliance folded within a year.

---

## TOP TEN MOST SUCCESSFUL
## COMMANDERS IN CHIEF

As far as fighting goes, Uncle Sam is proficient. In his first bout, he beat an empire, and he went undefeated in the next twenty major contests to follow. When he experienced defeat in Southeast Asia, by decision, his supporters feared that it would force his retirement. Yet fifteen years after that particular setback, the United States became the undisputed heavyweight champion of the world. Today he's a bit tired, a little pudgy, and worn from sparring, but he is still the champ.

Well-beaten metaphors aside, there are certain elements that make the United States an ideal fighting force. Geographically, the nation is in an ideal location, bordered by two relatively benevolent neighbors and buffered by two immense oceans. A multitude of natural ports lace both coasts, and its interior holds enormous mineral deposits. It has self-sustaining food production and self-replicating cheap labor. And all of it stands under a highly centralized popular government.

Armed with these riches, the country has fared well in war, and nearly every chief executive has presided over a military operation at home or abroad. In total, American forces have participated in more than two hundred military operations, from modest flotillas pressuring isolationist Japan during Millard Fillmore's presidency, to massive armies, armadas, and bombers crushing Imperial Japan during Franklin Roosevelt's time.

Worried that the nation would become fond of fighting, James Madison cautiously observed, "It is in war, finally, that laurels are to be gathered, and it is the executive brow that they are to encircle." As both a veteran and a politician, Madison knew that it was terribly easy, and incorrect, to credit the president alone for any military outcome. But the title of commander in chief does entail final responsibility for actions taken by the armed forces. Following are the most accomplished among them, ranked by the relative strength of their opponents, the scope of war aims achieved, and the extent to which they were able to limit losses. They are listed with their most successful military endeavor.[60]

## 1.  FRANKLIN D. ROOSEVELT
### SECOND WORLD WAR (1941–45)

In accepting his party's nomination for the 1936 presidential race, Franklin Roosevelt offered an unintentional vision of things to come. "This generation of Americans has a rendezvous with destiny," he said. A standard platitude, but on this occasion, neither the incumbent nor his listeners had any idea how correct he would be. The following year, a virus of wars began to germinate in Manchuria, as the ravenous empire of Japan began to feed on the limbs of a dying China. Two years later an undereducated painter from Austria led a revived Germany into the west plains of Poland. Weeks later, eastern Poland fell to invasion from the Soviet Union.[61]

Per American tradition, so long as each menace did not soil the Monroe Doctrine, the Roosevelt administration made no promise to become directly involved. One of the great myths of history contends that Roosevelt purposely allowed the Pacific fleet to be martyred at Pearl Harbor so that he might drag his isolationist country into the global fight. No such idiocy occurred. If he was guilty of anything, it was the failure to temper the traditional rivalry between his army and navy, a divisiveness that severely compromised readiness in Hawaii, the Philippines, Guam, Wake, and other areas Japan hit on that "day of infamy."

However unprepared the United States was on December 7, it soon became a model of forged coordination. Within weeks of entering the conflagration, FDR established a Combined Chiefs of Staff with Great Britain, far outweighing any cooperative effort ever attempted in the First World War. By the summer of 1942, a well-oiled Joint Chiefs of Staff was up and running. An army ranked seventeenth in the world in 1939 was nearing parity with Nazi Germany by 1942, and in that same year, the U.S. armaments industry was outproducing the entire Axis combined.[62]

Throughout the war, Roosevelt developed a talent for spotting military talent, the prime examples being Army Chief of Staff George C. Marshall, Supreme Allied Commander in Europe Dwight Eisenhower, and Commander in Chief of the Pacific Forces Chester Nimitz. While he promoted prima donnas of questionable skills (namely Douglas MacArthur),

FDR and Churchill met at Casablanca in 1943. During a press conference at the summit, Roosevelt announced to the world that the Allies would not stop fighting until every Axis power had surrendered unconditionally.

he entrusted and empowered only the best. It is fair to say that Adolf Hitler, Josef Stalin, and Winston Churchill did not display the same overall wisdom or luck in choosing senior military leaders.

It was Roosevelt who, in 1943, first declared the aim of unconditional surrender, providing a finite, definable, and shared goal previously lacking among the Allies. To achieve this grand strategy, he was neither haphazard (like Hitler), heartless (like Stalin), hesitant (like Churchill), nor a figurehead (like Hirohito). Throughout the conflict, the U.S. forces were the best fed and the best equipped, with twice the ratio of doctors to troops as the Germans or Soviets, three times the manpower of Britain, and ten times the combat survival rate of the Japanese.[63]

Roosevelt would not live to see the end of this global conflict, nor would 405,000 of his fellow Americans in the second bloodiest war in U.S. history. Yet American losses were comparatively modest. Thirteen nations lost more soldiers and civilians. And despite fighting on two fronts, with allies of widely divergent goals, against two of the most powerful nation-states in modern warfare, the president was able to lead his nation to victory and leave it stronger than any other country still standing.[64]

---

For every American killed in the Second World War, Japan lost nine, Germany lost seventeen, China lost thirty-five, and the Soviet Union lost sixty.

---

## 2.  JAMES K. POLK
### MEXICAN-AMERICAN WAR (1846–48)

Some presidents make wars. Others have wars thrust upon them. James K. Polk willingly rattled his saber while running for office in 1844, vowing to plow into Mexico and the Oregon Territory if his foreign opponents did not concede to his territorial demands. In the end, the would-be warrior chose to charge at the lesser of two windmills, and his gains were unparalleled in the country's brief history.

While he opted to negotiate a settlement over Oregon, he refused to accept the Mexican position that Texas ended at the Nueces River. Polk and his fellow Democrats argued that the southern border of *Tejas* stood at the Rio Grande, two hundred miles farther south, and stretched all the way north and west into modern-day New Mexico, Colorado, and

Polk's preemptive strike against Mexico reaped huge benefits for his government. The ensuing peace treaty expanded the U.S. land area by a third and shrank Mexico to half its original size.

Wyoming. Polk's halfhearted attempts to buy the disputed area, plus New Mexico and California, yielded nothing but more hostility.

In a blatant show of force, "Little Hickory" sent a contingent of officers and men, under the direction of Brig. Gen. Zachary Taylor, to guard the "U.S." side of the Rio. The event touched off a small battle and enabled Polk to ask for, and receive, a congressional declaration of war.

Polk wasted little time or effort reducing the unstable government of Mexico by initiating concurrent strikes on Santa Fe and Monterrey eight hundred miles to the southeast. Both cities fell, and within months, most of California was in U.S. hands. The following spring brought an amphibious assault upon Veracruz on the Gulf of Mexico. Driving west toward the Halls of Montezuma, Maj. Gen. Winfield Scott, assisted by able field officers such as Capt. Robert E. Lee, captured Mexico City by early autumn.

At the cost of thirteen thousand American dead (half the losses of their opponent), plus fifteen million dollars offered in compensation for lost lands, the United States grew by a third and reduced the size of Mexico by half. The degree of success was so great that an "All Mexico" movement grew in the United States, calling for the acquisition of the entire country, plus additional territory in the Caribbean and South America.[65]

A higher proportion of Congress voted for the declaration of war against Mexico in 1846 (93 percent) than did against Germany in the First World War (89 percent) or against Britain in 1812 (61 percent).

## 3.   HARRY S TRUMAN (FIRST TERM)
PACIFIC WAR (1945)

In the summer of 1945, American journalists stationed in the Pacific were betting on when the war would end. The earliest estimates were 1946. For troops leaving San Francisco for the Pacific theater, the optimistic phrase was "Golden Gate in '48." Even with the fall of Okinawa in late June, the military high command in Tokyo was planning to fight into the indefinite future.[66]

Harry Truman felt differently. He had first learned about the Manhattan Project and its "cosmic" or "atomic" devices in late April 1945, twelve days into his presidency, and he had known from his first reading of the top-secret reports that he was going to use them. The possibility of a shortened war seemed even brighter by mid-July after the Trinity Test in Alamogordo, New Mexico. Truman was in the aristocratic Berlin suburb of Potsdam when he received word of the successful detonation.[67]

From its inception, the Manhattan Project aimed to build several prototypes in an effort to find a reliable design. Two promising models emerged: one a sphere of plutonium compressed to critical mass (the Trinity type), and the simpler but less stable "Little Boy," which slammed two subcritical pieces of Uranium 235 together. When the project first began in 1939, Franklin Roosevelt envisioned the superweapons as an unassailable additive to conventional forces. In 1945 Truman believed the same, as did Gen. George Marshall and Secretary of War Henry Stimson. An invasion of Japan was set for November, but the bombs would start falling as soon as they were ready.

It is true that the cabinet of Prime Minister Suzuki Kataro wanted a cease-fire in the summer of 1945, but they were wholly against surrendering. Japan volunteered disarmament, yet insisted it would disarm itself. There was to be no foreign occupation, nor a replacement of the government. In addition, the empire was to retain Formosa, Korea, and Manchuria, encompassing three times the land and twice the population of Japan proper.[68]

The Allies refused. Conventional bombing of Japan's main islands continued, and the uranium device was prepared for use. To give the impression that the United States had a whole arsenal of ultraweapons, Truman ordered the destruction of Hiroshima on August 6, followed immediately by a public statement: "We are now prepared to obliterate more rapidly and completely every productive enterprise the Japanese have above ground in any city."[69]

When no word came of unconditional surrender, the president ordered the second device dropped on August 9, burning much of Nagasaki. Preparations were fast underway to assemble a third and fourth bomb when Tokyo capitulated.

Truman gambled and won. Fire and irradiation killed 170,000 in two cities, but it was a fraction of what Japan had already lost through incendiary bombings. Both sides were experiencing an exponential increase of losses as the United States neared the main islands. Manila alone cost 11,000 American and Japanese dead. Iwo Jima killed 25,000 altogether. Nearly 200,000 soldiers and civilians on all sides died in Okinawa. Estimates of a half-million casualties through the coming invasion were conservative, and the war would likely have ended no sooner than 1947.[70]

---

Japan's Minister of War Anami Korechika, previously committed to fight on after Hiroshima, feared the Americans had "one hundred atomic bombs" after he learned of the loss of Nagasaki.

---

## 4. GEORGE H. W. BUSH
### FIRST GULF WAR (1990–91)

George H. W. Bush could be pragmatic. For years the United States had backed Panama strongman Manuel Noriega. But when the diminutive general became closely associated with drug cartels, negated the 1989 Panamanian elections, and installed a crony as president, he became the target of a U.S. invasion. Under Bush's orders, Noriega was deposed, caught, and extradited for trial. It only took the U.S. armed forces a few weeks to complete the mission.

Bush could be compassionate. Food shortages and warlords reduced Somalia to a state of famine in 1992. The lame duck Bush ordered twenty-five thousand troops into the east African nation to secure the delivery of relief supplies. The operation saved possibly thousands of lives, and Bush made no attempt to turn the rescue mission into a permanent police force.

He also knew how to liberate a country. On August 2, 1990, Iraqi dictator Saddam Hussein invaded the nation of Kuwait. Smaller than New Hampshire, Kuwait was monarchial, wealthy, and not the friendliest country toward Washington, but it was nonetheless a sovereign nation and a key piece to the political stability and oil production of the Gulf. Judiciously, diplomatically, with the assistance of Secretary of State James Baker III and the National Security Council, Bush assembled the largest coalition of armies since the Second World War. Thirty nations amassed seven hundred thousand servicemen and women altogether, most of them American. A widely supported U.N. resolution demanded that Iraq withdraw by January 15, 1991, or face a military expulsion.

Ideally, Bush wanted an Iraqi withdrawal. Casualty estimates for the United States alone numbered in the tens of thousands. In a letter to his children, the president expressed a sincere desire that war could be averted. His worst fear, he wrote, was that a war would devolve into a protracted stalemate and an indefinite occupation. If that were to occur, he said, his impeachment was all but inevitable.[71]

Bush did not have to worry. A monthlong bombing campaign decimated a poorly led, poorly equipped, unmotivated Iraqi army. A multinational invasion in February needed only one hundred hours to crush Hussein's forces and liberate Kuwait. A cease-fire quickly took hold, and within four weeks, the Bush administration began withdrawing U.S. troops from the area. The entire affair lasted seven months. In terms of lives lost, the entire coalition experienced fewer than four hundred deaths. The financial commitment was approximately sixty-one billion dollars, most of which was paid by Kuwait.[72]

Despite its success, the war was not viewed as a great triumph. Exercising his trademark restraint, George Herbert Walker Bush refused to placate the hawks who wanted a full-scale invasion and the overthrow of a blowhard tyrant. In a rare instance of history answering "what if," Bush's eldest son decided to play out the invasion scenario in 2003. The result was almost exactly what George H. W. Bush had predicted in his memoirs, written years before George W. Bush was ever a presidential candidate:

I firmly believed that we should not march into Baghdad. . . . To occupy Iraq would instantly shatter our coalition, turning the whole Arab world against us, and make a broken tyrant into a latter-day Arab hero. It would have taken us way beyond the imprimatur of international law bestowed by the resolutions of the Security Council, assigning young soldiers to a fruitless hunt for a securely entrenched dictator and condemning them to fight in what would be an unwinnable urban guerrilla war. It could only plunge that part of the world into even greater instability and destroy the credibility we were looking so hard to reestablish.[73]

---

Number of U.S. troops killed in the First Gulf War: 297

Number of U.S. troops killed in the Second Gulf War: 3,800+

---

## 5.  WILLIAM McKINLEY
### SPANISH-AMERICAN WAR (1898)

To destroy an empire in a few months is no mean feat, and President McKinley did not want to do it in the first place. Before the Republican ever took office, it was clear that Cuba, the Caribbean jewel of the Spanish Empire, was nearing a point of total collapse. Years of imperial oppression and corruption had decimated the colony, causing widespread starvation and revolts. By the end of 1897, one in six Cubans—nearly a quarter of a million human beings—were dead from emaciation or plague. In the United States, farmers in the Midwest empathized with the plight of Cuba's rural poor, while investors in the Northeast salivated at the growth potential of the island's plantations, mines, and railroads.[74]

At the time, it was common practice for U.S. presidents to send the navy into troubled waters in an attempt to induce calm. McKinley's predecessor Grover Cleveland had warships pay a visit to Brazil, China, Korea, Nicaragua, and Samoa during periods of unrest. The otherwise isolationist McKinley followed suit and ordered the USS *Maine* into Havana Harbor.

After being anchored in port only a few weeks, the battleship exploded under mysterious circumstances. The detonation killed 266 crewmen on board. Eight more soon died of their wounds, and the public was screaming for revenge.

A distraught president, gentle and even-tempered by nature, offered alternatives to further bloodshed—an armistice on the island, humanitarian aid, arbitration, even the outright purchase of Cuba. Hungry for more decisive punishment, Congress declared war on Spain without McKinley's request.[75]

Pious and hesitant William McKinley had an easier time defeating the Spanish Empire than subduing a Filipino insurrection.

Fortunately for the placid man from Ohio, his navy was brand-new; the three-year-old *Maine* was the "oldest" of six battleships in the fleet. The navy was also well supplied (thanks to Assistant Secretary of the Navy Theodore Roosevelt). Facing an unmotivated and outdated opponent in Spain, U.S. warships decimated ten archaic vessels at Manila Bay in the Philippines and patiently awaited the arrival of ground troops from the states. In Cuba, an army of seventeen thousand (including recent volunteer Theodore Roosevelt) ran roughshod over a paltry imperial defense, while the USS *Texas* and company sank the remnants of Spain's once glorious armada. After barely seven months of fighting, Madrid was asking for an armistice.

In victory, the United States acquired Cuba, Puerto Rico, Guam, and the Philippines and annexed the peaceful island chain of Hawaii. McKinley also gained a new running mate in 1900, the nearsighted war hero of San Juan Hill.

The price was approximately thirty-three hundred dead American servicemen, lost primarily to viruses and bacteria rather than shells and bullets. Dysentery, malaria, typhoid, yellow fever, along with food poisoning from tainted canned beef killed just as many soldiers stateside as had fallen overseas. The United States would also choke on a chain of islands. After granting Cubans their freedom, McKinley decided to "civilize" the Filipino people and turn their vast archipelago into a protectorate. The caustic endeavor would result in the longer and deadlier PHILIPPINE-AMERICAN WAR, and push the United States into its own era of imperial rule.[76]

The Spanish-American conflict produced an overload of media sensational-
ism. The worst perpetrator of yellow journalism was the owner of the *New
York World*, Joseph Pulitzer, who would later establish an award for outstanding achievement in news reporting.

## 6.  WOODROW WILSON (SECOND TERM)
### FIRST WORLD WAR (1917–18)

"Why, by interweaving our destiny with that of any part of Europe, entan-
gle our peace and prosperity in the toils of European ambition, rivalship,
interest, humor or caprice?" George Washington's Farewell Address
never seemed more logical than in 1917, when Europe's royal houses
were attempting to cure medieval hate through modern warfare.

To his credit, Woodrow Wilson avoided the vortex for three years. He
even forbade the general staff from drawing up plans for mobilization,
lest they create some self-fulfilling prophecy. Yet when Germany resumed unrestricted submarine offensives on all Atlantic traffic in February 1917—and issued its bumbling "Zimmermann telegram" a month
later, offering Mexico support if it attacked the United States—the cautious Wilson had few options but to call for a declaration of war.[77]

The president knew combat on a personal level. As a little boy in Civil
War Georgia, he wrapped bandages for the stumps of soldiers, and he saw
the devastation wrought by armies scything through farmsteads and vil-
lages. In entering a conflict far worse than the Brothers' War, Wilson proceeded with a tangible sense of dread: "It is a fearful thing to lead this
great peaceful people into war, into the most terrible and disastrous of all
wars; civilization itself seems to be in the balance." He was not exaggerating. By 1917 the Great War had become the deadliest in human history.
But the time had come for the United States to end it.[78]

Wilson did not conduct himself as a beacon of justice, suppressing
basic civil rights through the SEDITION ACT OF 1918. But he did understand the concept of total war, establishing executive boards to direct the
country's growing industry—the Shipping Board, the War Industries
Board, plus commissions for food, coal and petroleum, and railroads. He
also established the first military draft since the Civil War. In less than a
year, the army was able to conscript, equip, train, supply, and transport

two million doughboys (including artillery officer Harry Truman) directly into the European theater. Heralded as a "War for Democracy," it was more to end the interminable butchering along the western front and to liberate the Atlantic Ocean from trade-killing torpedoes.[79]

Wilson's choice for field commander, Gen. John Pershing, may not have been the wisest. "Black Jack" had failed to subdue the insurgent Pancho Villa in 1917, and in Europe, he displayed an outdated faith in frontal assaults. But he did insist on keeping the American Expeditionary Force together rather than feed it piecemeal into the depleted ranks of the British and French armies. By 1918 the sheer weight of the U.S. contingent began to tip the scale in favor of the Allies. While Germany had not lost a foot of its own territory, sea blockades were starving it from the inside, and the front lines were bleeding it dry. A massive Allied assault upon the well-defended woodlands of the Meuse-Argonne in September 1918 cost American families nearly twenty-seven thousand dead in a few weeks, but it broke any chance of the German Empire's lasting through the winter. An armistice on November 11 closed the slaughterhouse for good.

The price had been high—fifty-three thousand American dead from combat and more than sixty-three thousand consumed by disease. But in a little over a year, the United States had stopped a war that was killing an average of four hundred thousand human beings per month. Millions were being maimed or starved to death. At least eight million European children were orphaned by the time the shooting stopped. Though the United States would not be a part of it, the president's dream of a League of Nations did come to fruition. Viewed as a failure, the peace did bury the warring empires of Austria, Germany, Russia, and the Ottomans, and the Atlantic was once again free.[80]

---

Though the fighting abated in November 1918, the dying did not. In their lungs, veterans of all nations returned to their homes carrying the pandemic Spanish influenza, which proceeded to kill twenty million people worldwide, including a half-million Americans.

---

## 7. DWIGHT EISENHOWER
### KOREA (1953)

The dominant issue of the 1952 elections was the bloody stalemate in Korea. Truman's changing objectives, the futility in negotiations, and the

As he promised during his campaign for the White House, President-Elect Dwight Eisenhower visited the war zone of Korea. The arduous terrain and grueling stalemate convinced him that a continuation of the conflict would be pointless for both sides.

EISENHOWER LIBRARY

mounting death toll (125,000 U.S. dead, wounded, missing, or captured by Election Day), doomed the Democrats to a landslide loss. Ike sealed his victory weeks before the polls opened by offering a solution to the Asian deadlock: "I shall go to Korea."[81]

Simple in dress and speech, Eisenhower sincerely wanted to be liked. When he smiled, which was often, his bright Kansas grin spanned the entirety of his friendly face. But there was something about the West Point graduate that struck people the moment they met him. He was efficient, no-nonsense, and he could get things done, mostly by way of relentless, prudent, teamwork.

He kept his promise to see the Korean Peninsula for himself and to push the negotiations forward (the largest impasse being repatriation of POWs). Upon his arrival, the former general was struck by the unforgiving mountainous terrain, the same kinds of geological obstacles that had pinned the Allies for so many years in Nazi-occupied Italy. Continuation of the same old conventional strategy was not going to break the Chinese-anchored North, Ike surmised. The only option left was to hold tight on the ground, look for an end-run in negotiations, and prepare to use nuclear weapons.

By May 1953, atomic bombs were forwarded to bases in Okinawa. The first nuclear artillery piece, "Atomic Annie," was successfully test-fired later that month at the Nevada Test Site. Meanwhile, officials in India began to work as mediators between Beijing and Washington, hinting at the possibility that Eisenhower would initiate nuclear strikes if China did not cooperate.[82]

Until the Beijing archives indicate either way, it is not yet known whether the nuclear threat or cumulative exhaustion broke the deadlock, but both North Korea and its Chinese allies agreed to a cease-fire in July. After six months in office, Eisenhower was able to fulfill his objective of ending the war with the existing boundaries of the two Koreas intact—without having to employ atomic devices.

Though a painful and costly struggle, the conflict had an unexpected benefit for the American military, namely, it never substantively downsized again. After every major conflict, the U.S. government traditionally dismantled its army and mothballed its navy, often by 90 percent or more, as was the case with the Civil War and the two world wars. By 1948, Truman had reduced the defense budget to less than fourteen billion dollars per year. After Korea, the Eisenhower administration funded the Pentagon at more than forty-five billion dollars annually.[83]

---

Among the troops Ike visited in Korea was his own son John, who was serving as an infantry officer near the front lines. He survived to become an accomplished historian and diplomat. John Eisenhower is also, to date, the last child of a president to serve in a war.

---

## 8. JOHN ADAMS
### QUASI WAR WITH FRANCE (1798–1800)

In the innate antagonism between France and Britain, the ethnically English John Adams always felt closer to the latter, and his country had commercially drifted back to her after achieving independence. The shift had pushed the "eternal ally" France to hire privateers, basically pirates, to raid U.S. merchant ships at will. In 1796 alone, French cruisers and raiders had plucked more than three hundred out of five thousand American vessels from the sea, mostly in the Caribbean. The following year brought more of the same, and the United States began to struggle from lack of trade.[84]

His cabinet, his country, and his wife were calling for all-out war against the tempestuous French. But Adams knew his people were vulnerable. They had won their Revolution in large part because they were able to play the two superpowers against each other. At present there was no such opportunity, and to fight alone against either one would likely mean that Adams would be the last president of a short-lived United States.

Playing every angle, Adams coldly suppressed dissent at home through the ALIEN AND SEDITION ACTS and tried to maintain open channels of diplomacy in the ill-fated XYZ AFFAIR. At the same time, he prepared to fight if needed, and for that he has been rightly called the "Father of the Navy."

The Quasi War, or the Half War against France, was never declared, and it was fought entirely on water, which was a bit of a problem for the Americans because they only had three modest warships. Long decommissioned were the Continental navy and their companion privateers. To rectify the problem, Adams signed into existence the Navy Department on April 30, 1798, and saw the construction of six frigates, the most celebrated being the USS *Constitution* with forty-four guns. They would be a small but formidable force.

There was no clear start to the fighting, and no conclusive final battle. By diligent pressure on both the high seas and the diplomatic front, Adams was able to save his fragile state and its precious navy from a major engagement. Working with tacit cooperation from Britain, his handful of frigates and smaller warships began to capture smaller French ships-for-hire, avoiding the larger battle frigates of the French navy. In February 1799 came the first true victory, as the thirty-six-gun *Constellation* defeated the equally outfitted *l'Insurgente* in the eastern Caribbean. By the end of the year, American crews caught twenty-six privateers hired by the French. In 1800 the haul more than doubled. In total, the U.S. Navy brought in nearly one hundred vessels, mostly raiders, losing only one frigate to enemy engagement in more than two years of fighting.[85]

The conflict came to an end with a regime change in France. Unwilling to tangle with the pesky Americans any further, Napoleon Bonaparte negotiated a settlement to a war that never was. The United States regained its neutrality on the high seas, the U.S. Navy was born—as were the marines. Armed with an experienced, confident, and expanded naval force, the country was prepared to fight its next foe: the Muslim city-states along the Barbary Coast of North Africa.

For the president, all his achievements went for naught. A month before the Senate ratified the treaty to bring the Quasi War to an end, Adams lost the ELECTION OF 1800 to his vice president, Thomas Jefferson.[86]

---

Suspecting France would invade, Congress authorized Adams to form an army of eighty thousand (four times larger than the Continental army ever was). Adams in turn named George Washington as commanding officer.

The invasion never came, the army was never formed, and Washington died a year after the nomination.

---

## 9.  THEODORE ROOSEVELT
### THE GREAT WHITE FLEET (1907–9)

Upon leaving office in 1910, the antagonistic Theodore Roosevelt was nonplussed that he had not presided over some great conflict. Looking back at other legacies, he contended, "If Lincoln had lived in times of peace, no one would know his name now."[87]

Contrary to Roosevelt's opinion, trial by fire does not guarantee presidential immortality. Among the most famous chief executives, Teddy stands well above James Polk and William McKinley, victors in major wars that greatly expanded the boundaries of American dominion. Wartime president James Madison was known more for his work in creating the Constitution, and the immortal George Washington avoided international tangles like the plague during his presidency.

While TR may have romanticized combat as the ultimate test of personal and national manhood, as president he was militarily active but not particularly belligerent. His ROOSEVELT COROLLARY justified limited engagements in Colombia, the Dominican Republic, Honduras, and Panama. In 1903 U.S. troops landed in Syria to protect the American consulate from a suspected attack by radical Muslims. On the other side of the globe, marines performed a similar duty in Korea as Japan fought (and defeated) Russia over control of the Korean Peninsula. In 1906 Roosevelt tried to stabilize Cuba by partial occupation. But his greatest success came from a peaceful use of power, one that would embody his worldview and earn the respect of continents.

The idea emerged as a reaction to racial tension on the California coast. A large influx of immigrants posed a threat to the white population. Willing to work longer hours for less pay, the outsiders were also placing their children into the school system. In October 1906, the board of education in San Francisco began to segregate these "outsiders," sparking riots in their native land. Gravely upset at the ethnic hatred within his own borders, the president called the whole affair "a wicked absurdity," and feared it would lead to greater violence. Relations between the United States and Japan had never been worse.[88]

Advisors suggested he transfer the bulk of the Atlantic fleet around the Horn of South America to San Francisco Bay. It would take perhaps three months, but it would work to calm both the local population and be seen as a show of force against any possible actions from Tokyo. Roosevelt had a better idea. Rather than make a slow, small, pugnacious demonstration for minimal gain, he envisioned a voyage for the history books.

It would be called the "Great White Fleet." With hulls painted in ivory and bows trimmed in gold, the mighty American warships would circumnavigate the globe. The world would see the iron might of the United States through a peaceful, headline-grabbing tour rather than from the barrel of a gun. When rival nations declared it could not be done, not on such a grand scale, TR became all the more committed. Navy officials asked how many of its sixteen battleships should be sent. Roosevelt responded with a simple order—all of them.[89]

The idea was not popular. Cities on the coast protested they were being stripped of their defense. Congressmen believed TR was secretly hoping to provoke a war with Japan and end his presidential career with a glorious victory. Teddy ignored them and ordered the fleet away.

Roosevelt's intuition proved correct. The armada was welcomed all along the shores of South America. By the time it reached California, the Tokyo government had warmly invited the vessels over. Eagerly accepting, U.S. sailors and marines reached Yokohama several weeks later and were serenaded by excited Japanese schoolchildren singing "The Star-Spangled Banner." Port after port, curious and admiring populations gawked at the spectacle of mighty craft drifting in.

The Great White Fleet's itinerary included visits to Trinidad, Brazil, Chile, Peru, Mexico, New Zealand, Australia, the Philippines, Japan, China, Ceylon, Egypt, and Gibraltar before returning to port in Hampton Roads. Total distance—forty-five thousand miles.

U.S. NAVAL HISTORICAL CENTER

By 1909 the ships were safely back at Hampton Roads. Without firing a shot in anger, and traversing more than forty-five thousand miles, they had achieved the seemingly impossible and earned the United States more goodwill and respect than it had since its inception. Welcoming them back in person was the same man who had seen them off, only he was fourteen months older and had but two weeks left in his final term as president. Beaming with immeasurably pride, Roosevelt assessed the trip and his legacy. "In my own judgment," he concluded, "the most important service that I rendered to peace was the voyage of the battle fleet round the world."[90]

---

In 1908, the lengthy voyage of the Great White Fleet convinced Theodore Roosevelt that the Philippines were too far away to be practicably defended. Seeking a more defensible position, he officially transferred the U.S. Pacific Naval Base from Manila Bay to the Hawaiian port of Pearl Harbor.

---

## 10. RONALD REAGAN
### THE BOMBING OF LIBYA (1986)

Born at a time when thousands of Civil War veterans were still alive, Ronald Reagan possibly heard a few of them mention the golden rule of shooting—aim low. The Gipper was a nationalist, a militarist, unworldly, and blindly patriotic, but he was not a warmonger. Though he took many opportunities to flex American muscle across the first, second, and third worlds, he never overcommitted nor overstayed an engagement, preferring instead to speak loudly and carry a small stick. In his first term alone, he deployed advisors, troops, and/or aircraft to Chad, Egypt, El Salvador, Granada, Lebanon, Libya, and the Persian Gulf. None of the engagements escalated beyond a few sorties, skirmishes, or short occupations. Even his IRAN-CONTRA operation, though immensely illegal, was minuscule compared to the arms and money that LBJ and Nixon poured into Saigon. Reagan meant it when he said "no more Vietnams." The consummate actor, Reagan knew when it was time to exit a scene.[91]

On October 23, 1983, a suicide bomber plowed through the gates of U.S. Marine barracks in Beirut, killing 241 of the peacekeeping forces and injuring more than 100. Within two days, Reagan ordered a military offensive, not in Lebanon, but against the tiny Caribbean island of Granada, fearing that 800 American medical students there were in danger of a violent Cuban Marxist takeover. It took forty hours for a carrier task force and army rangers totaling 5,000 officers and men to conquer the island and its 800 Cuban defenders. The short, successful invasion was widely popular among the U.S. population, and it masked the pain of Beirut. Three months later, in a move favored by his cabinet and his country, Reagan pulled all remaining U.S. Marines out of Lebanon.[92]

His most successful and least costly operations involved Libya and its verbose Islamic president, Muammar Qaddafi. Head of a country of fewer than three million, Qaddafi had enough oil in his country and anti-Americanism in his nationalistic veins to merit numerous public rants against Reagan. Intended more to impress everyone in Tripoli rather than anyone in Washington, the dictator's rhetoric still offended the sensitive Gipper. Claiming "freedom of navigation," Reagan sent a modest armada to the Gulf of Sidra in the spring of 1986, within miles of Libyan territorial waters. Qaddafi proclaimed a "line of death" across the gulf, and he all but dared the cowboy president to a shootout on Main Street. An exchange of rockets in late March upped the ante.[93]

When an American serviceman was killed by a bomb in a Berlin nightclub, Reagan had his cue to enter into a larger operation, from arm's length. Launching air strikes from bases in Britain on April 14, 1986, the U.S. Air Force and Navy dropped ninety tons of high explosives on Tripoli and Benghazi, killing more than one hundred people, including Qadaffi's adopted two-year-old daughter, but missing their main target. The strike nonetheless had the desired effect. With no losses on his own side, and no long-term occupation on the ground, Reagan effectively neutered the Libyan leader's war of words. Though the international community condemned the bombings, a majority of Americans viewed the strikes as a show of legitimate strength. From a line straight out of a dusty Western, Sheriff Reagan proudly announced to the townsfolk: "Every nickel-and-dime dictator the world over knows that if he tangles with the United States of America, he will pay a price."[94]

---

Under the War Powers Act of 1973, a president must first inform Congress if he plans to send U.S. forces into hostile areas. In his 1986 air strike against Libya, hours before U.S. bombers reached enemy airspace, Reagan told a few key legislators about the operation, thus obeying the letter of the law.

---

# TOP TEN LEAST SUCCESSFUL
# COMMANDERS IN CHIEF

When the drafted Constitution emerged in September 1787, not a few civilians were shocked to read of its ample provisions for making war. To the wary, the idea of having a standing army in peacetime ran counter to the revolutionary ideal, itself begun as a protest against quartered troops, military governorships, and imposed taxes to pay for them. In addition, to have a president serve as commander in chief seemed like an open invitation for another Julius Caesar or Oliver Cromwell or George III.

Fortunately, the framers knew to temper dictatorial lust by granting Congress sole responsibility to declare and finance wars. Adding to the checks and balances were a judiciary to monitor the use of war powers and an electorate capable of deposing militant executives through regularly scheduled elections.

In general, the collective effort has created a rather impressive war record, but presidents sometimes falter anyway, especially when it comes to their prewar objectives. During the course of conflicts, such goals are frequently compromised or abandoned altogether. The most glaring failures have involved the promises of short fights and modest loss of life—popular selling points that have proven difficult to deliver. While no leader has seen a military engagement go completely as planned (armed opponents rarely cooperate), some have faltered terribly through mismanagement and miscalculation.

Following are the least successful presidents based on the scope of their failed war aims, the duration of their wars, and the damages rendered in blood and money. Interestingly, nine of the following individuals served as officers in the armed forces before they became commander in chief, challenging the popular assumption that candidates with military experience are inherently better suited to lead the country in times of international unrest.

### 1. LYNDON B. JOHNSON
VIETNAM (1964–69)

Two years in, Lyndon Johnson realized he had no viable solution. In a private conversation with Lady Bird in March 1965, he painted himself as a

LBJ's secretary of defense, Robert McNamara, points to the sinkhole of Southeast Asia, where the United States was losing an average of thirty men a day in 1968.

victim of circumstance: "I can't get out. I can't finish it with what I have got. So what the hell can I do?"[95]

For starters, he could have realized he was responsible for causing rampant inflation. A master of domestic politics, LBJ knew very little about world history or international affairs, which led him to critically ignorant assessments of a perennial civil war in a third-world country that was of almost no geographic, economic, or material significance to U.S. national security. In the 1964 presidential elections, the electorate correctly perceived the insurgency in Southeast Asia a minor issue.[96]

Johnson was not the first to try to subdue the region, to force it into a form of rule to which it was not suited. Before LBJ, there were Kennedy, Eisenhower, Truman, the French Fourth Republic, Imperial Japan, the French Third Republic, and the Chinese. Johnson inherited fifteen thousand U.S. troops in Indochina. But the decision was ultimately his alone to balloon that number to more than a half-million troops and to transform an intraregional conflict into the supreme test of American will.

His impression of the region revealed an embarrassing lack of perspective, one that made him highly susceptible to the doomsday premonitions of National Security Advisor McGeorge Bundy and Secretary of Defense Robert McNamara (both holdovers from the JFK administration). "If I got out of Vietnam and let Ho Chi Minh run through the streets of Saigon," Johnson once claimed, "then I'd be doing exactly what Chamberlain did in World War II." He also believed the "loss of China" to be "chickensh-t compared with what might happen if we lost Vietnam."[97]

To equate the international leverage of Nazi Germany or Communist

China with provincial Vietnam takes a great deal of vivid imagination and false information, both of which LBJ had in abundance. His first critical mistake was to inflate a pair of small naval encounters in the GULF OF TONKIN in August 1964 into the worst possible offense to the dignity and safety of the United States imaginable. Poor marks go to Congress for consequently passing a resolution that surrendered most of its responsibilities in military management. But the legislators had incentive. At the time, Johnson had a public approval rating of 70 percent.

By the start of 1965, more than four hundred U.S. advisors and servicemen had died in Vietnam. In an attempt to prevent further loss, LBJ sent in the first of many combat battalions. He also unleashed Operation Rolling Thunder, a massive bombing campaign designed to bring the North Vietnamese to their knees. Reconnaissance and analysis soon revealed that the air strikes were having minimal effect on the largely rural and agricultural country. The president countered that all the strategy would work if the quantity and quality of the bombings were increased. He was soon going so far as to tell the air force what bridges to hit and escalating his troop levels. By the end of the year, eighty-two thousand American soldiers and marines were on the ground, U.S. deaths had climbed to twenty-two hundred, and Rolling Thunder would continue for the next two years.[98]

By the time Johnson left the presidency in early 1969, troop levels had surpassed five hundred thousand, fatalities were nearing forty thousand, and the Saigon government was under the control of a virtual dictator in Nguyen Van Thieu, a former military officer who ruled largely through political repression and U.S. aid.

The traditional view is that LBJ's biggest failure was his lack of a precise strategy for victory. The assessment is largely correct. Americans in 1776 and 1941 proved their country was capable of paying any price, bearing any burden, and meeting any hardship, so long as they had a well-defined goal. But as those two wars also demonstrated, any superpower can be beaten if subjected to the lethal weapons of time and attrition.[99]

Technically, Johnson did not lose the war. He would simply pass it on to his successor, just as he had received it from the president before him. But his decision to invest so much in a fight that offered so little in return cost him the White House and destroyed his dream of the "Great Society." His mistake also eventually ended the lives of fifty-nine thousand young Americans and nine hundred thousand Vietnamese.

In the five years Lyndon Johnson was in office, South Vietnam experienced seven different regime changes, mostly by way of coups.

## 2.   RICHARD NIXON
### VIETNAM, CAMBODIA, AND LAOS (1969–73)

October 1969, Camp David, Maryland—President Richard Nixon wrote a memo to Henry Kissinger. Scribbled on the paper, among other items for Kissinger's consideration, was a short, solitary question: "Is it possible we were wrong from the start on Vietnam?" The problem for Nixon and his national security advisor was not their support for the war in the past. It was their plan for going forward. Kissinger joked: "We will not make the same old mistakes. We will make our own."[100]

The Nixon plan had always been to establish a pro-West government in the south, regardless of its legitimacy or virtue, so long as it was not communist. To achieve this, Nixon initially maintained the Johnson strategy—saturation bombing, shifting the burden of ground security to the Saigon government (what Defense Secretary Melvin Baird dubbed "Vietnamization"), and waiting for the North Vietnamese to cave.

By November 1969 he had been in office nearly a year, and to his surprise, the old methods were not working. In his famous "Silent majority" speech, Nixon urged his two hundred million fellow Americans to stay the course. "This first defeat in our Nation's history would result in a collapse of confidence in American leadership, not only in Asia but throughout the world." A compelling notion, if leadership simply involved winning wars.[101]

By 1969, even the bright, optimistic face of Nixon could not raise American morale in Vietnam.

NIXON LIBRARY

To give the weak South Vietnamese government time to become self-sustaining, Nixon expanded the war into Cambodia, through which the North Vietnamese were infiltrating the South. In May 1970, he invaded Cambodia with 70,000 men to flush out suspected communist cells. He also accelerated troop withdrawals from Vietnam to appease the antiwar movement in the States. From a peak of 550,000 U.S. servicemen and women in 1969, he reduced the total to 334,600 by the end of 1970.

None of it worked. Campus protests at Kent State in May left four students dead. Civilian and military casualties climbed in Southeast Asia. The bloodthirsty Khmer Rouge attained power in Cambodia. Secret negotiations with North Vietnam produced nothing. Nixon responded by bombing suspected hostile bases in neutral Laos and hinted that he would be willing to use nuclear weapons on Hanoi to achieve peace.

By 1972, troop levels were below one hundred thousand, but the bombings continued. The tonnage dropped on Laos alone was nearing the amount the United States had used in all of World War II. When Hanoi refused to negotiate any further, Nixon launched the infamous Christmas bombings in December 1972—twelve days of air strikes totaling twenty thousand tons of ordnance (or five times what the Allies used in the firebombing of Dresden in 1944).[102]

In January 1973, the long-promised armistice was finally achieved. The Nixon phase of the conflict, often seen as a final act in a long tragedy, lasted as long as the American Civil War, and it culminated in defeat.

---

U.S. aircraft dropped approximately eight million tons of bombs on Vietnam, Cambodia, and Laos, making them respectively the first-, second-, and third-most bombed nations in the history of aerial warfare.

---

## 3. HARRY TRUMAN (SECOND TERM)
### KOREA (1950–53)

Shortly before Christmas in 1950, Harry Truman confided in his diary, "Formosa, Communist China, Chiang Kai-shek, Japan, Germany, France, India, etc. I've worked for peace for five years and six months and it looks like World War III is here." His fear of communism was genuine, bolstered by the 1948 blockade of West Berlin, the detonation of a Soviet atomic device in 1949, and the "fall of China" later that year. The anguish

Truman's counterinvasion of North Korea backfired dangerously, to the point where a frustrated commanding general Douglas MacArthur (right front) advocated the use of nuclear weapons and an all-out war with China. In April 1951, Truman fired the seditious MacArthur, but the quagmire of Korea was still firmly in place.

only worsened when the leftist dictatorship of Pyongyang invaded South Korea on June 25, 1950. Spearheading their attack of 135,000 men were 120 Soviet-made T-34 tanks, the very machine that broke the Wehrmacht on the eastern front only a few years before.[103]

To stop the offensive, Truman deployed U.S. forces under an emergency U.N. resolution (but without congressional authority). The rush to defend the Republic of Korea began badly. In a week, Seoul had fallen. Two months later, the late-arriving U.N. force and the ROK army held only the toe of the peninsula, an area less than 5 percent of the entire land mass of the two Koreas. The United States was about to experience its first defeat.

Then on September 15, Gen. Douglas MacArthur launched a daring and brilliant amphibious assault upon the west coast port of Inchon, nearly three hundred miles behind the lines of the North Korean People's Army. The reversal was almost instantaneous. At risk of being cut off and crushed between two fronts, the overextended NKPA retreated northward in a panic.

But it was at this point that Truman chose to change his main objective. At first he simply wanted to reestablish the territorial integrity of South Korea. In just one hundred days, the U.N. coalition forces accomplished that goal and were holding steady on the prewar dividing line of the thirty-eighth parallel. Instead of standing firm and negotiating a settlement, Truman authorized a counterinvasion, hoping to unify the entire peninsula under one rule, just as the authoritarian Kim Il Sung had aimed to do only months before. Within days, the plan backfired catastrophically.[104]

Mopping up the remnants of Kim's broken army, the ROK and the U.N. coalition sped to the Yalu River and the border of the People's Republic of China. Minor clashes erupted between South Korean and Chinese regiments, heightening tensions to critical levels. Fearing a U.N. takeover of the mainland, China attacked—with three hundred thousand soldiers—twice the entire Allied first wave on D-day.

Thus began "Mr. Truman's War," a conflict that could have ended after three months but eventually dragged on for more than three years, ending only after Truman's departure. The eventual death toll: more than 200 Canadian soldiers, 530 British, 49,000 Americans, 103,000 South Koreans, 315,000 North Koreans, and 422,000 Chinese. The losses pale in comparison to the number of civilians who perished—approximately two million (for a perspective, there are fewer than one million individual digits and letters in this book).[105]

---

The lowest approval rating for any American president recorded by a major poll was 22 percent, achieved by Harry Truman during the Korean War.

---

## 4.  GEORGE W. BUSH
### WAR ON TERROR (2001– )

"Our war on terror begins with al Qaeda, but it does not end there. It will not end until every terrorist group of global reach has been found, stopped and defeated." Noble and heartfelt, George W. Bush's September 20, 2001, address to Congress and the nation focused on Taliban-led Afghanistan, the known center of al Qaeda operations, and its leader, Osama bin Laden. Less than three weeks later, the United States began bombing operations. By mid-November, ground troops and CIA agents were mopping up the remnants of the Taliban government. The United States had yet to lose an agent or a soldier.[106]

Yet Bin Laden and most of the main figures in al Qaeda were not found, and the militant Taliban continued to operate on a limited basis. Rather than retain focus on Afghanistan, Bush looked to expand the war into Iraq on the premise that Saddam Hussein's regime possessed weapons of mass destruction and was harboring terrorists. The ensuing invasion in March 2003 achieved one stated objective—the capture of Hussein. The Iraqi president was later tried and executed by the provisional government in Baghdad. As for the other goals—finding weapons of mass destruction, proving a link between Hussein and international terrorism, and establishing a stable democratic government in Iraq— none were accomplished in any measurable sense.[107]

Throughout both wars, Bush proudly referred to himself as "a wartime president." He might have done better to remember that he had a degree in history, because he readily ignored the lessons of the past. He grossly manipulated intelligence to suit his needs (per Eisenhower in the Middle East). His "coalition" was 90 percent American (as with Truman in Korea). He overestimated a country's ability to rule itself (like McKinley in Cuba). He vastly underestimated the time, funds, and manpower necessary to complete his major objectives (thus Madison in the War of 1812). His worst failure was that he and his advisors engaged in a war that could not be won (like Johnson in Vietnam). "Fighting terror" was an objective with no parameters. His definition of "the enemy" was in continual flux. There was no capital city, no central government, no head of state to force into submission. Consequently, the option of an armistice, peace treaty, or decisive victory was not available.[108]

At the date of publication, U.S. losses in Afghanistan had surpassed three hundred, while the conflict in Iraq had consumed thirty-eight hundred men and women, plus an estimated fifty thousand civilians. The financial cost of hunting Bin Laden and "nation building" in Iraq was set to surpass one trillion dollars.[109]

> The highest approval rating for any American president recorded by a major poll was 90 percent, achieved by George W. Bush a week after September 11, 2001. The week before, his ratings were 51 percent and falling.

### 5.  ABRAHAM LINCOLN
#### AMERICAN CIVIL WAR (1861–65)

He was undoubtedly a brilliant wordsmith, and his speeches are among the most cherished in the country's rich anthology. Misconstrued as an idealist, he was in fact a shrewd moderate, daring to walk the middle path when others ran to the extremes. Supremely farsighted, he endorsed bills that gave birth to a transcontinental railroad, scores of land grant colleges, and millions of acres of humble homesteads. But as a commander in

During the Civil War, 650,000 were killed, unknown numbers were wounded and traumatized, debt escalated, and sectional hostilities were cemented for generations to come.

chief, Abraham Lincoln does not rank among the successful, despite having defeated a popular separatist movement within his own borders.

Questionable was his ability to spot military talent, especially in the critical eastern theater. In fact, no president has ever done as poorly in selecting commanding officers in wartime. His first choice was Irvin McDowell, who had never led troops in combat. Next came George B. McClellan, who reached the gates of Richmond in 1862, only to retreat after winning most of the battles of the Seven Days and outnumbering his opponent four to one. Next was John Pope, an insubordinate and incompetent braggart who was routed at Second Manassas by inferior numbers. Consequently, Lincoln reappointed McClellan, who proceeded to be a nonfactor at Antietam. Then there was Ambrose E. Burnside, appointed *after* leading his men to slaughter against a force one-tenth his size at the south end of the Antietam battlefield. Burnside would repeat the mistake of a frontal assault at Fredericksburg a few months later, suffering more than eleven thousand casualties in a single day. Six weeks went by before Lincoln found the sense to fire him.

Also worthy of reassessment is the president's willingness to delegate authority despite clear instances of incompetence. Only in the case of emancipation did he override the opinion of his subordinates. The rest of the time, he consented to the opinions of "experts."

Though he personally tested a few rapid-fire shoulder arms, he did not pressure the U.S. Army Ordnance Department to adopt the deadly weapons. He instead believed their assertions that soldiers armed with such rifles would waste ammunition. He never checked to see that it was taking an average of one thousand bullets from single-shot muzzle-loaders to score one kill.

When the prisoner exchange system broke down in 1863, causing camps and stockades to overflow with POWs on both sides, Lincoln chose not to intervene. Instead he followed the advice of War Secretary Edwin H. Stanton and refused to negotiate a settlement. In the following fifteen months, nearly fifty thousand troops perished in military prisons, mostly from disease and malnutrition. The death toll exceeded the number killed in action at the battles of Antietam, Chancellorsville, Chickamauga, Cold Harbor, Fredericksburg, Gettysburg, First and Second Manassas, Shiloh, Stones River, Spotsylvania, and the Wilderness combined.[110]

Lincoln also made no concerted effort to improve funding and supply for the medical corps, relying instead on help from civilian organizations, such as the U.S. Sanitary Commission and the Christian Commission. In total, more than forty-three thousand Union troops died in hospitals (close to the total U.S. deaths by all causes during the Korean War).[111]

Most significant, he imposed no grand strategy. Not until 1864, under the direction of Lt. Gen. U. S. Grant, did the Union war efforts coordinate simultaneous attacks on five different Confederate fronts, and most of these were based on the principle of costly attrition. While it is true that he ultimately reestablished the existing borders of the United States, Lincoln did so at the cost of more than 650,000 dead North and South, a price higher than the victories of the American Revolution, the Mexican-American War, the Spanish-American War, the First World War, and the Second World War put together.

> If the Civil War were fought in 2008, and the United States lost the same proportion of its population as had been killed in the War Between the States, the overall death count would be 5.5 million.

## 6. JAMES MADISON
### WAR OF 1812 (1812–15)

Since 1803 the legions of Napoleon had been quite busy, ruthlessly hacking away at the aging monarchies of Europe, creating a world war in the name of France. Fighting would eventually reach from the czarist gates of Moscow to the islands of the Caribbean, drawing British attention far away from the United States, which is exactly why James Madison found the courage to strike.

For years, Britain had tried to convince the United States to join its side, using that age-old method of imperial persuasion—abuse. Fostering Native American uprisings along the Great Lakes, forcing thousands of neutral American sailors into their depleted Royal Navy, and halting U.S. trade with France, the British were hoping to coerce the American states toward their way of thinking. Most offensive was the Orders in Council, a unilateral proclamation demanding all U.S. ships trading with Europe to first enter a British port for inspection.

By 1812 the normally timid "Jemmy" Madison had reached the breaking point. He resolved to declare war, quickly capture British Canada by taking its paltry few cities, and force Parliament into a speedy peace settlement. But the best laid plans of mice and Madisons often go awry.[112]

Although the United States had twenty-five times the population of Canada and held the element of surprise, Madison opted to invade with several small attacks at multiple points rather than go straight for Montreal or Quebec, Britain's right and left arm in North America. As a result, Detroit was lost without a shot, Native Americans rallied against settlers in Michigan, and forays into Ontario were driven back in short order.

By 1813 Madison was starting to lose the war, and with it, control of his own people. New York militia declined to fight outside its own borders. Clergy in New England denounced the widening conflict. Pro-British communities held fasting days in protest. Commercially connected to London more than Washington, Massachusetts considered seceding from the

The burned ruins of the Capitol stood as a glaring symbol of Madison's inability to protect citizens during the War of 1812.

Union. Lured by high profits, citizens smuggled foodstuffs to the British fleet blockading the eastern seaboard.[113]

In 1814, the president also experienced the shame of abandoning the national capital to enemy troops and losing most of the federal buildings in the city, including the White House, to looting and arson.

He had hoped to win quickly, yet it was the protraction of the war that ultimately saved Madison. By the end of 1814, the United States had been at war for nearly three years and had lost well over twenty-two hundred troops, but the British had been fighting in Europe for more than a decade and had lost approximately two hundred thousand dead and missing. Weary and ready for peace, both sides agreed to the Treaty of Ghent, which simply maintained the old Canada–U.S. border and did nothing to settle the issues that had precipitated the war in the first place.[114]

There was one saving grace for the Americans. In January 1815, on the Mississippi Delta, the Indian fighter Andrew Jackson and two thousand militia and mercenaries brutally thwarted ten thousand redcoats at the battle of New Orleans (the British attempted a massive frontal assault over open ground). The overwhelming victory transformed the War of 1812 from a tie into a great success, and it instilled a strange new emotion among Americans—a sense of nationalism. Basking in the light of triumph, few citizens bothered to notice that the battle had occurred several weeks after the peace treaty had been signed.

---

In the War of 1812, several U.S. frigates achieved a modicum of success. Their names would become immortal when attached to aircraft carriers in World War II—*Enterprise, Essex, Hornet, Saratoga*, and *Wasp*.

---

### 7.  WILLIAM McKINLEY
PHILIPPINE-AMERICAN WAR (1899–1901)

Quick victory against the Spanish Empire brought the United States rather large prizes of war—Cuba, Guam, and Puerto Rico. Foremost was the Philippines—seven thousand islands, seven million inhabitants, with a land area roughly equivalent to Italy. Acquisition of the thousand-mile-long archipelago would mark the initiation of the United States into the order of empires. It would also test the American commitment to the principle of self-determination.

Rather than immediately grant the islands independence, McKinley felt compelled to stay and stabilize the region. His goals were to implant Western forms of democracy and capitalism so that the "backward" and long-repressed Filipinos could rule themselves. For good measure, he also expressed the intent to convert everyone to Christianity (although missionaries had been spreading Catholicism in the region for hundreds of years).[115]

While Cuba achieved quasi independence, the Filipinos were rather upset to find the United States bringing an occupation force in 1898. Open rebellion to the American presence began in 1899, and the fighting soon descended into mutual barbarity. Guerrillas conducted hit-and-run operations. The United States established "reconcentration camps" for security purposes (much like the strategic hamlet system in Vietnam seventy years later). Both sides used torture. A common interrogation tactic for the Americans was the "water cure" (similar to CIA "water boarding" during the War on Terror).[116]

While McKinley was able to defeat the Spanish in less than four months, it took him more than two years to end the Filipino uprisings, and the conflict consumed forty-five hundred American dead. The number of Filipinos killed is unknown, but estimates range from two hundred thousand to six hundred thousand, mostly from starvation and disease.[117]

---

Among the many Americans adamantly opposed to the annexation of the Philippines were the industrialist Andrew Carnegie, the presidents of Stanford and Harvard, and author Mark Twain.

---

## 8. WOODROW WILSON (FIRST TERM)
### MEXICO (1914–17)

He is seen as the tragic defender of peace, the scholar who would rather change the world through ideals than through force. But a closer look reveals that Dr. Thomas Woodrow Wilson happened to be one of the most active commanders in chief the country has ever elected. In addition to the First World War, he sent armed forces into China, Croatia, Cuba, Guatemala, Panama, Russia, and Turkey, among other nations.

For such a studious man, Wilson knew little about Central and South

America, where most of his military injections were administered. Mexico especially perplexed him. He consequently became confused when the overthrow of Gen. Victoriano Huerta in 1914 produced a power struggle. In a rush to recognize someone as the new head of state, the Wilson administration chose to back strongman Venustiano Carranza, the archenemy of northern revolutionary Francisco "Pancho" Villa. In retaliation, Villa crossed into Columbus, New Mexico, and clashed with U.S. soldiers and civilians, killing seventeen and looting the town.[118]

The following American "expedition" to capture Villa lasted nearly a year and failed miserably. At one point, more than ten thousand U.S. soldiers, sailors, and marines were roaming through Mexico, slowly and loudly scouring the countryside in search of a solitary man, who later became a national hero in the wake of the bumbling manhunt. On several occasions, the expedition nearly caused a war between the two countries. Accidental clashes with the Carranza regime escalated into a mobilization of troops on both sides. In 1916, Wilson federalized the National Guard in all forty-eight states and ordered them to the southern border of Texas in preparation for a full scale conflict.

Fearing the worst, both sides moved toward deescalation, and Wilson agreed to withdraw. By February 1917, the search was canceled. The effort cost the United States more than $130 million and scores of lives.[119]

---

In 1961, the Department of Defense honored the memory of Woodrow Wilson by having a nuclear submarine named after him.

---

Pancho Villa (noted with an X) rose to prominence in Mexico. A falling out with Washington led to a massive manhunt by the U.S. Army, who failed to catch him. Villa was later murdered in 1923.

## 9.   JOHN F. KENNEDY
CUBA (1961, 1962)
VIETNAM (1961–63)

"How could I have been so stupid, to let them go ahead?" The question was rhetorical, but Jack Kennedy and close advisor Ted Sorensen knew it was also valid. False assumptions, poor intelligence, underestimation of Cuba's defense system, and simply bad planning led to complete failure at the Bay of Pigs on April 17, 1961. Kennedy had inherited the clandestine CIA operation from the Eisenhower administration, and when told the attack could not wait, he ordered it to proceed.[120]

Overwhelming defeat for the Cuban insurgents and the excessive embarrassment for United States provided Kennedy with a valuable lesson, one he would not soon forget. From then on, the president would be far more reserved in applying the KENNEDY DOCTRINE to "assure the survival and success of liberty."

The first test came in civil-war wracked Laos, where Dwight Eisenhower had warned him of a possible communist takeover. Comprehending the high risk and minimal benefits of getting involved in an unstable area, Kennedy opted for an international recognition of Laotian neutrality. Next was Thailand, where JFK deployed a security force of several thousand to prevent leftist infiltration. The operation lasted a modest ten weeks. Then came the potentially lethal CUBAN MISSILE CRISIS. Created in large part because of U.S. deployment of nuclear missiles in Turkey, the Soviet countermove threatened to end the existence of Washington itself. Rather than push for a confrontation, Kennedy wisely orchestrated a

On December 29, 1962, Kennedy appeared at a face-saving rally in Miami's Orange Bowl for the Cuban brigade that invaded the Bay of Pigs. When he received the unit's battle flag, he vowed, "This flag will be returned to this brigade in a free Havana."

naval "quarantine" of incoming Soviet ships, a less belligerent maneuver than a blockade (an internationally recognized act of war).

For a president who promised to "pay any price, bear any burden," he was showing considerable restraint—until Vietnam. In 1961 his administration was pumping in millions of dollars and hundreds of advisors to buttress the teetering regime of right-winger Ngo Dinh Diem. By 1963 the cash flow was into the billions, and a few hundred advisors had turned into more than fifteen thousand. Kennedy officials also permitted the ousting of Diem, who was overthrown and assassinated on November 2, 1963. When communist leader Ho Chi Minh heard of the destabilizing coup, he purportedly said, "I can scarcely believe the Americans would be so stupid."[121]

---

In 1955, Ngo Dinh Diem rigged the South Vietnamese elections and won the presidency with nearly 100 percent of the vote. In Saigon, he took over 130 percent. The following year, Senator Jack Kennedy called Vietnam "the cornerstone of the Free World in Southeast Asia."

---

## 10. JIMMY CARTER
### IRAN (1980)

Other presidents have rescued civilians and government workers from hostile situations—William Howard Taft in China, Lyndon Johnson in the Congo, Gerald Ford in South Vietnam. Jimmy Carter's failed attempt to liberate fifty-three American hostages from the U.S. embassy in Teheran resulted in the deaths of eight servicemen. But the blow to America's national morale and international prestige could hardly be measured.

The assignment was months in the making, and Carter reluctantly ordered it to commence on April 24, 1980. Daring and courageous, the plan was also exceedingly complex. Landing in a prescouted staging area deep inside an Iranian desert, eight minesweeper helicopters were to meet with six C-130 transport planes, load up with fuel and commandos, fly to the embassy, locate and extricate the captives, and fly to an air base *inside* Iran. At that point, the ground troops and hostages would transfer to additional C-130s and fly out of the country. The would-be rescuers never got past the first staging area.

Sandstorms and eyewitnesses doomed the secret mission from the outset. Two helicopters got lost, and a third suffered mechanical problems. Carter seconded the decision on the ground to pull out and try at another date. Blinded by the darkness and churning sand during takeoff, a chopper pilot accidentally ran into one of the planes. In seconds, the two vehicles were engulfed. The burning fuel and detonating ordnance quickly consumed five airmen and three marines. In the scramble to abort, the military contingent left behind several of their copters and sensitive intelligence on U.S.-friendly operatives in Iran.

While Carter addressed his country via live broadcast and accepted full responsibility, Iranian television transmitted images of the charred wreckage to the rest of the world. The hostages were quickly dispersed throughout Teheran, making a second rescue attempt all but impossible. Internment for the bulk of the prisoners eventually lasted 444 days and would not end until the very hour Carter stepped down from office.

The crash was an accident, but it gave the impression that the United States was utterly helpless against a small band of radicals. The spectacular failure cemented the supremacy of Ayatollah Ruhollah Khomeini in Iran and elevated the rhetoric of radical Shia in the Persian Gulf. Consequently, the U.S. government quietly supported an invasion of Iran five months later conducted by Iraq and its authoritarian president, Saddam Hussein.[122]

---

Soon after the failed rescue, the Carter administration authorized another attempt. During one of the practice runs, a transport plane crashed, and the whole mission was scrapped before it ever left the United States.

---

# 5

# THE INNER CIRCLE

## TOP TEN MOST INFLUENTIAL FIRST LADIES

For Martha Custis Washington, nothing in the Constitution or social protocol outlined what she was supposed to do as the wife of the nation's head of state. Under this entirely new form of government, customs had to be invented. Even her title was a matter of debate. The aristocratic Federalists chose to call her "Lady Washington," while the more democratically inclined Republicans preferred "Mrs. Washington" ("first lady" would not be used until 1877 and only became popular in the twentieth century). In the search for balance, both Martha and her husband relied on restraint. They showed respect for the office through formal dinners and upper-class attire, but they avoided behaving like royalty.

The challenge for every first lady thereafter lay in finding equilibrium, to serve in an unelected, undefined position in such a manner than satisfied both right and left, prince and pauper, fellow American and foreign visitor. Most presidential spouses soon realized that they were publicly criticized no matter what they did. But to do nothing was not an option, as they lived at the very center of the executive branch. By tradition, none of them were ever technically employed by the government, yet all were expected to accept what Pat Nixon called "the hardest unpaid job in the world."

Ascertaining their respective "greatness" depends on the criteria one chooses. Ambition ran high in Florence Harding, whereas none were more independent from the federal circus than Bess Truman. In speaking one's mind, Betty Ford stands above, while Laura Bush is the model of compliance. None guarded a spouse with more militant resolve than Nancy Reagan, or herself more than Pat Nixon. Few were as scholarly as the bibliophile Abigail Fillmore, or as worldly and cerebral as geologist Lou Hoover, or as warm and kind as Lucy Hayes or Grace Coolidge.[1]

Arguably the primary role of the first ladies has always been public relations, promoting the image, policies, and public appeal of their significant other. Whether through correspondence and social gatherings in the nineteenth century, or through mass media and fund-raising in the twenty-first, wives were the first and most personal link between the politician and the population. The success of any given career depended heavily on how well the spouse connected to the body politic. Ranked here are the most effective partners ever to hold the rank of first lady and the means by which they supported their president.

## 1.  ANNA ELEANOR ROOSEVELT
(NEW YORK, 1884–1962)

Since the Great Depression, it has never been a question as to which first lady had the greatest impact on the presidency and the nation. In any poll of the president's wives, she is eternally first by a wide margin.[2]

It is often contended that Franklin Roosevelt, who grew up in wealth and comfort, developed his sympathy for the downtrodden when he was stricken with polio at age thirty-nine. In reality, his change in character came decades before, when his girlfriend Eleanor introduced him to a world he had never seen. Also a member of society's elite, she was a debutant and a graduate of a prestigious girls' academy outside London. But she chose to be a social worker in the decrepit slums of New York's East Side. In 1902, she brought him to where she worked. As he walked among the destitute, seeing and smelling the repressive filth in which they lived, he became profoundly aware of what suffering did to people. The experience never left him.[3]

When polio struck FDR in 1921, the person most altered by it may have been Eleanor. Shy and worrisome by nature, she developed a sense of inner strength by helping him conquer a deep depression. Through her diligence and encouragement, he was back among his Democratic colleagues and practicing law by 1924. He would never walk on his own power again, but she could campaign where he could not, acting as his legs, his eyes, and his ears. In 1928 they completed the miracle comeback when he won the race for New York governor. Four years later, he would be president, and she would redefine what it meant to be first lady.

Eleanor Roosevelt was the first wife of a president to hold press conferences, write a syndicated column, and give national radio addresses on a regular basis. In the first year alone, she traveled more than forty thousand miles to monitor the progress of the New Deal. If FDR was the mastermind of the new government, she was the conscience, spending time with coal miners, sharecroppers, the displaced, and the unemployed. She also publicly ended her membership in the Daughters of the American Revolution because of the organization's segregationist practices.

During the war, she unsuccessfully pressed the State Department to issue visas to European Jews seeking asylum and failed in her protests against internment of Japanese Americans. She succeeded in her case to get more women in the workplace and African Americans in the military. Though she loathed travel, the first lady flew into the war zones of Britain and the South Pacific. She visited wounded GIs, conferred with royalty, and reassured the British high brass of America's continued support. At one point in her ambassadorial duties, she was covering twenty-five thousand miles per month.[4]

Millions adored her, especially enlisted men, minorities, and the British. Others found her relentless drive and liberal idealism worthy of ridicule, particularly white conservative southerners and anti–New Deal Republicans. Regardless of her means, she ultimately and conspicuously placed the interests of the country far above her own. Over the course of twelve years, in a government that promised to restore dignity to common Americans, no one in the administration pursued that end with greater honesty and commitment than Eleanor.

As a paid public speaker and columnist, First Lady Eleanor Roosevelt sometimes made more money than her presidential husband. Much of what she earned was donated to charity.

## 2.  CLAUDIA TAYLOR "LADY BIRD" JOHNSON
(TEXAS, 1912–2007)

 Lyndon Johnson knew he had met his perfect match in 1934. He proposed to her within hours of their first meeting. Extremely intelligent, Claudia Taylor had finished high school at age fifteen and graduated with honors from Texas University, attaining degrees in history and journalism. She possessed a remarkable memory for faces and details, and she balanced him. He was profane; she was lyrical. He intimidated; she listened. He was another Bull Moose; she was the original Lady Bird.[5]

They began their political ascendance battling illiteracy through the New Deal's National Youth Administration. He moved up through the ranks to become a U.S. representative, heavily dependent on her moral, financial, and political support. She ran his Washington office while he served in the Pacific War.

She wept when her senator husband lost the 1960 Democratic presidential nomination to a lower-ranked senator from Massachusetts. But when Jack Kennedy named LBJ as his running mate, Lady Bird Johnson canvassed the country on their behalf, conducting more than 150 public appearances. Her hectic efforts helped to reduce the burdens of campaigning for the reticent and very pregnant Jacqueline Kennedy (who gave birth to John Jr. two weeks after the election).

While some wives withdrew from politics when their spouses became president, Claudia became more involved, if that were possible. A prime example was her support for the 1964 Civil Rights Act. The late Kennedy felt reluctant to impose the controversial measure upon the segregated South, where his political capital was marginal. LBJ was able to get it passed, but the backlash threatened to destroy everything the law was trying to achieve. To quell the dissent, Claudia set out on a seventeen-hundred-mile rail tour into her native Deep South. Stop after stop aboard the "Lady Bird Special," she defended the new law and extolled its virtues. Only in South Carolina did she experience any meaningful resistance, and that soon dissipated under the public support for the first lady.[6]

She was best known for her community and highway "beautification project," which was effectively an environmental movement, planting millions of flowers and thousands of trees, reducing litter, junkyards, and highway billboards. As the program's official spokesperson, she logged more than two hundred thousand miles in forty separate trips. Critics dismissed it as a vast aesthetic makeover, trivializing the true substance of the woman and her work. But criticism was something to which she had grown accustomed. Traditionalists attacked Claudia's stance on civil rights, progressives denounced her slavish loyalty to her husband, and the shallow chided her age and middle-class wardrobe.

Yet as the national chair of Head Start, a voice for historic preservation, a devout conservationist, and a highly effective political campaigner, she maintained both her own agenda as well as her husband's and still managed to appeal to the majority. For a woman straddling the breakpoint of feminism, and operating in the tumultuous 1960s, to be a convincing and respected voice of compromise was no small achievement.[7]

---

When Claudia Taylor Johnson was a little girl, her nanny called her "Bird." Claudia hated the nickname immensely, but it stuck.

---

## 3.  SARAH CHILDRESS POLK
### (TENNESSEE, 1803–91)

The first truly political first lady, Sarah Polk had no children, no pet causes, no pressing obligations beyond her own interests in politics and the desire to work with her equally driven spouse. Highly educated for her era, she had studied history and geography as a teenager at the prestigious Moravian Academy in North Carolina, and she read voraciously throughout her life. Playing hostess was not for her. When her husband became the Democratic nominee for president in 1844, Sarah reportedly declared, "If I get to the White House, I expect to live on $25,000 a year and I will neither keep house nor make butter."[8]

True to her word, the young forty-one-year-old made no attempt to host lavish galas or redecorate. What was good enough for the Tylers, she contended, was good enough for the Polks. Instead she insisted that the White House take on an atmosphere befitting its purpose—serious, focused, and sober. A strict Presbyterian, she forbade dancing and drinking, and though she received the nickname "Sahara Sarah" for her temperance, she charmed her critics by turning the mansion's dining hall into a roundtable of meaningful discussion. Having cultivated friendships in Washington while her husband was Speaker of the House, Sarah Polk simply solidified her network as first lady. Among her closest personal friends were Supreme Court Justice Joseph Story, the widow Dolley Madison, and Brig. Gen. Franklin Pierce.[9]

While Sarah was generally healthy, her husband was not. Eight years her elder, he worked incessantly and refused vacations. To work faster, he often had his wife read through piles of governmental paperwork to mark only those passages worthy of his attention. She also edited his major speeches, wrote correspondence for him, and gathered valuable insights in her conversations with congressional guests.

That he became president, and a successful one, did not surprise Sarah. Yet as perceptive and farsighted as she was, she did not anticipate his untimely death only months after leaving office. She lived out her days in Nashville, surviving her partner by forty-two years. Symbolic of her stature in the country, her home was declared neutral territory during the Civil War, respected and visited by Union and Confederate officers alike.[10]

---

When she was growing up, Sarah Childress frequently had the pleasure of spending time with family friend Andrew Jackson.

---

## 4.  DOROTHEA "DOLLEY" PAYNE TODD MADISON
(VIRGINIA, 1768–1849)

Lucky for James Madison he was born before the age of mass media. The shortest president at five feet four inches, a hundred pounds, and with a low and whispery voice, he was also terribly shy, a virtual opposite of the man who would succeed him. But he married well, and when the time came to move from secretary of state to head of state, he had an astute wife to guide him along the way.

Dolley had but one liability—her son JOHN PAYNE TODD from a previous marriage. Otherwise, she was everything Madison was not: charming, extroverted, embracing, and a skilled conversationalist. She was also a veteran of

White House affairs before the couple ever moved in, having served as acting first lady for widower and fellow Virginian Thomas Jefferson.

To casual observers, Dolley's worth resided in the superficial—extravagant parties, haut French attire, the first to have an inaugural ball, the first to serve ice cream at state dinners. A graceful woman, seventeen years younger than James, she certainly warmed the room with her deep azure eyes, porcelain skin, curled raven locks, and Botticelli buxomness.

A closer examination revealed a woman of far greater depth, one who understood the power of political networking far better than her mousy man "Jemmy." She was the first first lady to grant a newspaper interview and the first to use her fame to promote a philanthropic cause (in her case, the Washington Orphans Asylum). She also hosted large dinners for the wives of legislators, establishing good relations with the families of Capitol Hill and gathering valuable insights on the inner workings of Congress. At diplomatic soirées, she knew to soothe rivalries with her charisma (especially between the British and the French), while the antisocial James Madison often showed dangerous indifference. As Washington Irving described the president, when it came to social settings, "he is but a withered little applejohn."[11]

Dolley was also a woman of conspicuous courage, never more so than in 1814, when British forces were marching on the national capital. Madison departed to direct troops in the field, while she stayed behind in the Executive Mansion. Hours before the city fell, and long after most of the guards had fled, she resolved to leave her home, but not before taking every vital document she could stow into a single carriage. She also managed to save Gilbert Stuart's masterpiece portrait of George Washington, one of the few works of art to survive the ensuing fire.[12]

For six years, Dolley Madison made the White House the social epicenter of Washington, a feat not repeated until Julia Dent Grant in the 1870s. She also softened the opposition to her withdrawn and reclusive husband. Foremost, Dolley accomplished something most first ladies never could. As historian Betty Boyd Caroli observed, Dolley presented a presidency as both democratic and regal, open to the whole of the spectrum, rather than just the party in power.[13]

---

In 1794, Dolley Payne Todd and James Madison were formally introduced to each other by mutual friend Aaron Burr.

---

## 5. JACQUELINE LEE BOUVIER KENNEDY
(NEW YORK, 1929–94)

"What does my hairdo have to do with my husband's ability to be President?" Actually, Jacqueline Kennedy knew the unfortunate answer. Even George Washington knew the power of appearances, although he opted for stately stoicism rather than a fabulous bouffant and sultry sophistication. For the Kennedys, the emergence of television only solidified the importance of style in lieu of substance.[14]

Only thirty-one when she entered the White House, she was the youngest first lady of the twentieth century. She was also exquisitely photogenic, physically fit, and had immaculate taste in French fashion. After eight years of the traditional Mamie Eisenhower, the country and the media were ready for regal sophistication. Never mind that Jackie did not champion a single philanthropic cause, other than art and furniture restoration in the White House. "Why should I traipse around to hospitals playing Lady Bountiful when I have so much to do around here?" she said. The fact that she did not pander to the public seemed to add to her mystique.[15]

If she brought class and respectability to the Executive Mansion, she did the same for her husband. For a wealthy man, he was notoriously stingy, and his tastes were solidly pedestrian. But she imposed her elegance upon the both of them, entertaining the elites of the fine arts world and staging grand White House performances featuring celebrated musicians. She knew better than he did the enormous leverage of the presidential image.

Her impact may have been greater in foreign affairs. A former student at the Sorbonne, she enchanted the gruff Charles DeGaulle with her fluency in French language and culture. At the 1961 Vienna summit, her husband performed poorly, appearing timid and inexperienced in front of the Soviet delegation. Jackie, however, utterly dazzled the smitten Nikita Khrushchev with her graceful charms. She conducted repeat performances in Central and South America, Greece, India, and Italy, giving her husband second and third chances to work with nations otherwise suspicious of American intentions.[16]

Unquestionably the greatest contribution to her husband's presidency came after it had ended. In describing their shortened life at the White House, Jacqueline christened the administration "Camelot." With the help of many sympathetic journalists and biographers, she proceeded to weave that idealized image into the collective conscience, turning a marginally successful conservative Democrat, who was less than respectful of his marital vows and who escalated U.S. involvement in Vietnam, into a youthful idealist, struggling for all that was right and just. Her title for the time was definitely perfect, as it was a story of wandering knights, adored damsels, and fiction.[17]

---

In 1962, Jacqueline Kennedy's personal wardrobe bill was $121,000, which was more than the president's gross salary for the year.

---

## 6.  ELEANOR ROSALYNN SMITH CARTER
(GEORGIA, 1927– )

In 1982, the Siena Research Institute asked a number of historians to rate the qualities of the first ladies. Not surprisingly, Eleanor Roosevelt ranked first in nearly every category, from integrity to leadership. But in the role of "Value to the President," Mrs. Roosevelt finished second—to Rosalynn Carter.[18]

Looking back on their marriage, Rosalynn observed, "Jimmy and I were always partners." When her husband first entered politics, the couple soon realized they could canvass twice as much ground when they campaigned separately. To stay informed, she often conferred with him on all political matters. In adopting a cause as first lady of Georgia, she chose the substantive issue of mental health, and she served on a commission that scrutinized medical facilities in the state.[19]

When entering the White House, she continued to pursue her goal of greater public awareness toward psychological illness. She was the first first lady since Eleanor Roosevelt to speak before a congressional panel, and her testimony influenced the passage of the Mental Health Systems Act of 1980.

Unlike other presidential wives of the era, she refused to confine herself to the role of simple advocate. In the first two years alone, she gave

154 interviews, took part in 641 briefings, and traveled to three dozen countries. She hired 20 percent more staff than her predecessor, and created EAST WING offices to handle her research and press. She also insisted that her chief of staff receive pay and rank equal to her husband's. From 1978 onward she regularly attended cabinet meetings.[20]

As a national figure, she was not adored. She did not possess the refined glamour of a Jackie Kennedy or the edgy punch of a Betty Ford. Her involvement in political affairs brought much criticism from more conservative elements of the press and electorate. But she brought an element of intelligence and professionalism not seen since the Second World War, and at times, her approval ratings were twice as high as her husband's. Her well-earned credibility enabled and inspired her husband to do something not yet attempted by a president. For the first time, nearly one in four executive appointments went to women, including three cabinet positions.[21]

---

The 1980 Mental Health Systems Act, which Rosalynn Carter championed, eventually lost most of its funding under the Reagan administration.

---

## 7.  EDITH BOLLING GALT WILSON
### (VIRGINIA, 1872–1961)

It is a myth that Edith Galt Wilson ran the country after her husband's stroke. But she did literally save the man and his legacy—twice.

In 1914, on the very day a global war drew its first breath in Europe, Woodrow Wilson lost his first wife, Ellen. She was only fifty-four, a first lady for only seventeen months, and her passing sent the already emotional and needy Woodrow into a cavernous depression. For months he wallowed in mourning, and he neglected his work. At one point he mentioned in private that he welcomed the idea of being assassinated.[22]

When his cousin Helen Bones brought along a friend to the White House, the president's spirits immediately lifted. Those close to him were guarded. His wife had been dead for less than five months. For him to suddenly develop a giddy fascination with Edith Galt, a forty-three-year-old widow, was potentially dangerous to his public image, if not a sign of erratic behavior. But the love-struck man would not be deterred from his "special gift from Heaven." The two began exchanging love letters, and he soon proposed marriage. Only the interference from his closest advisors delayed the wedding for several months.[23]

From then on, Edith spent a great deal of time with him, often going over mails and dispatches in the morning, sharing a working lunch, and taking long breaks for billiards and outings to the theater. Their easy schedule ended with the U.S. entry into the First World War. Thereafter, Edith was the consummate patriot, volunteering for the Red Cross and greeting troops at the Washington rail station. She introduced meatless and heatless days at the White House, hosted bond drives, and kept a herd of twenty sheep on the south lawn, auctioning their wool for the war effort.

She became far more involved after the Armistice. In September 1919, Wilson frantically toured the country to garner support for the Versailles Treaty. While in Colorado, he suffered a mild stroke. Upon his immediate return to Washington, a second stroke occurred, and he was clearly in trouble, ashen, weak, trembling. For fear of placing the country in a panic, his doctors refused to state publicly the extent of his condition. They ordered full rest, no visitors, and an absolute minimum of work. Their first line of defense was the first lady.

Days stretched into weeks. Washington grew suspicious. Letters went unanswered, bills unsigned, appointments placed in limbo. When a few official papers came back with scribbled signatures, some began to wonder if they were forged. No one saw the chief executive, save for his doctors, his personal secretary, and Edith. She took it upon herself to screen every paper that came his way.

The cabinet led the country in the interim, meeting regularly but without their chief member. Several of them had no idea how sick he was. For six months, much of the executive duties went undone. Wilson slowly recovered, but never fully. Capable of working only in ten-minute increments, he lingered through his last year in office and was barely able to attend Warren Harding's inauguration.[24]

In shielding her husband from paperwork and outside contact, Edith Wilson contended: "I myself, never made a single decision regarding the disposition of public affairs. The only decision that was mine was what was important and what was not." Of course, to filter who and what reached him was a monumental interference, but it spared the nation from seeing their president in the morbid throws of paralysis, and it prevented Woodrow Wilson from being the first president ever to resign from office.[25]

---

While Wilson was hidden from public view, a few people saw bars on a White House window and deduced that he had gone insane and was being held captive. The bars were actually installed by Theodore Roosevelt. His kids liked to play ball indoors.

---

### 8. ABIGAIL SMITH ADAMS
(MASSACHUSETTS, 1744–1818)

While John Adams was away in Philadelphia, helping craft a declaration of separation from the British Empire, his wife wrote to him the famous caveat: "Remember the Ladies. . . . Do not put such unlimited power into the hands of the Husbands. Remember all Men would be tyrants if they could."[26]

Abigail Adams is the darling of many historians of the early Republic, and rightly so. She was a true manifestation of the revolutionary ideal. Independent, cerebral, she carried a sense of equality that was centuries before its time. When many women, including first ladies, burned personal correspondence to preserve their privacy, she saved her writings. Alone she authored more than two thousand letters still in existence, offering rare and vivid insights into the world of a fledgling United States. In addition, she could take credit for creating two of its first six presidents.

While John Adams built his career in the Continental Congress, she managed the family and property back in Quincy. Well read and skilled with money, she was thoroughly aware of the connections between micro- and macroeconomics. Her husband learned to trust her observations and her accounting, as she generally operated in the black, a skill that neither George Washington nor Thomas Jefferson possessed. For years she traveled with John as he acted as the American representative in France and Britain. Thereafter, she became his most trusted advisor on foreign affairs.

As first lady in Philadelphia and later in Washington, she knew her role in political spheres was limited to private interaction—hosting dinners for congressmen, diplomats, and cabinet members, receiving up to sixty callers a day—but that fact did not prevent her from speaking her mind. "I will never consent to have our Sex considered in an inferior point of light. . . . If man is Lord, woman is *Lordess*," she insisted. Mrs. Adams also displayed an acute awareness of the nation's worst internal fissures. Repulsed by the prevalence of slave labor in the District of Columbia, she deduced that the institution was the main reason the city perpetually ran behind schedule and overbudget. "I hope we may be held together," she wrote in 1798, "but I know not how long, for oil and water are not more contrary in their nature than North and South." Such insightful honesty made her the president's main political confidant throughout his four years in office.[27]

Her better nature may have failed her only once, regarding the strained U.S. relations with France. Angered by the bloodshed of their revolution, she pushed her husband to ask for a declaration of war. He instead erred on the side of caution, expanding the navy to protect American interests on the high seas but resisting the popular demand to lunge into the Louisiana Territory or French holdings in the Caribbean or against France itself, for fear of losing too much blood and money against yet another empire.[28]

The bitter loss of reelection in 1800 left Abigail angrier than her husband, and it placed her once close relationship with Thomas Jefferson on hiatus for nearly a decade. But it did grant the resolute woman one opportunity she rarely had in thirty-six years of marriage, the chance to spend time in Quincy with the one man who treated her as his equal.

---

First Lady Abigail Adams was so popular, especially in New England, that she had a company of Massachusetts militia named after her: the "Lady Adams Rangers."

---

## 9. HILLARY RODHAM CLINTON
(NEW YORK, 1947– )

It was nothing new for a first lady to be accused of coopting the office. To pressure cabinet members on whom they hired or promoted, one spouse illegally used War Department stationery and the signature "Mrs. President Lincoln." The early 1920s saw a White House marriage so dominated by the female half that the couple were known as "The President and Mr. Harding." Nor was it unusual for wives to remain with their husbands long after the discovery of extramarital affairs, as was the case with Lucretia Garfield, Florence Harding, Eleanor Roosevelt, Jackie Kennedy, and Lady Bird Johnson.[29]

But Hillary Clinton was unique in that she was the first wife of a president to ever have a West Wing office. No first lady before her had attained a law degree or had been as professionally independent. None had imposed the level of discipline into her husband's work as she did. And none had rescued her husband's career so often.

The fact that Bill Clinton's career needed rescuing was a testament to his coy nature. While such behavior was marginally survivable in 1980s Arkansas, it was politically unsafe in 1990s Washington. Were it not for Hillary's diligent defense of his character, especially against allegations that he had a longtime affair with Jennifer Flowers, Clinton might not have been nominated in 1992, let alone elected. In many ways, he operated a generation behind, as if accompanied by the discreet press corps of JFK or LBJ. In contrast, she was a generation ahead, keenly aware that the general public and the media had assumed the role of Big Brother. Proving her point, she would be the subject of more major opinion polls than nearly all of her forerunners combined.

Even in failure she spared his reputation. Heading the administration's number-one priority of universal health care, she assembled a task force that grew to several hundred people. Relying on a natural ability to stay focused and organized, she engineered a plan that would have provided basic services for the thirty-seven million Americans who had no coverage whatsoever. But the program would have cost in excess of one hundred billion dollars. In addition, she was only the first lady, neither elected nor appointed, and thereby possessed no constitutional authority to dictate policy. Financially, politically, and legally, the plan was bound for failure. Yet it was Hillary who took the brunt of the blame, rather than the man who had promised to deliver universal health care in the first place.[30]

She was living proof of her gender's progress in the social and professional worlds, and she had tested the limits more than any of her predecessors. But the presidency still contained its rigid checks and balances. True to her character, Hillary weathered the disappointment and managed to rescue a career. In 2000, she became the first wife of a president to run for political office, winning a seat in the U.S. Senate.

When she was growing up, Hillary Rodham's parents were devoted Republicans, and she was as well. As a youngster she supported the 1964 candidacy of Barry Goldwater.

## 10. LOUISA CATHERINE JOHNSON ADAMS
### (ENGLAND, 1775–1852)

For all of its hidden influence, the role of first lady cannot be declined. The duties, obligations, and the burning scrutiny that comes with it are all part of the post. Some have been more involved than others. A select few truly enjoyed their time in service. For the wife of John Quincy Adams, the experience pushed her into physical illness, fragmented her family, and reduced her marriage to a cold obligation. Yet she endured commendably, as the only first lady born outside of the United States.

Louisa Johnson had first met her future spouse when she was four and he was twelve. Her father was an American diplomat, her mother an English aristocrat. Together they lived in Nantes, France, nervously awaiting the outcome of the American Revolution, when they met with consul John Adams and his young son. Reconnected on several other occasions, the families became close. In 1797, the twenty-two-year-old Louisa married the thirty-year-old John Quincy. She would follow him to Berlin, where he served for four years as the minister to Prussia. Worldly, fluent in several languages, she was immensely popular. When she came to the United States in 1801, her audience was less welcoming.

Mother-in-law Abigail Adams openly disliked her, believing that John Quincy could have married better. Others found her foreign birth to be worthy of suspicion. But when her husband moved into the Senate and later became secretary of state, she developed her inherent skills in diplomacy, compensating heavily for a spouse who was too brash and bookish to be effective in social settings. She stayed informed by watching Senate debates, one of the first women ever to do so. She also hosted weekly dinners for prominent guests. When her husband was mentioned as a possible candidate for the presidency in 1824, she staged a dinner party for sixty-eight congressmen to bolster his chances.[31]

Her political skills were tested to their limits when John won the White House under the specter of the alleged CORRUPT BARGAIN OF 1824. Without a clear mandate, his administration struggled. She attempted to calm animosities by resuming the custom of visiting legislators' wives, taking several hours every day to traverse the unpaved streets of Washington and Georgetown. She publicly tried to dismiss rumors that her husband had supplied a mistress to the Romanov Court years before. At times, invitations to her White House parties were virtually ignored, as a slight against her husband rather than her. But by sheer diligence, and the willingness to be more congenial than the proud and confrontational John Quincy, she was able to maintain what little support he had left in government.

In 1828, Louisa worked harder than her husband to gain his reelection, and she was infuriated by the way Andrew Jackson's supporters attacked them both. The following year proved even worse with the premature death of her troubled son GEORGE WASHINGTON ADAMS. But she would return to prominence in Washington when John Quincy was elected to the House of Representative in 1830. A forgiving and generous person, she quickly reestablished old friendships and happily reconciled with those who had slighted her years before.

---

When Louisa Adams died in 1852, the Senate and House of Representatives adjourned for a day of mourning. It was the first time Congress had ever honored the passing of a former first lady.

---

## TOP TEN VEXING FAMILY MEMBERS

"Madam, I may be President of the United States," said Chester A. Arthur to an inquisitive citizen, "but my private life is nobody's damn business." Unfortunately for widower Arthur and his two children, the first family is America's royalty by proxy and is therefore a popular subject for gossipers and journalists alike. Fortunately for the country, while some relatives have provided theatrics reminiscent of *The Taming of the Shrew*, none have roused a tragedy on the scale of *Hamlet*.

On the contrary, many have played integral roles in the national support system. Lacking an adequate staff, early presidents relied heavily upon siblings, nieces, nephews, and children to help with official business. Long before Robert Kennedy became attorney general or Hillary Clinton chaired her husband's health care initiative, George Washington depended on nephew Bartholomew Dandridge for accounting and secretarial work. All four of Martin Van Buren's sons worked as his office assistants. James Polk's physician was his brother-in-law.[32]

Sometimes trouble arises at home, and the country is reminded that the first family can be just as imperfect as any other. Considering the never-ending scrutiny under which they live, and the tendency for critics to magnify every misstep, these households often show a commendable amount of tenacity. But every family tree has a few nuts. The following are among the more troubling figures in the domestic affairs of the chief executives.

### 1.  JOHN PAYNE TODD (1792–1852)
STEPSON OF JAMES MADISON

 Thus far James Madison is one of six presidents to have no biological children. At times, he may have wished that his dear bride, Dolley Todd, a widow, had also been childless. She brought to the marriage her two-year-old, John Payne Todd, who would grow up to curse the house of Madison with interminable shame and debt.

At first the tyke showed great promise. Graced with his mother's blue eyes and raven locks, John appeared to have inherited her innate wit and intelligence as well. Quite naturally his mother adored him. By the time his stepfather reached the presidency, John Todd had reached puberty, standing nearly six feet tall and brimming with charm and confidence. He was also a habitual slacker. To test the young man, Madison made him an attaché to a vital diplomatic mission to St. Petersburg, where the Romanov Court had offered to mediate an end to the War of 1812. John spoke French. The Russians negotiated in French. It seemed logical.

Once in St. Petersburg, the young diplomat neglected to write his parents, but he somehow found time to become physically involved with a countess. When the Russian deal fell apart, the American delegation headed to Gothenburg in search of another summit. Instead of going along, John bid them adieu, deciding he would rather take a holiday in Paris. Meanwhile, Britain continued to wage war on the United States, tightening its blockade on American ports, and setting Washington, D.C. on fire.[33]

Evidently unconcerned with the safety of his country, his relatives, or his fellow emissaries, John stretched his getaway into a three-month vacation, spending time and small fortunes at opera houses, casinos, restaurants, and brothels. A trip to London inspired a shopping spree for paintings, sculptures, and busts. The drifter paid on credit, assuring that the U.S. government would reimburse every franc and pound.[34]

In 1815 John Todd finally returned home, more than a year overdue and nearly ten thousand dollars in debt (when the median income was less that four hundred dollars per year). A beaming mother greeted him with open arms. A furious stepfather started transferring family funds to cover John's pricey escapades.

For the remainder of the Madison administration, and for years thereafter, John simply increased his consumption of hard drink, easy money, and loose women. To escape punishment, he often disappeared for weeks, writing home only when he needed more cash. Two stints in debtors' prison failed to induce remorse.

When James Madison passed away in 1836, he willed almost everything to Dolley, including a letter. In it he explained why their estate was smaller than expected. She had thought John had cost the family around twenty thousand dollars over the years. Only in death did her husband have the courage to tell her it was closer to forty thousand dollars (nine hundred thousand dollars in 2008).[35]

After James Madison's death, his stepson John Payne Todd illegally tried to sell his valuable private and public papers. His mother and Congress intervened. Facing bankruptcy, Dolley Madison eventually had to sell the papers herself, and she gave to her son the family home of Montpelier.

## 2.  GEORGE WASHINGTON ADAMS (1801–29)
### SON OF JOHN QUINCY ADAMS

Named after the first president, he was grandson to the second, and son to the sixth, yet he could never be president himself. Not that George

Washington Adams was lacking in intellect or achievement. A graduate of Harvard who studied in law, he had the brains, the breeding, and the connections to rise far. But he had been born overseas, Berlin to be exact. George was therefore ineligible for the presidency. He would also fail to acquire another trait necessary for election. He would never reach thirty-five years of age.

His father, John Quincy Adams, had a parenting style much like Thomas Jefferson's. He was strict, quick to criticize, and he expected success. He was also frequently absent, penning parental advice from a world away in consulates and embassies.

By 1825 George's father had become president. The pressure for the son to perform was greater than ever, as were the setbacks. First, George's fiancée dumped him for his brother John. Then, on July 4, 1826, his hero and grandfather John Adams passed away. Soon after, George was elected to the Massachusetts legislature, where he performed so poorly that he was eventually voted out. When a collapsing law practice left him deep in debt, he began to drink, womanize, and hallucinate.

It is not clear whether some progressive mental illness, pressure from his father, or an accident caused George's early death. On April 29, 1829, George started off from Boston to Washington to visit his dad, who had recently lost the presidency to Andrew Jackson. Traveling on a slow-rolling steamer off the coast of Long Island, George became erratic, wandered the decks, and asked to be taken into port. Sometime that evening, he either fell or jumped overboard. Six weeks later, his body washed ashore, providing closure but little comfort to his grieving father.[36]

---

George Washington Adams's brother John, the man who married his fiancée, would die five years after his brother at the age of thirty-one, apparently from the effects of alcoholism. The sole surviving brother, Charles Francis Adams, would become an accomplished author and Abraham Lincoln's ambassador to Britain.

---

## 3. ANDREW JACKSON JR. (1808–1865)
### ADOPTED SON OF ANDREW JACKSON

Meet John Payne Todd's twin. Andrew and Rachel Jackson produced no children, so they adopted Rachel's infant nephew. The tyke grew up on the Jackson's Tennessee plantation, the Hermitage, basking in opulence, which may have led to his complete lack of work ethic.

Money was never an issue. When pubescent Andrew Jr. left for boarding school, he was given a horse, a personal servant, and wardrobe of the finest imported clothes. Still the mediocre student managed to rack up a personal debt of several hundred dollars in a few months through carousing and socializing. Figuring boys will be boys, Andrew Sr. covered the bill.[37]

The young man never really grew up, and when his father became president, twenty-one-year-old Andrew made no effort to stop his trademark drinking binges and flirtatious behavior. Marriage to a bright Philadelphia Quaker in 1831 offered some hope, and the newlyweds operated the Hermitage while their father managed the country. But Junior's incompetence with farming and his expensive tastes in food, clothes, and alcohol soon had the homestead running deep in the red. Father bailed him out time and again, wondering if the cycle would ever cease.

Retiring in 1837, Old Hickory tried to reeducate his son, but to no avail. Even in death, Jackson Sr. continued to pay dearly. Passing away in 1845, he left the thousand-acre Hermitage to Andrew. Within a year, the indebted heir began selling off small plots to pay creditors. Soon the entire property was mortgaged. By 1855 he was selling over half the property to the state of Tennessee. Mercifully, the state permitted Andrew and his family to remain on the property as caretakers.

In 1865 his ineptitude finally caught up with him. Careless with guns as well as with money, Andrew Jackson Jr. accidentally shot himself while hunting. He died soon after.

---

No other administration came closer to eliminating the national debt than Andrew Jackson's. In early 1835, the debt was down to a few thousand dollars. At one point, the U.S. federal government owed creditors less than what Andrew Jackson Jr. did.

---

## 4.  JANE MEANS APPLETON PIERCE (1806–63)
### FIRST LADY

She was emotional, selfish, and passive aggressive. If she could, she would have voted against her husband in the 1852 elections, for Mrs. Franklin Pierce never wanted to see him in public office, let alone the presidency.

Jane Means Appleton was born in 1806 to sternly religious parents, and early on she displayed a conspicuous lack of mental and physical toughness. In the parlance of the times, she also suffered from depressions of the mind. But when Jane was twenty, she fell in love with a handsome lawyer from New Hampshire, and they courted for eight years.

It was a hard road. Her family were staunch Federalists; he was a Democrat. She was a teetotaler; he drank. She was shy; he was outgoing. She hated politics; he had ambitions. They loved each other, but soon after their wedding in 1834, their continuous fighting began to strain the relationship.

The marriage struggled further when two of their sons died in infancy. Jane thereafter became extremely possessive of her husband and their last surviving child, eldest son Bennie. Against her wishes, Franklin accepted the nomination of his party for the presidency in 1852. His surprise victory only filled her with misery, which deepened interminably when the Pierce family took a train ride to a friend's funeral. Along the way, the cars derailed at high speed. The president-elect and his wife were slightly injured. Eleven year-old Bennie was not as fortunate. His head was crushed in the wreckage, and he died instantly. Mentally, his mother never recovered. She later rationalized that God took her son away so that her husband could devote all of his time to being president.[38]

Jane chose not to attend the inauguration or most of Franklin's public events. She instead spent most of her time secluded in the second story of the White House, sporadically consulting spiritualists to contact her dead sons and writing long letters to Bennie. Most of the social duties of first lady were taken over by Varina Davis, wife of War Secretary Jefferson Davis.

A rare moment of joy came when the Democrats refused to renominate her husband in 1856, and the couple retired to their home in Concord, New Hampshire. Subsequent trips to the Bahamas and Europe failed to bring Jane out of her deep depression, and she died of pneumonia at the height of the Civil War.

---

To get away from the White House, Jane Pierce would occasionally take boats trips on the Potomac with family friend Nathaniel Hawthorne.

---

## 5.  MARY TODD LINCOLN (1818–82)
FIRST LADY

He was no treat to live with—slightly manic depressive, prone to brooding, excessively folksy and disheveled. In the words of his wife, "You can see he is not pretty."[39]

She was worse—materialistic, controlling, jumpy, a portly pixie with a belly full of issues. Perhaps her least pleasant trait, she was an incurably envious creature. Mary frequently accused her husband of being unfaithful, going so far as to throw him out of their Springfield home. On more than one occasion she physically attacked him.

More like counterweights than a couple, the Lincolns stumbled up the sociopolitical ranks, tempering each other's worst elements along the way. He might have never reached the presidency had it not been for his wife's unique ability to simultaneously love and prod him. But once in the White House, Mary was out of her element, and critics let her know it. From a slave-owning Kentucky family, she was too Dixie for Republicans and too Midwest for Washingtonians. Southerners damned her for the unforgivable sin of being Mrs. Abraham Lincoln.

Had there been no Civil War, she might have weathered such predictable barbs. But the conflict only intensified the pressure, and she stumbled often. She meddled in political appointments, publicly criticized cabinet members, and labeled U. S. Grant "a butcher" for his costly performance at Shiloh. Suspecting she was a Southern sympathizer and possibly a spy, a congressional committee secretly investigated her connections. One of the few character witnesses to speak on Mary's behalf was her husband.[40]

In her defense, she had lost several relatives in the war, plus her beloved eleven-year-old son Willie to typhoid in 1862. Constant media attacks against her husband only eroded her fragile state, and she lost most of her few friends.

But she utterly failed to connect with the suffering American public, embarrassing her husband time and again with expensive shopping sprees and public tantrums. Her worst move was to stage a major redecoration of the White House when others were struggling to get by without their husbands and sons. From the finest suppliers in Europe, she bought custom furnishings, brass fixtures, and ornate carpets. She also insisted on adorning herself in custom silk dresses for every occasion, when the nation was losing an average of two thousand soldiers a week. Unbeknownst to the struggling country, the president's wife had also gone 30 percent overbudget on the federally funded redecoration project.[41]

Little wonder why she had such a difficult time finding someone to accept her invitation to Ford's Theatre less than a week after the triumph of Appomattox. Rejection followed rejection, until a senator's daughter and her fiancé consented to go. As the couples enjoyed the play, Mary grew suspicious that Lincoln was trying to flirt with their young female guest. Moments before a bullet ripped through his brain, the president told his wife to not be so possessive.

> Before she settled on Lincoln, the young Mary Todd was briefly courted by a shorter but more famous Illinois politician named Stephen Douglas.

## 6. ALICE ROOSEVELT (1884–1980)
### DAUGHTER OF THEODORE ROOSEVELT

"I can either run the country or attend to Alice," Theodore Roosevelt admitted. "I cannot possibly do both." For a city that lived on intrigue, TR's eldest daughter was an eternal feast. Rightly christened "Washington's other monument," she was an alluring and insatiable debutant who faithfully lived by her mantra: "If you haven't anything good to say about someone, come and sit by me."[42]

Entering the White House at seventeen, Alice possessed the assured countenance of a monarch and the sinewy outline of a poet's siren. Much to the dismay of her father, she was also extremely independent. She smoked in public, drove fast cars, flirted with older men, and kept the media guessing on her many romances. When speeding through the countryside, she adopted TR's habit of shooting pistols at trees. Vocally irreverent to high society, yet perpetually in it, she would wake at the crack of noon to attend premier parties on a nightly basis, where she would adorn herself in long gowns of "Alice Blue" and mingle while her pet garter snake slithered along the embroideries of her bodice. An adoring press accurately named her escapades "Alice's Adventures in Wonderland."[43]

She was undeniably Theodore's daughter—but he could not bring himself to look at her. He never could, not since she was two days old.

St. Valentine's Day, 1884, New York Assemblyman Roosevelt had just returned to his home in Manhattan to see his beloved wife and their new-born daughter. They appeared to be doing well, when word came from downstairs that his mother was dying. She had been suffering from a se-vere cold—more than likely it was typhoid. Sometime around 3:00 a.m., Mittie Roosevelt passed away. Inconsolable, Teddy returned upstairs to discover that his wife was experiencing kidney failure. Hours later, she died in his arms.[44]

From then on, TR repressed all traces of his bride, blotting her name from diaries, removing her photo from scrapbooks, refusing to mention her name in his autobiography. He would marry again, this time with guarded affection. His second wife, Edith, would give him five more chil-dren, all of whom he adored. But his relationship with Alice was forever strained.

She found it all confusing and painful. "Father doesn't care for me," she confided, often wondering what she or her mom had done to deserve such alienation. It may have never dawned on her that she and her mother shared the same name and that Alice represented the only thing Theodore Roosevelt ever feared—the memory of the worst day of his life.[45]

---

To avoid speaking her name, Theodore Roosevelt called Alice by a myriad of nicknames, including "Sister," "Baby Lee," and "Mousie."

---

## 7.  JOSEPH PATRICK KENNEDY SR. (1888–1969)
FATHER OF JOHN F. KENNEDY

A ruthless businessman, flagrant womanizer, and anti-Semite, he endorsed appeasement with Adolf Hitler and financially backed Senator Joe McCarthy. Yet his son became president largely because of Joseph Patrick Kennedy rather than in spite of him.[46]

Early on, the patriarch taught his nine children the supremacy of image, especially winning. It mattered not what was involved—Wall Street, touch football, sexual conquest, or federal politics—so long as the family came out in front. As Joe once said to a young Jacqueline Bouvier, "All of us Kennedys don't like second prize."[47]

The drive came at a price. When twenty-three-year-old daughter Rosemary showed signs of mental illness, which sometimes manifested in violent outbursts, Joe submitted her to a lobotomy on the assumption it would make her more manageable. The procedure instead reduced her to permanent vegetative state. When second son Jack won the Navy and Marine Corps Medal for heroics in the Pacific theater, the father showered the young man with praise. The blatant and sudden favoritism motivated eldest son Joseph to volunteer for several dangerous missions over occupied France, one of which resulted in his death.

Because of his own transgressions, Joe Sr. knew he could never win the White House, but he assumed he could make his dashing and charismatic eldest son the first-ever Catholic president. Rather than surrender his vicarious dream when Joseph Jr. died, Joe Sr. simply turned to the next in line, who until then had no inclination to enter public service.

Ascendancy through the House of Representatives and the Senate brought Jack marginal notoriety, mostly for his relative youth and powerful surname. Despite a lackluster record (in fourteen years, his name never appeared in a major piece of legislation that passed), he still managed to appear on the cover of a 1957 issue of *Time*. Other favorable articles appeared in major papers, television reports, *Look*, and elsewhere, in no small part because of Joe's many connections and generous gifts to the media. Candidate Jack entered only seven presidential primaries, but he won them all.[48]

The 1960 Democratic Convention was almost anticlimactic, "prearranged" said a disappointed Harry Truman. Eleanor Roosevelt, an Adlai Stevenson supporter, alluded that the frontrunner Kennedy was "second best." Senator Lyndon Johnson fumed that he had no chance for the nomination. In turn, he verbally attacked the Kennedy wealth and made references to Joe Sr.'s sordid past, especially concerning appeasement and McCarthyism.[49]

For once, tragedy actually helped the Kennedy family. During Jack's first year in office, a week before Christmas, Joe Kennedy went from a political lightning rod to a beacon of sympathy when he suffered a massive stroke. Mute and confined to a wheelchair, he would never again be a target for his many detractors. The president would last see his dad in October 1963, at the sprawling Kennedy estate at Hyannis Port, Massachusetts. Before leaving, Jack turned to look at his father, and he said to an aide, "He's the one who made all this possible."[50]

---

Joseph P. Kennedy outlived four of his nine children.

---

## 8.  BILLY CARTER (1937–88)
### BROTHER OF JIMMY CARTER

Any family tree can bear strange fruit. Jimmy Carter's lineage contained a great-great-grandfather who had been acquitted of murder, a great-grandfather and grandfather who were killed in violent altercations, and a nephew arrested and sentenced for armed robbery while on drugs.[51]

Jimmy's younger brother was among the less conventional members of the family. A former marine who had attended college, Billy was far more intelligent and hardworking than his inane persona and well-documented drinking problem led people to believe, but he was not particularly close to his brother. Most of the Carters were relatively distant to each other. But this lack of contact led Billy to engage in behavior that was, in a word, peculiar.

In 1978 Billy began traveling to Libya. He also hosted Libyan dignitaries in the States. In July 1980, one month before the Democratic National Convention, the Justice Department discovered why. The younger Carter was working as a lobbyist for the Libyan government, and he failed to notify Washington—a violation of the U.S. Foreign Agents Registration Act. In addition, he had received a number of payments from Tripoli, totaling a hefty $220,000.[52]

A Senate subcommittee investigated whether the White House was connected with Billy's activities and whether he was influencing U.S. foreign policy. After nine weeks of gathering testimonies, documents, and depositions, the subcommittee found no evidence of legal wrongdoing, but it did criticize the Carters for their general lack of discretion.

The episode was one more nail in the administration's coffin, and it all but ensured a landslide defeat in the November election. Reduced to a pitiable figure in politics and pop culture, William Alton Carter would live just eight more years, succumbing to cancer in 1988.

> Often bragging about his ability to consume large quantities of draft, Billy Carter agreed to endorse Billy Beer in 1977. Though millions of cans were produced, sales were very poor, and the seventy-year-old company that made the brew was forced into bankruptcy.

### 9.  PATRICIA "PATTI DAVIS" REAGAN (1952– )
DAUGHTER OF RONALD REAGAN

Patti Davis did not invent teen angst, nor did her parents invent posturing, but both parties were extremely adept at their chosen craft. The resulting battles were particularly intense and well publicized, ending only when a crippling disease began to claim her father.

Ronald Reagan had been married to Nancy Davis only seven months when their daughter Patricia was born. His third child and her first, little Patti developed into an intelligent but strong-willed youth. She fought with her mother often, and on occasion the confrontations became physical. Her father rarely intervened, due to his innate aversion to confrontation.[53]

During the sixties, as Reagan's star rose among West Coast conservatives, Patti dropped out of school, experimented with drugs, protested the Vietnam War, and followed her parents' footsteps into the entertainment industry. She also dropped her father's surname name in favor of her mother's.

When Reagan won the 1980 ELECTION in a landslide, Patti became a highly visible critic of his prolife stance and nuclear weapons program. She also remained distant and removed from the entire family, with the exception of her younger brother Ron Jr., a Democrat, AIDS research advocate, and at the time, contributing editor to *Playboy*. The two of them certainly loved their parents, but they were paramount examples that the Reagan-era mantra of "family values" was more rhetoric than substance.

The feud lasted until her aging father was diagnosed with Alzheimer's in 1994. Davis gradually reconciled with the Reagans, especially her father, and in his last years she transformed from adversary to confidant. As a final paradox to their troubled relationship, she became closest to him when the disease robbed him of all memory of her.

---

In 1994, Patti Davis published an adult thriller entitled *Bondage*. The following year, after her father's diagnosis, she wrote *Angels Don't Die: My Father's Gift of Faith*.

---

## 10. ROGER CLINTON JR. (1956– )
### HALF BROTHER OF BILL CLINTON

In a classic case study of nature versus nurture, his half brother led the free world while he pursued a career in the entertainment business, heading a rock band appropriately called *Politics* and acting in such cinematic gems as *National Lampoon's Scuba School* and *Pumpkinhead II: Blood Wings* (as Mayor Bubba).

Roger Clinton Jr. did not enjoy a pleasant childhood, enduring mental and physical abuse from an alcoholic father. The older and much taller Bill tried to protect him as much as possible, but they were only four and fourteen years old when the worst of the beatings transpired.[54]

Their mother finally left Roger Sr. in 1962, but it was clear that only one of the boys would be able to psychologically distance himself from the past. In 1984, while Bill served as governor of Arkansas, Roger served time in the federal penal system, convicted on a charge of cocaine possession and sentenced to a year in prison. Oddly, his arrest came from a sting operation initiated by Bill's administration.

After the 1992 election, Roger Jr. provided the public with a marginally bemusing sidebar to his more charismatic relative. Undereducated, uncouth, and eager for attention, he diluted the credibility of the already precarious Clinton image. But aside from the occasional appearance in a television sitcom, musical gig, or comedy club, he generally succeeded in avoiding trouble.

Strangely enough, Roger became the topic of scandal on the last day of the presidency when his half brother decided to create a problem where one did not exist. Among the 140 names in Bill Clinton's controversial list of eleventh-hour pardons, including convicted tax evaders, perjurers, and drug dealers, Clinton added his half brother Roger, who had already paid his debt to society fifteen years before.

One month after Bill Clinton left office, Roger Clinton was arrested for driving while under the influence of alcohol. He pleaded guilty to a lesser charge.

# TOP TEN ALTERATIONS TO
# THE WHITE HOUSE

The mansion resembles the presidency—initially grand, then overrun
with obligations, and now heavily insulated from the general public. Creating the building was very much George Washington's brainchild, though
he would be the only president never to reside in it. While he served out
his second term, residing on High Street in Philadelphia, work began on
the Federal City 150 miles to the southwest.

Chosen primarily for its central location along the eastern seaboard,
the District of Columbia did not rest on ideal land. Carved from the
marshlands of Maryland's soft underbelly, its hundred square miles were
susceptible to oppressively humid summers, wet windswept winters, and
annual visitations from bloodsucking mosquitoes.

The Executive Mansion was the first government structure built in the
city. Up to the Civil War, it was the largest family home in the country, and
over time, it continued to grow. Today it is a sprawling estate of several buildings on eighteen acres. The main residence alone consists of 132 rooms with
35 bathrooms, and possesses over 55,000 square feet of floor space (an area
larger than a football field). Despite its many changes, two facets remain the
same. Most of the outer wall is original, and despite its ever-increasing security network, the house provides only a marginal amount of privacy for its inhabitants. Ronald Reagan equated it with "living over the store."[55]

Following, in chronological order, are the greatest changes to the
complex that now houses the first family. Known by many names over the
years—the President's House, the President's Palace, the President's
Mansion—it is better known by a less exclusive title, popularized by the
first Roosevelt and made official by the second: the White House.

## 1.  CONSTRUCTION (1791–1800)

Democratically inclined figures such as Thomas Jefferson were hoping for
a more modest capital city, along the lines of Williamsburg. Washington

refused. A greater statement was in order, something like Rome with open spaces. To accomplish his vision, he hired his military engineer from the Revolution, Pierre L'Enfant.

Aiming for a palace on par with the great monarchies of Europe, L'Enfant initially planned to build a White House nearly five times larger than its eventual size. Washington reminded him that the young government did not have the means for such an enthusiastic enterprise. When the engineering artiste persisted, Washington fired him.[56]

Taking the reins was Irish-born James Hoban, who submitted and won a design competition for a scaled-down model. Hoban's vision was just taking shape when Washington retired in 1797. By late 1800, President John Adams and wife Abigail were able to move in, with four months left in his presidency. The experience was, at best, unpleasant. The plaster walls were still wet and would not cure for weeks, requiring the few functioning fireplaces to burn warm all day, every day. Few rooms were complete. The first lady had to dry laundry in the barren East Room.

Comparatively, the building was further along than most of the city of three thousand residents. One wing of the Capitol was partially done. Roads were little more than cart paths, meandering over hills and traversing bogs. The great mall (which would not be created until the twentieth century) was a patchwork of common fields, policed by grazing cows. The ragged, muddy, frontier vista inspired Mrs. Adams to call it "the very dirtiest hole I ever saw." Still, the city and the house were very much like the rest of the nation, sitting restlessly along the Atlantic, ready to grow up and outward.[57]

---

James Hoban's design for the White House was based heavily on an existing mansion in Ireland called the Leinster House, which today is home to the Parliament of the Republic of Ireland.

---

## 2.  THE BURNING (1814)

The true White House lived but fourteen years, only to become one of thousands of buildings destroyed during the War of 1812. When American soldiers set fire to the Canadian city of York (later Toronto), British troops advanced up the Potomac to execute revenge upon Washington. Chasing American soldiers and militia from the city streets, redcoats en-

After the British burned the city in August 1814, all that remained of the White House was a fire-gutted shell. Ensuing months of rain and snow further deteriorated the charred stone walls.

tered 1600 Pennsylvania Avenue and proceeded to ransack the place, tossing furniture and breaking glass. They stole silverware, clothes, paintings, and James Madison's love letters to his wife. After raiding the wine racks and toasting the deposed president, the officers and enlisted filed outside to throw torches through the tall pane windows. In minutes the entire building was aflame, matching the hundreds of house fires rising throughout much of the city. Citizens could see the glow of their burning capital from thirty miles away.[58]

Separated during the melee, James and Dolley Madison would not find each other for two nights, reuniting at a place called Wiley's Tavern, Virginia. When they returned to their abandoned home days later, all that remained were most of the four main outer walls and a few chimneystacks. Madison would serve the remainder of his term living in various homes nearby, but he and many others began to contemplate moving the Federal City for a fourth time, perhaps to Ohio, where it would be safer from foreign intrusions.[59]

The government decided to stay, and Madison aimed to rebuild the Executive Mansion to its original specifications, rehiring James Hoban to repeat his most famous work. The project did not begin until the war was fully over in 1815, by which time rain and snow had further deteriorated the shell.

It took nearly a year to clean out the charred debris and reconstruct the roof. By March 1817 white lead paint coated the stone exterior and most of the floorboards were in place as James Monroe took the oath of office within sight of the recovering mansion. He would finally move into the building later that year, but work would not be completed until 1820. In what would become a tradition for Washington, D.C., reconstruction took longer than expected, and it went 60 percent over budget.[60]

---

Britain's act of arson totally consumed the White House roof. Much of the new roofing material, consisting of copper and slate, ironically had to be imported from Britain.

---

### 3. TWO PORTICOS AND MANY DREAMS UNREALIZED (1824, 1829)

If the political will and necessary funds had been available, the White House would have looked far different than it does. The Monroe administration initially wanted to double the width of the building, but a nationwide financial panic in 1819 delayed those plans indefinitely. In his last year in office, Monroe opted for something more modest—a rectangular portico to the north side of the building. Two presidencies later, Andrew Jackson took pity on journalists waiting outside in the rain and added a curved portico to the south-side entranceway in 1829. For the ornate stonework, he borrowed Italian artisans working on the ever-expanding Capitol to the east. These two grand awnings would be the last significant changes to the face of the complex for nearly a lifetime.

In the 1880s, Chester Arthur wanted to tear the whole structure down and start anew. After sixty years, the house was showing structural and aesthetic signs of weakness, primarily from the piecemeal reconstruction performed during the Madison-Monroe years. Comparing the ex-

The South Portico, added in 1829, enhances this c. 1846 image of the White House. During the Truman restoration, a second-story balcony was added.

pense of needed repairs to the lower cost of a new building, Arthur lobbied for the latter. A depleted treasury assured him that even minor renovations were not possible, and the poor structure continued to age.[61]

In 1890, the Benjamin Harrison family, all thirteen of them, felt im-
mobilized by the growing number of staff workers carving out office
space on the family's second floor. First Lady Caroline Harrison envisioned tripling or quadrupling the floor space, and she collected prospec-
tive designs from various architects to make the dream a reality. One of
her favorite sketches proposed two grand wings extending from each end
of the main building, with three-story domed rotundas anchoring both
sides. Another popular plan called for the creation of a great quadrangle,
with the existing structure acting as the south side. The Harrisons requested an initial investment of $950,000 to get started; Congress gave
them $35,000 for minor renovations.[62]

> During her scaled-down renovating, Caroline Harrison came across dis-
> carded White House china in an old cabinet. Adding to the set herself, she
> began the tradition of displaying past china patterns to visiting tourists.

## 4.  THE ROOSEVELT RECONSTRUCTION AND THE WEST WING (1902)

Over the course of the nation's first century, as the number of executive
employees increased, their offices began to encroach onto the second
floor where the first family resided. This was not a major issue for child-
less William and Ira McKinley. But their successors, the larger-than-life

Theodore Roosevelt's new
office space, as seen in this
1909 photograph, has since
become known as the West
Wing.

This 1909 image shows the East Wing before the structure became a building in its own right in the 1940s—complete with bomb shelter.

Roosevelt family, found the accommodations untenable. The house itself was also beginning to protest, with peeling wallpaper, foot-worn carpets, and kitchens glazed with decades of hardened grease. The floors visibly sagged. Every time there was to be a large gathering in one of the main areas, carpenters had to construct temporary buttressing in the rooms below.[63]

To correct the problems, TR commandeered the services of New York architectural firm McKim, Mead, and White. Charles McKim directed the effort in person. Typical TR, he gave his architects months, not years, to get the work done.

Inside the house, exposed pipes were tucked behind the walls, unneeded partitions were removed to create open space, bright white paint and natural woods lightened the very air of the once dank structure. The house began to resemble the presidency and the country itself, shedding the dark and compartmentalized past for the open view of modernity.

Outside, large greenhouses flanking both sides of the building were torn down. Intended to supply the White House with fresh flowers year-round, they gave the wings a cluttered look and masked the long, elegant colonnades built during the Jefferson administration. A public entrance was added to the end of the east colonnade. On the west side, an entirely new one-story building emerged, connected to the house by the west colonnade gallery. Containing telegraph and telephone offices, the Cabinet Room, a press area, the mail room, a reception area, and TR's main office, the complex successfully siphoned away the staff and busywork from the elegant main house.

Though built in 1902, the office building wasn't commonly called the West Wing until the 1930s.

## 5.  THE 180-TON ROOF (1926–27)

During the constructing of the West Wing, crews also expanded the State Dining Room in the main residence by knocking out a dividing brick wall. The end result was stunning. The expanded room resembled a grand lodge, with rich green carpets and deep velvet drapes and moose and elk heads staring down on the spacious hall. Unfortunately, the wall that was removed turned out to be load-bearing.

Years later, during the Coolidge administration, the missing wall's importance became evident when the full weight of the ceiling began to crack the wooden support beams. Informed that the roof had become unsafe, penny-pinching Calvin Coolidge suggested that if it was truly unstable, it would have already fallen down.

Credit Grace Coolidge, the more aggressive spouse, for showing initiative. She recommended solving both the structural problem and the building's chronic lack of space by adding a third floor. Congress consented to her wisdom and granted the money. Renovators tore apart the decaying attic area, lowered the floor, increased the pitch of roof, and replaced aged lumber beams with reinforced steel and concrete. Skylights illuminated the hallways, and an electric elevator was installed. In all, eighteen rooms were added, providing much-needed space for guests, servants, and storage. Crews also constructed a new room for the first lady, a sunroom that offered a majestic view of the south grounds and the slow-rolling Potomac River beyond.[64]

An engineer who helped designed the White House roof reconstruction was Ulysses S. Grant III, grandson of the eighteenth president.

## 6.  WEST WING RENOVATION AND THE FINAL OVAL OFFICE (1933–34)

The eminent chamber of the executive branch, the Oval Office did not exist until the twenty-seventh presidency, when William Howard Taft had an internal rectangular room converted into an ellipse in 1909. Emulating

The West Wing underwent a complete overhaul in 1934 under the direction of the Roosevelt administration.

the grand oval rooms of the White House's south side, the shape also served as an homage to George Washington, who preferred curved walls for formal reception rooms. The shape allowed for a natural balance, where the president could stand at one center of the room and the people the other, symbolizing the two sources of American governance.

Taft also placed the room in a central location, allowing for workers in the West Wing to have equal access to him and vise versa. When Franklin Roosevelt became president in 1933, the idea of the ellipse remained, but the locality bugged him, because it offered almost no quiet or privacy. FDR resolved to have the whole floor plan changed, and while he was at it, he threw on a second floor for good measure.

Reconstruction expanded the basement, doubled the area of the main floor, and perched a subdued second floor atop most of the first.

This 1938 image captures the renovated West Wing, which received a new second story and a transfer of the Oval office to the southeast corner (lower right).

The Oval Office was moved to the extreme southeast corner. With a taller ceiling, spacious windows, and a magnificent view of the south grounds, it provided a statelier locale than Taft's confined den. It also allowed the president to slip out onto the south lawn or into the main residence without being seen or bothered by staffers or White House journalists.

---

In 1929, on Christmas Eve night, an electrical fire broke out in the original West Wing, requiring Herbert Hoover to replace the roof and refurbish the offices. This may have given FDR added reason to provide the Oval Office with several quick exits. Due to his challenged mobility, Roosevelt had an acute fear of house fires.

---

## 7.  EAST WING–BOMB SHELTER (1942)

White House security tightened considerably after Pearl Harbor. Soldiers patrolled the locked gates. Antiaircraft guns bristled from the rooftops and the lawns. No one entered the premises without a pass. All house tours stopped. FDR understood the need for added precautions, but he detested the tense atmosphere it created. When Treasury Secretary Henry Morgenthau, in charge of the Secret Service, called for tanks to ring the perimeter, Roosevelt quickly overruled the measure as overkill. When Morgenthau insisted the president use the treasury vault as a bomb shelter, Roosevelt said he would be happy to, but only if he could play poker with the gold down there.[65]

Given that an air raid or naval bombardment against the White House was considered a real possibility, the secretary and others felt it necessary to build a bomb shelter on site. They chose an area just east of the main residence. When it was completed, FDR took one look at the confined subterranean tube and decided that he would rather take his chances above ground. All that work did not go to waste, however. To cover the structure, crews built a two-story East Wing with a large entrance foyer and ample office space for wartime staff.

The East Wing later became the headquarters of the White House Social Office and the main entrance for tour groups. In 1977, Rosalynn Carter was the first to officially establish the wing as the office of the first lady, a role it has retained ever since, except when Hillary Clinton opted for an office in the West Wing. Also located in the building is a narrow but comfortable movie theater for the first family (seating capacity: thirty).

The bomb shelter still exists. It is currently referred to as the Presidential Emergency Operations Center (PEOC). Used during situations of high alert, it can hold a dozen people or more. It also has a private bathroom, a few sleeping cots, emergency rations, and can reportedly withstand an airburst from a nuclear warhead.

During 9/11, several members of the executive branch were ushered into the PEOC, including Vice President Dick Cheney, National Security Advisor Condoleezza Rice, Transportation Secretary Norman Mineta, Deputy Chief of Staff Josh Bolton, and Cheney's chief of staff Lewis "Scooter" Libby.

## 8.  THE TRUMAN OVERHAUL (1948–52)

Bess Truman knew it was time to move out when her piano broke through the second floor of the main residence. The walls bulged. Cracks webbed the plaster ceilings. Plumbing and electricity were convoluted and substandard. After inspecting the structure, the city's building commissioner commented that the floors were "staying up there purely from habit." Age, inherent structural weaknesses, and the hefty new roof were conspiring to implode the whole place. The only ones not complaining about the conditions were the rats.[66]

While the Trumans moved across the street to the Blair House, construction crews set about gutting the entire structure, except for the

By the 1940s, the support beams of the original structure were so weak that floor boards actually swayed beneath people as they walked through the rooms. So during the Truman restoration, the whole building was gutted and rebuilt.

ABBIE ROWE, WHITE HOUSE

In this view, the entire substructure of the North Portico undergoes an overhaul, including the installation of a two-lane bowling alley.

ABBIE ROWE, WHITE HOUSE

newer third floor. In went a new foundation, two subfloors, steel framing, a gym, a new pantry, uniform plumbing and wiring, plus an updated air-conditioning system and a two-lane bowling area below the North Portico. For the first time, guest rooms had adjoining baths.

The project consumed nearly six million dollars and took almost all of Truman's second term to complete. When it was finished in 1952, the president led the first-ever televised tour of the building, escorting Walter Cronkite and other members of the media on a room-to-room expedition. Some thirty million viewers tuned in to see the new digs.

> To expedite the process of dismantling the mansion's interior, engineers brought in a bulldozer. Truman refused to let them knock a hole in the wall large enough to drive it through, so workers dismantled the dozer piece by piece and reassembled it inside the house.

### 9.   THE KENNEDY RESTORATION (1961)

Dwight and Mamie Eisenhower were military through and through. Accustomed to formal dinners and proper etiquette, they were also hardwired to live on a budget. As a consequence, they kept a rather frugal house. For middle-class America, this was all well and good. For incoming First Lady Jacqueline Lee Bouvier Kennedy, the decor was hideously gauche. To her, it looked like "a wholesale furniture store during a January clearance."[67]

Poring over books from the Library of Congress, Jackie researched every lost facet of the historic building. "Everything in the White House must have a reason for being there," she insisted. "It would be sacrilege merely to 'redecorate it'—a word I hate. It must be restored." She quickly cofounded the White House Historical Association and established a committee of restoration and fine arts scholars to assist. She also had the house designated as a museum, making it eligible for donations of historic artifacts and original furniture, all of which were to remain permanently under the care of a full-time curator. The entire project, she vowed, would be done with private funds and the sales of an official White House guidebook.[68]

In the spirit of Truman, but with somewhat more panache, she conducted a televised tour of her own. It aired on Valentine's Day, 1962, and attracted more than forty million viewers. In the following months, tourism to the mansion increased 67 percent.

---

Among the items restored was a desk carved from timbers of a British frigate. The piece was a gift to Rutherford B. Hayes from Queen Victoria in 1877. Jackie Kennedy found it in a storage area in the White House basement. The desk had been rescued once before, by First Lady Caroline Harrison in the early 1890s, who found it in the attic.

---

## 10. THE SITUATION ROOM (1961)

With painfully slow reports, no central communications hub, and no way to see the big picture, Jack Kennedy viewed the Bay of Pigs operation as a blur of confusion, in addition to being a crushing disappointment. To prevent the dangerous mayhem from happening again, he ordered the construction of a "Situation Room," from which he could monitor critical events as they unfolded.

Constructed in the southwest corner of the West Wing basement, the initial arrangement was Spartan, consisting of small offices with mahogany walls and low ceilings. The entire area had a dark, echoing gloom that Henry Kissinger described as "essentially oppressive." A main conference area served as the meeting room for the NATIONAL SECURITY COUNCIL. Communications consisted of a few telephones, televisions, and direct links to the CIA, the Pentagon, and the State Department. Two or three aides manned the adjacent and cramped "Watch Room," collecting information from intelligence agencies and departments and sorting reports into file folders. The "real time" arrangement may have had an effect on Kennedy's foreign policy. Rather than view international problems as long-term issues, he increasingly treated them as short-term "situations" to be addressed ad hoc.

During the ensuing Vietnam escalation, Lyndon Johnson frequented the complex often, hovering over maps and micromanaging ground and air forces in Southeast Asia.

Later presidents rarely visited, except for the occasional NSC meeting and during actual crises. Most preferred instead to receive daily reports from the Watch Room staff.

In 2006 the Sit Room underwent a major overhaul, complete with brighter lights, sound-dampening walls, cell-phone detectors, and larger work areas. The Watch Room was provided with two ergonomic workstations with multiscreen visuals, allowing the five rotating crews to work in greater speed and comfort. In the main conference room, old TVs were replaced with six flat-screen LCD and plasma monitors with secure connections and a direct feed to *Air Force One*. The overall floor space expanded to five thousand square feet, or about the area of two ranch homes. Unlike the Presidential Emergency Operations Center beneath the East Wing, the Situation Room remains merely a subbasement and is not bombproof.[69]

> In 2005, Hurricane Katrina revealed a major shortcoming with the Situation Room. Configured for international emergencies, the complex was conspicuously lacking in domestic communications, greatly retarding its ability to gather information from and dispense instructions to sites within the United States.

## TOP TEN MOST POWERFUL OFFICES IN THE WEST WING

Grover Cleveland called the presidency "a responsibility almost beyond human strength." Novelist John Steinbeck observed, "We give the President more work than a man can do, more responsibility than a man should take, more pressure than a man can bear." Gerald Ford's chief of staff Dick Cheney said of every chief executive, "No matter how hard he works or how smart he might be, he can't do it by himself."[70]

For decades, presidents tried to do it on their own, because they had to. Congress used to keep the executive branch on a tight fiscal leash, providing almost nothing for administrative assistance. Consequently, Lincoln often worked sixteen hours a day. A typical shift for Benjamin Harrison and his cabinet was 9:00 a.m. to midnight. Herbert Hoover ate his meals in ten minutes or less so he could get back to work.[71]

Finally showing some mercy, the legislature passed the Reorganization Act of 1939, establishing the Executive Office of the President (EOP) and doubling Franklin Roosevelt's staff from forty to eighty. Considered by many scholars as the start of the "modern presidency," the EOP should be called the beginning of the modern bureaucracy. The prime motivation, of course, was not to create a top-heavy paper mill but to expand federal services to satisfy voters. As the appetite of the populace grew, so grew the executive branch. William McKinley functioned with a staff of twenty-seven. William Clinton had more than three hundred full-time advisors and administrators. Add consultants, volunteers, security, and interns, and his total was closer to six thousand.

The Executive Office is a paradox in many ways. It is not one office but many. It allows a president to delegate busywork, yet it enables him to take on more responsibilities. The EOP provides greater control over the civil service, but it also adds one more layer to the bureaucracy. It is a product of democracy, yet most of its staff members "serve at the pleasure of the president" and are officially accountable only to him.

In this "White House community," only a select group of directors and deputies are given precious office space in the West Wing. Consequently, they are among the few citizens who get consistent face time with the president. And in Washington, time equals power. Following are the ten people who commonly have the greatest amount of presidential access. As George H. W. Bush's press secretary Marlin Fitzwater said, "You're really talking about twenty people, a very small group . . . a very personal kind of thing."[72]

## 1.   CHIEF OF STAFF

When Harry Truman assumed the Oval Office, he was shocked by the chaotic nature of operations. Franklin Roosevelt thrived in the informal environment. Truman could not tolerate such discord and redundancy.

The Nixon administration produced perhaps the tightest inner circle ever to command the White House: (from left to right) President Nixon, Chief of Staff Bob Haldeman, international relations guru Henry Kissinger, and John Ehrlichman, assistant to the president for domestic affairs.

WHITE HOUSE

Determined to transform the circus into a drill team, he hired former Labor Department specialist and FDR assistant John Steelman to be his "assistant to the president." The title would soon become something more imposing—the chief of staff.

The COS is the manager of the West Wing and gatekeeper to the Oval Office. Most any message, request, or problem must first pass through this guardian before it is deemed worthy of a president's attention. In turn, orders from the top usually pass through the COS. As Gerald Ford saw it, "You need a filter, a person that you have total confidence in who works so closely with you that in effect he is almost an alter ego." Commonly, a president meets every morning with the chief of staff and deputies before continuing with the rest of the day.[73]

The power of the position depends heavily on the governing style of the president. Truman, Eisenhower, and LBJ preferred obedient lieutenants in their chain of command. As a way of staying in control, Nixon demanded absolute loyalty from H. R. Haldeman and later Alexander Haig, and then proceeded to circumvent their authority at every turn. "I had these problems with Nixon; so did everyone else who worked for him," said Haig. Rather than trust a single deputy, noticed Haig, the bowling president chose to play "six or seven alleys."[74]

Hands-on executives Ford, Carter, and Clinton initially tried to operate their office on their own and consequently experienced chronic inefficiency and infighting. They solved the problem by hiring assertive individuals to take control. Ford first turned to conservative hawk Donald Rumsfeld (future secretary of defense) and later to authoritarian Dick

Cheney (future vice president). Clinton's administration wandered for more than a year until Leon Panetta assumed the role of disciplinarian. When Erskine Bowles took over in Clinton's second term, even Hillary needed an appointment to see the president.[75]

> The only recent president who never had a chief of staff was Jack Kennedy. To manage the West Wing, he preferred a "brain trust" of close colleagues rather than a single individual.

## 2. DEPUTY CHIEF OF STAFF

The COS manages the office. Deputies are the chief advisors. The position is a relatively new invention, made to liberate the primary consultants from any other duties and prevent them from becoming highly visible lightning rods. In hindsight, Lincoln's William H. Seward, Eisenhower's John Foster Dulles, and Gerald Ford's Henry Kissinger might have operated with more focus and less controversy if they had been deputized out of the spotlight. Instead, they worked in the very public position of secretary of state, where they had to juggle serving the president, managing an entire federal department, and catering to the press.

The first de facto deputy was John Ehrlichman, Nixon's assistant for domestic affairs. Before Watergate made him infamous, Ehrlichman worked in splendid anonymity, having round-the-clock access to the president while preventing others from having the same privilege. Ehrlichman and chief of staff H. R. Haldeman were so possessive of Nixon's time that they were known inside the White House as "the Berlin Wall."

More recent Republicans have moved toward multiple deputies as the central core of their administration. In his first term, Ronald Reagan entrusted much his policy making to COS James Baker III, deputy COS Michael Deaver, and White House counsel Ed Meese. George H. W. Bush often had two deputies, one for political strategy and the other for domestic policy. In his second term, George W. Bush added a third, designating high-school graduate Karl Rove officially as an additional deputy. In reality, Rove was the lead advisor of the entire administration.

> Illustrating the growth of bureaucracy in the West Wing, chief of staff James Baker III, while working for George H. W. Bush, had two deputies

under him, plus an executive assistant, an administrative assistant, a staff assistant, a special assistant, and a staff assistant to the special assistant.

### 3. THE WHITE HOUSE COUNSEL

The attorney general is the nation's lawyer. The White House counsel is the attorney for the executive branch. Established in 1943, the office has steadily grown in size and influence, reflecting an increasingly litigious political system.

Anything that is potentially a legal issue (which is everything) requires an examination from the counsel's office. From hiring practices to war powers, pardons, ethics regulations, and executive orders, it all falls under their purview. Before a president or any cabinet member gives a major speech, this office will have gone through it line by line, looking for any statement that might constitute a breech of law. Before a president ever signs a bill, the counsels will ensure the act would in fact be legal. Before presidents claim executive privilege, they will usually consult with this group first to see if they have a case.

Armed with attorney-client privilege, in charge of preventing legal problems and solving them if they arise, chief counsels are frequently among the most trusted members of a president's inner circle. Consequently, they hold a great deal of prestige in the eyes of their employer. The first official counsel, Samuel Rosenman, was also one of FDR's key speechwriters. Truman's confidant and the architect of his miraculous 1948 victory was Clark Clifford, who would go on to become a private attorney for Jack Kennedy and LBJ's secretary of defense. Few people saw the honest side of Kennedy more often than his counsel Theodore Sorenson, the man who wrote much of his inaugural address and played a central role in the CUBAN MISSILE CRISIS. Nixon involved John Dean in the most sordid elements of the Watergate cover-up. Reagan's White House counsel Ed Meese, and later attorney general, was like a second chief of staff.[76]

When he was thirty-four, Fred Fielding had the distinction of serving as deputy counsel under John Dean during Watergate. He became lead counsel in his early forties for the Reagan presidency. In his later sixties, he returned as lead counsel for George W. Bush.

## 4.  NATIONAL SECURITY ADVISOR

A product of the cold war, the National Security Council was officially created by the National Security Act of 1947 (the same measure that made the CIA and the Department of Defense). The idea was to form a centralized command structure in place of the divergent State, War, and Navy Departments. Initially, the council met in the Old Executive Office Building, across the street from the West Wing.

Chaired by the president and vice president, its members included the secretaries of defense, state, and treasury. In consulting roles were the chairman of the Joint Chiefs of Staff and the director of the CIA. A national security advisor acted as overall director. Truman thought the group unwieldy but turned to it often during the Korean War. Eisenhower was quite comfortable with its backroom feel, where politics and military concerns cohabitated. He attended nearly 90 percent of the meetings.

JFK brought it firmly under his wing, literally. After the Bay of Pigs fiasco, he moved the meetings to the newly constructed SITUATION ROOM in the basement of the West Wing and elevated the power of his national security advisor. McGeorge Bundy operated what many called the "Little State Department," often forming policy with minimal input from the Joint Chiefs or the CIA. Suspicious that even this truncated group was causing leaks, LBJ reduced the working council still further to his "Tuesday lunch" group of Bundy, Secretary of State Dean Rusk, and Secretary of Defense Robert McNamara.

By the Nixon administration, policy decisions were dictated almost exclusively by the president and National Security Advisor Henry Kissinger.

ABBE ROWE, NATIONAL PARK SERVICE

JFK confers with National Security Adviser McGeorge Bundy, a major advocate for increased involvement in Vietnam.

Nixon's national security adviser, Henry Kissinger, dominated foreign affairs to the point that the State Department became a bit player in the administration.

Carter followed Nixon's lead with NSA Zbigniew Brzezinski. During the Reagan administration, even the president was out of the picture, resulting in a near total loss of oversight and the debacle of the IRAN-CONTRA AFFAIR.

The position recovered its dignity and prestige during the tenure of George H. W. Bush with the return of Ford's NSA Brent Scowcroft. Like Bush, Scowcroft had professional experience in the intelligence field and the armed forces, and he became one of the chief architects in the multinational victory of the First Gulf War.[77]

> Colin Powell had the distinction of serving on the National Security Council in three different capacities—as national security advisor under Ronald Reagan, as chairman of the Joint Chiefs of Staff under George H. W. Bush, and as secretary of state under George W. Bush.

## 5. DIRECTOR OF THE OFFICE OF MANAGEMENT AND BUDGET

Normally, Congress surrenders its obligations to the executive in small steps. One giant leap came in 1921. Before then, the House Ways and Means Committee and the Senate Finance Committee dictated what the government was going to spend in any given year. From the executive branch, individual departments and agencies would come with hat in hand, requesting a portion of available funds. The president had minimal influence on the process, except in wartime.

It was during the Great War that Capitol Hill felt it could no longer control its own spending. Under the advice of Warren Harding's treasury secretary Andrew Mellon, Congress passed the Budget and Accounting Act, essentially putting the presidency in charge of figuring the cost of running the country. For a while the system seemed to work. Under the executive Bureau of the Budget, the debt fell from twenty-six billion dollars to sixteen billion dollars in less than a decade.[78]

The unforeseen trauma of the Great Depression quadrupled the debt, but the Budget Office remained small. Even in 1939, when it officially transferred from the Treasury Department to the Executive Office of the president, the organization had a modest staff of forty-five. The monumental money pit of the Second World War boosted its payroll to five hundred employees.[79]

Since then, the count has stayed roughly the same, only the name and strategy have changed. In 1970 the bureau became the Office of Management and Budget, and instead of reducing costs, the political incentive has been to procure more revenues for popular programs. Charged with defending the president's fiscal agenda, the OMB has the power to shift discretionary funds from one area of the government to another, determine allowances for federal agencies, and make recommendations to the president as to which programs and agencies should receive the most funding.

An odd reversal of fortune, so to speak, since the submissive executive branch used to approach Congress for money. Today, every autumn, the legislature, the judiciaries, the executive agencies, and the cabinet departments humbly submit their budget requests to the OMB.

---

Directors of the OMB have gone on to become secretary of state (George Schultz), secretary of defense (Caspar Weinberger), and chief of staff (Leon Panetta and Josh Bolton).

---

### 6.  THE PRESS SECRETARY

"The White House spokesman is the second most visible person in the country," said Reagan's press contact Larry Speakes, "which can be not only an honor but a headache." Rarely involved in decision making, but almost always the earliest to know, the press secretary is the link between the president and the national news.[80]

Acknowledging the power of the papers, Theodore Roosevelt was the first to truly cater to them, building a pressroom in the newly built West

Wing. TR was also his own media front man. Presidents to follow were not so gregarious. Herbert Hoover was less inclined to speak to the press than Silent Cal Coolidge, so he hired an assistant to do it for him. FDR, conscious of the emerging influence of radio, created an entire group to work with journalists, and the White House Press Office was born.[81]

As the age of information manifested itself through live television, the office became even more active and visible. Handling breaking news, plus giving briefings twice a day, the spokesperson is the first to present the official White House line on any given subject and the lightning rod for questions from the press corps. Marlin Fitzwater said it was like serving two masters, the White House and the media.[82]

At times, they are instructed to lie. To explain Kennedy's sudden cancellation of a trip to Seattle, Pierre Salinger told the media that JFK had a respiratory infection and had to return to Washington. In reality Kennedy was rushing back to deal with the escalating CUBAN MISSILE CRISIS. Jimmy Carter's spokesman Jody Powell knew about the impending (and doomed) military rescue operation for the Iranian hostages. But when reporters inquired about a possible rescue mission, Powell maintained secrecy by denying that any rescue plan existed.[83]

Constant pressure to perform well, even when the administration does not, can create a high rate of attrition. Nixon's Ron Ziegler, the youngest press secretary to date at age twenty-nine, toughed it out the whole way. In contrast, George W. Bush was on his third press secretary in his final years. Lyndon Johnson had four. Truman went through them like a plate of pork ribs, using five.

Ronald Reagan's press secretary Larry Speakes (right) called the press job an honor and a headache. Speakes was one of three press secretaries to serve under Reagan during the president's eight years in office.

REAGAN LIBRARY

Chief executives initially hired journalists to fill the position. Recently the tendency is to select political insiders with speaking experience. Bill Clinton made the freshman mistake of choosing neither. Opting for novelty over know-how, he paid the price in bad press. At thirty-one, Dee Dee Myers was one of the youngest and the first female to hold the job. But she had virtually no media background and minimal access to the president. Amiable but underinformed, she adapted and held on for two years.[84]

---

The Class of 1901 at Independence (MO) High School included Harry S Truman, Elizabeth V. Wallace, and Charles Griffith Ross. The country would get to know all three as Mr. President, the first lady, and Mr. Press Secretary.

---

## 7.   DIRECTOR OF COMMUNICATIONS

Selling the presidency, the Office of Communications is the public relations firm of the White House. Clinton's first director, George Stephanopoulos, exaggerated only a little when he said, "By definition, if the President isn't doing well, it's a communications problem."[85]

From the beginning, administrations knew the vital importance of presenting their worldview to the masses. Initially, it was done covertly through partisan newspapers. Later on, presidencies became more aggressive in disseminating their brand of information, especially in wartime. During U.S. involvement in the First World War, the Wilson administration hired "Four-Minute Men," public speakers who gave prepared short speeches at movie houses before the main feature. During World War II, FDR's Office of War Information delivered newsreel footage.[86]

The office truly came into its own under Nixon, who separated its duties from the Press Office. Disseminating favorable information through television, radio, periodicals, photography, and speechwriting, checking the nation's pulse through polls, research, news analysis, and public liaisons, his administration was able to sidestep the press and appeal directly to the "great silent majority." For Dick, it worked wonders, especially in damage control. Despite Cambodia, Kent State, Laos, Vietnam, Watergate, and a slowing economy, he won reelection by a landslide in 1972.

In contrast, Ford, Carter, and George H. W. Bush reduced staff, wrote and edited most of their own speeches, depended on personal appearances to reach the people, and let their work ethic do most of the talking.

In the age of high-dollar marketing and high-speed media, their methods proved slow and unresponsive. In turn, Reagan offered a lesson in how it should have been done. His communications staff released thousands of warm, colorful, patriotic photos of the president every month. They carefully edited video pieces to show the septuagenarian hard at play at his California ranch. They perfected the sound bite, stayed in tune with his ratings, and kept him away from the press.[87]

Generally, Republican administrations also tend to perform better than their opposition in presenting a united front. As Dick Cheney insisted: "You're there to run an effective presidency. And to do that, you have to be disciplined in what you convey to the country." Through internal briefings, media handlers, and carefully prepared responses to difficult questions, they often appear in lockstep, presenting a greater appearance of control, all of which falls under the jurisdiction of the Office of Communications. It is a high-stress job, and most directors last an average of eighteen months before they step down or are replaced.[88]

---

Bill Clinton's Office of Communications was the first to set up an official White House Web site.

---

## 8. DIRECTOR OF LEGISLATIVE AFFAIRS

Presidents can appeal directly to the public for moral support on an issue, but they communicate their official position through the director of legislative affairs. Proposing bills in the House, getting treaties passed in the Senate, mending fences after vetoes, getting appointees approved, it all takes live bodies from the Executive Office working directly on Capitol Hill.

Familiar with the dangers of poor communication between allies, Eisenhower established the first legislative liaison office. Small, informal, and bipartisan, it was effective enough for his administration's modest agenda. Kennedy and Johnson were more aggressive in their efforts, and their directors emphasized party loyalty to sway voters. Carter reduced his liaison staff, and he famously struggled for his first two years, mystified that party members were not more obedient. Publicly, Reagan could be downright abusive toward the Hill, but his liaison office was one of the most organized and cooperative, using generous bargaining to win over lawmakers. The tactic often backfired, however. Reagan's budget director

David Stockman remembered the irony of convincing legislators to back the 1981 tax cut bill by enticing them with huge tax breaks for corporations, real estate developers, and oil companies in their districts.[89]

Part of the job is mathematic—tracking vote counts, calculating the required majorities, determining margins of error. It also requires teaching skills—explaining to lawmakers the wisdom of voting a particular way, keeping cabinet members and senior staff informed on the personalities and issues involved. Sometimes, it involves playing Santa Claus—offering support for pet projects, sending invitations to White House functions, and the ultimate prize, scheduling face time with the president.

Typically, the work gets harder as the administration ages. Presidents start off with a high level of political capital in Congress, but this honeymoon invariably ends, and the legislature rediscovers a sense of independence. Conditions only get worse after midterm elections, when voters get impatient. The party of the incumbent almost always loses seats (thirty-three out of thirty-seven times since the Civil War). Consequently, no matter how hard the liaisons and the president try, they almost always see a decline in support. Eisenhower was getting 89 percent of his preferred legislation passed in his first year and only 65 percent in his last. Nixon went from 74 to 60. Reagan fell from 82 to 47 over the course of his administration. The Democratic darling Clinton initially won nearly 90 percent of his favored bills, only to see his poor management of the White House damage his credibility. Some months he was only getting 30 percent of his bills passed.[90]

---

During the Clinton administration, one of the many interns in the Office of Legislative Affairs was Monica Lewinsky.

---

## 9.   THE NATIONAL ECONOMIC ADVISOR

It used to be that the president received most of his fiscal advice from a dream team of economists, many of whom were professors on loan from prestigious universities. A three-person panel with a support staff of a dozen fellow academics and statisticians, they focused on the long term, delving into macroeconomic issues of unemployment, inflation, debt, and taxation. This Council of Economic Advisors still exists, but its influence has waned since the 1990s. Now the practice is to think in much shorter terms and follow the lead of business advisors in the National Economic Council.

Created by Bill Clinton in his first week as president and headed by investment banker Robert Rubin (formerly of Goldman Sachs), the NEC was the financial equivalent to the National Security Council, grouping together several cabinet secretaries and federal agencies, including the old economic advisors. Members included the secretaries of agriculture, commerce, energy, housing and urban development, labor, and transportation, the U.S. trade representative, the head of the Environmental Protection Agency, and others. The NEC was given the responsibility to not only formulate policy but to force it into action, demanding the cooperation of otherwise disparate and often competing offices. The council itself is armed with a staff of thirty and views domestic and internal trade policy in more concrete terms—such as housing markets, Medicare and Medicaid, Social Security, existing trade agreements, and tax laws.

The formula appeared to work. Concentrating on the micro- instead of the macroeconomic, the short-term stimulus packages and resulting growth in the economy signaled an end to a recession that had begun in the previous presidency. For three years in a row, the government operated in the black, and the NEC had the unusual pleasure of contemplating what to do with an annual budget surplus. Assuming as many did that this economic trend would continue for years to come, Clinton declared his NEC "the single most significant organizational innovation that our administration has made in the White House."[91]

George W. Bush tacitly agreed. A businessman himself, Bush favored the NEC over the Council of Economic Advisors. In his West Wing, he gave first-floor office space to the director and deputy director of the NEC, while the economic advisors worked far off-site, and were left understaffed for much of Bush's second term.

---

George W. Bush's third director of the National Economic Council was Allan Hubbard. The two men were classmates in Harvard Business School, and Hubbard later became one of Bush's major campaign contributors.

---

## 10. DIRECTOR OF THE OFFICE OF MANAGEMENT AND ADMINISTRATION

The power is indirect. The Office of Management and Administration has no policy-making powers whatsoever, and yet every building and every human body in the White House complex completely depends upon it to operate smoothly.

With one of the largest employee bases in the Executive Office system (more than two hundred full-time staff members), it has quite a few ongoing assignments, such as keeping all computer and communication equipment updated and working, controlling the EOP budget, processing thousands of White House visitors each day, and acting as White House liaisons to the Secret Service. They are also in charge of salaries, building maintenance, staff orientation, the travel office, telephone operators, the motor pool, and the White House intern program. Arguably one of the most difficult of duties involves distributing limited West Wing office space to a legion of type-A personalities. The prime real estate is on the first floor with the Oval Office, followed by the second story and the basement (where the OMA director and deputy are usually located).[92]

Created by Carter, streamlined under Reagan, and receiving its current title from George H. W. Bush, it is usually the least partisan office in the White House complex. If its workload was not ample enough, it also oversees the White House Military Office. With more than two thousand full-time and part-time employees, the Military Office handles the operations for *Air Force One*, the *Marine One* helicopter squadron, the 221 acres of Camp David (managed by the navy), the West Wing mess (also under the navy), the White House Medical Unit (twenty doctors and the president's personal physician), honor guards, the Marine Band, plus five military aides (all lieutenant colonels or higher) that carry the "Football"—the briefcase that contains the launch codes for U.S. weapons of mass destruction. On top of it all, the Office of Management and Administration also determines who gets the best parking spots outside the West Wing.[93]

---

Indicative of their vital position in presidential operations, OMA directors are paid almost the same as the chief of staff.

---

## TOP TEN BIGGEST SCANDALS

Corruption comes in a multitude of genres—blackmail, graft, insider trading, espionage, sex. It mostly resides in the lower depths of society. The higher it ascends, the greater the scandal when it surfaces.

In examining instances of executive intrigue, a few observations can be made. Generally, citizens hold their leaders to a higher ethical standard than themselves. They may or may not care for a particular president, but as a whole, the electorate holds the presidency in high regard, and the public wrath has been most pronounced when officeholders do not express similar respect.

Also, the populace will seek retribution, to a point. When implicated, the president in question must offer disclosure, accept responsibility, or suffer a certain amount of humiliation. Once the public appetite for reprisal has been satiated, regardless of the letter of the law, forgiveness pervades, and political capital is gradually reinstated. If the nation ever wanted to adopt a new motto that best reflects its basic nature, it would do well to consider Ronald Reagan's favorite proverb: "Trust, but verify."

Lastly, as the following cases clearly illustrate, the executive branch has been generally inept at engineering conspiracies. Subject to the watchtowers of free speech and free press, populated with rivals, rogues, saints, and squealers, the White House consistently fails to hide so much as an office break-in without half the planet eventually hearing about it. Below in chronological order are the worst episodes of political scandal that directly involved the executive branch, measured by the number and illegality of acts committed, and their measurable consequences.

## 1.  XYZ AFFAIR (1797)

During the French and Indian War, the colonies sided with Mother England. Fifteen years later, rebellious Americans paired up with the French to shun the British yoke. Fifteen years after that, the United States became chummy trade partners with Britain again.

Not surprisingly, Paris found this two-step rather tiresome. In 1796, French magistrates and media reminded the Yanks that it was France who came to the rescue during their little revolution, signing a treaty of eternal cooperation, and eventually providing most of their ammunition, gunpowder, and navy. At Yorktown, half the troops were from *l'armée française*. In rebuttal, many Americans, including President John Adams, reminded the French that the Treaty of Alliance applied to the France of Louis XVI, and that particular head of state had been chopped off years ago.

John Adams tried to invoke executive privilege in the XYZ Affair. His prudence initially caused a national crisis but ultimately led to his vindication.

Battles in print soon turned to seizures on the high seas, as French privateers began confiscating American ships by the dozen. Hoping to calm the swelling tempest, Adams sent Charles C. Pinckney, John Marshall, and Elbridge Gerry to Paris on a mission of peace. Greeting them were three dignitaries who said they would let the Americans speak with the French foreign minister, providing the Adams administration pony up $250,000, plus a loan of $10 million, and a formal apology from Adams himself for his chides against the French people. It is unlikely the demands were serious, and they would remain secret, for a while.

When the American public heard that the mission had failed, those sympathetic to the French (including Vice President Thomas Jefferson) accused Adams of sabotaging the negotiations, and they demanded to see all the records pertinent to the case. Adams claimed executive privilege and refused, which only cemented suspicions. Grudgingly, the president released the sordid details to the Senate, and someone leaked the news to the public. The French and their blackmail, slurs, and affronts—it was all there in ink and parchment. The only unknowns were the names of the French diplomats, who were simply called X, Y, and Z.

Red with rage, the pro-British majority called for an immediate declaration of war. Congress appropriated millions for warships, coastal forts, and a larger army. Cities began to collect money to build gunboats. The undeclared QUASI WAR ensued, which dragged on precariously for two years, costing the lives of at least twenty American sailors and terminating all existing treaties between the two countries. The scandal, which initially threatened to destroy Adams's credibility, ultimately made him look like a sage, and inspired Congress to pass the dictatorial ALIEN AND SEDITION ACTS.[94]

---

Hundreds of merchant vessels were captured by both sides during the two-year Quasi War. As a result, insurance rates for overseas shipping went up nearly 500 percent.

---

## 2.   THE PETTICOAT AFFAIR (1828–31)

The president's cabinet is sometimes called the official first family, and as with any household, the children will squabble from time to time. For Andrew Jackson's administration, one fight involved a woman who some deemed unworthy to include. The resulting fight sent nearly the entire clan packing.

She was extroverted and sociable Margaret O'Neale who had a spouse in the navy. Washington gossipers claimed she also had a lover in the Senate, John Henry Eaton, a friend of Andrew Jackson. Saucy stuff. Then in 1828, news came that Margaret's husband, while serving at sea, took his own life. By custom, Margaret was supposed to mourn for a year. She decided not to wait, and she married her alleged lover. Barely two months after that, newly elected President Andrew Jackson named Eaton as his secretary of war.

It was all too much for Floride Calhoun, wife of Vice President John C. Calhoun. Obliged to socialize with the Eatons, the second lady initially demonstrated a cold civility and then avoided them altogether. Soon every cabinet member's wife refused to be seen with the new Mrs. Eaton, a snub that grossly offended Jackson, whose own wife was the target of heartless ridicule (see ELECTION OF 1828). Within a year, nearly all of "polite society" had ostracized Margaret, including Jackson's niece Emily Donelson, the acting first lady. Jackson responded to the insult by banishing his niece from the White House.[95]

Steadily, the intrigue and alienation of half of Washington took a toll on the president. His hair turned from gray to white, his eyes sank and turned permanently bloodshot. He cried easily. He lost weight. By 1830 he was losing patience, threatening to fire his entire cabinet and banning congressmen from the White House. He even threatened to dismiss ambassadors who did not openly accept the war secretary and his wife.

When warned of the possible international ramifications of such an act, the president angrily responded, "I will show the world that Jackson is still the head of the government."[96]

The only person to show any sincere kindness toward Margaret was Secretary of State Martin Van Buren. A widower like Jackson, Van Buren was positive and friendly by nature, a cherry tree compared to Old Hickory. Already fond of the little New Yorker, Jackson began to view him as the next best hope for the presidency.

The deadlock finally broke in 1831 when department heads started to resign one by one. Triumphant, the president readily accepted. To save face, both Eaton and Van Buren also took their leave, much to Jackson's disappointment. With the exception of his postmaster general, his entire cabinet had been cleaned out.

Remarkably, nothing illegal took place, and yet the event forced more high-level retirements than any scandal except for Watergate. The shake-up, involving nothing more than social posturing and gossip, also changed the course of presidential history. Rejuvenated by his victory over the social elite, Jackson ran for reelection in 1832 and won. For his vice president and successor, he chose Martin Van Buren, the one man who stood by him and Margaret O'Neale Eaton.

---

At one point during the dispute, Secretary of War John Eaton brandished a loaded pistol and began wandering the streets of Washington, threatening to duel with anyone who dared insult his wife.

---

Peggy Eaton was the lady in question during the Jackson administration. High society in Washington could not come to terms with her past, and the fallout from this rejection led to the disintegration of the president's cabinet.

## 3.   BLACK FRIDAY (1869)

U. S. Grant's eight years in office were so mired by corruption that they were dubbed the "Era of Good Stealings." Part of the problem was Grant's practice of doling out government jobs to relatives and Union veterans regardless of ability, leading one senator to call the administration "a dropsical nepotism swollen to elephantiasis." Had Grant surrounded himself with better men, he might not have been susceptible to the likes of Jay Gould and "Jubilee Jim" Fisk.[97]

Two Wall Street speculators in their early thirties, Gould and Fisk owned the expansive Erie Railway, a conglomerate they had wrested from Cornelius Vanderbilt. In 1869 they set their sights much higher and schemed to corner the U.S. gold market with the help of anyone who had influence with the president.[98]

The plan was to purchase as much gold as possible, driving up the price, while simultaneously preventing the government from selling its reserves. Once the market could no longer sustain the inflated value, Gould and Fisk would sell all of their holdings and make a hideously huge profit. The flooded market would consequently plummet, ruining anyone else who had invested in the precious metal.

With their plot underway, they tried to ensnare Washington insiders—bankers, a secretary to the president, even the first lady. No one was biting, except Grant's brother-in-law, Abel Rathbone Corbin. Grant had known the sixty-seven-year-old Corbin for decades, but the president was unaware he had recently accepted a free "loan" of ten thousand dollars from Gould and Fisk.

As the summer of '69 wore on, Corbin orchestrated several seemingly innocent meetings between his presidential brother-in-law and Gould and Fisk, who in idle conversation, attempted to indoctrinate Grant on the wisdom of high gold prices. At the same time, they asked if he was about to release gold reserves anytime soon. Through all of this, Grant remained silent, but he did enjoy visiting Corbin's posh New York home and traveling on Fisk's luxury steamboat.[99]

By September, gold certificates were climbing from $130 to $138 then $144 per share. Foreign imports and exports, payable only in gold specie, virtually stopped. Banks, which conducted most of their major transactions via the precious metal, could not conduct business. Gould and Fisk's hoarding was pushing the entire economy to the brink. Then came September 24—Black Friday.

That morning, scarce certificates were rising by the hour: $150, $155, $160. Gould and Fisk owned $100 million worth, and they were making millions more with each passing moment. Finally realizing what his new-found friends had done, Grant torpedoed their scheme by dumping tons of treasury gold on the market. In minutes the price collapsed to $133.

Unfortunately, the president's intended targets emerged relatively unscathed. Gould had quietly sold a part of his holdings while buying smaller amounts, keeping up appearances. Fisk lost millions but still had his original fortune. Though indicted, both men paid handsomely for the finest lawyers and walked. As for the rest of the country, stock prices fell 20 percent across the board as jittery traders avoided investing. Grain prices dropped more than 30 percent in the face of unstable currency. Many greedy speculators and totally innocent farmers lost everything they had.[100]

---

A congressional committee investigated the Gold Panic of 1869, and despite allegations that the president and the first lady were heavily involved, the panel absolved the Grants of any wrongdoing. The chairman of the committee was Union veteran James Garfield.

---

## 4.　THE WHISKEY RING (1874–75)

Tax evasion is as old as the Republic, especially when it comes to taxed liquor. To defray the cost of defending the colonies during the French and Indian War, the British Empire imposed a tax on colonial production of rum. Activists like Samuel Adams protested, and importers such as John Hancock turned to smuggling. When the American Revolution saddled the country with debt, Treasury Secretary Alexander Hamilton put a duty on hard alcohol. In response, frontier distillers in Pennsylvania fomented the WHISKEY REBELLION.

The grotesquely expensive Civil War caused authorities to once again impose a levy on alcohol. Once again the masses resisted, yet this time they were joined by members of the government.

To legally sell their wares, distillers and bottlers had to pay exorbitant fees that often cost many times what their product was worth. Poorly paid civil servants, assigned to the unpleasant task of enforcing the hated law, became targets of hostility from buyers and sellers alike. Rather than resort to violence, the opposing sides often formed small alliances, especially in the brewery capitals of Chicago, Milwaukee, and St. Louis. In exchange for modest bribes, revenue collectors sold tax stamps far below price, greatly underreported factory outputs, and failed to report shipments. In St. Louis alone, approximately two-thirds of all alcohol went untaxed.[101]

In 1874, Benjamin Bristow, the newly appointed secretary of the Treasury Department, began digging into rumors of wholesale corruption. With President Grant's blessing, Bristow proceeded to clean house across the Midwest, confiscating record books, seizing ledgers, and closing down whole factories. More than 350 indictments were issued. Some of the guilty worked at the highest levels of the Treasury Department and the Internal Revenue Service.

"Let no guilty man escape," insisted Grant—until the trail led to the White House. Bristow had uncovered circumstantial evidence connecting a ringleader in Missouri to Brig. Gen. Orville Babcock. The likable Babcock had served with Grant and was one of the officers present at Robert E. Lee's surrender at the McLean house in Appomattox. His current occupation was just as prestigious. He was the president's personal secretary.[102]

Sensing that Bristow had joined some Democratic smear campaign, Grant stoutly defended his comrade. He also launched an independent inquiry and offered to personally testify at Babcock's trial.

In the end, his secretary was acquitted of all charges. But the pervasiveness of corruption in his administration, which was evident from his first to his last years in office, all but confirmed Grant's own guilt of

Orville Elias Babcock was a West Point graduate, an engineer, and a Union officer. He served at the siege of Vicksburg and worked as Grant's aide-de-camp from the Wilderness campaign onward. As President Grant's private secretary, Babcock was implicated in the Whiskey Ring but was eventually acquitted. Upon his death, he was interred at Arlington National Cemetery.

negligence in running the government. Because of the multiple scandals, many historians rank Grant's presidency as a failure.[103]

---

In order to spare his friend from further accusations, Grant reassigned Orville Babcock to be a federal inspector of lighthouses. Years later, while performing his job along the coast of Florida, Babcock fell into the sea and drowned.

---

## 5.　TEAPOT DOME (1922–24)

One of President Warren Harding's closest poker buddies was Interior Secretary Albert Fall, a gun-toting, backslapping, face-punching cowboy-type who first befriended Harding when they were both freshmen in the Senate. New Mexico's first senator, Fall had made a name for himself as a defense lawyer specializing in adultery and murder cases. Florence Harding took an instant liking to him.[104]

Though the president was a cretin to his wife, he was an otherwise friendly man, outgoing, and rather needy. He trusted easily, and therefore saw nothing suspicious when Fall asked to have certain oil fields officially transferred from the Navy Department to his Interior Department, such as the Teapot Dome field in Wyoming. The president also obliged when Fall sold drilling rights to those areas to a select few poker guests, such as Harry Sinclair, a multimillionaire oil tycoon (and founder of Sinclair Petroleum).[105]

Legislators became concerned when Fall made no attempt to entertain competitive bids from other companies. Inquiries initially turned up nothing. But then it was discovered that Fall had received a one-hundred-thousand-dollar "loan" from his oil associates. After years of formal investigations, the U.S. Senate Committee on Public Lands unearthed a number of gifts in livestock and cash to the senator, totaling nearly a half-million dollars.

After years of formal hearings, the U.S. government eventually regained the drilling rights plus some six million dollars in lost oil revenues, a fraction of what had gone into the pockets of Fall and his associates. Sinclair was found guilty of contempt and jury tampering, for which he served three months, while Fall was convicted of bribery and spent a year in prison, making him the first-ever sitting cabinet member to be convicted of a crime.[106]

Warren Harding once said, "If Albert Fall isn't an honest man, I'm not fit to be President of the United States."

## 6.  THE VETERANS BUREAU SCANDAL (1923)

Harding's wife, Florence, had a cold streak ten miles wide, but she was empathetic to the downtrodden, especially victims of abuse. Herself beaten as a child, and later impregnated and abandoned by an alcoholic first husband, she found love in a second marriage, until he cheated on her—repeatedly. Some solace came when he became president in 1920, enabling her to act as a guardian to the powerless.

Of her many causes, Mrs. Harding was most devoted to "her boys," three hundred thousand disabled American veterans of the Great War. She would visit area wards and hospitals, host picnics for the wounded, support charity events, and champion their cause within the White House. When her husband's industrious friend Charlie Forbes became head of the Veterans Bureau, Florence was understandably elated. He was a retired colonel and Distinguished Service Medal recipient. Under Forbes's direction, the bureau quickly spent thirty-six million dollars on new hospitals, distributed medicines and supplies to survivors in need, and oversaw the well-being of millions of former doughboys. Oddly though, his accomplishments were only showing up on paper.

Suspicions arose when Forbes, who made a modest ten thousand dollars per year, began to hold swank parties at lavish venues and developed a penchant for high-stakes gambling. Investigations soon unearthed multiple cases of kickbacks from unscrupulous contractors. Manifests showed the government paying twenty times the market price for a century's worth of cleaning supplies. Millions of dollars' worth of blankets, sheets, gauze, pajamas, alcohol, and drugs were being classified as "surplus" or "damaged" and sold to private buyers for next to nothing. So incensed was the president by the level of betrayal that he invited Forbes to the White House, called him into the Red Room for a chat, and proceeded to choke him.[107]

While the Senate commenced official hearings, Forbes resigned and left the country. It was soon discovered that, along with being a thief, Forbes had never served in the First World War. He had deserted the army in 1914. He also had a history of spousal abuse. For his shameless

Florence Harding's advocacy for veterans included welcoming Confederate veterans to the White House in the summer of 1922.

graft, which cost the government millions and caused undue suffering upon thousands of disabled veterans, Charles Forbes was eventually fined ten thousand dollars and sentenced to several years in prison. He was released after serving eighteen months.[108]

> Forbes's legal advisor Charles Cramer, who was also involved in the Veterans Bureau scandal, committed suicide before he could be tried. He took his own life in the very home he bought from a couple named Warren and Florence Harding.

## 7.  THE CORRUPT SPIRO AGNEW (1973)

The vice presidency has seen two resignations, and John C. Calhoun did so because he could no longer tolerate the authoritarian Andrew Jackson. The other retiree had few options but to leave. It was either that or prison.

In April 1973, Dick Nixon enjoyed an approval rating of 60 percent, but he suspected it would fall as more information about hush money, wiretaps, and a certain burglary began to point toward the Oval Office. When his vice president expressed concerns about an investigation in Maryland involving construction contracts and bribery, Nixon dismissed the comment as irrelevant.

By May, Attorney General Elliot Richardson discovered why Agnew, the former governor of Maryland, was so worried about an innocuous inquiry about alleged kickbacks. Agnew was involved—heavily. The head of the Justice Department claimed to have never seen such damning evidence, speculating that the vice president could be indicted on at least forty counts. Nixon believed there was modest cause for concern, but he had his own worries. The FBI was beginning to deploy agents within the White House to monitor the movement of documents and staff.[109]

By August, the entire ship of state was foundering. Nixon's ratings were down to 31 percent, carpet bombing in Cambodia was having no effect on the influx of enemy troops into South Vietnam, and the public was becoming aware of the White House tapes. On top of it all, the *Wall Street Journal* exposed the extent of Agnew's probable crimes in Maryland, including extortion, kickbacks, tax evasion, and bribery. Information arose that he was still receiving dirty money. To Nixon's face, Agnew denied the allegations, and he repeated his statements in a news conference soon after. The public support for the popular veep was overwhelming.[110]

But so was the evidence, and Agnew could no longer hide it. In October, he agreed to plea no contest to one count of tax evasion, pay a fine of ten thousand dollars, and serve three years probation. He would also step down from the vice presidency on October 10, 1973. When he broke the news to Nixon, the two men shook hands, parted company, and never said a word to each other for the rest of their lives.[111]

---

Two months after Spiro Agnew's resignation, Gerald Ford was confirmed as the vice president. In the interim, the line of presidential succession temporarily passed to Speaker of the House Carl Albert—a Democrat.

---

## 8.  WATERGATE (1972–74)

Interviewed years after the fact, former president Gerald Ford concluded, "If Nixon had destroyed the tapes, there would have been no solid, concrete evidence of a cover-up." Ford was incorrect on two counts. Had Nixon attempted to obliterate the tapes (improbable since the Secret Service possessed them), the act itself could have constituted an obstruction of justice. In addition, recordings or not, the conversations on them still took place, and every participant was a witness.[112]

Among them was H. R. "Bob" Haldeman, Nixon's former chief of staff and one of the first to discuss the Watergate break-in with the president. Nixon's number-two man was John Ehrlichman, his assistant for domestic affairs and architect of THE PLUMBERS, an outfit instructed to stop all White House leaks. Close behind was young legal counsel John Dean, with whom Nixon discussed bribing the five Watergate burglars and laundering the money they would receive. Then there was the Committee to Re-Elect the President (CREEP), including former attorney general John Mitchell, G. Gordon Liddy, who coordinated the break-in, and former CIA agent E. Howard Hunt, who had organized the wiretapping of the Democratic National Committee Office in the Watergate building. And so on and so on.

Nixon neither authorized the burglary nor knew about it ahead of time, but the ensuing year found him scheming with the above cadre to block all investigations into the matter. Part of his downfall was his eagerness to find a scapegoat, even if it included the very people trying to protect him.

Month after month, conversations revolved around ways to quiet the burglars, impede the FBI, hide earlier wiretappings, collect hush money, and blame Mitchell or Hunt or the CIA. The sheer volume and complexity of Nixon's efforts, more than any recorded conversation, was what condemned him to failure. By late summer of 1974, even Nixon acknowledged he had done the exact opposite of what he intended, making a bad situation far worse by attempting to cover it up. On the evening of August 8, in a televised address from the Oval Office, Nixon offered his resignation to the American public. They abruptly accepted.

When looking back at what had transpired, Gerald Ford was partially correct in emphasizing the impact of the infamous tapes, because they revealed something as damaging as any testimony. Emanating from the

NIXON LIBRARY

Richard and Pat Nixon prepare to board Marine One for the last time as president and first lady.

thousands of hours of muffled static and pregnant pauses was the undeniably acidic nature of a profane, somewhat paranoid, and thoroughly manipulative individual who was willing to do virtually anything to stay in power. What Ford and many others failed to recognize, however, was that this man had risen to power *because* of his reputation for ruthlessness. He made a career out of publicly dismantling Democrats, vowing law and order on American streets, and acting as the toughest anticommunist since Joe McCarthy and Barry Goldwater. And for his imperial appeal, the American public reelected him in one of the biggest landslides in U.S. history, five months *after* a minor burglary in a Washington office building.

---

In total, twenty individuals either pleaded guilty or were convicted for taking part in the Watergate scandal. Their average maximum sentence—five years. Average time spent in prison—twelve months.

---

### 9.  IRAN-CONTRA (1985–87)

While the Carter administration struggled to free the Iranian hostages, candidate Ronald Reagan campaigned on a "tough on terrorism" theme. Once in office, the Gipper had just as much trouble liberating captives as Carter did. In Reagan's case, Hezbollah was the perpetrator, and the Lebanese organization was in possession of several Americans, including journalists, clergy, government workers, and CIA Beirut chief William Buckley.[113]

In contrast to the micromanaging Carter, Reagan simply instructed a few staff members, primarily National Security Advisor Robert "Bud"

Third-level characters in Iran-Contra included (from left to right) Defense Secretary Caspar Weinberger, Secretary of State George Schultz, White House Counsel Ed Meese, Chief of Staff Don Regan, and President Reagan.

REAGAN LIBRARY

McFarlane, to get the hostages out by any peaceful means available. Those means eventually involved breaking U.S. law.

The idea was to sell weapons to Iran, who in gratitude would supposedly instruct their ally Hezbollah to release the Americans. Acting in what might be described as good faith, McFarlane commenced the secret shipments in the summer of 1985 without a guarantee that anything would be done about the captives. The plan did not go well. Though hundreds of shoulder-fired rockets were sent, the scheme produced only one freed hostage, and it wasn't CIA agent Buckley, the man the administration most desperately wanted back. In frustration, McFarlane resigned.

Replacing him was John Poindexter, who continued the program. Assisting him on the NATIONAL SECURITY COUNCIL was Lt. Col. Oliver North, who suggested illegally channeling profits from the arms sales to a right-wing insurgency in Nicaragua. If the Iranian deal was not bearing results, reasoned North, at least the revenues could help combat leftist governments—a prime objective of the REAGAN DOCTRINE.

On November 4, 1986, the Lebanese periodical *Al Shiraa* leaked the weapons-for-hostages deal, and the Iranian government confirmed the details. Nine days later, in a televised address from the Oval Office, Reagan assured the American public that no such trade had taken place but that defensive weapons and parts had been sent to the Iranians as a goodwill gesture. He added, "These modest deliveries, taken together, could easily fit into a single cargo plane." Later that week, North began shredding documents. The shipments were far greater than Reagan had insinuated.[114]

Before the month was out, the White House sacked North and accepted Poindexter's resignation. Ensuing investigations revealed at least six deliveries to Iran totaling more than two thousand shoulder-fired rockets and seventeen medium-range HAWK surface-to-air missiles. Also discovered was the transfer of millions of dollars to the Contra rebels in Central America, an organization whose members, by most definitions, were terrorists.[115]

Oliver North was convicted on three minor counts but did not serve time. His staunch defense of supporting the Contras made him a hero among many archconservatives. John Poindexter was found guilty of multiple felonies, including obstruction of justice and conspiracy. The charges were overturned on appeal. In 1987, Robert McFarlane attempted suicide.

In a sworn statement, Reagan insisted he was unaware of the illegal activities. A joint congressional commission found his testimony flawed but did not press charges. His approval ratings fell to 40 percent. Two years later, with the assistance of a strong economy, Reagan's numbers were back up to 60 percent.[116]

> In spite of all the clandestine activities, the arms-for-hostages deal secured the release of only three Americans. Not among them was CIA agent William Buckley. In 1985, he died of heart failure while undergoing torture at the hands of Hezbollah.

## 10. THE LEWINSKY AFFAIR (1997)

He was forty-nine, she was twenty-two. Both craved validation, among other things. Unbeknownst to either of them, they would one day get officially probed.

Extramarital sex in the White House was nothing new. Warren Harding met Nan Britton when he was a senator and she was five years out of high school. In 1919, she gave birth to his daughter. In 1921, he became president. They continued to explore their love in various rooms in the White House until his death in 1923. Franklin Roosevelt first started sleeping with Eleanor Roosevelt's personal secretary Lucy Page Mercer when he was deputy secretary to the navy. Mercer was with him at Warm Springs, Georgia, when he passed away in 1945. Jack Kennedy had more extramarital affairs than most presidents had state dinners, but the escapades would not become public knowledge until well after his death.[117]

Then there was Bill Clinton, who made a career of surviving accusations of promiscuity. Among many, one came from former Arkansas state employee Paula Jones, who filed a sexual harassment suit against the former governor. CLINTON V. JONES reached the Supreme Court during his second term as president.

It was this case that brought up the name of Monica Lewinsky, previously an intern at the White House and later an employee at the Pentagon. Under oath during the Jones case, Clinton was asked if he ever had sexual relations with Lewinsky, to which he answered in the negative. Evidence then emerged of a certain blue dress belonging to Lewinsky that contained DNA belonging to Clinton. Further evidence indicated that he had instructed her to deny their relationship. Regardless of his marriage vows, the defendant had essentially committed perjury, obstruction of justice, and witness tampering. He was held in contempt. The Arkansas bar suspended his license. He was fined.[118]

Congress, then under Republican control, initiated impeachment proceedings in October 1998, culminating in a Senate trial early the next year. With arguments for and against conviction, mostly along party lines, much of Clinton's tawdry behavior and disregard for the office became evident to the most casual observer. But nothing legally surfaced that constituted "Treason, Bribery, or other High Crimes and Misdemeanors." Right before Valentine's Day, the Senate failed to reach a two-thirds majority needed for removal.

In short, Clinton's worst mistake, aside from the affair, was denial. If he had studied his presidential history, he would have known that Americans do not tolerate a presidential cover-up. Whether by negligence, perjury, or plot, the obstruction of justice is generally regarded as worse than ignoring international law, inducing wars, or cooperating with countries of ill repute.

In turn, he escaped full punishment for a number of reasons—a blatantly supportive first lady, a strong economy, and a weak prosecution. In addition, four months of congressional infighting had given the public impeachment fatigue.[119]

---

During Bill Clinton's presidency, his approval ratings were at their highest during his impeachment and trial.

---

# Epilogue

IT WAS SHORTLY AFTER midday, July 4, 1826, on the fiftieth anniversary of the Declaration of Independence, when ninety-year-old John Adams began to slip in and out of consciousness. Pneumonia was about to complete the miserable work that heart disease had begun years before. Lying in bed on the second floor of the family home in Quincy, the ailing Adams struggled to breathe. His once lucid blue eyes, murky with cataracts, slowly began to close. But his mind, the greatest part of his bald, short, portly being, was still clear.

Demonstrating his tenacious will and the wisdom to realize his time had come, Adams rallied for a moment and whispered, "Thomas Jefferson still survives." He drifted to sleep. Shortly after 6:00 p.m., his heart finally stopped beating.

In his last declaration, John Adams was wrong. Five hundred miles to the southwest, at Monticello, the eighty-two year-old Jefferson was dead. He had passed away a few hours earlier. A painful fight with crippling rheumatism and digestive complications had finally broken the lanky planter, inventor, and writer. Only the day before, the cataleptic Jefferson awoke to ask if it was the Fourth, hoping he would reach his most cherished day. His doctor told him the moment was near. Comforted by the assurance, Jefferson fell asleep and never woke again.

And yet Adams was right in his final assessment. So long as the United States still stood, so lived Jefferson and Washington and himself and all who had laid the stones of a monument that would long endure. When dignitaries visited the aging statesman a few days before his passing so that he might write some invocation for the upcoming Independence Day celebration, the exhausted Adams subtly reminded his visitors that he had already given them independence itself. Fitting that he reserved his last words for his dear companion, for the two men together had brought forth a new nation, and their friendship faithfully represented it in innumerable ways.

They were born subjects, and proudly so, of the greatest empire the world had yet seen, connected to heaven through a king, and governed on earth by a parliament of laws and men. In the course of human events, the Americans matured and labored to break the bonds of an overly possessive Mother England. After seven years, they were free and adrift.

With the common enemy of George III out of the picture, the two parties soon discovered a basic inability to work together. Though they came from the same political lineage, they were two completely different beings. One was the blustery North—cold, conceited, and puritanical, yet capable of a most revolutionary bravery. The other was the agrarian South—warm, open, and eloquent, but incapable of ridding itself of slavery.

Inherently different in temperament, they soon developed irreconcilable differences. The breaking point came in a presidential election, in 1800, as it would be in 1860, both seen as all-or-nothing referendums on which way the country would go—along the existing path of conservatism or toward a wholly new republic. The outcome was too much to bear for the defeated, causing an acrimonious separation that lasted for years.

Just as North and South took ages to reconcile, Adams and Jefferson let ten years pass before they ended their personal war. It was John who broke the silence, writing Tom in January 1812 to wish him a happy new year. The surprise correspondence heartened the Virginian, and the two soon reconnected. Still fundamentally worlds apart, the retirees sometimes wrote on completely different planes. Adams preferred ethereal topics, while Jefferson leaned toward the sciences. But they found enough common ground to forge a lasting and heartfelt bond that would endure to their very final moments.

They were preceded in death by the man who had sacrificed his last vestige of health to breathe life into the government. George Washington lived not three years into retirement. On December 14, 1799, a sudden bout of pneumonia killed him, though the bleeding and blistering his doctors performed on him did not help matters. He died and was entombed at his beloved Mount Vernon, finally achieving his own dream, not to be the head of a country, but to be at home and at peace.

Now the second and third presidents were gone. For many of their fellow citizens, Adams's and Jefferson's departures on the Fourth of July was proof of the Republic's blessed and unique standing among the family of nations. James Monroe's death five years later, also on July 4, seemed to confirm the notion that nothing less than divine providence was at work.

In reality, Monroe succumbed to heart failure. Several months of choking tuberculosis had reduced him to a coughing, fragile ghost of his former self. Monroe was buried in the city where he died—New York. In 1858 he was reinterred in Hollywood Cemetery in Richmond, Virginia, where in 1862 former president John Tyler was laid to rest very near him, albeit under a Confederate flag as an elected member of their Congress. Attesting to the cost of that terrible epoch, eighteen thousand Confederate soldiers were buried in the same cemetery, many of whom were never identified. Their president, Jefferson Davis, former secretary of war under his close friend Franklin Pierce, is buried there as well, having died a free man after serving two years' confinement in a fort named after James Monroe.

James Madison nearly became the fourth former president to die on the country's birthday. Legend has it that the bedridden Madison, suffering from crippling rheumatism, was given the option of stimulants to live until the national anniversary. He declined. On June 28, 1836, his eighty-five-year-old heart went into arrest, and the last of the Revolutionaries was gone.

In their place came a new generation, mere children when the experiment began. John Quincy Adams was only eight when he watched the slaughter of Bunker Hill from a nearby ridge. Andrew Jackson was nine when illiterate neighbors asked him to read a newspaper containing a report of a "Declaration of Independence." At the time, Martin Van Buren was not yet born, and William Henry Harrison was three years old and living in rural Virginia. He would be the last president born a colonial.

From Washington, Adams, Jefferson, Madison, and Monroe came the descendants Bush, Clinton, Reagan, Carter, Ford, and Nixon. If the latter names ring less than regal in the contemporary ear, then what is the reason? Do they all lack the noble qualities and altruism of the original class? Have their scandals, intrigues, and egos jaded the office beyond repair?

Popular is the notion that these recent administrations have mutated into an imperial presidency, assuming rights and privileges far beyond what the Founding Fathers ever intended. George Washington led a country through its formative years without so much as a paid secretary. Now chief executives are surrounded by an undisclosed number of guards and served by hundreds of loyal assistants. They command a standing army of more than a million men and women, preside over a budget that has reached into the trillions of dollars, and possess the ability to destroy the earth many times over.

To call them imperial is grave, accusatory, and inflammatory. And it is correct—in part.

The sun no longer sets upon Old Glory. Its states and protectorates reach far into the Atlantic and Pacific. With the territories of American Samoa, Guam, parts of the Marianas, Puerto Rico, and the U.S. Virgin Islands, the federal government holds more square miles of territory than any other nation in the world. Its corporations and properties span the planet. The armed forces remain in places long since mollified—Kuwait, Bosnia, South Korea, Japan, Italy, Okinawa, the Philippines, Cuba. The United States has eighteen military bases in Germany alone, despite the fact the cold war has been over for nearly twenty years.

By all intents and measures, the nation has become an empire, with one great peculiarity—"We the People" are the emperor.

In 1787, "the People" were fifty-five delegates who had gathered in the Pennsylvania State House to form a more perfect union. They created a government based on the concept of representation, but in practice the electorate was less than one-fourth of the white male population. Today the People number more than three hundred million, over two-thirds of whom are guaranteed the right to register and vote in federal elections. Through freedom of speech, press, petition, and assembly, they can advance their cause to the highest office of the land. They choose from among themselves the representatives who will have the sole power of executive impeachment and the senators who advise and consent on presidential appointments. Congress alone has the power to establish and collect federal taxes, to borrow federal funds, to declare or permit the country to enter into a state of war.

The People are the presidents themselves, chosen from among the native-born, thirty-five years old or more. If the chief executives have attained powers vastly greater than their forefathers, it is because the population has done the same. Through their unprecedented political leverage, the electorate has allowed, requested, or demanded services from its chief executives far beyond what previous generations even considered. Per capita, the current generation of Americans consumes more food and fuel than any other before it. In the last century, life expectancy has increased 50 percent among the middle and lower classes, and yet one of the key issues for the 2008 elections is universal health care. President Washington was not unique in having less than a year of formal education. Abraham Lincoln had about the same. Andrew Johnson had none at all. Today every citizen has access to a free public education from kindergarten through high school, and the electorate demands more, including increases in federal grants for the thirteen million students attending colleges and universities.

In their annual messages to Congress, the first presidents frequently used the word *legislature* when addressing the audience. With the invention of the radio and the establishment of universal suffrage, the word became *people*.

The relationship has never been perfect. During his administration, George Washington labored to visit every state in the Union, a slow and arduous endeavor. His aged and aching body cringed against the rutted roads of eighteenth-century America, but he felt compelled to see and be seen by his people. And for his troubles, he was accused of behaving like a monarch checking on his fiefdoms. When he signed the Jay Treaty averting war with Britain, he was chastised for courting the former enemy. When he dispersed the unlawful Whiskey Rebellion by calling out the militia, he was deemed a tyrant.

The worst came from a fellow revolutionary. In a publicly printed letter, the great agitator Thomas Paine bade Washington a mean farewell in his last year in office, writing, "The world will be puzzled to decide whether you are an apostate or an imposter, whether you have abandoned good principles, or whether you ever had any?"

And so it went for the presidents to follow—Adams "the monarchist," Jefferson "the atheist," Madison "the puppet of Jefferson," Monroe "the mediocrity." In addition to his four years as president, John Quincy Adams served another seventeen in the House of Representatives, for which he was condemned for opposing the annexation of Texas, criticizing slavery, and defending the captives of the *Amistad*.

Andrew Jackson's ancient body was so wracked with headaches, intestinal disorders, and war wounds, people assumed he would die in office, and quite a few wished he would. His successor, Martin Van Buren, a.k.a. "Van Ruin," wrestled hopelessly with an economic depression caused by

Jackson. He never lost his cheery demeanor, but he was never elected again, despite running in 1840, 1844, and 1848. Comparatively, Van Buren's successor, William Henry Harrison, suffered far less abuse because he died very early in his first term.

Regrettably, death in office is the only sure path to appreciation. The fate has befallen eight chief executives thus far, four by murder. For those who had the audacity to stay alive during their administration, they were commonly expected to be all things to all people. In addition, they were held responsible, said William Howard Taft, "for all the sins of omission and of commission of society at large." The paradox was not lost on Lyndon Johnson: "They geld us first, and then expect us to win the Kentucky Derby."

Alas, after the sedative of time takes effect, a critical public can treat even the least popular presidents with a measure of gratitude and respect. Past mistakes and party animosities are taken in context, and the character of the individual becomes the overriding measure.

If the presidents of the distant past appear so grand in comparison to the more recent versions, it is because so much of the negative has faded, and all that is left to the general observer is the noble aura. These once living, breathing, imperfect beings take on the stoic perfection and marble strength of the very monuments that bear their likeness.

One must take into consideration just how long it took for those stone and metal memorials to emerge. The George Washington Monument, that mighty obelisk of ancient design, which appears as the regal axis upon which the whole national capital turns, was actually started in 1848, nearly fifty years after the death of its namesake. Because of funding problems and construction delays, it was not completed until 1884. A president's portrait did not appear on a U.S. coin until 1909, when Abraham Lincoln's profile was affixed to the humble penny. Work on Mount Rushmore did not begin until 1927, nearly 140 years after the creation of the executive branch. People were finally willing to construct these tributes in large part because many of them never knew the presidents as real people, never voted against them, never had to pay their taxes or fight their wars or weather the constant feuds that invariably danced around their administrations.

The only accurate monuments have been built by the presidents themselves—the laws they signed, the programs they championed, the treaties they forged, the precedents they established, with all their flaws and strengths.

Has the presidency usurped rights and authorities far beyond what the Founding Fathers ever intended? That would depend on which Father was asked. Perhaps none would be more pleased than Alexander Hamilton to see the United States of 2008, with a strong executive leading a commercial giant—a country industrialized, incorporated, and capital rich, with an almost boundless line of credit. To know that his face was on federal currency would only add to his sense of victory. But his mood would dampen considerably to know that the elite no longer have total control over nominations and elections.

Benjamin Franklin would probably divide his wonderment equally between the creation of a space program and the rise of women in the executive branch. Female astronauts would send him into absolute euphoria. Incurably flirtatious, even in his final years, Franklin showered women with attention in part because he recognized their worth when few others could.

As for the recent ascendancy of religion in the White House, no one would be more worried than Thomas Jefferson or more pleased than Patrick Henry. Probably none of them would view a war in the Middle East as a desirable enterprise, least of all Jefferson, who knew the difficulty of fighting Islam during the Barbary Wars.

The proudest of the Fathers might be the men who emerged from the Pennsylvania State House in September 1787, men like James Madison and George Washington, who offered to the struggling country a new Constitution. How would they feel to realize that their experiment lives and nothing has yet stopped it, not assassinations, not scandals, not rebellions, not economic collapse, not global wars? What might they say when learning that the nation's presidents have been planters, teachers, merchants, lawyers, soldiers, and statesmen, and not one of them became a Caesar, a Cromwell, or a king?

It is impossible to know, but it is fair to guess that these creative and hopeful Founding Fathers would not be entirely disappointed by what they saw. And after a toast of American beer, perhaps brewed in a city they had never heard of—like Madison—they might share a little American wine as well, bottled in a state equally mysterious to them—like Washington. Indeed, they might ask for a map and trace their fingers along the expansive borders and marvel at the immensity of it all. Inevitably, one of them would spot a familiar surname and another and another. Would they laugh and make a game of it, to find all the rivers, lakes, cities, and towns bearing their names? And as Hamilton showed his ten-dollar bill to everyone, might they inquire if more money could be found and jest when they discovered that some faces were more valuable than others? What would the reaction be to realize that these bills and coins number in the trillions and reside on almost every person and exist in every home and business and bank.

After the initial rush of excitement, perhaps one of the more serious members, someone like Washington, would pose the question of whether the presidency and its Constitution would possibly last another 220 years. Being realists, these men would know full well that every nation hoped and believed it was eternal—Sparta, Rome, Byzantium, the Holy Roman Empire, monarchial France. They might calculate that after more than two centuries, the United States was probably into its middle age. As a lone superpower, it might have not yet peaked. Yet most assuredly, it would some day fall, as every domain eventually does.

An astute observer of history, John Adams once wrote of the inevitable fate of great nations: "When they have reached the summit of grandeur, some minute and unsuspected cause commonly affects their ruin, and the empire of the world is transferred to some other place." Fittingly, he wrote this in 1755, as the subject of the British Empire. Ten years later, an imperial tax on paper would set into motion a great rebellion. Ten years after that, Adams himself would help his friend Jefferson craft the very document that would mark the birth of a new nation.

Until that time, they would hope that their fellow citizens, the heirs of their creation, would labor as passionately and as rigorously as they did to study their history, to improve the present, and to select the best leaders for the future, so that they might continue to form a more perfect union of people and presidents.

# Lists of the Presidents

| TERM | PRESIDENT | PARTY | VICE PRESIDENT |
|------|-----------|-------|----------------|
| 1789–93 | George Washington | None | John Adams |
| 1793–97 | George Washington | None | John Adams |
| 1797–1801 | John Adams | Federalist | Thomas Jefferson |
| 1801–5 | Thomas Jefferson | Dem-Rep | Aaron Burr |
| 1805–9 | Thomas Jefferson | Dem-Rep | George Clinton |
| 1809–13 | James Madison | Dem-Rep | George Clinton (d. 1812) |
| 1813–17 | James Madison | Dem-Rep | Elbridge Gerry (d. 1814) |
| 1817–21 | James Monroe | Dem-Rep | Daniel Tompkins |
| 1821–25 | James Monroe | Dem-Rep | Daniel Tompkins |
| 1825–29 | John Quincy Adams | Dem-Rep | John C. Calhoun |
| 1829–33 | Andrew Jackson | Democrat | John C. Calhoun (resigned 1832) |
| 1833–37 | Andrew Jackson | Democrat | Martin Van Buren |
| 1837–41 | Martin Van Buren | Democrat | Richard M. Johnson |
| 1841–45 | William H. Harrison (d. 1841) | Whig | John Tyler |
| | John Tyler | Whig | None |
| 1845–49 | James Knox Polk | Democrat | George M. Dallas |
| 1849–53 | Zachary Taylor (d. 1850) | Whig | Millard Fillmore |
| | Millard Fillmore | Whig | None |
| 1853–57 | Franklin Pierce | Democrat | William R.D. King (d. 1853) |
| 1857–61 | James Buchanan | Democrat | John C. Breckinridge |
| 1861–65 | Abraham Lincoln | Republican | Hannibal Hamlin |
| 1865–69 | Abraham Lincoln (d. 1865) | Union | Andrew Johnson |
| | Andrew Johnson | Democrat | None |
| 1869–73 | (Hiram) Ulysses Grant | Republican | Schuyler Colfax |
| 1873–77 | (Hiram) Ulysses Grant | Republican | Henry Wilson (d. 1875) |
| 1877–81 | Rutherford Birchard Hayes | Republican | William A. Wheeler |
| 1881–85 | James Abram Garfield (d. 1881) | Republican | Chester Alan Arthur |
| | Chester Alan Arthur | Republican | None |
| 1885–89 | (Stephen) Grover Cleveland | Democrat | Thomas Hendricks (d. 1885) |
| 1889–93 | Benjamin Harrison | Republican | Levi P. Morton |
| 1893–97 | (Stephen) Grover Cleveland | Democrat | Adlai E. Stevenson |
| 1897–1901 | William McKinley | Republican | Garret A. Hobart (d. 1899) |
| 1901–5 | William McKinley | Republican | Theodore Roosevelt |
| | Theodore Roosevelt | Republican | None |
| 1905–9 | Theodore Roosevelt | Republican | Charles W. Fairbanks |
| 1909–13 | William Howard Taft | Republican | James S. Sherman (d. 1912) |
| 1913–17 | (Thomas) Woodrow Wilson | Democrat | Thomas R. Marshall |
| 1917–21 | (Thomas) Woodrow Wilson | Democrat | Thomas R. Marshall |

| TERM | PRESIDENT | PARTY | VICE PRESIDENT |
|------|-----------|-------|----------------|
| 1921–25 | Warren Gamaliel Harding (d. 1923) | Republican | (John) Calvin Coolidge |
| | (John) Calvin Coolidge | Republican | None |
| 1925–29 | (John) Calvin Coolidge | Republican | Charles G. Dawes |
| 1929–33 | Herbert Clark Hoover | Republican | Charles Curtis |
| 1933–37 | Franklin D. Roosevelt | Democrat | John N. Garner |
| 1937–41 | Franklin D. Roosevelt | Democrat | John N. Garner |
| 1941–45 | Franklin D. Roosevelt | Democrat | Henry A. Wallace |
| 1945–49 | Franklin D. Roosevelt (d. 1945) | Democrat | Harry S Truman |
| | Harry S Truman | Democrat | None |
| 1949–53 | Harry S Truman | Democrat | Alben W. Barkley |
| 1953–57 | (David) Dwight Eisenhower | Republican | Richard M. Nixon |
| 1957–61 | (David)Dwight Eisenhower | Republican | Richard M. Nixon |
| 1961–65 | John Fitzgerald Kennedy (d. 1963) | Democrat | Lyndon Baines Johnson |
| | Lyndon Baines Johnson | Democrat | None |
| 1965–69 | Lyndon Baines Johnson | Democrat | Hubert H. Humphrey Jr. |
| 1969–73 | Richard Milhous Nixon | Republican | Spiro Agnew |
| 1973–77 | Richard Milhous Nixon (res. 1974) | Republican | Spiro Agnew, Gerald Ford |
| | Gerald Rudolph Ford | Republican | Nelson Rockefeller |
| 1977–81 | James Earl Carter | Democrat | Walter F. Mondale |
| 1981–85 | Ronald Wilson Reagan | Republican | George H. W. Bush |
| 1985–89 | Ronald Wilson Reagan | Republican | George H. W. Bush |
| 1989–93 | George Herbert Walker Bush | Republican | James Danforth Quayle |
| 1993–97 | William Jefferson (Blythe) Clinton | Democrat | Albert Gore |
| 1997–2001 | William Jefferson (Blythe) Clinton | Democrat | Albert Gore |
| 2001–5 | George Walker Bush | Republican | Richard Cheney |
| 2005–9 | George Walker Bush | Republican | Richard Cheney |

# PRESIDENTIAL RANKINGS

Ranking the presidents started in 1948 when Arthur M. Schlesinger invited fifty-five authorities, most of them professional historians, to rate the presidents from best to worst. Schlesinger repeated the effort fourteen years later with more stringent criteria and a slightly larger pool of academics. The U.S. Historical Society tried its hand in 1977, as did the *Chicago Tribune* in 1982. By the 1990s dozens of formal and informal polls had tried to discern the greats from the failures.

Among the most vigorous and reputable lists have been the Siena Research Institute review and the *Wall Street Journal*–Federalist Society analysis. Both involved scores of historians, political scientists, and law experts with diverse outlooks who graded the executives on a multitude of criteria, ranging from domestic policy to court appointments, imagination, and luck. Following are their rankings compared to this author's, who places the greatest scrutiny on foreign policy, economic initiatives, labor and land management, and response to crises.

| WALL STREET JOURNAL (2000) | SIENA POLL (2002) | THOMAS R. FLAGEL (2007) |
|---|---|---|
| 1. George Washington | Franklin Roosevelt | Theodore Roosevelt |
| 2. Abraham Lincoln | Abraham Lincoln | Franklin Roosevelt |
| 3. Franklin Roosevelt | Theodore Roosevelt | George Washington |
| 4. Thomas Jefferson | George Washington | Thomas Jefferson |
| 5. Theodore Roosevelt | Thomas Jefferson | James K. Polk |
| 6. Andrew Jackson | Woodrow Wilson | John Adams |
| 7. Harry Truman | Harry Truman | Abraham Lincoln |
| 8. Ronald Reagan | James Monroe | Grover Cleveland |
| 9. Dwight Eisenhower | James Madison | James Monroe |
| 10. James K. Polk | Dwight Eisenhower | William Clinton |
| 11. Woodrow Wilson | James K. Polk | George H.W. Bush |
| 12. Grover Cleveland | John Adams | Dwight Eisenhower |
| 13. John Adams | Andrew Jackson | James Madison |
| 14. William McKinley | John F. Kennedy | William H. Taft |
| 15. James Madison | Lyndon Johnson | Harry Truman |
| 16. James Monroe | Ronald Reagan | Woodrow Wilson |
| 17. Lyndon Johnson | John Quincy Adams | William McKinley |
| 18. John F. Kennedy | William Clinton | Andrew Jackson |
| 19. William H. Taft | William McKinley | Lyndon Johnson |
| 20. John Quincy Adams | Grover Cleveland | Zachary Taylor |
| 21. George H.W. Bush | William H. Taft | Ronald Reagan |
| 22. Rutherford B. Hayes | George H.W. Bush | John F. Kennedy |
| 23. Martin Van Buren | George W. Bush | Martin Van Buren |
| 24. William Clinton | Martin Van Buren | John Quincy Adams |
| 25. Calvin Coolidge | James Carter | Herbert Hoover |
| 26. Chester A. Arthur | Richard Nixon | Calvin Coolidge |

| WALL STREET JOURNAL (2000) | SIENA POLL (2002) | THOMAS R. FLAGEL (2007) |
|---|---|---|
| 27.  Benjamin Harrison | Rutherford B. Hayes | George W. Bush |
| 28.  Gerald Ford | Gerald Ford | James Carter |
| 29.  Herbert Hoover | Calvin Coolidge | Rutherford B. Hayes |
| 30.  James Carter | Chester A. Arthur | Chester A. Arthur |
| 31.  Zachary Taylor | Herbert Hoover | Gerald Ford |
| 32.  Ulysses S. Grant | Benjamin Harrison | James Garfield |
| 33.  Richard Nixon | James Garfield | James Buchanan |
| 34.  John Tyler | Zachary Taylor | Benjamin Harrison |
| 35.  Millard Fillmore | Ulysses S. Grant | William H. Harrison |
| 36.  Andrew Johnson | William H. Harrison | John Tyler |
| 37.  Franklin Pierce | John Tyler | Richard Nixon |
| 37.  Warren Harding | Millard Fillmore | Millard Fillmore |
| 39.  James Buchanan | Franklin Pierce | Andrew Johnson |
| 40. | Warren G. Harding | Ulysses S. Grant |
| 41. | James Buchanan | Franklin Pierce |
| 42. | Andrew Johnson | Warren G. Harding |

# AGE AT DEATH

### (ASTERISK DENOTES DIED IN OFFICE)

| | | | |
|---|---|---|---|
| Ford | 93 | W. H. Harrison | 68° |
| Reagan | 93 | Washington | 67 |
| J. Adams | 90 | B. Harrison | 67 |
| Hoover | 90 | Wilson | 67 |
| Truman | 88 | A. Johnson | 66 |
| Madison | 85 | Taylor | 65° |
| Jefferson | 83 | Pierce | 64 |
| Nixon | 81 | L. B. Johnson | 64 |
| J. Q. Adams | 80 | Grant | 63 |
| Van Buren | 79 | F. D. Roosevelt | 63° |
| Eisenhower | 78 | Coolidge | 60 |
| Jackson | 78 | T. Roosevelt | 60 |
| Buchanan | 77 | McKinley | 58° |
| Fillmore | 74 | Harding | 57° |
| Monroe | 73 | Arthur | 57 |
| Taft | 72 | Lincoln | 56° |
| Tyler | 71 | Polk | 53 |
| Cleveland | 71 | Garfield | 49° |
| Hayes | 70 | Kennedy | 46° |

# BIRTH STATES OF THE PRESIDENTS

## VIRGINIA

Washington
Jefferson
Madison
Monroe
W. H. Harrison
Tyler
Taylor
Wilson

## OHIO

Grant
Hayes
Garfield
B. Harrison
McKinley
Taft
Harding

## MASSACHUSETTS

J. Adams
J. Q. Adams
Kennedy
G. H. W. Bush

## NEW YORK

Van Buren
Fillmore
T. Roosevelt
F. Roosevelt

## NORTH CAROLINA

Polk
A. Johnson

## TEXAS

Eisenhower
L. Johnson

## VERMONT

Arthur
Coolidge

## ARKANSAS

Clinton

## CALIFORNIA

Nixon

## CONNECTICUT

G.W. Bush

## GEORGIA

Carter

## ILLINOIS

Reagan

## IOWA

Hoover

## KENTUCKY

Lincoln

## MISSOURI

Truman

## NEBRASKA

Ford

## NEW HAMPSHIRE

Pierce

## NEW JERSEY

Cleveland

## PENNSYLVANIA

Buchanan

## SOUTH CAROLINA

Jackson

# PRESIDENTIAL HEALTH

Like most Americans, few presidents enjoyed pristine health. Undoubtedly the fittest among them were Millard Fillmore, Gerald Ford, and George W. Bush. Listed here are the major illnesses that beset the presidents in their lifetimes. Names with an asterisk indicate that the ailment was the leading cause of death.

## ADDISON'S DISEASE

Kennedy

## ALZHEIMER'S DISEASE

Reagan°

## ARTHRITIS

Madison
Eisenhower
Reagan
George H.W. Bush

## BRIGHT'S DISEASE

Arthur°

## CANCER

Grant°
Cleveland
Hoover
Eisenhower
Reagan

## CHOLERA

Polk°
Taylor°

## CORONARY EMBOLISM

Theodore Roosevelt°

## DEPRESSION

Washington
J. Adams
Jefferson
Jackson
Pierce
Lincoln
B. Harrison

Coolidge
Nixon

## DYSENTERY

Washington
Jefferson°
Jackson
Taylor
Buchanan

## ENLARGED PROSTATE

Jefferson
Taft
Reagan

## GOUT

Van Buren
Cleveland
Taft

## GUNSHOT WOUND

Monroe
Jackson
Lincoln°
Garfield°
McKinley°
T. Roosevelt
Kennedy°
Reagan

## HEADACHES/MIGRAINES

Jefferson
Taft
Wilson
Truman

## HEART DISEASE/FAILURE

J. Adams°
Madison°
Van Buren°
Garfield
Arthur
Hayes°
Taft°
Wilson
Harding°
Coolidge°
F. Roosevelt
Truman°
Eisenhower°
L. Johnson°
Ford°
George H.W. Bush
Clinton

## HEMORRHAGING

Hoover°
F. Roosevelt°

## MALARIA

Washington
Monroe
Taylor
Lincoln

## PNEUMONIA

Washington°
W. H. Harrison°
B. Harrison°
Harding
Ford
Reagan

## POLIO

F. Roosevelt

## RESPIRATORY INFECTION

J. Adams
Monroe°
Van Buren
Tyler
Garfield

B. Harrison
Taft
Wilson
Ford
Reagan

## RHEUMATISM

J. Adams
Jefferson
Buchanan°
T. Roosevelt

## SMALLPOX

Washington
Jackson
Lincoln

## STROKE

J. Q. Adams°
Tyler°
Fillmore°
A. Johnson°
Wilson°
Eisenhower
Nixon°
Ford

## SEVERE TOOTH DECAY

Washington
Adams
B. Harrison
Wilson

## TUBERCULOSIS

Washington
Jackson°
Pierce°
A. Johnson

## TYPHOID

A. Johnson
Cleveland
Taft

## YELLOW FEVER

Taylor

# PRESIDENTIAL SITES

## GENERAL SITES AND ATTRACTIONS

American Presidential Museum
3107 West Highway 76
Branson, MO 65616
(417) 334-8683
www.americanpresidentialmuseum.com

Hall of Presidents
789 Baltimore Street
Gettysburg, PA 17325
(717) 334-5717
www.gettysburgbattlefieldtours.com

Mount Rushmore History Association
13000 Highway 244, Building 31, Suite 2
Keystone, SD 57751
(800) 699-3142
www.mtrushmorebookstore.com

The Museum of American Presidents
130 North Massanutten Street
Strasburg, VA 22657
(540) 465-5999
www.waysideofva.com/presidents

The Presidential Museum and
Leadership Library
4919 East University
University of Texas
Odessa, TX 79761-8144
(432) 363-7737

United States Vice Presidential Museum
Dan Quayle Center
815 Warren Street
Huntington, IN 46750
(260) 356-6356
www.quaylemuseum.org

## PRESIDENTIAL MONUMENTS, MUSEUMS, AND LIBRARIES

Washington Birthplace National Monument
1732 Popes Creek Road
Washington's Birthplace, VA 22443
(804) 224-1732
www.nps.gov/gewa

Mary Washington House
1200 Charles Street
Fredericksburg, VA 22401
(540) 373-1569

Historic Mount Vernon
Post Office Box 110
3200 Mount Vernon Memorial Highway
Mount Vernon, VA 22121
(703) 780-2000
www.mountvernon.org

Adams National Historic Park
135 Adams Street
Quincy, MA 02169-1749
(617) 773-1177
www.nps.gov/adam/

Thomas Jefferson Foundation
Post Office Box 316
Charlottesville, VA 22902
(434) 984-9822,
www.monticello.org

The James Madison Museum
129 Caroline Street
Orange, VA 22960-1532
(540) 672-1776
www.jamesmadisonmus.org

James Monroe Museum and Memorial Library
908 Charles Street
Fredericksburg, VA 22401
(540) 654-1043
www.umw.edu/jamesmonroemuseum

Andrew Jackson's Hermitage
4580 Rachel Lane
Hermitage, TN 37076
(615) 889-2941
www.hermitage.org

Martin Van Buren National Historic Site
1013 Old Post Road
Kinderhook, NY 12106
(518) 758-9689
www.nps.gov/mava/home.htm

William Henry Harrison Mansion
3 West Scot Street
Vincennes, IN 47591
(812) 882-2096
www.grouselandfoundation.org

Tippecanoe Battlefield
200 Battle Ground Avenue
Battle Ground, IN 47920
(765) 567-2147
www.tcha.mus.in.us

James K. Polk Memorial Association
301-305 West Seventh Street
Columbia, TN 38402
(931) 388-2354
www.jamespolk.com

President James K. Polk State Historic Site
12031 Lancaster Highway
Box 475
Pineville, NC 28134
(704) 889-7145
www.ah.dcr.state.nc.us/sections/hs/polk/

Lincoln Museum and Library
112 North Sixth Street
Springfield, IL 62701
(800) 610-2094
www.nps.gov/abli

The Lincoln Museum
200 East Berry Street
Fort Wayne, IN 46802
(260) 455-3864
www.thelincolnmuseum.org

Abraham Lincoln Museum
Lincoln Memorial University
Cumberland Gap Parkway
Harrogate, TN 37752
(615) 869-6235
www.lmunet.edu/museum/

Andrew Johnson National Historic Site
College & Depot Streets
Post Office Box 1088
Greeneville, TN 37744
(423) 638-3551
www.nps.gov/anjo

General Grant National
Memorial: Grant's Tomb
Riverside Drive and 122nd Street
New York, NY 10027
(212) 666-1640
www.nps.gov/gegr/

The Rutherford B. Hayes Presidential Center
Spiegel Grove
Fremont, OH 43420-2796
(419) 332-2081
www.rbhayes.org

James A. Garfield National Historic Site
8095 Mentor Avenue
Mentor, OH, 44060
(440) 255-8722
www.nps.gov/jaga/

President Benjamin Harrison Home
1230 North Delaware Street
Indianapolis, IN 46202
(317) 631-1888
www.presidentbenjaminharrison.org

William McKinley Presidential
Library and Museum
800 McKinley Monument Drive NW
Canton, OH 44708
(330) 455-7043
www.mckinleymuseum.org

Sagamore Hill National Historic Site
20 Sagamore Hill Road
Oyster Bay, NY 11771-1807
(516) 922-4788
www.nps.gov/sahi/home.htm

William Howard Taft National Historic Site
2038 Auburn Avenue
Cincinnati, OH 45219
(513) 684-3262
www.nps.gov/wiho/

Woodrow Wilson Presidential Library
18-24 North Coalter Street
Post Office Box 24
Staunton, VA 24402-0024
(540) 885-0897
www.woodrowwilson.org

Herbert Hoover Presidential
Library and Museum
210 Parkside Drive
West Branch, IA 52358
(319) 643-5301
hoover.archives.gov

Calvin Coolidge Presidential
Library and Museum
Forbes Library
20 West Street
Northampton, MA 01060
(413) 587-1014
www.forbeslibrary.org

Franklin D. Roosevelt Presidential
Library and Museum
4079 Albany Post Road
Hyde Park, NY 12538
1-800-FDR-VISIT
www.fdrlibrary.marist.edu

Truman Presidential Library and Museum
500 West US Highway 24
Independence, MO 64050
(816) 268-8200
www.trumanlibrary.org

Dwight Eisenhower Presidential
Library and Museum
200 Southeast Fourth Street
Abilene, KS 67410
(877) RINGIKE
www.dwightdeisenhower.com/library-museum

Eisenhower National Historic Site
250 Eisenhower Farm Lane
Gettysburg, PA 17325
(717) 338-9114
www.nps.gov/eise

John Fitzgerald Kennedy Presidential
Library and Museum
Columbia Point
Boston, MA 02125
(866) JFK-1960
www.jfklibrary.org

The Sixth Floor Museum
411 Elm Street, Suite 120
Dallas, TX 75202-3301
(888) 485-4854 ext. 6681 or 6682
www.jfk.org

LBJ Library and Museum
2313 Red River Street
Austin, TX 78705
(512) 721-0200
www.lbjlib.utexas.edu

Richard Nixon Library and Birthplace
18001 Yorba Linda Boulevard
Yorba Linda, CA 92886
(714) 93-5075
www.nixonfoundation.org

Gerald R. Ford Museum
303 Pearl Street NW
Grand Rapids, MI 49504-5353
(616) 254-0400
www.ford.utexas.edu/museum

Jimmy Carter Library and Museum
441 Freedom Parkway
Atlanta, GA 30307-1498
(404) 865-7131
www.jimmycarterlibrary.org

Ronald Reagan Presidential Library
40 Presidential Drive
Simi Valley, CA 93065
(800) 410-8354
www.ronaldreaganmemorial.com

George H.W. Bush Library and Museum
1000 George Bush Drive W
College Station, TX 77845
(979) 691-4000
www.bushlibrary.tamu.edu

Clinton Presidential Library and Museum
1200 President Clinton Avenue
Little Rock, AR 72201
(501) 374-4242
www.clintonfoundation.org

# Notes

*Full bibliographic data can be found in the Bibliography*

## CHAPTER 1: PRESIDENTIAL CHARACTER

1. Of those presidents not included in this list, Millard Fillmore established a militia unit after his presidency, when the Civil War began, and James Buchanan was a private (not an officer) in the Pennsylvania militia.

2. Sievers, *Benjamin Harrison: Hoosier Statesman*, 2:361.

3. Kane, Podell, and Anzovin, *Facts About the Presidents*, 583. See also Gross, *America's Lawyer-Presidents*.

4. Binkley, *President and Congress*, 381–82.

5. DeGregorio, *The Complete Book of U.S. Presidents*, 673–74.

6. Ford, *A Time to Heal*, 66–67, 96.

7. Johnson quoted in Bush and Gold, *Looking Forward: An Autobiography*, 101.

8. Barry Burden, "United States Senators as Presidential Candidates," *Political Science Quarterly* 117, no. 1 (2002): 81, 86.

9. Adams quoted in Walch, *At the President's Side: The Vice Presidency in the Twentieth Century*, 1; Garner quoted in Reeves, *The Life of Chester A. Arthur*, 45.

10. McCullough, *John Adams*, 38; Rayback, *Millard Fillmore*, 6; Karabell, *Chester Alan Arthur*, 12.

11. Goodwin, *Lyndon Johnson and the American Dream*, 64–69; Garfield quoted in Peskin, *Garfield*, 21.

12. U. S. Grant is not included as a cabinet member, though he was acting secretary of war under Andrew Johnson. Grant's interim capacity came as a result of Johnson's attempted removal of Edwin M. Stanton from the post, for which Johnson was impeached.

13. Socolofsky and Spetter, *The Presidency of Benjamin Harrison*, 162. Polk, Jefferson, and Clinton quoted in Richard Ellis, "The Joy of Power: Changing Conceptions of the Presidential Office," *Presidential Studies Quarterly* (June 2003): 269, 277.

14. Whitcomb and Whitcomb, *Real Life at the White House*, 296, 466.

15. Moore, *The Madisons*, 470.
16. Jeffries, *In and Out of the White House*, 138.
17. Judith Weaver, "Edith Bolling Wilson as First Lady: A Study in the Power of Personality," *Presidential Studies Quarterly* (Winter 1985): 54.
18. Lincoln quoted in DeGregorio, *The Complete Book of U.S. Presidents*, 228.
19. Thomas, *Abraham Lincoln*, 304.
20. Truman quoted in Brogan and Mosley, *American Presidential Families*, 30.
21. DeGregorio, *The Complete Book of U.S. Presidents*, 584.
22. Watterson, *The Games Presidents Play: Sports and the Presidency*, 111–12; DeGregorio, *The Complete Book of U.S. Presidents*, 125.
23. Adams quoted in DeGregorio, *The Complete Book of U.S. Presidents*, 22.
24. Morris, *Theodore Rex*, 173.
25. See also Wiltse, *Contested Waters: A Social History of Swimming Pools in America*.
26. Roberts, *Rating the First Ladies*, 64.
27. See also Pierce and Ashley, *Pierce Piano Atlas*.
28. Grant quoted in Ward, *The Civil War*, 280.
29. Wilson quoted in DeGregorio, *The Complete Book of U.S. Presidents*, 412.
30. Whitcomb and Whitcomb, *Real Life at the White House*, 342.
31. Ibid., 357.
32. See also Watterson, *The Games Presidents Play: Sports and the Presidency*.
33. Morris, *Theodore Rex*, 236.
34. Lambert, *The Founding Fathers and the Place of Religion in America*, 282.
35. Washington quoted in Gaustad, *A Documentary History of Religion in America to the Civil War*, 276
36. Grant quoted in Menendez, *Religion at the Polls*, 28–29; Hoogenboom, *Rutherford B. Hayes: Warrior and President*, 268.
37. For additional sources on the role of religion in U.S. politics, see Wilson, *Church and State in America: A Bibliographical Guide*.
38. Stuckey, *Defining Americans: The Presidency and National Identity*, 272; Reichley, *Faith in Politics*, 142.
39. Reichley, *Faith in Politics*, 290; Eisenhower quoted in Alley, *So Help Me God: Religion and the Presidency*, 83.
40. Reichley, *Faith in Politics*, 320–21. Statistics on denominational votes from 2004 Religion and Politics Post-election Survey, University of Akron. Bush quoted in Frum, *The Right Man: An Inside Account of the Bush White House*, 283.
41. Frum quoted in D. Jason Berggren and Nicol C. Rae, "Jimmy Carter and

George W. Bush: Faith, Foreign Policy, and an Evangelical Presidential Style," *Presidential Studies Quarterly* (December 2006): 614.

42. Ibid., 606. See also Singer, *The President of Good and Evil: The Ethics of George W. Bush*.

43. Andrew R. Flint and Joy Porter, "Jimmy Carter: The Re-Emergence of Faith-Based Politics and the Abortion Rights Issue," *Presidential Studies Quarterly* (March 2005): 30.

44. "We have a responsibility" from ibid., 32; convention quote from ibid.; Ford quoted in Hutcheson, *God in the White House: How Religion Has Changed the Modern Presidency*, 96; "I'll be a better president . . ." from Pippert, *The Spiritual Journal of Jimmy Carter*, 117.

45. National Archives and Records Administration, *Public Papers of the Presidents: James Carter, Book 1*, 812–14.

46. Flint and Porter, "Jimmy Carter: The Re-Emergence of Faith-Based Politics and the Abortion Rights Issue," 37.

47. Reichley, *Faith in Politics*, 257–58.

48. McKinley quoted in Bonnell, *Presidential Profiles: Religion in the Life of American Presidents*, 175.

49. Handy, *Undermined Establishment: Church-State Relations in America, 1880–1920*, 8.

50. McKinley quoted in ibid., 7.

51. McKinley quoted in ibid., 81.

52. Reagan quoted in Edel, *Defenders of the Faith: Religion and Politics from the Pilgrim Fathers to Ronald Reagan*, 140.

53. Reagan quoted in Schlesinger and Israel, *The History of American Presidential Elections*, 4145. Reichley, *Faith in Politics*, 297, 301–2. Falwell quoted in Flint and Porter, "Jimmy Carter: The Re-Emergence of Faith-Based Politics and the Abortion Rights Issue," 47. On the use of *God* in annual addresses, see Elvin Lim, "Five Trends in Presidential Rhetoric," *Presidential Studies Quarterly* (June 2002): 336, fig. 2.

54. NCC quoted in Reichley, *Faith in Politics*, 258–59; Edel, *Defenders of the Faith: Religion and Politics from the Pilgrim Fathers to Ronald Reagan*, 169.

55. Reagan quoted in Edel, *Defenders of the Faith: Religion and Politics from the Pilgrim Fathers to Ronald Reagan*, 150.

56. Reichley, *Faith in Politics*, 259–60, 303.

57. DiNunzio, *Woodrow Wilson: Essential Writings and Speeches of the Scholar-President*, 2–4; Weinstein, *Woodrow Wilson: A Medical and Psychological Biography*, 263–64. On TR's view on the existence of moral absolutism, see Watts, *Rough Rider in the White House: Theodore Roosevelt*

*and the Politics of Desire*. Historian John Milton Cooper Jr. contends that Wilson was not necessarily religious in his political operations and instead worked to separate the two. Cooper also contends that between Theodore Roosevelt and Wilson, Roosevelt alone possessed a "brand of political evangelism." See Cooper, *The Warrior and the Priest: Woodrow Wilson and Theodore Roosevelt*.

58. Wilson quoted in Weinstein, *Woodrow Wilson: A Medical and Psychological Biography*, 21.

59. Wilson quoted in Stuckey, *Defining Americans: The Presidency and National Identity*, 167.

60. Wilson quoted in Weinstein, *Woodrow Wilson: A Medical and Psychological Biography*, 263, and in Stuckey, *Defining Americans: The Presidency and National Identity*, 167.

61. Clemenceau quoted in Berggren and Rae, "Jimmy Carter and George W. Bush: Faith, Foreign Policy, and an Evangelical Presidential Style," 607. Lloyd George quoted in ibid., 608. Hoover quoted in ibid., 609.

62. Wilson's Holy Land statement quoted in Handy, *Undermined Establishment: Church-State Relations in America, 1880–1920*, 178. Wilson's "Divine Will" statement quoted in Stuckey, *Defining Americans: The Presidency and National Identity*, 167.

63. TR quoted in McPherson, *"To the Best of My Ability,"* 172.

64. Harrison quoted in Calhoun, *Benjamin Harrison*, 13.

65. Harrison and Quay quoted in Sievers, *Benjamin Harrison: Hoosier Statesman*, 2:426.

66. Anthony, *America's First Families*, 225; Calhoun, *Benjamin Harrison*, 4; Socolofsky and Spetter, *The Presidency of Benjamin Harrison*, 23.

67. Socolofsky and Spetter, *The Presidency of Benjamin Harrison*, 163.

68. Dulce and Richter, *Religion and the Presidency*, 77.

69. Reichley, *Faith in Politics*, 331.

70. Ibid.

71. Summers, *The Arrogance of Power: The Secret World of Richard Nixon*, 310.

72. Anthony, *America's First Families*, 225; Summers, *The Arrogance of Power: The Secret World of Richard Nixon*, 12.

73. Strober and Strober, *The Nixon Presidency: An Oral History of the Era*, 185.

74. Ibid., 12–13.

75. Nixon quoted in Summers, *The Arrogance of Power: The Secret World of Richard Nixon*, 448.

76. Coyle, *Ordeal of the Presidency*, 29.

77. Dear, *The Oxford Companion to World War II*, 632–34; Maney, *The Roosevelt Presence*, 160–61.

78. Black, *Franklin Delano Roosevelt: Champion of Freedom*, 722–25.

79. Maney, *The Roosevelt Presence*, 160–61; Mencken quoted in Rubenzer and Faschingbauer, *Personality, Character, and Leadership in the White House: Psychologists Assess the Presidents*, 253.

80. Jefferson quoted in Rubenzer and Faschingbauer, *Personality, Character, and Leadership in the White House: Psychologists Assess the Presidents*, 86.

81. Jackson quoted in James, *The Life of Andrew Jackson*, 617.

82. Jackson quoted in ibid., 622.

83. Lincoln quoted in Oates, *Abraham Lincoln: The Man Behind the Myths*, 106.

84. For the gradual transformation of the proclamation from first draft to final signature, see Thomas, *Abraham Lincoln: A Biography*, 333–64.

85. Goodwin, *Lyndon Johnson and the American Dream*, 39; Reedy quoted in Rubenzer and Faschingbauer, *Personality, Character, and Leadership in the White House: Psychologists Assess the Presidents*, 102.

86. Rubenzer and Faschingbauer, *Personality, Character, and Leadership in the White House: Psychologists Assess the Presidents*, 103.

87. Tonkin Resolution quoted in Goodwin, *Lyndon Johnson and the American Dream*, 198.

88. Link, *Wilson*, 2:67.

89. Venzon, *The United States in the First World War*, 536–37.

90. Ibid., 536.

91. Reeves, *Richard Nixon: Alone in the White House*, 348.

92. Ibid., 369.

93. Rubenzer and Faschingbauer, *Personality, Character, and Leadership in the White House: Psychologists Assess the Presidents*, 300–302.

94. "U.S. Secretary of State Colin Powell Addresses the U.N. Security Council," February 5, 2003, http://www.whitehouse.gov/news/releases/2003/02/20030205-1.html.

95. Washington letter from Mount Vernon to attorney general of the United States, August, 26, 1792, in Fitzpatrick, *The Writings of George Washington*, 32:135.

96. Hanna quoted in Walch, *At the President's Side: The Vice Presidency in the Twentieth Century*, 10.

97. *New York Times* reporter quoted in Ellis, "The Joy of Power: Changing Conceptions of the Presidential Office," 283.

98. Morris, *Theodore Rex*, 161.

99. Ibid., 165–66.
100. Taylor quoted in Brinkley and Dyer, *The Reader's Companion to the American Presidency*, 35.
101. For the text of the Alien and Sedition Acts, see Bruun and Crosby, *Our Nation's Archive: The History of the United States in Documents*, 195–97.
102. Risjord, *Thomas Jefferson*, 110–11.
103. Ibid.; McCullough, *John Adams*, 504–7, 536–37.

CHAPTER 2: ELECTIONS

1. Melder, *Hail to the Candidate: Presidential Campaigns from Banners to Broadcasts*, 124–25.
2. For general overviews on the changing nature of campaigning, see Melder, *Hail to the Candidate: Presidential Campaigns from Banners to Broadcasts*; Austin, *Political Facts of the United States Since 1789*; Kelly, *Election Day*.
3. Ferling, *Adams vs. Jefferson: The Tumultuous Election of 1800*, 177.
4. James Bayard to John Adams, February 19, 1801, "Papers of James A. Bayard, 1796–1815," *Annual Report of the American Historical Association* 2 (1913): 129–30.
5. For background on the role of Supreme Court Justices in the 1876 election, see Rehnquist, *Centennial Crisis: The Disputed Election of 1876*.
6. Ibid., 104–5.
7. In 2000, many Democrats blamed Green Party nominee Ralph Nader for "taking" 97,488 Florida votes that likely would have gone to the environmentalist Gore. Yet the same could be said of George W. Bush's losing Iowa (7 electoral votes) by 4,144 votes to right-wing Reform Party candidate Pat Buchanan, who collected 5,731. In New Mexico (5 electoral votes), where Bush lost by only 366, Buchanan and Libertarian Harry Browne won a combined 3,450. And in Wisconsin (11 electoral votes), Bush lost by 5,708, while Buchanan and Browne collected a combined 18,111.
8. Ames letter to Oliver Wolcott quoted in Smith, *The Republic of Letters: The Correspondence Between Thomas Jefferson and James Madison*, 2:940.
9. Ferling, *Adams vs. Jefferson: The Tumultuous Election of 1800*, 248. Jefferson quoted in Randall, *Thomas Jefferson*, 521.
10. Smith, *The Republic of Letters: The Correspondence Between Thomas Jefferson and James Madison*, 2:943.
11. Ibid., 2:944.
12. TR and Taft quoted in Schlesinger and Israel, *History of American Presidential Elections*, 2246, 2247.
13. Perret, *Eisenhower*, 375; McCullough, *Truman*, 887–89.

14. See also Denton, *The 2004 Presidential Campaign: A Communication Perspective.*

15. Morris, *The Rise of Theodore Roosevelt*, 186–88.

16. Congressional Quarterly, *Presidential Elections, 1789–2000*, 42.

17. Morris, *The Rise of Theodore Roosevelt*, 291.

18. Presidential Proclamation 4311 of September 8, 1974, *Record Group 11: General Records of the United States Government, 1778—1992* (Washington, DC: National Archives and Records Administration, 1993).

19. Pomper, *The Election of 1976: Reports and Interpretations*, 65–66, 70–72.

20. Taylor quoted in Smith, *The Presidencies of Zachary Taylor and Millard Fillmore*, 39.

21. Ibid., 27.

22. Ibid., 50.

23. Truman quoted in *New York Times*, November 7, 1960.

24. Ambrose, *Nixon*, 1:604–6.

25. Roper quoted in the *New York Times*, November 8, 1960.

26. Franklin quoted in Bowen, *Miracle at Philadelphia*, 60.

27. Franklin quoted in Isaacson, *Benjamin Franklin: An American Life*, 462.

28. Letter from Washington to Charles Pettit on August 16, 1788, from Fitzpatrick, *The Writings of George Washington*, 30:42. Washington letter to Benjamin Lincoln from ibid., 30:119.

29. Washington quoted in Ellis, *His Excellency: George Washington*, 149.

30. Washington quoted in Fitzpatrick, *The Writings of George Washington*, 30:174.

31. Ibid., 30:268.

32. Washington quoted in Tebbel and Watts, *The Press and the Presidency*, 12.

33. Ellis, *His Excellency: George Washington*, 190–91.

34. Fitzpatrick, *The Writings of George Washington*, 30:45, 310

35. Cunningham, *The Presidency of James Monroe*, 106.

36. William Plumer quoted in ibid., 107.

37. Singer, *Campaign Speeches of American Presidential Candidates, 1928–1972*, 125.

38. Davis, *FDR: The New Deal Years, 1933–1937*, 645.

39. Ibid., 646.

40. Reagan's bombing gaffe and other misquotes from "McCain Jokes About Bombing Iran," ABC News, July 26, 2007, http://www.abcnews.go.com/Politics/wireStory?id=3056994.

41. Schlesinger and Israel, *The History of American Presidential Elections*, 4162.

42. Ibid., 4168.

43. Abramson, Aldrich, and Rohde, *Change and Continuity in the 1984 Elections*, 67.

44. Kennedy quoted in Schlesinger and Israel, *The History of American Presidential Elections*, 3871.

45. Pomper, *The Election of 1976: Reports and Interpretations*, 70.

46. White, *The Making of the President, 1972*, 198–204.

47. Pomper, *The Election of 1976: Reports and Interpretations*, 61.

48. Schlesinger and Israel, *The History of American Presidential Elections*, 160–65.

49. Ibid., 162.

50. Jefferson quoted in ibid., 168.

51. Emerson quoted in Waugh, *Reelecting Lincoln*, 357.

52. Lincoln quoted in Donald, *Lincoln*, 529.

53. Sears, *The Civil War Papers of George B. McClellan*, 588.

54. Letter to Samuel Barlow, November 10, 1864, in ibid., 618.

55. Schaller, *Reckoning with Reagan*, 28–29.

56. Morris, *Jimmy Carter: American Moralist*, 286.

57. Schlesinger and Israel, *The History of American Presidential Elections*, 4135.

58. Johnson quoted in Dallek, *Flawed Giant: Lyndon Johnson and His Times, 1961–1973*, 136.

59. Goldwater quoted in Schlesinger and Israel, *The History of American Presidential Elections*, 3574, 3585.

60. Dallek, *Flawed Giant: Lyndon Johnson and His Times, 1961–1973*, 138.

61. John B. Martin quoted in Schlesinger and Israel, *The History of American Presidential Elections*, 3565.

62. Melder, *Hail to the Candidate: Presidential Campaigns from Banners to Broadcasts*, 140; McPherson, *Ordeal by Fire*, 599.

63. *Richmond Daily Whig*, "Reflect Well and Vote Wisely," November 5, 1860; *St. Louis News* quoted in *Richmond Daily Whig*, October 4, 1860; *Hopkinsville (KY) Mercury* quoted in ibid. Texas media rumors from McPherson, *Battle Cry of Freedom*, 228. Banner in New York parade quoted in ibid., 224.

64. Lincoln officially received zero votes in Alabama, Arkansas, Florida, Georgia, Louisiana, Mississippi, North Carolina, Tennessee, and Texas, as well as no electoral votes from the legislature of South Carolina. For a breakdown of results, see Dubin, *United States Presidential Elections: The Official Results by County and State*, 159, 168.

65. *Richmond Daily Whig*, November 12, 1860; South Carolina Convention, *Journal of the Convention of the People of South Carolina, Held in 1860*,

*1861, and 1862, Together with the Ordinances, Reports, Resolutions, etc.*, 461–66.

66. Georgia newspaper quoted in McPherson, *Battle Cry of Freedom*, 230.

67. Boller, *Presidential Campaigns*, 134.

68. Hoogenboom, *Rutherford B. Hayes: Warrior and President*, 259; McPherson, *Ordeal by Fire*, 593–95, 598.

69. Boller, *Presidential Campaigns*, 136; Rehnquist, *Centennial Crisis: The Disputed Election of 1876*, 106–8.

70. Rehnquist, *Centennial Crisis: The Disputed Election of 1876*, 203.

71. Remini, *The Election of Andrew Jackson*, 102–5, 116–18.

72. Ibid., 150–51.

73. Jackson quoted in James, *The Life of Andrew Jackson*, 483.

74. Adams quoted in Ferling, *Adams vs. Jefferson: The Tumultuous Election of 1800*, 326.

75. Madison quoted in Randall, *Thomas Jefferson*, 520.

76. Jefferson quoted in Akers, *Abigail Adams*, 107.

77. Jefferson quoted in Malone, *Jefferson and His Time*, 1:275; Hamilton quoted in Lambert, *The Founding Fathers and the Place of Religion in America*, 275; *Connecticut Courant* quoted in Kelly, *Election Day*, 47. See also Menendez, *Religion at the Polls*, 25.

78. Jefferson quoted in Ferling, *Adams vs. Jefferson: The Tumultuous Election of 1800*, 181–82; Smith, *The Republic of Letters: The Correspondence Between Thomas Jefferson and James Madison*, 2:1138.

79. Abigail Adams quoted in Akers, *Abigail Adams*, 139.

80. Remini, *Henry Clay*, 652–55.

81. Dulce and Richter, *Religion and the Presidency*, 24–25; Menendez, *Religion at the Polls*, 26.

82. Dulce and Richter, *Religion and the Presidency*, 26.

83. Ibid., 27; O'Clay anecdote from Boller, *Presidential Campaigns*, 83.

84. Boller, *Presidential Campaigns*, 322.

85. Ribicoff quoted in Schlesinger and Israel, *History of American Presidential Elections*, 647.

86. Reeves, *President Nixon: Alone in the White House*, 513.

87. Reverend Ball quoted in Boller, *Presidential Campaigns*, 128.

88. Congressional Quarterly, *Presidential Elections, 1789–2000*, 42–43.

89. Ibid., 42.

90. "Rum" slogan quoted in Menendez, *Religion at the Polls*, 31; Fischer, *Tippecanoe and Trinkets Too: The Material Culture of American Presidential Campaigns*, 128.

91. Boller, *Presidential Campaigns*, 157–58, 165–66.
92. Stephens quoted in Boller, *Presidential Campaigns*, 129.
93. *New York Sun* quoted in Boller, *Presidential Campaigns*, 129.
94. Fischer, *Tippecanoe and Trinkets Too: The Material Culture of American Presidential Campaigns*, 100.
95. Greeley quoted in Boller, *Presidential Campaigns*, 130; Brown drinking noted in Kohn, *American Scandal*, 58.
96. On disenfranchised minority voters, see Rakove, *The Unfinished Election of 2000*, 28, 92–95, 236–37.
97. Robert Dudley, "The Presidential Election of 2000," *Presidential Studies Quarterly* (September 2001): 508. Rigorous data analysis suggests that as many as two thousand people from Palm Beach intended to vote for Gore on the butterfly ballot but instead voted for the archconservative Pat Buchanan instead. See Jacobsen and Rosenfeld, *The Longest Night: Polemics and Perspectives on Election 2000*, 50–68.
98. Weisberg and Wilcox, *Models of Voting in Presidential Elections: The 2000 U.S. Election*, 184. See also Dover, *The Disputed Presidential Election of 2000: A History and Reference Guide*.
99. Atwater quoted in Boller, *Presidential Campaigns*, 378–79; Maryland campaign pamphlet in ibid.
100. Democratic ad quoted in Boller, *Presidential Campaigns*, 381.

## CHAPTER 3: THE DOMESTIC SPHERE

1. Elvin Lim, "Five Trends in Presidential Rhetoric," *Presidential Studies Quarterly* (June 2002): 343.
2. National debt estimates from U.S. Office of Management and Budget, *Budget of the United States Government: Historical Tables, Fiscal Year 2007* and U.S. Commerce Department, *Statistical Abstract of the United States*.
3. Lincoln quoted in Boritt, *Lincoln and the Economics of the American Dream*, 94.
4. McPherson, *Battle Cry of Freedom*, 443–48.
5. Boritt, *Lincoln and the Economics of the American Dream*, 206–7.
6. Ibid., 251.
7. Hammond, *Sovereignty and the Empty Purse: Banks and Politics in the Civil War*, 134–35; Lawson, "Let the Nation Be Your Bank: The Civil War Bond Drives and the Construction of National Patriotism," 90–91.
8. Kennedy, *The Rise and Fall of the Great Powers*, 267.
9. Treasury Report on Finance, *Annual Report of the Secretary of the Treasury* (1919), 736; Ferguson, *The Pity of War: Explaining World War I*, 336.

10. Hendricks, *The Federal Debt: 1919–1930*, 108.

11. Treasury Report on Finance, *Annual Report of the Secretary of the Treasury* (1928), 416–19; Hendricks, *The Federal Debt: 1919–1930*, 1, 157.

12. FDR quoted in Lyons, *Herbert Hoover: A Biography*, 295.

13. Roosevelt quoted in Davis, *FDR: The New Deal Years, 1933–1937*, 641.

14. Kelly, *The National Debt: From FDR (1941) to Clinton (1996)*, 1.

15. Ibid., 23.

16. Reagan quoted in Walter Isaacson, "America's Incredible Day," *Time*, February 2, 1981.

17. U.S. Office of Management and Budget, *Budget of the United States Government: Historical Tables, Fiscal Year 2007*, 31.

18. Stockman quoted in Schaller, *Reckoning with Reagan*, 46.

19. Gordon, *Hamilton's Blessing*, 167; Abramson, Aldrich, and Rohde, *Change and Continuity in the 1984 Elections*, 196.

20. Malkin, *The National Debt*, 37.

21. Schick, *The Federal Budget: Politics, Policy, Process*, 17.

22. Kelly, *The National Debt: From FDR (1941) to Clinton (1996)*, 82–83, 135.

23. Hamilton quoted in Gordon, *Hamilton's Blessing*, 20.

24. Ibid., 30–31.

25. LeLoup, *Parties, Rules, and the Evolution of Congressional Budgeting*, 182–85.

26. Bush quoted in Alan K. Ota, "Deadlocked Tax Cut Proposals Expose Rift in GOP Ideology," *Congressional Quarterly Weekly Report* (May 3, 2003): 1029–33; LeLoup, *Parties, Rules, and the Evolution of Congressional Budgeting*, 194–95.

27. Official and academic estimates on costs of Second Gulf–Iraq War from Jamie Wilson, "Iraq War Could Cost over $2 Trillion, Says Nobel Prize-Winning Economist," *Guardian*, January 7, 2006; Scott Wallsten, "The Economic Cost of the Iraq War," *Economists' Voice*, 3 (2006): 2, art. 1, http://www.bepress.com/ev/v013/iss2/art1. Estimated adjusted dollar comparison of aid to Britain based on $34.1 billion 1945 Lend-Lease dollars plus $4.34 billion 1945 dollars in postwar loans, times conservative inflation adjustment of six 2008 dollars for every 1945 dollar.

28. Federalist legislator quoted in Hickey, *The War of 1812: A Forgotten Conflict*, 111.

29. Madison quoted in ibid., 120; Federalists quoted in ibid., 120.

30. Ibid., 124.

31. Rutland, *The Presidency of James Madison*, 196.

32. Gordon, *Hamilton's Blessing*, 190; Greene, *The Presidency of George Bush*, 79–80.

33. John Woolley and Gerhard Peters, *The American Presidency Project*, University of California, Santa Barbara, http://www.presidency.ucsb.edu/ws/?pid=17744.

34. Kelly, *The National Debt: From FDR (1941) to Clinton (1996)*, 141.

35. Ibid., 160.

36. Wilson quoted in Watson, *Presidential Vetoes and Public Policy*, xi; Truman quoted in Truman, *Where the Buck Stops: The Personal and Private Writings of Harry S. Truman*, 102.

37. Franklin quoted in Truman, *Where the Buck Stops: The Personal and Private Writings of Harry S. Truman*, 102.

38. Madison quoted in Watson, *Presidential Vetoes and Public Policy*, 10.

39. Phelps, *George Washington and American Constitutionalism*, 150–51; Watson, *Presidential Vetoes and Public Policy*, 16.

40. For a list of specific vetoes rendered up to 1988, see U.S. Senate Library, *Presidential Vetoes, 1789–1988*. For statistics on vetoes (by issue, overrides, challenges, etc.) to 1984, see King and Ragsdale, *The Elusive Executive: Discovering Statistical Patterns in the Presidency*, 88–102; Kane, Podell, and Anzovin, *Facts About the Presidents*, 669.

41. FDR quoted in Spitzer, *The Presidential Veto: Touchstone of the American Presidency*, 66.

42. On the Will Rogers Memorial, see Rosenman, *The Public Papers and Addresses of Franklin D. Roosevelt*, 6:337. On renaming the Chemical Warfare Service, see Rosenman, *The Public Papers and Addresses of Franklin D. Roosevelt*, 6:320–21. For information on the CWS during FDR's tenure, see Kleber and Birdsell, *The Chemical Warfare Service: Chemicals in Combat*.

43. Rosenman, *The Public Papers and Addresses of Franklin D. Roosevelt*, 13:80–81.

44. December 7 veto quoted in Rosenman, *The Public Papers and Addresses of Franklin D. Roosevelt*, 12: 528–29.

45. Jong R. Lee, "Presidential Vetoes from Washington to Nixon," *Journal of Politics* 37 (May 1975): 528.

46. Jackson, *Presidential Vetoes, 1792–1945*, 149. See also "Pensions: The Law and Its Administration," *Harper's Monthly*, January 1893.

47. Henig and Niderost, *A Nation Transformed: How the Civil War Changed America Forever*, 388; Spitzer, *The Presidential Veto: Touchstone of the American Presidency*, 61. Cleveland quoted in Congressional Quarterly, *Presidential Elections, 1789–2000*, 43.

48. On Cleveland's loss of the 1888 election connecting to his frequent vetoes of pensions, see Fischer, *President and Congress: Power and Policy*, 97; Spitzer, *The Presidential Veto: Touchstone of the American Presidency*, 60–67.

49. Megan J. McClintock, "Grover Cleveland: Civil War Pensions and the Reconstruction of Union Families," *Journal of American History* (September 1996): 456–80.

50. Vandenberg quoted in Truman, *Harry S. Truman*, 217.

51. McCullough, *Truman*, 358–59.

52. Truman quoted in Dallek, *Hail to the Chief: The Making and Unmaking of American Presidents*, xvii.

53. Truman, *Where the Buck Stops*, 70.

54. David Cole, "Enemy Aliens," *Stanford Law Review* (2002): 953.

55. Estimate of farmhouse cost in 1870s from Varhola, *Everyday Life During the Civil War*, 77. Salt works bill from 1873, S161. East Tennessee University claim from 1873 S490. Paducah bill from Jackson, *Presidential Vetoes*, 132–37; Grant quoted in Jackson, *Presidential Vetoes*, 134.

56. Jackson, *Presidential Vetoes*, 137.

57. Morison, *The Letters of Theodore Roosevelt*, 4:1264.

58. Jackson, *Presidential Vetoes*, 165.

59. Nathaniel Nash, "Campaign to Kill SBA Is Scrapped," *New York Times*, August 28, 1986; Ellie McGrath, "Survivor of the Budget Cuts," *Time*, August 31, 1981; Spitzer, *The Presidential Veto: Touchstone of the American Presidency*, 89–90.

60. "Senate Overrides Veto of Medical Research," *New York Times*, November 21, 1985; Senate Library, *Presidential Vetoes, 1789–1988*, 492–509.

61. HR4042 "To continue in effect the current certification requirements with respect to El Salvador"; Senate Library, *Presidential Vetoes, 1789–1988*, 496–97. On the Apartheid sanction veto, see *New York Times*, September 13, 1986; *New York Times*, October 3, 1986; Spitzer, *The Presidential Veto: Touchstone of the American Presidency*, 96–100.

62. Ford quoted in Spitzer, *The Presidential Veto: Touchstone of the American Presidency*, 155, n2.

63. Ford aide quoted in Light, *The President's Agenda*, 111–12.

64. Ford veto statements in John Woolley and Gerhard Peters, *The American Presidency Project*, University of California, Santa Barbara. For Vocational Rehabilitation Act, see www.presidency.ucsb.edu/ws/?pid=4528; for Vietnam Era Veterans' Education and Training Benefits Legislation, see www.presidency.ucsb.edu/ws/?pid=4591; for National School Lunch Act, see www.presidency.ucsb.edu/ws/?pid=5304.

65. Dan Lopez et al., eds., "Veto Battle 30 Years Ago Set Freedom of Information Norms," *National Security Archive Electronic Briefing Book No. 142* (Washington, DC: George Washington University, 2004), see www.gwu.edu/~nsarchiv/NSAEBB/NSAEBB142/index.htm; Alan Cranston, "Veto Reveals Watergate Blind Spot," *Congressional Record–Senate*, November 19, 1974, 36535.

66. Bill for war widow pensions—1924 S5, Senate Library, *Presidential Vetoes, 1789–1988*, 227.

67. Parmet, *George Bush: Life of a Lone Star Yankee*, 431–32; Greene, *The Presidency of George Bush*, 93–95. Benjamin Harrison, Woodrow Wilson, and George H. W. Bush all issued forty-four vetoes, but Bush is placed on this list because he had more regular vetoes than Harrison and more vetoes sustained than Wilson.

68. Schwartz, *A History of the Supreme Court*, 33, 37–38.

69. Jefferson quoted in Smith, *The Republic of Letters: The Correspondence Between Thomas Jefferson and James Madison*, 2:888; Marshall quoted in Scigliano, *The Supreme Court and the Presidency*, 25.

70. Smith, *John Marshall: Definer of a Nation*, 300–302.

71. Jefferson quoted in Scigliano, *The Supreme Court and the Presidency*, 29.

72. Ibid., 30.

73. Jefferson quoted in Melton, *Aaron Burr: Conspiracy to Treason*, 194.

74. Jefferson quoted in Scigliano, *The Supreme Court and the Presidency*, 30.

75. Edwin Miles, "After John Marshall's Decision: *Worcester v. Georgia* and the Nullification Crisis," *Journal of Southern History* (1973): 524; Marshall quoted in Beveridge, *The Life of John Marshall*, 4:550.

76. Cherokee quoted in Miles, "After John Marshall's Decision: *Worcester v. Georgia* and the Nullification Crisis," 529; Lumpkin quoted in Beveridge, *The Life of John Marshall*, 4:551.

77. Jackson quoted in Horace Greeley, *The American Conflict*, 106. Jackson biographer Robert Remini suggests Jackson did not say it, noting that the supposed witness to Jackson's alleged statement had reason to defame the president; see Remini, *Andrew Jackson and the Course of American Freedom*, 276–77.

78. Marshall quoted in Newmyer, *John Marshall and the Heroic Age of the Supreme Court*, 386.

79. McPherson, *Battle Cry of Freedom*, 285.

80. Abraham Lincoln, "To Winfield Scott [authorizing suspension of the Writ, April 27. 1861]," in Basler, *The Collected Works of Abraham Lincoln*, 4:347.

81. Lincoln quoted in Schwartz, *A History of the Supreme Court,* 129.

82. David L. Martin, "When Lincoln Suspended Habeas Corpus," *American Bar Association Journal* (January 1974): 99.

83. Sydney G. Fisher, "The Suspension of the Writ of Habeas Corpus During the War of the Rebellion," *Political Science Quarterly* (September 1888): 456–57; Monroe Johnson, "Taney and Lincoln," *American Bar Association Journal* (August 1930): 501.

84. Taney quoted in Johnson, "Taney and Lincoln," 501.

85. Bates quoted in Randall, *Constitutional Problems Under Lincoln,* 132; *New York Tribune,* May 30, 1861; *New York Times* quoted in Johnson, "Taney and Lincoln," 502.

86. Schwartz, *A History of the Supreme Court,* 232.

87. Roosevelt quoted in *New York Times,* March 10, 1937.

88. Ibid.

89. Abraham, *Justices and Presidents: A Political History of Appointments to the Supreme Court,* 208; Sumners quoted in Baker, *Back to Back: The Duel Between FDR and the Supreme Court,* 8; Hoover quoted in ibid., 28. See also Rosenman, *The Public Papers and Addresses of Franklin D. Roosevelt,* 6:113.

90. Truman quoted in Baker, *Back to Back: The Duel Between FDR and the Supreme Court,* 21.

91. McCullough, *Truman,* 898–901.

92. Schwartz, *A History of the Supreme Court,* 254.

93. Ibid.

94. Genovese, *The Supreme Court, the Constitution, and Presidential Power,* 264.

95. Nixon, *The Memoirs of Richard Nixon,* 508; Justice Department restraining order quoted in Sheehan, *The Pentagon Papers,* x; *New York Times* editorial quoted in ibid., 653.

96. Nixon, *The Memoirs of Richard Nixon,* 511; Abshire, *Triumphs and Tragedies of the Modern Presidency,* 287.

97. Rosenberg and Karabell, *Kennedy, Johnson, and the Quest for Justice: The Civil Rights Tapes,* xi; Reeves, *President Nixon: Alone in the White House,* 505.

98. Reagan quoted in Irons, *A People's History of the Supreme Court,* 462.

99. *School District of the City of Grand Rapids v. Ball,* 473 U.S. 373 (1985); *Thornburg v. American College of Obstetricians and Gynecologists,* 476 U.S. 747 (1986); Reagan, State of the Union Address, February 4, 1986.

100. Biskupic and Witt, *Guide to the U.S. Supreme Court,* 1:58–59.

101. *Clinton v. Jones,* 520 U.S. 681 (1997). See also Rozell and Wilcox, *The*

*Clinton Scandal and the Future of American Government*; and Mary E. Stuckey and Shannon Wabshall, "Sex, Lies, and Presidential Leadership," *Presidential Studies Quarterly* (September 2000): 514–33.

102.  Thomas, *Abraham Lincoln*, 302.

103.  Federalist Papers No. 74, *New York Packet*, March 25, 1788.

104.  Hogeland, *The Whiskey Rebellion*, 213; Slaughter, *The Whiskey Rebellion*, 217–19.

105.  Hogeland, *The Whiskey Rebellion*, 238; Slaughter, *The Whiskey Rebellion*, 218.

106.  For Hamilton's involvement and reaction to the Whiskey Rebellion, see Chernow, *Alexander Hamilton*, 475–78.

107.  Benedict, *The Impeachment and Trial of Andrew Johnson*, 43.

108.  Johnson quoted in Peter Browning, "Amnesty for All," *Nation*, January 15, 1977, 41.

109.  Russell, *The Shadow of Blooming Grove: Warren G. Harding in His Times*, 462–63, 487.

110.  Nixon, *The Memoirs of Richard Nixon*, 658.

111.  Ford, *A Time to Heal*, 174.

112.  Ibid., 175.

113.  O'Neill quoted in Cannon, *Time and Chance: Gerald Ford's Appointment with History*, 382.

114.  Ford quoted in ibid., 381.

115.  Ibid., 384–85.

116.  Browning, "Amnesty for All," 39–41.

117.  David Shichor and Donald R. Ranish, "President Carter's Vietnam Amnesty: An Analysis of a Public Policy Decision," *Presidential Studies Quarterly* (Summer 1980): 444.

118.  For a transcript of the first presidential debate between Ford and Carter, see Commission on the Presidential Debates, *The First Carter-Ford Presidential Debate*, at www.debates.org/pages/trans76a.html.

119.  Shichor and Ranish, "President Carter's Vietnam Amnesty: An Analysis of a Public Policy Decision," 443; Browning, "Amnesty for All: To Begin a New Life," 39–42. See also Baskir and Strauss, *Chance and Circumstance: The Draft, the War and the Vietnam Generation*.

120.  Ronald Reagan, "Statement on Granting Pardons to W. Mark Felt and Edward S. Miller" (Austin: University of Texas Archives, 1981), at www.reagan.utexas.edu/archives/speeches/1981/41581d.htm.

121.  "Notes on People; Congratulations and Champagne from Nixon," *New York Times*, April 30, 1981.

122. Bush pardon in Kornbluh and Byrne, *The Iran-Contra Scandal: The Declassified History*, 374.

123. Greene, *The Presidency of George Bush*, 26.

124. Ibid. Gallop Poll from Frank Newport and Joseph Carroll, "Americans Generally Negative on Recent Presidential Pardons," www.galluppoll.com /content/default.aspx?ci=26830&pg=1.

125. George W. Bush, 2003 State of the Union Address, www.whitehouse.gov /news/releases/2003/01/20030128–19.html.

126. "Russert Says He Didn't Give Libby Agent's ID," CNN.com, February 8, 2007, www.cnn.com/2007/POLITICS/02/07/cia.leak/index.html.

127. George W. Bush, "Grant of Executive Clemency: A Proclamation by the President of the United States of America," White House, July 2, 2007, www.whitehouse.gov/news/releases/2007/07/20070702–4.html. Bush's clemency record in Texas from Adam Liptak, "For Libby, Bush Seemed to Alter His Texas Policy," *International Herald Tribune*, July 7, 2007, www.iht.com /articles/2007/07/08/america/08commute.php.

128. Garfield quoted in Peskin, *Garfield*, 593.

129. For details on the evolution of White House security, see *Public Report of the White House Security Review* (Washington, DC: U.S. Treasury Department, 1995), and Seale, *The President's House*.

130. For more information on government assessments of presidential safety, see *Report of the Select Committee on Assassinations, U.S. House of Representatives, 95th Congress, Second Session: Findings and Recommendations* (Washington, DC: U.S. Government Printing Office, 1979).

131. Jackson quoted in Davis, *Old Hickory*, 345.

132. Ibid., 345–46; Remini, *Andrew Jackson and the Course of American Democracy, 1833–1845*, 228.

133. Brands, *Andrew Jackson: His Life and Times*, 503–5; Burstein, *The Passions of Andrew Jackson*, 202–3.

134. Davis, *Old Hickory*, 345–46; Booth letter quoted in Remini, *Andrew Jackson and the Course of American Democracy, 1833–1845*, 227.

135. Weichmann, *A True History of the Assassination of Abraham Lincoln and the Conspiracy of 1865*, 148; Steers, *Blood on the Moon: The Assassination of Abraham Lincoln*, 104–5.

136. Robert Todd Lincoln quoted in Baker, *Mary Todd Lincoln: A Biography*, 321. Excerpt on Robert Todd Lincoln from Goff, *Robert Todd Lincoln: A Man in His Own Right*, 234.

137. Peskin, *Garfield*, 583–86.

138. Ibid., 588–89.

139. Guiteau quoted in ibid., 592.

140. Garfield quoted in ibid., 597.

141. Ibid., 600–602.

142. For an examination of the anarchist movement from 1890 to 1914, see Tuchman, *The Proud Tower*, 63–113.

143. Czolgosz quoted in ibid., 106.

144. McKinley quoted in Gould, *The Presidency of William McKinley*, 251.

145. Theodore Roosevelt quoted in Dalton, *Theodore Roosevelt: A Strenuous Life*, 221; Czolgosz execution described in Grossman, *Encyclopedia of Capital Punishment*, 67–68.

146. Calder, *The People's War: Britain, 1939–1945*, 27; Jakob B. Madsen, "Agricultural Crises and the International Transmission of the Great Depression," *Journal of Economic History* (June 2001): 328.

147. Black, *Franklin Delano Roosevelt: Champion of Freedom*, 263–64.

148. Freidel, *Franklin D. Roosevelt: A Rendezvous with Destiny*, 87–88. Foley connection to McKinley shooting in Black, *Franklin Delano Roosevelt: Champion of Freedom*, 264ff.

149. Wagenheim, *Puerto Rico: A Profile*, 79–80.

150. Truman, *Where the Buck Stops: The Personal and Private Writings of Harry S. Truman*, 94ff.

151. McCullough, *Truman*, 810–11.

152. Truman quoted in Hamby, *Man of the People: A Life of Harry S. Truman*, 472.

153. Nellie Connally's account from U.S. Warren Commission, *Report of the Warren Commission on the Assassination of President Kennedy*, 62–63.

154. *New York Times* editor quoted in Harrison E. Salisbury, "An Introduction to the Warren Commission Report," in ibid., xvi.

155. U.S. Warren Commission, *Report of the Warren Commission on the Assassination of President Kennedy*, 177–83; Posner, *Case Closed: Lee Harvey Oswald and the Assassination of JFK*, 473–82.

156. Posner, *Case Closed: Lee Harvey Oswald and the Assassination of JFK*, ix. For a list of questioned witnesses, see U.S. Warren Commission, *Report of the Warren Commission on the Assassination of President Kennedy*, 455–71.

157. Fearey quoted in "Terrorism: 'Growing and Increasingly Dangerous,'" *Newsweek*, September 29, 1975, 77.

158. Fromme quoted in Clarke, *American Assassins*, 153.

159. Ford quoted in "Ford on Stump" *Newsweek*, September 22, 1975, 19.

160. Clarke, *American Assassins*, 161.

161. Ibid., 156–62.

162. National Archives and Records Administration, *Public Papers of the Presidents of the United States: Gerald R. Ford*, 1519.

163. Moore quoted in Clarke, *American Assassins*, 165.

164. Reagan quoted in Cannon, *Reagan*, 403.

165. Morris, *Dutch: A Memoir of Ronald Reagan*, 428–29.

CHAPTER 4: FOREIGN AFFAIRS

1. Truman quoted in Lee Hamilton, "Congress and Foreign Policy," *Presidential Studies Quarterly* (Winter 1982): 133.

2. Ford, "The Work of John Quincy Adams," 40–48.

3. Smith, *The Last Years on the Monroe Doctrine, 1945–1993*, 3, 24–25.

4. TR quoted in Scholes, *United States Diplomatic History*, 2:13.

5. TR quoted in Gould, *The Presidency of Theodore Roosevelt*, 175.

6. TR's Colombia comments in Scholes, *United States Diplomatic History*, 13; Dominican Republic comment from Hagedorn, *The Works of Theodore Roosevelt*, 20:496.

7. TR on the Dominican Republic quoted in Hagedorn, *The Works of Theodore Roosevelt*, 20:176; TR's comment on Cuba in Scholes, *United States Diplomatic History*, 2:14.

8. Scholes, *United States Diplomatic History*, 2:194–97.

9. Eisenhower quoted in Kegley and Wittkopf, *American Foreign Policy*, 43.

10. Pach and Richardson, *The Presidency of Dwight D. Eisenhower*, 90; Kelly, *The National Debt: From FDR (1941) to Clinton (1996)*, 82–83.

11. Humphrey quoted in Pach and Richardson, *The Presidency of Dwight D. Eisenhower*, 161.

12. For the final draft of the 1964 Democratic Convention Platform, see Schlesinger and Israel, *The History of American Presidential Elections*, 43.

13. Herring, *America's Longest War: The United States and Vietnam*, 71–72; Gordon Gray memorandum, September 14, 1959, Eisenhower Papers, "Cleanup" File Box 5.

14. Nixon, *The Memoirs of Richard Nixon*, 395.

15. Ibid., 395, 410.

16. Yergin, *The Prize*, 566, 644.

17. Correlation between Lord Lansdowne's statement and Carter's made in ibid., 702.

18. Carter quoted in Papp, Johnson, and Endicott, *American Foreign Policy*, 175.

19. Percentages of defense spending from U.S. Office of Management and Budget, *Budget of the United States Government: Historical Tables, Fiscal Year 2007*, 47, 49–50.

20. Reagan quoted in Chester Pach, "The Reagan Doctrine: Principle, Pragmatism, and Policy," *Presidential Studies Quarterly* (March 2006): 79; Reagan's State of the Union quoted in Kegley and Wittkopf, *American Foreign Policy*, 117.

21. Pach, "The Reagan Doctrine: Principle, Pragmatism, and Policy," 79.

22. Lincoln quoted in Schlesinger, *The Imperial Presidency*, 42.

23. Nancy Kassop, "The War Power and Its Limits," *Presidential Studies Quarterly* (September 2003): 511–13.

24. Singer, *The President of Good and Evil: The Ethics of George W. Bush*, 180–81; Glenn Kessler, "U.S. Decision on Iraq Has Puzzling Past," *Washington Post*, January 12, 2003.

25. Coyle, *Ordeal of the Presidency*, 14.

26. For the text on Washington's proclamation, see Rhodehamel, *George Washington: Writings*, 840.

27. Coyle, *Ordeal of the Presidency*, 13.

28. Knox quoted in ibid., 20; Jefferson quoted in Smith, *The Republic of Letters: The Correspondence Between Thomas Jefferson and James Madison*, 2:944; anecdote of Adams and the War Department from Coyle, *Ordeal of the Presidency*, 17.

29. Kastor, *The Louisiana Purchase: Emergence of an American Nation*, 58–60.

30. Kukla, *A Wilderness So Immense: The Louisiana Purchase and the Destiny of America*, 280, 305.

31. Kastor, *The Louisiana Purchase: Emergence of an American Nation*, 183–85.

32. Jefferson quoted in Risjord, *Thomas Jefferson*, 147. See also Rodrigues, *The Louisiana Purchase: A Historical and Geographic Encyclopedia*.

33. Hagedorn, *The Works of Theodore Roosevelt*, 20:501.

34. TR quoted in Hagedorn, *The Works of Theodore Roosevelt*, 20:503; Dalton, *Theodore Roosevelt: A Strenuous Life*, 255.

35. *Evening Post* quoted in Gould, *The Presidency of Theodore Roosevelt*, 98.

36. Oliver and White, *Selected Speeches from American History*, 250–51; Dear, *The Oxford Companion to World War II*, 680–82.

37. For more detail on the implementation of Lend-Lease, see Dawson, *The Decision to Aid Russia, 1941*; Kimball, *The Most Unsordid Act: Lend-Lease, 1939–1941*.

38. Truman, *Where the Buck Stops: The Personal and Private Writings of Harry S. Truman*, 233.

39. George Bush, "Remarks to the Citizens in Mainz," U.S. Embassy, Bonn, Germany, 1989, http://usa.usembassy.de/etexts/ga6–890531.htm.

40. Nash, *The Other Missiles of October: Eisenhower, Kennedy, and the Jupiters, 1957–1963*, 1–3.

41. Frankel, *High Noon in the Cold War: Kennedy, Khrushchev, and the Cuban Missile Crisis*, 14–15; Eubank, *The Missile Crisis in Cuba*, 21–24.

42. Sorensen, *Kennedy*, 676–85; see also Kennedy, *Thirteen Days*.

43. Kennedy, *Thirteen Days*, 97; Frankel, *High Noon in the Cold War: Kennedy, Khrushchev, and the Cuban Missile Crisis*, 163.

44. Nixon quoted in Reeves, *President Nixon: Alone in the White House*, plate 9; Moorer quoted in Strober and Strober, *The Nixon Presidency: An Oral History of the Era*, 428.

45. Macmillan, *Nixon and Mao*, xix.

46. Mann, *About Face: A History of America's Curious Relationship with China*, 28.

47. Nixon quoted in Macmillan, *Nixon and Mao*, 3.

48. Mann, *About Face: A History of America's Curious Relationship with China*, 45.

49. Quandt, *Camp David: Peace Making and Politics*, 235.

50. Ibid., 222.

51. Kaufman, *The Presidency of James Earl Carter, Jr.*, 119.

52. Ibid., 117; Quandt, *Camp David: Peace Making and Politics*, 222.

53. Haig quoted in Strober and Strober, *Reagan: The Man and His Presidency*, 571.

54. Gennadi Gerasimov quoted in ibid., 347.

55. Brownlee and Graham, *The Reagan Presidency*, 144.

56. Ridgeway quoted in Strober and Strober, *Reagan: The Man and His Presidency*, 357.

57. Barilleaux and Rozell, *Power and Prudence: The Presidency of George H. W. Bush*, 125; Bush and Scowcroft, *A World Transformed*, 234–35; Parmet, *George Bush: Life of a Lone Star Yankee*, 385.

58. George H. W. Bush, "Remarks to the Citizens in Mainz," U.S. Embassy, Bonn, Germany, 1989, http://usa.usembassy.de/etexts/ga6-890531.htm.

59. Kohl quoted in Barilleaux and Rozell, *Power and Prudence: The Presidency of George H. W. Bush*, 123.

60. Madison quoted in David Gray Adler, "Presidential Greatness as an Attribute of Warmaking," *Presidential Studies Quarterly* (September 2003): 468.

61. Roosevelt quoted in Singer, *Campaign Speeches of American Presidential Candidates, 1928–1972*, 129.

62. Kaufman, *Arms Control During the Pre-Nuclear Era*, 190; Kennedy, *The Rise and Fall of the Great Powers*, 352.

63. Linderman, *The World Within War: America's Combat Experience in World War II*, 39; Krivosheev, *Soviet Casualties and Combat Losses in the Twentieth Century*, 88; Sorge, *The Other Price of Hitler's War: German Military and Civilian Losses Resulting from World War II*, 65.

64. Smith, *The War's Long Shadow*, 82.

65. Vandiver, *How America Goes to War*, 22. For details on U.S. opposition to the war with Mexico, see Schroeder, *Mr. Polk's War: American Opposition and Dissent, 1846–1848*.

66. Hogan, *Hiroshima in History and Memory*, 60. War Minister Anami quoted in Maddox, *Weapons for Victory: The Hiroshima Decision Fifty Years Later*, 148.

67. McCullough, *Truman*, 376.

68. For a detailed chronology of Japan's switch from aggressive defense to capitulation, see Feis, *Japan Subdued: The Atomic Bomb and the End of the War in the Pacific*. For a balanced historiography of the use of the atomic devices, both for and against, see Walker, *Prompt and Utter Destruction: Truman and the Use of Atomic Bombs Against Japan*.

69. National Archives and Records Administration, *Public Papers of the Presidents of the United States: Harry S. Truman*, 212.

70. Newman, *Truman and the Hiroshima Cult*, 2–7; Toland, *The Rising Sun*, 830; Astor, *Operation Iceberg*, 508; Hogan, *Hiroshima in History and Memory*, 60; War Minister Anami quoted in Maddox, *Weapons for Victory: The Hiroshima Decision Fifty Years Later*, 148.

71. Bush and Scowcroft, *A World Transformed*, 435.

72. U.S. Department of Defense, *Conduct of the Persian Gulf War: The Final Report to the U.S. Congress*, app. P.

73. Bush and Scowcroft, *A World Transformed*, 464.

74. John L. Offner, "McKinley and the Spanish-American War," *Presidential Studies Quarterly* (March 2004): 51.

75. Ibid., 57.

76. Ibid.

77. Williams, *The History of American Wars: From 1745 to 1918*, 382.

78. Wilson quoted in Cooper, *The Warrior and the Priest: Woodrow Wilson and Theodore Roosevelt*, 322.

79. Kendrick A. Clements, "Woodrow Wilson and World War I," *Presidential Studies Quarterly* (March 2004): 68.

80. Davies, *Heart of Europe*, 112–13; Howard, "The Legacy of the First World War," 38; Kitchen, *Europe Between the Wars: A Political History*, 22–24;

see also Kendrick A. Clements, "Woodrow Wilson and World War I," *Presidential Studies Quarterly* (March 2004).

81. Pach and Richardson, *The Presidency of Dwight D. Eisenhower*, 45–46.
82. Perret, *Eisenhower*, 455.
83. U.S. Office of Management and Budget, *Budget of the United States Government: Historical Tables, Fiscal Year 2007*, 314–15.
84. Palmer, *Stoddert's War: Naval Operations During the Quasi-War with France, 1798–1801*, 5.
85. Ibid., 235.
86. See also DeConde, *The Quasi War*.
87. TR quoted in David Gray Adler, "Presidential Greatness as an Attribute of Warmaking," *Presidential Studies Quarterly* (September 2003): 471.
88. TR quoted in Miller, *Theodore Roosevelt: A Life*, 479.
89. Ibid., 480–81.
90. Van Sant, Mauch, and Sugita, *Historical Dictionary of United States-Japan Relations*, 13; TR quoted in Miller, *Theodore Roosevelt: A Life*, 482.
91. Reagan quoted in Cannon, *President Reagan: The Role of a Lifetime*, 339.
92. Ibid., 448–49.
93. Schaller, *Reckoning with Reagan*, 138–39.
94. Reagan quoted in Cannon, *President Reagan: The Role of a Lifetime*, 654.
95. LBJ quoted in Anthony, *First Ladies: The Saga of the Presidents' Wives and Their Power*, 2:133.
96. Fredrik Logevall, "Lyndon Johnson and Vietnam," *Presidential Studies Quarterly* (March 2004): 100.
97. LBJ quoted in Goodwin, *Lyndon Johnson and the American Dream*, 252–53.
98. Logevall, "Lyndon Johnson and Vietnam," 101.
99. Davidson, "How We Lost the War," 335.
100. Nixon quoted in Reeves, *President Nixon: Alone in the White House*, 142; Kissinger quoted in Herring, *America's Longest War*, 221.
101. Reeves, *President Nixon: Alone in the White House*, 143.
102. Summers, *Vietnam War Almanac*, 227; Tucker, *Encyclopedia of the Vietnam War*, 7.
103. Fisher, *Presidential War Power*, 85; Truman quoted in Ferrell, *Harry S. Truman: A Life*, 329.
104. Tucker, *Encyclopedia of American Military History*, 467–68; Morris, *Readings in American Military History*, 276–79.
105. Death tolls from Brogan, *World Conflicts*, 217.
106. George W. Bush, "Address to a Joint Session of Congress and the American

People," September 20, 2001, www.yale.edu/lawweb/avalon/sept_11 /president_025.htm.

107. State Department Washington File quoted in Kassop, "The War Power and Its Limits," 524; Andrew Rudalevige, "The Structure of Leadership," *Presidential Studies Quarterly* (June 2005): 334.

108. Kassop, "The War Power and Its Limits," 509; James M. Lindsay, "Deference and Defiance: The Shifting Rhythms of Executive-Legislative Relations in Foreign Policy," *Presidential Studies Quarterly* (September 2003): 537.

109. Associated Press, "U.S. Deaths in Afghanistan, Region," June 11, 2007, www.boston.com/news/nation/articles/2007/06/11/us_deaths_in_afghanistan _region. Official and academic estimates on costs of Second Gulf–Iraq War from Jamie Wilson, "Iraq War Could Cost over $2 trillion, Says Nobel Prize-Winning Economist," *Guardian*, January 7, 2006; Scott Wallsten, "The Economic Cost of the Iraq War," *Economists' Voice* 3, no. 2 (2006): art. 1, http://www.bepress.com/ev/v013/iss2/art1.

110. Hesseltine, *Civil War Prisons: A Study in War Psychology*, 137; Flagel, *The History Buff's Guide to the Civil War*, 263–64; see also Speer, *Portals to Hell: Military Prisons of the Civil War*.

111. Adams, *Doctors in Blue*, 135–36; Johnson, *Muskets and Medicine*, 131.

112. Stagg, *Mr. Madison's War: Politics, Diplomacy, and Warfare in the Early American Republic, 1783–1830*, 227.

113. Donald Hickey, *The War of 1812: A Forgotten Conflict*, 117; Stagg, *Mr. Madison's War*, 265.

114. For losses in the Napoleonic Wars, see Dumas, *Losses of Life Caused by War*.

115. Handy, *Undermined Establishment: Church-State Relations in America, 1880–1920*, 7.

116. Kennedy and Bailey, *The American Pageant*, 321; Tucker, *Encyclopedia of American Military History*, 675.

117. See also Silbey, *A War of Frontier and Empire: The Philippine-American War, 1899–1902*.

118. Tucker, *Encyclopedia of American Military History*, 708.

119. Ibid., 709.

120. Kennedy quoted in Sorensen, *Kennedy*, 309.

121. Kelly, *The National Debt: From FDR (1941) to Clinton (1996)*, 82; Ho quoted in Moyar, *Triumph Forsaken: America's Descent into Vietnam*, 286; Fishel, *Vietnam: Anatomy of a Conflict*, 144.

122. Yergin, *The Prize*, 705.

CHAPTER 5: THE INNER CIRCLE

1. One of the more reputable surveys of the first ladies is that of the Siena Institute at Siena College, New York. Since 1982, it has conducted scholarly assessments of the presidents' partners based on the following measures: intelligence, background for the position, service to country, service to presidency, service to her own values, integrity, accomplishments, leadership, courage, and public image.
2. Ladybird Johnson quoted in Lewis Gould, "Modern First Ladies in Historical Perspective," *Presidential Studies Quarterly* (Summer 1985): 533.
3. DeGregorio, *The Complete Book of U.S. Presidents*, 484.
4. Goodwin, *No Ordinary Time, Franklin and Eleanor Roosevelt: The Home Front on World War II*, 10.
5. Gould, "Modern First Ladies in Historical Perspective," 534.
6. Anthony, *First Ladies: The Saga of the Presidents' Wives and Their Power*, 2:124.
7. Ibid., 2:121.
8. Sarah Polk quoted in Caroli, *First Ladies*, 62.
9. Ibid., 61.
10. Although their correspondence was relatively limited, considering they spent a large amount of time together, an insightful sampling of John and Sarah Polk's letters can be found in Sarah Agnes Wallace, ed., "Letters of Mrs. James K. Polk to Her Husband," *Tennessee Historical Quarterly* 11 (1952): 180–91.
11. Roberts, *Rating the First Ladies*, 28–29; Irving quoted in Caroli, *First Ladies*, 14.
12. Moore, *The Madisons*, 291.
13. Caroli, *First Ladies*, 16.
14. Jackie Kennedy quoted in Beasley, *First Ladies and the Press*, 73.
15. Jackie Kennedy quoted in Whitcomb and Whitcomb, *Real Life at the White House*, 351.
16. Beasley, *First Ladies and the Press*, 76–78.
17. Gould, "Modern First Ladies in Historical Perspective," 534.
18. Caroli, *First Ladies*, 437.
19. Rosalynn Carter quoted in Gould, "Modern First Ladies in Historical Perspective," 536.
20. Ibid., 536.
21. Roberts, *Rating the First Ladies*, 153–54.
22. DeGregorio, *The Complete Book of U.S. Presidents*, 413.
23. Wilson quoted in Hamilton, *The Presidents*, 232.

24. Judith Weaver, "Edith Bolling Wilson as First Lady: A Study in the Power of Personality," *Presidential Studies Quarterly* (Winter 1985): 55.
25. Caroli, *First Ladies*, 149; Edith Wilson quoted in Weaver, "Edith Bolling Wilson as First Lady: A Study in the Power of Personality," 51, 55; *New York Tribune*, October 14, 1919.
26. Abigail Adams quoted in Beasley, *First Ladies and the Press*, 30.
27. Akers, *Abigail Adams: An American Woman*, 143, 152.
28. Roberts, *Rating the First Ladies*, 17.
29. Ibid., 111.
30. Marton, *Hidden Power: Presidential Marriages that Shaped Our Recent History*, 308–10.
31. Caroli, *First Ladies*, 21; Roberts, *Rating the First Ladies*, 41.
32. Anthony, *America's First Families*, 150–51.
33. Moore, *The Madisons*, 298–99, 335; Wead, *All the Presidents' Children*, 333–34.
34. Wead, *All the Presidents' Children*, 333–34; Moore, *The Madisons*, 335.
35. Rutland, *James Madison*, 236.
36. Wead, *All the Presidents' Children*, 16.
37. Ibid., 61.
38. Roberts, *Rating the First Ladies*, 93–95; Angelo, *First Families*, 11.
39. Mary Todd quoted in Roberts, *Rating the First Ladies*, 107.
40. Thomas, *Abraham Lincoln*, 298–99.
41. Ibid., 299.
42. TR quoted in Wead, *All the President's Children*, 45.
43. Morris, *Theodore Rex*, 401.
44. Morris, *The Rise of Theodore Roosevelt*, 240–44.
45. Alice Roosevelt quoted in Morris, *Theodore Rex*, 251.
46. Maier, *The Kennedys: America's Emerald Kings*, 130–31, 259–60.
47. Joe Kennedy Sr. quoted in ibid., 264.
48. Lasky, *JFK: The Man and the Myth*, 260.
49. Harry Truman and Eleanor Roosevelt quoted in ibid., 394–95.
50. JFK quoted in Maier, *The Kennedys: America's Emerald Kings*, 445.
51. Brogan and Mosley, *American Presidential Families*, 720.
52. Kohn, *The New Encyclopedia of American Scandal*, 70–72.
53. Wead, *All the Presidents' Children*, 285.
54. Hamilton, *Bill Clinton: An American Journey*, 106–9.
55. Reagan quoted in Whitcomb and Whitcomb, *Real Life at the White House*, xvii.
56. Ibid., 3.

57. Abigail Adams quoted in Freidel and Pencak, *The White House: The First Two Hundred Years*, 17.

58. Moore, *The Madisons*, 320–21.

59. Whitcomb and Whitcomb, *Real Life at the White House*, 35.

60. Ibid., 143, 152.

61. Ibid., 233.

62. Roberts, *Rating the First Ladies*, 165.

63. Whitcomb and Whitcomb, *Real Life at the White House*, 233.

64. Coolidge quoted in ibid., 287.

65. Burns, *Roosevelt: The Soldier of Freedom*, 173, 198.

66. D.C. building commissioner quoted in Kessler, *Inside the White House*, 4.

67. Jackie Kennedy quoted in Roberts, *Rating the First Ladies*, 278.

68. Jackie Kennedy quoted in Schlesinger, *A Thousand Days*, 670.

69. See Bohn, *Nerve Center: Inside the White House Situation Room*.

70. Cleveland quoted in Richard Ellis, "The Joy of Power: Changing Conceptions of the Presidential Office," *Presidential Studies Quarterly* (June 2003): 281; Cheney quoted in Kumar and Sullivan, *The White House World: Transitions, Organization, and Office Operations*, 111; Steinbeck quoted in Robert Gilbert, "Personality, Stress and Achievement: Keys to Presidential Longevity," *Presidential Studies Quarterly* (Winter 1985): 33.

71. Socolofsky and Spetter, *The Presidency of Benjamin Harrison*, 85.

72. Fitzwater quoted in Charles Walcott et al., "The Chief of Staff," *Presidential Studies Quarterly* (September 2001): 469.

73. Ford quoted in Kumar and Sullivan, *The White House World: Transitions, Organization, and Office Operations*, 111.

74. Haig quoted in Strober and Strober, *The Nixon Presidency: An Oral History of the Era*, 464. For bibliography and further detail on the office, see Charles Walcott et al., "The Chief of Staff," 464–89.

75. Marton, *Hidden Power: Presidential Marriages that Shaped Our Recent History*, 320.

76. Kumar and Sullivan, *The White House World: Transitions, Organization, and Office Operations*, 120.

77. Andrew Preston, "The Little State Department," *Presidential Studies Quarterly* (December 2001): 649.

78. Kelly, *The National Debt: From FDR (1941) to Clinton (1996)*, 15.

79. Edwards and Wayne, *Presidential Leadership: Politics and Policy Making*, 421.

80. Speakes quoted in Nelson, *Who Speaks for the President? The White House Press Secretary from Cleveland to Clinton*, vii.

81. Malthese, *Spin Control: The White House Office of Communications and the Management of Presidential News*, 4.
82. Nelson, *Who Speaks for the President? The White House Press Secretary from Cleveland to Clinton*, 1.
83. Ibid., 2.
84. Ibid., 248–49.
85. Stephanopoulos quoted in Martha Joynt Kumar, "The Office of Communications," *Presidential Studies Quarterly* (December 2001): 610.
86. Malthese, *Spin Control: The White House Office of Communications and the Management of Presidential News*, 7–9.
87. Kolb, *White House Daze: The Unmaking of Domestic Policy in the Bush Years*, 2–4; Malthese, *Spin Control: The White House Office of Communications and the Management of Presidential News*, 160.
88. Cheney quoted in Malthese, *Spin Control: The White House Office of Communications and the Management of Presidential News*, 2.
89. Edwards and Wayne, *Presidential Leadership: Politics and Policy Making*, 329.
90. Nelson, *Guide to the Presidency*, 1761.
91. Clinton quoted in Patterson, *The White House Staff: Inside the West Wing and Beyond*, 95.
92. Peri Arnold et al., "The White House Office of Management and Administration," *Presidential Studies Quarterly* (June 2001): 190.
93. Ibid., 195–203.
94. McCullough, *John Adams*, 503–5.
95. Roberts, *Rating the First Ladies*, 49.
96. Jackson quoted in James, *The Life of Andrew Jackson*, 572.
97. Senator quoted in Boller, *Presidential Campaigns*, 127.
98. Smith, *Grant*, 482–83.
99. Perret, *Ulysses S. Grant: Soldier and President*, 390–91.
100. Smith, *Grant*, 489; Perret, *Ulysses S. Grant: Soldier and President*, 392–93.
101. Smith, *Grant*, 582–83.
102. Simpson, *Ulysses S. Grant*, 432–33; Grant quoted in Smith, *Grant*, 590.
103. Perret, *Ulysses S. Grant: Soldier and President*, 441–42.
104. Anthony, *Florence Harding*, 127–28; Russell, *The Shadow of Blooming Grove: Warren G. Harding and His Times*, 447.
105. Anthony, *Florence Harding*, 305.
106. Dunn, *The Scarlet Thread of Scandal: Morality and the American Presidency*, 72.

107. Russell, *The Shadow of Blooming Grove: Warren G. Harding and His Times*, 522–25; Anthony, *Florence Harding*, xix.

108. Kohn, *The New Encyclopedia of American Scandal*, 139–40.

109. Ambrose, *Nixon*, 3:108, 140; Strober and Strober, *The Nixon Presidency: An Oral History of the Era*, 89–92.

110. Ambrose, *Nixon*, 207.

111. Ibid., 231–32.

112. Ford quoted in Strober and Strober, *The Nixon Presidency: An Oral History of the Era*, 460–61.

113. Busby, *Reagan and the Iran-Contra Affair*, 57.

114. Reagan's November 13, 1986, address quoted in ibid., 60.

115. Busby, *Reagan and the Iran-Contra Affair*, 60.

116. Approval ratings in ibid., 144.

117. Marcia L. Whicker, "Sexual Probity and Presidential Character," *Presidential Studies Quarterly* (Fall 1998): 882. See also Mary E. Stuckey and Shannon Wabshall, "Sex, Lies, and Presidential Leadership," *Presidential Studies Quarterly* (September 2000): 514–33.

118. Abshire, *Triumphs and Tragedies of the Modern Presidency*, 294–97.

119. Ibid., 298–99. See also Rozell and Wilcox, *The Clinton Scandal and the Future of American Government*.

# Bibliography

## NEWSPAPERS

Augusta Daily Constitutionalist
Charleston Mercury
Cincinnati Gazette
Chicago Times
Chicago Tribune
Des Moines Register
Harper's Weekly Illustrated
London Times
New York Evening Post
New York Herald
New York Times
New York Tribune

Omaha World Herald
Philadelphia Inquirer
Philadelphia Journal
Philadelphia Weekly Times
Pravda
Richmond Daily Dispatch
Richmond Daily Whig
Richmond Enquirer
Richmond Examiner
Richmond Whig
Washington Chronicle
Washington Post

## PERIODICALS

American Bar Association Journal
American Historical Review
American Journal of Economics
   and Sociology
Atlantic Monthly
Civil War History
Congressional Quarterly Weekly Report
Current History
Diplomatic History
The Economist
English Historical Review
German History

Journal of Asian History
Journal of Asian Studies
Journal of American History
Journal of Contemporary History
Journal of Economic History
Journal of Military History
Journal of Modern History
Journal of Politics
Journal of Southern History
Nation (US)
Political Science Quarterly
Presidential Studies Quarterly

*The Guardian*                              *Tennessee Historical Quarterly*
*History*                                   *Time (US)*
*History and Memory*                        *War and Society*
*History Today*


## BOOKS


Abraham, Henry J. *Justices and Presidents: A Political History of Appointments to the Supreme Court*. New York: Oxford University Press, 1985.

Abramson, Paul, John H. Aldrich, and David W. Rohde. *Change and Continuity in the 1984 Elections*. Washington, DC: Congressional Quarterly, 1986.

Abshire, David, ed. *Triumphs and Tragedies of the Modern Presidency*. Westport, CT: Praeger, 2001.

Adams, George W. *Doctors in Blue*. Baton Rouge: Louisiana State University Press, 1952.

Akers, Charles W. *Abigail Adams: An American Woman*. Boston: Little, Brown, and Co., 1980.

Alley, Robert S. *So Help Me God: Religion and the Presidency*. Richmond, VA: John Knox, 1972.

Ambrose, Stephen E. *Nixon*. 3 vols. New York: Simon and Schuster, 1987–91.

Angelo, Bonnie. *First Families*. New York: Morrow, 2005.

Anthony, Carl S. *America's First Families*. New York: Touchstone, 2000.

———. *First Ladies: The Saga of the Presidents' Wives and Their Power*. 2 vols. New York: William Morrow, 1990–91.

———. *Florence Harding*. New York: William Morrow, 1998.

Astor, Gerald. *Operation Iceberg*. New York: Dell, 1995.

Austin, Erik W. *Political Facts of the United States Since 1789*. New York: Columbia University Press, 1986.

Baker, Jean H. *Mary Todd Lincoln: A Biography*. New York: Norton, 1987.

Baker, Leonard. *Back to Back: The Duel Between FDR and the Supreme Court*. New York: Macmillan, 1967.

Barilleaux, Ryan, and Mark Rozell. *Power and Prudence: The Presidency of George H. W. Bush*. College Station: Texas A&M University Press, 2004.

Baskir, Leonard, and William Strauss. *Chance and Circumstance: The Draft, the War and the Vietnam Generation*. New York: Random House, 1978.

Basler, Roy P., ed. *The Collected Works of Abraham Lincoln*. 9 vols. New Brunswick, NJ: Rutgers University Press, 1953.

Beasley, Maurine. *First Ladies and the Press*. Evanston, IL: Northwestern University Press, 2005.

Benedict, Michael Les. *The Impeachment and Trial of Andrew Johnson*. New York: Norton, 1973.

Berkin, Carol. *A Brilliant Solution: Inventing the American Constitution*. New York: Harcourt, 2002.

Beveridge, Albert J. *The Life of John Marshall*. 4 vols. Boston: Houghton Mifflin, 1919.

Binkley, Wilfred. *President and Congress*. New York: Knopf, 1947.

Biskupic, Joan, and Elder Witt. *Guide to the U.S. Supreme Court*. 7 vols. Washington, DC: Congressional Quarterly, 1997.

Black, Conrad. *Franklin Delano Roosevelt: Champion of Freedom*. New York: Perseus, 2003.

Bohn, Michael. *Nerve Center: Inside the White House Situation Room*. Washington, DC: Potomac Books, 2004.

Boller, Paul, Jr. *Presidential Campaigns*. New York: Oxford University Press, 2004.

Bonnell, John S. *Presidential Profiles: Religion in the Life of American Presidents*. Philadelphia: Westminster, 1971.

Boritt, Gabor S. *Lincoln and the Economics of the American Dream*. Memphis, TN: Memphis State University Press, 1978.

Bowen, Catherine D. *Miracle at Philadelphia*. Boston: Little, Brown and Co., 1966.

Brands, H. W. *Andrew Jackson: His Life and Times*. New York: Doubleday, 2005.

Brinkley, Alan, and Davis Dyer, eds. *The Reader's Companion to the American Presidency*. Boston: Houghton Mifflin, 2000.

Brogan, Hugh, and Charles Mosley. *American Presidential Families*. New York: Macmillan, 1993.

Brogan, Patrick. *World Conflicts*. Lanham, MD: Scarecrow Press, 1998.

Brownlee, W. Elliot, and Hugh Davis Graham, eds. *The Reagan Presidency*. Lawrence: University Press of Kansas, 2003.

Bruun, Erik, and Jay Crosby, eds. *Our Nation's Archive: The History of the United States in Documents*. New York: Black Dog and Leventhal, 1999.

Burns, James M. *Roosevelt: The Soldier of Freedom*. New York: Harcourt Brace Jovanovich, 1970.

Burstein, Andrew. *The Passions of Andrew Jackson*. New York: Knopf, 2003.

Busby, Robert. *Reagan and the Iran-Contra Affair*. New York: St. Martin's 1999.

Bush, George H. W., and Brent Scowcroft. *A World Transformed*. New York: Knopf, 1998.

Bush, George H. W., and Victor Gold. *Looking Forward: An Autobiography*. New York: Doubleday, 1987.

Butterfield, L. H., ed. *Adams Family Correspondence*. The Adams Papers, ser. 2. 8 vols. Cambridge, MA: Belknap Press of Harvard University Press, 1963–2007.

Calder, Angus. *The People's War: Britain, 1939–1945*. New York: Pantheon, 1969.

Calhoun, Charles W. *Benjamin Harrison*. New York: Henry Holt, 2005.

Cannon, James. *Time and Chance: Gerald Ford's Appointment with History*. New York: HarperCollins, 1994.

Cannon, Lou. *Reagan*. New York: Putnam, 1982.

Caroli, Betty Boyd. *First Ladies*. New York: Oxford University Press, 2003.

Chernow, Ron. *Alexander Hamilton*. New York: Penguin Press, 2004.

Clarke, James W. *American Assassins*. Princeton, NJ: Princeton University Press, 1982.

Cole, David D. *Ordeal of the Presidency*. Westport, CT: Greenwood Press, 1973.

Congressional Quarterly. *Presidential Elections, 1789–2000*. Washington, DC: Congressional Quarterly, 2002.

Cooper, John M., Jr. *The Warrior and the Priest: Woodrow Wilson and Theodore Roosevelt*. Cambridge, MA: Belknap Press of Harvard University Press, 1983.

Coyle, David C. *Ordeal of the Presidency*. Westport, CT: Greenwood Press, 1973.

Cunningham, Noble E., Jr. *The Presidency of James Monroe*. Lawrence: University Press of Kansas, 1996.

Dallek, Robert. *Flawed Giant: Lyndon Johnson and His Times, 1961–1973*. New York: Oxford University Press, 1998.

Dalton, Kathleen. *Theodore Roosevelt: A Strenuous Life*. New York: Knopf, 2002.

Davidson, Phillip B. "How We Lost the War." In *Readings in American Military History*. Edited by James M. Morris. Upper Saddle River, NJ: Prentice Hall, 2004.

Davies, Norman. *Heart of Europe*. Oxford, UK: Oxford University Press, 1986.

Davis, Burke. *Old Hickory*. New York: Dial Press, 1977.

Davis, Kenneth S. *FDR: The New Deal Years, 1933–1937*. New York: Random House, 1986.

Dawson, Raymond H. *The Decision to Aid Russia, 1941*. Chapel Hill: University of North Carolina Press, 1959.

Dear, I. C. B., ed. *The Oxford Companion to World War II*. Oxford, UK: Oxford University Press, 1995.

DeConde, Alexander. *The Quasi War*. New York: Scribner, 1966.

DeGregorio, William A. *The Complete Book of U.S. Presidents*. New York: Wings Books, 1993.

Denton, Robert E., ed. *The 2004 Presidential Campaign: A Communication Perspective*. New York: Rowman and Littlefield, 2005.

DiNunzio, Mario, ed. *Woodrow Wilson: Essential Writings and Speeches of the Scholar-President*. New York: New York University Press, 2006.

Donald, David H. *Lincoln*. New York: Simon & Schuster, 1995.

Dover, E. D. *The Disputed Presidential Election of 2000*. Westport, CT: Greenwood, 2003.

Dubin, Michael J. *United States Presidential Elections: The Official Results by County and State*. Jefferson, NC: McFarland, 2002.

Dulce, Berto, and Edward Richter. *Religion and the Presidency*. New York: Macmillan, 1962.

Dumas, Samuel. *Losses of Life Caused by War*. London: Milford, 1923.

Dunn, Charles. *The Scarlet Thread of Scandal: Morality and the American Presidency*. Lanham: MD: Rowman and Littlefield, 2000.

Edel, Wilbur. *Defenders of the Faith: Religion and Politics from the Pilgrim Fathers to Ronald Reagan*. New York: Praeger, 1987.

Edwards, George C., III, and Stephen J. Wayne. *Presidential Leadership: Politics and Policy Making*. New York: St. Martin's, 1997.

Ellis, Joseph J. *His Excellency: George Washington*. New York: Knopf, 2004.

Eubank, Keith. *The Missile Crisis in Cuba*. Malabar, FL: Krieger, 2000.

Feis, Herbert. *Japan Subdued: The Atomic Bomb and the End of the War in the Pacific*. Princeton, NJ: Princeton University Press, 1961.

Ferguson, Niall. *The Pity of War: Explaining World War I*. New York: Basic Books, 1999.

Ferling, John E. *Adams vs. Jefferson: The Tumultuous Election of 1800*. New York: Oxford University Press, 2004.

———. *The First of Men: A Life of George Washington*. Knoxville: University of Tennessee Press, 1988.

———. *John Adams: A Life*. Knoxville: University of Tennessee Press, 1992.

Ferrell, Robert H. *Harry S. Truman: A Life*. Columbia: University of Missouri Press, 1994.

Fischer, Roger A. *Tippecanoe and Trinkets Too: The Material Culture of American Presidential Campaigns*. Urbana: University of Illinois Press, 1988.

Fishel, Wesley, ed. *Vietnam: Anatomy of a Conflict*. Itasca, IL: Peacock, 1968.

Fisher, Louis. *Presidential War Power*. Lawrence: University Press of Kansas, 1995.

Fitzpatrick, John C., ed. *The Writings of George Washington*. 39 vols. Washington, DC: U.S. Government Printing Office, 1931–44.

Flagel, Thomas R. *The History Buff's Guide to the Civil War*. Nashville: Cumberland House, 2003.

Ford, Gerald. *A Time to Heal*. New York: Berkeley Books, 1980.

Ford, Worthington C. "The Work of John Quincy Adams." In *The Monroe Doctrine*, edited by Armin Rappaport. New York: Holt, Rinehart, and Winston, 1964.

Frankel, Max. *High Noon in the Cold War: Kennedy, Khrushchev, and the Cuban Missile Crisis*. New York: Ballantine Books, 2004.

Freidel, Frank. *Franklin D. Roosevelt: A Rendezvous with Destiny*. Boston: Little, Brown, and Co., 1990.

———, and William Pencak, eds. *The White House: The First Two Hundred Years*. Boston: Northeastern University Press, 1994.

Frum, David. *The Right Man: An Inside Account of the Bush White House*. New York: Random House, 2003.

Gaustad, Edwin S., ed. *A Documentary History of Religion in America to the Civil War*. Grand Rapids, MI: Eerdmans, 1982.

*General Records of the United States Government, 1778–1992*. Washington, DC: National Archives and Records Administration, 1993.

Genovese, Michael. *The Supreme Court, the Constitution, and Presidential Power*. Lanham, MD: University Press of America, 1980.

Goff, John S. *Robert Todd Lincoln: A Man in His Own Right*. Norman: University of Oklahoma Press, 1969.

Goodwin, Doris Kearns. *Lyndon Johnson and the American Dream*. New York: St. Martin's Press, 1991.

———. *No Ordinary Time, Franklin and Eleanor Roosevelt: The Home Front on World War II*. New York: Simon and Schuster, 1994.

Gordon, John S. *Hamilton's Blessing*. New York: Walker and Co., 1997.

Goss, Norman, ed. *America's Lawyer-Presidents*. Chicago: Northwestern University Press, 2004.

Gould, Lewis. *The Presidency of Theodore Roosevelt*. Lawrence: University Press of Kansas, 1991.

———. *The Presidency of William McKinley*. Lawrence: Regents Press, 1980.

Greeley, Horace. *The American Conflict: A History of Great Rebellion in the United States of America*. Hartford, CT: Case, 1865.

Greene, John R. *The Presidency of George Bush*. Lawrence: University Press of Kansas, 2000.

Grossman, Mark. *Encyclopedia of Capital Punishment*. Santa Barbara, CA: ABC-CLIO, 1998.

Hagedorn, Hermann, ed. *The Works of Theodore Roosevelt*. 20 vols. New York: Scribner, 1926.

Hamby, Alonzo. *Man of the People: A Life of Harry S. Truman*. New York: Oxford University Press, 1995.

Hammond, Bray. *Sovereignty and the Empty Purse: Banks and Politics in the Civil War*. Princeton, NJ: Princeton University Press, 1970.

Hamilton, Neil. *The Presidents*. New York: Facts on File, 2001.

Hamilton, Nigel. *Bill Clinton: An American Journey*. New York: Random House, 2003.

Handy, Robert T. *Undermined Establishment: Church-State Relations in America, 1880–1920*. Princeton, NJ: Princeton University Press, 1991.

Hendricks, Henry G. *The Federal Debt: 1919–1930*. Washington, DC: Mimeoform Press, 1933.

Henig, Gerald S., and Eric Niderost. *A Nation Transformed: How the Civil War Changed America Forever*. Nashville, TN: Cumberland House, 2007.

Herring, George C. *America's Longest War: The United States and Vietnam*. New York: Knopf, 1986.

Hesseltine, William B. *Civil War Prisons: A Study in War Psychology*. Columbus: Ohio State University Press, 1930.

Hickey, Donald. *The War of 1812: A Forgotten Conflict*. Urbana: University of Illinois Press, 1989.

Hogan, Michael, ed. *Hiroshima in History and Memory*. Cambridge, UK: Cambridge University Press, 1996.

Hogeland, William. *The Whiskey Rebellion*. New York: Scribner, 2006.

Hoogenboom, Ari. *Rutherford B. Hayes: Warrior and President*. Lawrence: University Press of Kansas, 1995.

Howard, Michael. "The Legacy of the First World War." In *Paths to War*, edited by Robert Boyce and Esmonde M. Robertson. London: Macmillan, 1989.

Hutcheson, Richard, Jr. *God in the White House: How Religion Has Changed the Modern Presidency*. New York: Macmillan, 1988.

Hutson, James H. *Religion and the Founding of the American Republic*. Washington, DC: Library of Congress, 1998.

Irons, Peter. *A People's History of the Supreme Court*. New York: Viking, 1999.

Isaacson, Walter. *Benjamin Franklin: An American Life*. New York: Simon and Schuster, 2003.

Jacobsen, Arthur J., and Michel Rosenfeld, eds. *The Longest Night: Polemics and Perspectives on Election 2000*. Berkeley and Los Angeles: University of California Press, 2002.

Jackson, Carlton. *Presidential Vetoes, 1792–1945*. Athens: University of Georgia Press, 1967.

James, Marquis. *The Life of Andrew Jackson*. Indianapolis, IN: Bobbs-Merrill, 1938.

Jeffries, Ona Griffin. *In and Out of the White House*. New York: Wilfred Funk, 1960.

Johnson, Charles Beneulyn. *Muskets and Medicine*. Philadelphia: F.A. Davis Co., 1917.

Kane, Joseph N., Janet Podell, and Steven Anzovin, eds. *Facts About the Presidents*. 7th ed. New York: H. W. Wilson, 2001.

Karabell, Zachary. *Chester Alan Arthur*. New York: Henry Holt, 2004.

Kastor, Peter, ed. *The Louisiana Purchase: Emergence of an American Nation*. Washington, DC: Congressional Quarterly, 2002.

Kaufman, Burton. *The Presidency of James Earl Carter, Jr.* Lawrence: University Press of Kansas, 1993.

Kaufman, Robert G. *Arms Control During the Pre-Nuclear Era*. New York: Columbia University Press, 1990.

Keegan, John Keegan. *A History of Warfare*. New York: Knopf, 1993.

Kegley, Charles, Jr., and Eugene Wittkopf. *American Foreign Policy*. 4th ed. New York: St. Martin's, 1991.

Kelly, Kate. *Election Day*. New York: Facts on File, 1991.

Kelly, Robert E. *The National Debt: From FDR (1941) to Clinton (1996)*. Jefferson, NC: McFarland, 2000.

Kennedy, David M., and Thomas A. Bailey. *The American Pageant: A History of the Republic*. Lexington, MA: D. C. Heath, 1986.

Kennedy, Paul. *The Rise and Fall of the Great Powers*. New York: Random House, 1987.

Kennedy, Robert. *Thirteen Days*. New York: Norton, 1971.

Kessler, Ronald. *Inside the White House*. New York: Pocket Books, 1995.

Kimball, Warren F. *The Most Unsordid Act: Lend-Lease, 1939–1941*. Baltimore: Johns Hopkins University Press, 1969.

King, Gary, and Lyn Ragsdale. *The Elusive Executive: Discovering Statistical Patterns in the Presidency*. Washington, DC: Congressional Quarterly, 1988.

Kitchen, Martin. *Europe Between the Wars: A Political History*. London: Longman, 1988.

Kleber, Brooks E., and Dale Birdsell, *The Chemical Warfare Service: Chemicals in Combat*. United States Army in World War II: The Technical Services, vol. 6, pt. 7, vol. 3. Washington, DC: U.S. Government Printing Office, 1966.

Koch, Adrienne Koch. *Jefferson and Madison: The Great Collaboration*. New York: Oxford University Press, 1964.

Kohn, George C., ed. *The New Encyclopedia of American Scandal*. New York: Facts on File, 2001.

Kolb, Charles. *White House Daze: The Unmaking of Domestic Policy in the Bush Years*. New York: Free Press, 1994.

Kornbluh, Peter, and Malcolm Byrne, eds. *The Iran-Contra Scandal: The Declassified History*. New York: New York Press, 1993.

Krivosheev, G. F., ed. *Soviet Casualties and Combat Losses in the Twentieth Century*. London: Greenhill, 1997.

Kukla, Jon. *A Wilderness So Immense: The Louisiana Purchase and the Destiny of America*. New York: Knopf, 2003.

Kumar, Martha J., and Terry Sullivan, eds. *The White House World: Transitions, Organization, and Office Operations*. College Station: Texas A&M University Press, 2003.

Lambert, Frank. *The Founding Fathers and the Place of Religion in America*. Princeton, NJ: Princeton University Press, 2003.

Lasky, Victor. *JFK: The Man and the Myth*. New York: Macmillan, 1963.

Lawson, Melinda. "Let the Nation Be Your Bank: The Civil War Bond Drives and the Construction of National Patriotism." In *An Uncommon Time: The Civil War and the Northern Home Front*, edited by Paul A. Cimbala and Randall M. Miller. New York: Fordham University Press, 2002.

LeLoup, Lance T. *Parties, Rules, and the Evolution of Congressional Budgeting*. Columbus: Ohio State University Press, 2005.

Light, Paul C. *The President's Agenda*. Baltimore, MD: Johns Hopkins University Press, 1982.

Linderman, Gerald F. *The World Within War: America's Combat Experience in World War II*. New York: Free Press, 1997.

Link, Arthur. *Wilson*. 40 vols. Princeton, NJ: Princeton University Press, 1947–65.

Lyons, Eugene. *Herbert Hoover: A Biography*. New York: Doubleday, 1964.

McCullough, David. *John Adams*. New York: Simon and Schuster, 2001.

———. *Truman*. New York: Simon and Schuster, 1992.

McPherson, James. *Battle Cry of Freedom*. New York: Oxford University Press, 1988.

———. *Ordeal by Fire*. New York: Knopf, 1982.

———, ed. *"To the Best of My Ability."* London: Dorling Kindersley, 2000.

Macmillan, Margaret. *Nixon and Mao*. New York: Random House, 2007.

Maddox, Robert James. *Weapons for Victory: The Hiroshima Decision Fifty Years Later*. Columbia: University of Missouri Press, 1995.

Maier, Thomas. *The Kennedys: America's Emerald Kings*. New York: Perseus, 2003.

Malkin, Lawrence. *The National Debt*. New York: Henry Holt, 1987.

Malone, Dumas. *Jefferson and His Time*. 6 vols. Boston: Little, Brown, and Co., 1948–81.

Malthese, John A. *Spin Control: The White House Office of Communications and the Management of Presidential News*. Chapel Hill: University of North Carolina Press, 1994.

Maney, Patrick. *The Roosevelt Presence*. New York: Twayne, 1992.

Mann, James. *About Face: A History of America's Curious Relationship with China*. New York: Knopf, 1999.

Martin, Fenton S., and Robert U. Goehlert. *How to Research the Presidency*. Washington, DC: Congressional Quarterly, 1996.

Marton, Kati. *Hidden Power: Presidential Marriages That Shaped Our Recent History*. New York: Pantheon, 2001.

Melder, Keith. *Hail to the Candidate: Presidential Campaigns from Banners to Broadcasts*. Washington, DC: Smithsonian Institution Press, 1992.

Melton, Buckner, Jr. *Aaron Burr: Conspiracy to Treason*. New York: Wiley and Sons, 2002.

Menendez, Albert. *Religion at the Polls*. Philadelphia: Westminster, 1977.

Miller, Nathan. *Theodore Roosevelt: A Life*. New York: William Morrow, 1992.

Moore, Virginia. *The Madisons*. New York: McGraw Hill, 1979.

Morison, Elting E., ed. *The Letters of Theodore Roosevelt*. 8 vols. Cambridge, MA: Harvard University Press, 1951–54.

Morris, Edmund. *Dutch: A Memoir of Ronald Reagan*. New York: Random House, 1999.

———. *The Rise of Theodore Roosevelt*. New York: Ballantine Books, 1979.

———. *Theodore Rex*. New York: Random House, 2001.

Morris, James, ed. *Readings in American Military History*. Upper Saddle River, NJ: Pearson, 2004.

Morris, Kenneth E. *Jimmy Carter: American Moralist*. Athens: University of Georgia Press, 1996.

Moyar, Mark. *Triumph Forsaken: America's Descent into Vietnam*. New York: Perseus, 2006.

Nash, Philip. *The Other Missiles of October: Eisenhower, Kennedy, and the Jupiters, 1957–1963*. Chapel Hill: University of North Carolina Press, 1997.

National Archives and Records Administration. *Public Papers of the Presidents of the United States: Gerald R. Ford*. Washington, DC: Government Printing Office, 1956–.

———. *Public Papers of the Presidents of the United States: Harry S. Truman*. Washington, DC: Government Printing Office, 1956–.

———. *Public Papers of the Presidents: James Carter, Book 1*. Washington, DC: Government Printing Office, 1956–.

Nelson, Michael, ed. *Guide to the Presidency*. 3rd ed. Washington, DC: Congressional Quarterly, 2002.

Nelson, W. Dale. *Who Speaks for the President? The White House Press Secretary from Cleveland to Clinton*. Syracuse, NY: Syracuse University Press, 1998.

Newman, Robert P. *Truman and the Hiroshima Cult*. East Lansing: Michigan State University Press, 1995.

Newmyer, R. Kent. *John Marshall and the Heroic Age of the Supreme Court*. Baton Rouge: Louisiana State University Press, 2001.

Nixon, Richard. *The Memoirs of Richard Nixon*. New York: Grosset and Dunlap, 1978.

Oates, Stephen B. *Abraham Lincoln: The Man Behind the Myths*. New York: Signet, 1984.

Oliver, Robert T., and Eugene E. White, eds. *Selected Speeches from American History*. Boston, MA: Allyn and Bacon, 1966.

Pach, Chester J., and Elmo Richardson. *The Presidency of Dwight D. Eisenhower*. Lawrence: University of Kansas Press, 1991.

Palmer, Michael A. *Stoddert's War: Naval Operations During the Quasi-War with France, 1798–1801*. Columbia: University of South Carolina Press, 1987.

Papp, Daniel S., Loch Johnson, and John Endicott. *American Foreign Policy: History, Politics, and Policy*. New York: Pearson Longman, 2005.

Parmet, Herbert S. *George Bush: Life of a Lone Star Yankee*. New York: Scribner, 1997.

Patterson, Bradley, Jr. *The White House Staff: Inside the West Wing and Beyond*. Washington, DC: Brookings Institute, 2000.

Perret, Geoffrey. *Eisenhower*. New York: Random House, 1999.

———. *Ulysses S. Grant: Soldier and President*. New York: Random House, 1997.

Peskin, Allan. *Garfield*. Kent, OH: Kent State University Press, 1999.

Peterson, Mark A. *Legislating Together: The White House and Capitol Hill from Eisenhower to Reagan*. Cambridge, MA: Harvard University Press, 1990.

Phelps, Glenn. *George Washington and American Constitutionalism*. Lawrence: University Press of Kansas, 1993.

Pierce, Bob, and Larry Ashley. *Pierce Piano Atlas*. 11th ed. Albuquerque, NM: Larry Ashley, 2003.

Pippert, Wesley. *The Spiritual Journal of Jimmy Carter*. New York: Macmillan, 1978.

Pomper, Marlene M., ed. *The Election of 1976*. New York: David McKay, 1977.

Posner, Gerald R. *Case Closed: Lee Harvey Oswald and the Assassination of JFK*. New York: Random House, 1993.

Quandt, William. *Camp David: Peace Making and Politics*. Washington, DC: Brookings Institute, 1986.

Rakove, Jack, ed. *The Unfinished Election of 2000*. New York: Basic Books, 2001.

Randall, James G. *Constitutional Problems Under Lincoln*. Urbana: University of Illinois Press, 1952.

Randall, Willard Sterne. *Thomas Jefferson*. New York: Henry Holt, 1993.

Rayback, Robert. *Millard Fillmore*. Buffalo, NY: Henry Stewart, 1959.

Reeves, Richard. *President Nixon: Alone in the White House*. New York: Simon and Schuster, 2001.

Reeves, Thomas. *The Life of Chester A. Arthur*. New York: Knopf, 1975.

Rehnquist, William H. *Centennial Crisis: The Disputed Election of 1876*. New York: Knopf, 2004.

Reichley, A. James. *Faith in Politics*. Washington, DC: Brookings Institute, 2002.

Remini, Robert V. *Andrew Jackson and the Course of American Freedom, 1822–1832*. New York: Harper and Row, 1981.

———. *The Election of Andrew Jackson*. Philadelphia, PA: Lippincott, 1963.

———. *Henry Clay*. New York: Norton, 1991.

Rhodehamel, John H., comp. *George Washington: Writings*. New York: Library of America, 1997.

Risjord, Norman. *Thomas Jefferson*. Madison, WI: Madison House, 1994.

Roberts, John B., II. *Rating the First Ladies*. New York: Citadel, 2003.

Rodrigues, Junius, ed. *The Louisiana Purchase: A Historical and Geographic Encyclopedia*. Santa Barbara, CA: ABC-Clio 2002.

Rosenberg, Jonathan, and Zachary Karabell. *Kennedy, Johnson, and the Quest for Justice: The Civil Rights Tapes*. New York: Norton, 2003.

Rosenman, Samuel I., comp. *Public Papers and Addresses of Franklin D. Roosevelt*. 13 vols. New York: Random House, 1938–50.

Rozell, Mark, and Clyde Wilcox, eds. *The Clinton Scandal and the Future of American Government*. Washington, DC: Georgetown University Press, 2000.

Rubenzer, Steven J., and Thomas R. Faschingbauer. *Personality, Character, and Leadership in the White House: Psychologists Assess the Presidents*. Washington, DC: Brassey's, 2004.

Russell, Francis. *The Shadow of Blooming Grove: Warren G. Harding in His Times*. New York: McGraw-Hill, 1968.

Rutland, Robert. *James Madison*. New York: Macmillan, 1987.

———. *The Presidency of James Madison*. Lawrence: University Press of Kansas, 1990.

Sandburg, Carl. *Abraham Lincoln*. New York: Harcourt, Brace, and World, 1954

Schaller, Michael. *Reckoning with Reagan: America and Its President in the 1980s*. New York: Oxford University Press, 1992.

Schick, Allen. *The Federal Budget: Politics, Policy, Process*. Washington, DC: Brookings Institute, 2000.

Schlesinger, Arthur M., Jr. *The Imperial Presidency*. Boston: Houghton Mifflin, 1973.

———. *A Thousand Days*. Boston, MA: Houghton Mifflin, 1965.

————, and Fred L. Israel, eds. *The History of American Presidential Elections*. Philadelphia: Chelsea House, 2002.

Scholes, Walter V., ed. *United States Diplomatic History*. 2 vols. New York: Houghton Mifflin, 1973.

Schroeder, John H. *Mr. Polk's War: American Opposition and Dissent, 1846–1848*. Madison: University of Wisconsin Press, 1973.

Schwartz, Bernard. *A History of the Supreme Court*. New York: Oxford University Press, 1993.

Scigliano, Robert. *The Supreme Court and the Presidency*. New York: Free Press, 1971.

Seale, William. *The Presidents House*. Washington, DC: White House Historical Association, 1986.

Sears, Stephen W., ed. *The Civil War Papers of George B. McClellan*. New York: Ticknor and Fields, 1989.

Sheehan, Neil. *The Pentagon Papers*. New York: Quadrangle Books, 1971.

Sievers, Harry. *Benjamin Harrison: Hoosier Statesman*. 3 vols. Chicago: Regnery, 1952–68.

Silbey, David J. *A War of Frontier and Empire: The Philippine-American War, 1899–1902*. New York: Hill and Wang, 2007.

Simpson, Brooks. *Ulysses S. Grant*. Boston: Houghton Mifflin, 2000.

Singer, Aaron, ed. *Campaign Speeches of American Presidential Candidates, 1928–1972*. New York: Frederick Unger, 1976.

Singer, Peter. *The President of Good and Evil: The Ethics of George W. Bush*. New York: Dutton, 2004.

Slaughter, Thomas P. *The Whiskey Rebellion*. New York: Oxford University Press, 1986.

Smith, Bradley F. *The War's Long Shadow*. New York: Simon and Schuster, 1986.

Smith, Elbert B. *The Presidencies of Zachary Taylor and Millard Fillmore*. Lawrence: University Press of Kansas, 1988.

Smith, Gaddis. *The Last Years on the Monroe Doctrine, 1945–1993*. New York: Hill and Wang, 1994.

Smith, James Morton, ed. *The Republic of Letters: The Correspondence Between Thomas Jefferson and James Madison*. 3 vols. New York: Norton, 1995.

Smith, Jean E. *John Marshall: Definer of a Nation*. New York: Henry Holt, 1996.

Socolofsky Homer E., and Allan B. Spetter. *The Presidency of Benjamin Harrison*. Lawrence: University Press of Kansas, 1987.

Sorensen, Theodore. *Kennedy*. New York: Harper and Row, 1965.

Sorge, Martin K. *The Other Price of Hitler's War: German Military and Civilian Losses Resulting from World War II*. New York: Greenwood Press, 1986.

South Carolina Convention. *Journal of the Convention of the People of South*

*Carolina, Held in 1860, 1861, and 1862, Together with the Ordinances, Re-ports, Resolutions, etc.* Columbia, SC: R. W. Gibbes, 1862.

Speer, Lonnie R. *Portals to Hell: Military Prisons of the Civil War.* Mechanics-burg, PA: Stackpole Books, 1997.

Spitzer, Robert. *The Presidential Veto: Touchstone of the American Presidency.* New York: State University of New York Press, 1988.

Stagg, J. C. A. *Mr. Madison's War: Politics, Diplomacy, and Warfare in the Early American Republic, 1783–1830.* Princeton, NJ: Princeton University Press, 1983.

Steers, Edward, Jr. *Blood on the Moon: The Assassination of Abraham Lincoln.* Lexington: University Press of Kentucky, 2001.

Strober, Deborah H., and Gerald S. Strober. *The Nixon Presidency: An Oral His-tory of the Era.* Washington, DC: Brassey's, 2003.

———. *Reagan: The Man and His Presidency.* Boston: Houghton Mifflin, 1998.

Stuckey, Mary E. *Defining Americans: The Presidency and National Identity.* Lawrence: University Press of Kansas, 2004.

Summers, Anthony. *The Arrogance of Power: The Secret World of Richard Nixon.* New York: Viking, 2000.

Summers, Harry, Jr. *Vietnam War Almanac.* New York: Facts on File, 1985.

Tebbel, John, and Sarah M. Watts. *The Press and the Presidency.* New York: Ox-ford University Press, 1985.

Thomas, Benjamin P. *Abraham Lincoln: A Biography.* New York: Modern Li-brary, 1968.

Toland, John. *The Rising Sun.* New York: Random House, 1970.

Treasury Report on Finance. *Annual Report of the Secretary of the Treasury.* Washington, DC: U.S. Treasury Department, 1919.

———. *Annual Report of the Secretary of the Treasury.* Washington, DC: U.S. Treasury Department, 1928.

Tucker, Spencer C., ed. *Encyclopedia of American Military History.* New York: Facts on File, 2003.

———. *Encyclopedia of the Vietnam War.* New York: Oxford University Press, 1998.

Truman, Margaret. *Harry S. Truman.* New York: William Morrow, 1973.

———, ed. *Where the Buck Stops: The Personal and Private Writings of Harry S. Truman.* New York: Warner Books, 1989.

Tuchman, Barbara. *The Proud Tower.* New York: Macmillan, 1966.

U.S. Commerce Department. *Statistical Abstract of the United States.* Washing-ton, DC: U.S. Government Printing Office, 2005.

U.S. Department of Defense. *Conduct of the Persian Gulf War: The Final Report to the U.S. Congress.* Washington, DC: Government Printing Office, 1992.

U.S. Office of Management and Budget. *Budget of the United States Government: Historical Tables, Fiscal Year 2007*. Washington, DC: U.S. Government Printing Office, 2006.

U.S. Senate Library. *Presidential Vetoes, 1789–1988*. Washington, DC: Government Printing Office, 1992.

U.S. Warren Commission. *Report of the Warren Commission on the Assassination of President Kennedy*. New York: McGraw-Hill, 1964.

Vandiver, Frank E. *How America Goes to War*. London: Praeger, 2005.

Van Sant, John, Peter Mauch, and Yoneyuki Sugita. *Historical Dictionary of United States–Japan Relations*. Lanham, MD: Scarecrow, 2007.

Varhola, Michael J. *Everyday Life During the Civil War*. Cincinnati: Writer's Digest Books, 1999.

Venzon, Anne Cipriano, ed. *The United States in the First World War*. New York: Garland, 1995.

Wagenheim, Kal. *Puerto Rico: A Profile*. New York: Praeger, 1975.

Walch, Timothy, ed. *At the President's Side: The Vice Presidency in the Twentieth Century*. Columbia: University of Missouri Press, 1997.

Walker, J. Samuel. *Prompt and Utter Destruction: Truman and the Use of Atomic Bombs Against Japan*. Chapel Hill: University of North Carolina Press, 1997.

Ward, Geoffrey C. *The Civil War*. New York: Knopf, 1990.

Watson, Richard A. *Presidential Vetoes and Public Policy*. Lawrence: University Press of Kansas, 1993.

Watterson, John S. *The Games Presidents Play: Sports and the Presidency*. Baltimore: Johns Hopkins University Press, 2006.

Watts, Sarah. *Rough Rider in the White House: Theodore Roosevelt and the Politics of Desire*. Chicago: University of Chicago Press, 2003.

Waugh, John C. *Reelecting Lincoln: The Battle for the 1864 Presidency*. New York: Crown, 1997.

Wead, Doug. *All the Presidents' Children*. New York: Atria, 2003.

Weichmann, Louis. *A True History of the Assassination of Abraham Lincoln and the Conspiracy of 1865*. New York: Knopf, 1975.

Weinstein, Edwin A. *Woodrow Wilson: A Medical and Psychological Biography*. Princeton: Princeton University Press, 1981.

Weisberg, Herbert, and Clyde Wilcox, eds. *Models of Voting in Presidential Elections: The 2000 U.S. Election*. Stanford, CA: Stanford University Press, 2004.

Whitcomb, John, and Claire Whitcomb. *Real Life at the White House*. New York: Routledge, 2000.

White, Theodore H. *The Making of the President, 1972*. New York: Atheneum, 1973.

Williams, T. Harry. *The History of American Wars: From 1745 to 1918*. New York: Knopf, 1981.

Wilson, John F., ed. *Church and State in America: A Bibliographical Guide*. New York: Greenwood, 1987.

Wiltse, Jeff. *Contested Waters: A Social History of Swimming Pools in America*. Chapel Hill: University of North Carolina Press, 2007.

Yergin, Daniel. *The Prize*. New York: Simon and Schuster, 1991.

# Index